TE PUEA

*'When my life is written I want the truth told
and nothing but the truth ...'*

Te Puea Herangi

TE PUEA

A LIFE

Michael King

RAUPO

For

Irihapeti Merenia Ramsden

A RAUPO BOOK
Published by the Penguin Group
Penguin Group (NZ), 67 Apollo Drive, Rosedale,
North Shore 0632, New Zealand (a division of Pearson New Zealand Ltd)
Penguin Group (USA) Inc., 375 Hudson Street,
New York, New York 10014, USA
Penguin Group (Canada), 90 Eglinton Avenue East, Suite 700, Toronto,
Ontario, M4P 2Y3, Canada (a division of Pearson Penguin Canada Inc.)
Penguin Books Ltd, 80 Strand, London, WC2R 0RL, England
Penguin Ireland, 25 St Stephen's Green,
Dublin 2, Ireland (a division of Penguin Books Ltd)
Penguin Group (Australia), 250 Camberwell Road, Camberwell,
Victoria 3124, Australia (a division of Pearson Australia Group Pty Ltd)
Penguin Books India Pvt Ltd, 11, Community Centre,
Panchsheel Park, New Delhi – 110 017, India
Penguin Books (South Africa) (Pty) Ltd, 24 Sturdee Avenue,
Rosebank, Johannesburg 2196, South Africa

Penguin Books Ltd, Registered Offices: 80 Strand, London, WC2R 0RL, England

First published by Hodder & Stoughton 1977, reprinted 1978 (twice)
Second edition published 1982, reprinted 1984
Third edition published by Sceptre 1987, reprinted 1990, 1993
Fourth edition published by Reed Publishing (NZ) Ltd 2003
Reprinted 2004, 2005 (twice), 2006
This edition reprinted 2006 (twice), 2007

First published by Penguin Group (NZ) 2008
5 7 9 10 8 6

Copyright © Michael King 2003

The right of Michael King to be identified as the author of this work in terms of
section 96 of the Copyright Act 1994 is hereby asserted.

Text designed by Graeme Leather
Cover designed by Craig Violich
Cover photo by Te Uira Manihera
Printed in China by Nordica

ISBN: 978 0 14 301142 2

A catalogue record for this book is available
from the National Library of New Zealand.

www.penguin.co.nz

Contents

The animus in its most developed form sometimes connects the woman's mind with the spiritual evolution of her age, and can thereby make her even more receptive than a man to new creative ideas. It is for this reason that . . . women were used by many nations as diviners and seers. The creative boldness of their positive animus at times expresses thoughts and ideas that stimulate men to new enterprises.

M.L. Franz

Preface

The writing of this, my first major book and first biography, came about by virtue of a series of coincidences.

In 1965, when I was a university student, I read *The Maori and New Zealand Politics* edited by John Pocock, then professor of political science at Canterbury University. His introduction identified Te Puea Herangi as 'possibly the most influential woman in our political history' and lamented the absence of 'a full study of that remarkable woman'. I attempted further research on Te Puea's life and public career but could find nothing about her in existing literature — neither the full study proposed by Pocock nor, even, a short one. What, I wondered, was the justification for Pocock's assessment of her?

Three years later I found myself in Hamilton working as Maori roundsman for the *Waikato Times*, my first post-university job. Now I was hearing stories about Te Puea on a weekly basis as I attended hui, poukai and tangihanga throughout the Tainui rohe. She had at this time been dead for only sixteen years. Her presence and influence were strong in the memories of those who had known her. Accounts of things she did and what she said were related frequently by kuia and kaumatua in justification of previous or current Tainui policies. Again I had cause to share Pocock's regret about the absence of a full study of the woman to help me place these stories in context and more fully understand the significance of this unusually active and interesting life.

It dawned on me slowly that I might be in a position to write such a study. Over four years I came to know well Te Puea's surviving associates and protégés: Tumokai Katipa, her husband, a man of immense generosity and moral authority; Ngeungeu Zister, who had grown up with her at Mercer and would eventually outlive her by more than thirty years (dying at the age of 103); Piri Poutapu, one of the first of her 'children' at Mangatawhiri; the Jones brothers, Mick and Pei Te Hurinui, who had worked with and for her over three decades; Heeni Wharemaru and Te Uira Manihera, gathered into her orbit in the 1930s and with her till the end of her life; Tumate and Robert Mahuta, members of her extended family.

Once I had established in the early 1970s that Pei Te Hurinui Jones did not plan to write a biography of Te Puea — he produced several major books on Tainui history and considered himself the 'scribe' of the tribe — I set about seeking the authority and resources to write such a book myself. After several years of unsuccessful applications (I was, after all, an author with no track record), I was eventually awarded modest grants from the New Zealand Literary Fund and the Arts Council. With this backing, I approached Dame Te Atairangikaahu and members of the kahui ariki for formal permission to work in partnership with Tainui on researching and writing a life of Te Puea. I was given that permission.

This, the resulting study, is one in biography, not hagiography. In it, Te Puea's actions discredit her only to the extent that it is discreditable to be human. The principle I have adopted is that attributed to Voltaire: that to the living one owes respect, but to the dead one owes the truth. I was mindful of the comment Te Puea herself made to Eric Ramsden when he proposed writing such a book: 'When my life is written I want the truth told and nothing but the truth …'

There was a degree of anxiety in Waikato that some of the events with which Te Puea was associated, particularly those involving spiritual or apparently psychic phenomena, would not be believed by Europeans and would undercut whatever reputation she had accumulated for more conventional accomplishments. This had led to a reluctance to talk about her and a discouragement of the ambitions of earlier would-be biographers.

There was a further reason for delay: many of the people who knew Te Puea well were either illiterate, or simply more comfortable with oral than with written communication. This meant that a book about her had to incorporate a large quantity of oral research, especially interviewing surviving family and associates at considerable length.

One of the problems about this kind of research is that it cannot be done precipitately or coldly. It can only arise out of a relationship of ease and trust. Further, the resulting narrative can unintentionally take on the character of a series of loosely strung homilies; because it is the homily kind of story — the anecdotes that preserve maxims and morals — that flourish most readily in an oral climate, nurtured by frequent oratory and pointed story-telling that seek to reinforce the myths and values of a culture rather than to recount what actually happened.

Unaided memory can also prove to be fallible. Recollection may distort history because people forget things and are unwilling to admit it; or because they may be inclined to remember events as they would have liked them to have taken place — for the sake of tidiness, or so that posterity might view them in a favourable light.

On the other hand it should be stressed that the purely documentary approach to history is hazardous too. European newspaper and parliamentary reports of encounters with Maori groups were frequently compiled by people who neither spoke Maori nor identified what was important about proceedings from a Maori point of view. This led to the accumulation of what Maharaia Winiata called 'Pakeha-coloured' history.

Such colouring has given disproportionate attention to Maori leaders who were intelligible and appealing to Europeans, or whose careers included military adventures. Figures who have won an earlier place in school curricula and popular Pakeha mythology — Tamati Waka Nene, Te Rauparaha, Rewi Maniapoto and the like — are frequently not the ones most highly regarded by Maori posterity, those whose vision and injunctions continue to engage Maori attention. In Hokianga, for example, one is more likely to hear of Aperahama Taonui than Waka Nene; on Waikato maraes, of Tawhiao; in the King Country, of Wahanui Huatare; where is the story of these men in textbooks?

I suspect too that studies that have emphasised the contributions of twentieth-century, Western-educated leaders like Carroll, Ngata, Pomare, Buck and Bennett tell considerably less than the whole story of Maori adaptation and survival. It seems to me now that the influence of a community leader like Te Puea was more potent and more durable. Which is not to dismiss the contributions of the legislators — just to establish that their objectives could not have taken root without locally based hereditary leaders like Eru Ihaka, Te Puea and Tai Mitchell. In the case of Ngata, his direct influence did not extend far beyond Ngati Porou; in the case of some of his colleagues, they did not seem to have even a local hold beyond an ability to win elections.

Relevant and accurate history is most likely to arise from the matching of oral account against documentary, and vice versa. Neither approach is exclusively satisfactory. Here, wherever possible, I have compared oral description with the Maori written record, and preferably with the record compiled by Te Puea herself. Where I have had to use secondary sources I've tried to make them as direct as possible — first-hand rather than second or third, and from people who were close to Te Puea and viewed her as a human being rather than as a deity.

I have leaned most heavily on Maori informants, especially Te Puea's husband Tumokai Katipa, Piri Poutapu, Pei Te Hurinui and Mick Jones, Te Uira Manihera, Heeni Wharemaru, Winara Samuels and Robert Mahuta; and on Maori documents, particularly those written by Te Puea herself and others in Maori hands, like the papers of Maharaia Winiata and Mick Jones.

The fact that this book was written at all with any degree of comprehensiveness is attributable to three coincident factors rare in the case of Maori leaders: Te Puea's own prolific activity (she was a determined correspondent and kept a diary almost daily for the last thirty years of her life); the vast quantity of letters and interview notes preserved in the Ramsden Papers in the Alexander Turnbull Library; and the survival and full cooperation of the people who knew Te Puea most intimately, especially her husband. (The knowledge that this would not always be so infused the project with a sense of urgency; three major informants died during the preparation of the book and twenty-five years after publication all but one were gone.)

There were some complications about the use of Te Puea's own records. She was fluent in written and spoken Maori, and reasonably so in spoken English. Her written English, however, was not strong; unless it was refined by one of the group of people who acted as secretaries for her, it tended to be ungrammatical. To circumvent this, I have confined myself as far as possible to translations of her own views from Maori. In rare instances where her meaning is clear but the expression clumsy, I have 'tidied' her English; I have identified this interference in chapter footnotes.

I have written an additional note on sources which can be found after the text of this book. The footnotes are numbered and grouped according to chapters. Those that provide additional information that I judge might interest or assist the reader are asterisked and placed at the foot of the relevant text pages.

The Prologue is intended to shed light on the origin of the Maori King Movement and the state of Waikato at the time Te Puea emerged as a tribal leader; it is a summary of a complexity of events that took place over half a century. Because it is an outline only, it lacks the continuity of narrative and the interest of characterisation. Those interested solely in the story of Te Puea may prefer to begin reading at Chapter 1.

As I have noted, this book had its origins in my years in Waikato, 1967 to 1971, in associations with the people who came to be its protagonists. Its preparation was eventually made possible by a series of grants that allowed me to work on research and writing over two and a half years. For providing such assistance I am indebted to the Arts Council of New Zealand, the New Zealand Literary Fund, the Maori Purposes Fund Board, the Kelliher Charitable Trust and the University of Waikato's Centre For Maori Studies and Research; to the trustees of the Katherine Mansfield Fellowship for an uninterrupted spell in Menton, France, where I wrote the bulk of the manuscript; and to Ruth Brassington, Phyllis Gant, James and Helen McNeish and Anton and Birgitte Vogt for shelter and encouragement.

My task was also made easier by the agreement of the University of Waikato to my writing a doctoral thesis in association with this biography. For that decision I am indebted primarily to my major supervisor, Professor James Ritchie; and to Professor Peter Freyberg and Vincent O'Sullivan.

Even more fundamentally, the writing of this book depended on the cooperation of Waikato informants. I acknowledge with immense gratitude the assistance of Te Arikinui Dame Te Atairangikaahu, Whatumoana Paki, Tumokai Katipa, Robert Mahuta, Piri Poutapu, Alex McKay, Michael Rotohiko Jones, Pei Te Hurinui Jones, Ngeungeu Zister, Te Uira Manihera, Winara Samuels, Whitiora Cooper, Heeni Wharemaru, Charlie Mahuta, Wetere and Emily Paki and Ces Badley; and the earlier informants, Hori Paki, Paraire Herewini, Ngakahikatea Whirihana and Kirikino Epiha.

Other major contributors included Irihapeti Ramsden, Kingi Ihaka, Frances Winiata, Sister F.I. Hobbs, the Rev. G.I. Laurenson, C.G. Scrimgeour, Frank Monk, the Rev. Kingi Ihaka, Sam Karetu, Tiahuia Gray, Dr Margaret McDowall, B.E. Woodhams, Ted Williams, Dr H.B. Turbott, Mel Taylor, Sir Henry Kelliher, Lord Ballantrae, Rhys Richards, Ann Parsonson, Judith Binney, Dick Scott, M.P.K. Sorrenson, Raewyn Dalziel, A.G. Bagnall and E.A. Aubin.

Jim Traue, Tom Wilsted, June Stark, Margery Walton, Sharon Dell, Allison Buchan and Hillary Stace of the Alexander Turnbull Library provided generous assistance with research and logistic support, as did Joan Robinson of the University of Waikato's Centre For Maori Studies and Research. Judith Hornabrook and the staff of the National Archives, H. de S.C. MacLean and the staff at the General Assembly Library, the staff of the Auckland Institute and Museum Library and Ellen Ellis also helped with research. I offer a special thanks to all librarians, archivists and research assistants who undertake many of the less spectacular but utterly necessary aspects of research, for which authors frequently take the applause.

The absence of satisfactory biographies of other Maori leaders and politicians at the time of writing made the researching of this book both demanding and rewarding: demanding because there was a paucity of information about the people with whose lives Te Puea's was bound up; and rewarding because of the need to break new ground — to define and elaborate some of the themes of Maori adaptation to Western values and institutions. It has always been my hope that the existence of this book would encourage the writing of companion volumes. The fact that a biography of Apirana Ngata by Ranginui Walker appeared in 2001 was a source of much gratification and celebration.

Michael King
Coromandel Peninsula
2002

He Waiata Tangi a Tawhiao

Ka titiro whakaoro au te riu o Waikato
Ahakoa ma te pupuri ia i roto o taku ringa
Me takamiri tona atahua
Tena etahi mea matomato ngawari

Ka totoro atu au ki te tihi o Pirongia
Ahakoa ma te uhia me tiaki i tona matu I toku ake
Katea titia pewhea te pahu ma roto i te uma
O Maungatautari me Maungakawa
Nga puke o oku oha

Te awa o te ora ia piko nui atu te ataahua o te whakamutunga
Ka whakawhiti au i te awaawa o Kirikiriroa
O nga rauwiri i pai ana
Te renga o nga mea pai

Ki mua ki te waahi tutakitanga ki Ngaruawahia
I reira kei runga I te tuahu haumoko
Ka okioki au toku matenga
Ka titiro ma roto I nga heke o Taupiri

Ki reira ki te waahi o nga hanga katoa
Tukuna tenei kingi kia haere mai

Tawhiao's Lament for Waikato

I look down on the valley of Waikato,
As though to hold it in the hollow of my hand
And caress its beauty
Like some tender verdant thing.

I reach out from the top of Pirongia
As though to cover and protect its substance
With my own.
See how it bursts through
The full bosoms of Maungatautari and Maungakawa,
Hills of my inheritance:

The river of life, each curve
More beautiful than the last.
Across the smooth belly of Kirikiriroa,
Its gardens bursting with the fullness of good things,

Towards the meeting place at Ngaruawahia.
There on the fertile mound I would rest my head
And look through the thighs of Taupiri.

There at the place of all creation
Let the King come forth.

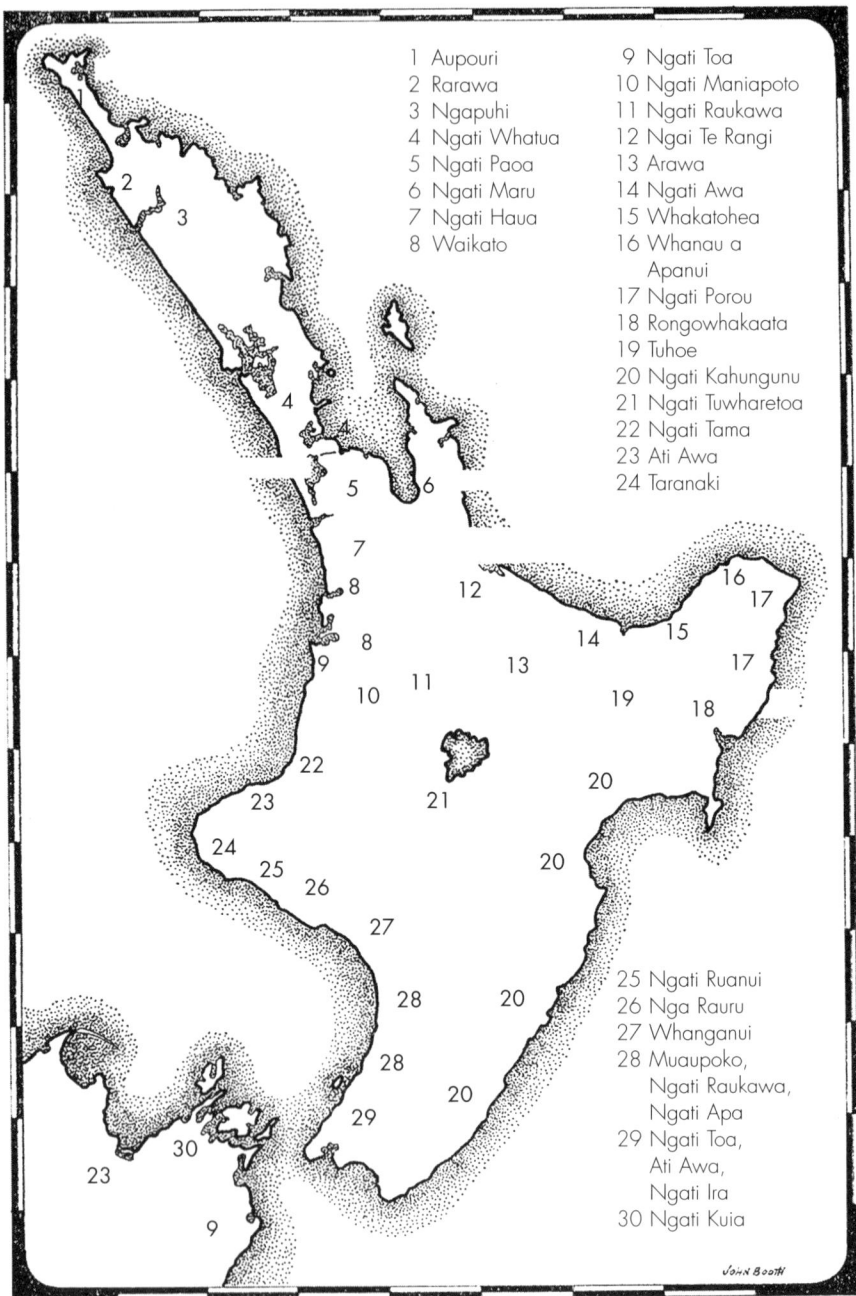

Major tribal areas. AJHR, 1870, D-23.

1 Aupouri
2 Rarawa
3 Ngapuhi
4 Ngati Whatua
5 Ngati Paoa
6 Ngati Maru
7 Ngati Haua
8 Waikato
9 Ngati Toa
10 Ngati Maniapoto
11 Ngati Raukawa
12 Ngai Te Rangi
13 Arawa
14 Ngati Awa
15 Whakatohea
16 Whanau a Apanui
17 Ngati Porou
18 Rongowhakaata
19 Tuhoe
20 Ngati Kahungunu
21 Ngati Tuwharetoa
22 Ngati Tama
23 Ati Awa
24 Taranaki
25 Ngati Ruanui
26 Nga Rauru
27 Whanganui
28 Muaupoko, Ngati Raukawa, Ngati Apa
29 Ngati Toa, Ati Awa, Ngati Ira
30 Ngati Kuia

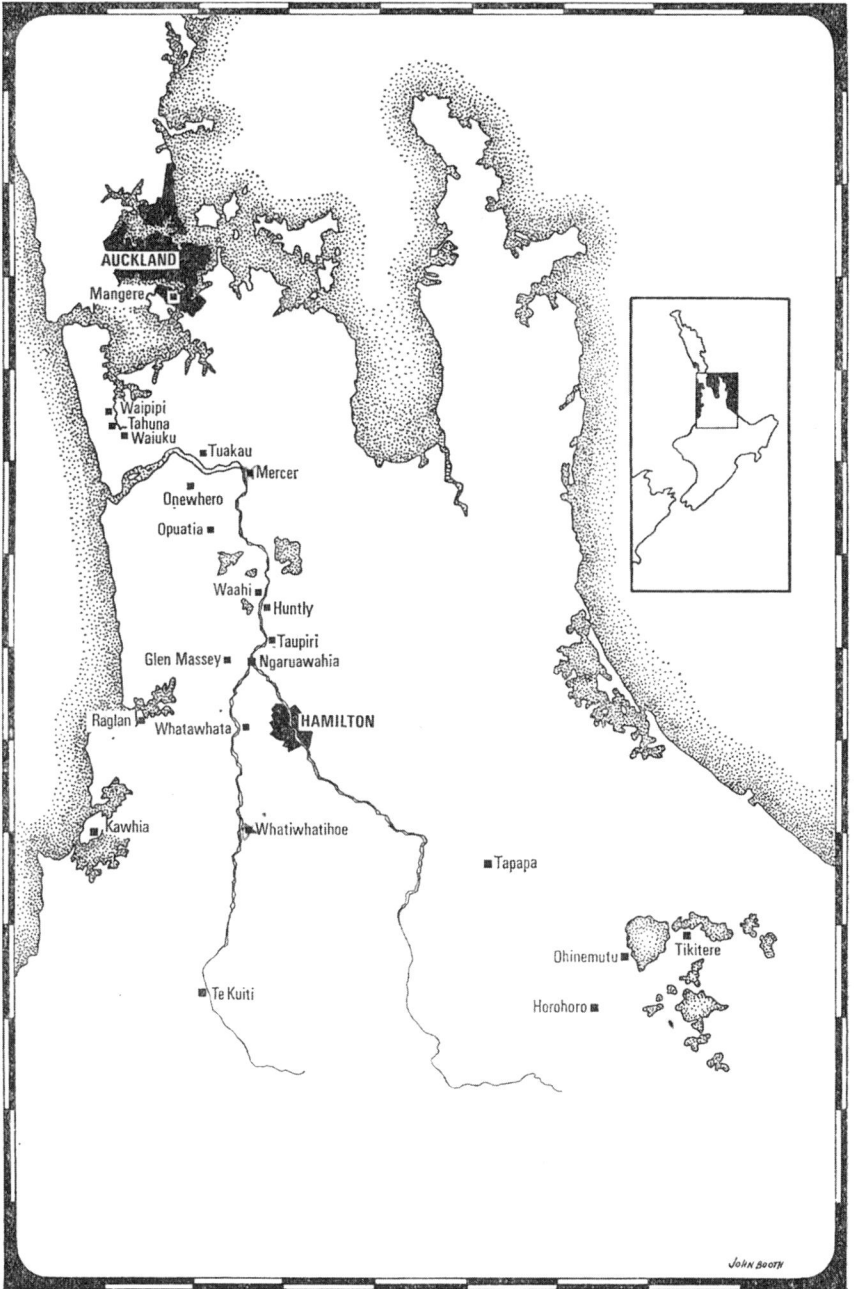

Principal places mentioned in the text.

Prologue

To most nineteenth-century European observers the idea of a Maori kingship seemed incongruous, even comical. It should not have done: Maori concepts of the mana and tapu of rangatiratanga or hereditary aristocracy were not far removed from the connotations of the Divine Right of Kings; and the idea that leadership should be cloaked in costume, rhetoric and ritual was already seemly in the Polynesian mind. Indeed, the institution of ariki or paramount chief was close to that of kingship. It is not surprising that four groups of Polynesian islands established dynastic monarchies within sixty years of one another, coincidentally and without consultation.

What was novel was the 'Maori' part of the concept. A tribal people isolated for centuries from other races had no traditional idea of race or culture. And they were vulnerable when they were confronted with people who not only carried such concepts but also believed that their own brands were superior to others. It was not only technology that enabled the Europeans to be more commanding than the indigenous peoples they colonised; it was also confidence, the kind of confidence that came with membership of a worldwide empire.

The major impulse behind the establishment of the Maori kingship was that of giving 'New Zealand Natives' a matching sense of brotherhood and confidence, a view of themselves as 'Maori', and of Maori as something worthy of self-respect.[†] Without these things they had been at a constant and demonstrable disadvantage in dealings with Europeans. As tribal fragments they were played off against one another, out-manoeuvred in negotiation, targets for land-seeking colonists. The institutions of government which had promised to protect their interests were in the hands of the same colonists (there was no Maori representation in Parliament until 1868). And the process of disintegration that had begun with cultural demoralisation and the collapse

---

[†] I do not propose to discuss the origins of the King Movement in detail, nor the immediate causes of the Waikato war. These have been well documented elsewhere (see Jones 1960 and 1968; Kelly 1949; Gorst 1864; Sinclair 1961; Sorrenson 1963; Belich 1986; Stokes 2002). I give only sufficient nineteenth-century background to indicate the nature of the movement and the conditions in Waikato that Te Puea inherited when she assumed a leadership role.

of customary laws was exacerbated by a lack of immunity to European diseases. When they fought among themselves, the consequences were more drastic because of firearms willingly supplied by Europeans; and when they quarrelled with Europeans they could not hope, in the long run, to win.

And yet there was hope, and Maori statements from the mid-nineteenth century are fragrant with it. The same process of colonisation that promised extinction for Maori had also offered them intimations of other possibilities: the imposition of British law made them (they were told) the equal of any man; they believed that the Treaty of Waitangi guaranteed that Queen Victoria would protect their 'lands and estates, forests, fisheries and other properties' as long as Maori wished to retain them; the Bible had confirmed the suggestion of individual worth, offered access to a more potent deity, and promised deliverance for the disinherited; voyages to England resulted in the exhibition of chiefs in London as gentle savages who demonstrated the refining effects of British colonisation.

This last factor, which enabled Maori leaders to see the English monarchy at first hand, sowed seeds in ground that was already fertile. In Maori circles in the 1840s and 1850s the view evolved that the key to European pre-eminence was their unity under the mana of the Queen. Should Maori achieve a similar unity under their own monarch, it was argued, they would be able to match European cohesion; to conserve what remained of customary law and leadership; to end the pay-back wars among families and tribes; to prevent the further sale of land to Europeans with its consequent loss of livelihood and break-up of communities.

These were the justifications for a Maori king raised at North Island meetings in the 1850s. There were few expressions of aggressive intention, no subversive threats; just a seeking of an equal partnership for the sharing and development of the country that the Europeans had been unable to establish (and perhaps did not want to establish — for most colonists, a far more hopeful outlook was eventual Maori extinction that would release every acre of land capable of production in the interests of personal and national prosperity).

The problem was how to select this king. The European precedent of dynastic wars was no answer — Pax Britannica would make it difficult, and the abolition of fighting was one of the major objectives of the king-makers. Instead, the matter was subjected to the process of interminable Maori debate that some have characterised as agreement by exhaustion. The names of the most highly regarded chiefs were canvassed at a series of hui. Candidates were considered in the light of genealogy, current standing and their ability to act as hosts for large and representative Maori gatherings. One by one leading contenders dropped away, voluntarily or as a result of elimination by discussion.

Among them were Te Heuheu Iwikau of Tuwharetoa, Te Kani a Takirau of Ngati Porou, Te Hapuku of Ngati Kahungunu, and Tamati Waka Nene of Ngapuhi. Finally a candidate achieved unanimity. In November 1856, at Pukawa on the shores of Lake Taupo, a meeting called by Te Heuheu agreed upon Te Wherowhero of Waikato (whose own unwillingness to accept the title on the ground that he had eaten human flesh had kept him away from the hui). He was considered high-ranking by those who proposed him: he was descended from Hoturoa, captain of the Tainui canoe, whose crew provided the major antecedents of the Tainui tribes; he also had genealogical connections with other tribes and especially strong ones with Te Arawa. He came from a line of successful fighting chiefs. He had been an outstanding combatant himself in the days of tribal warfare and had excelled at hand-to-hand duelling. In 1845 he had become a friend of Governor George Grey and his long residence in Auckland was credited with protecting the capital from attack by Ngapuhi from the north and Hauraki from the east.[†] He regarded himself as a friend of the Pakeha.

In addition to these personal advantages, Te Wherowhero was considered to have the resources needed to maintain the kingship. He was able to call upon the assistance of some 5000 followers. And his immediate territory, Waikato, was wealthy: there was food in its rivers and lakes and vast acres of potatoes in its cultivated fields; its Maori-operated granaries were supplying Auckland with flour and exporting to Australia and California. The clinching proverb cited at Pukawa in Te Wherowhero's favour referred to the Waikato River as a personification of the tribe and its resources: 'Waikato taniwharau, he piko he taniwha.' Waikato, river of a hundred bends, and at every bend a taniwha or powerful chief.

At first Te Wherowhero declined the kingship. He was in his mid-eighties, he was tired, he did not want to undertake new ventures (Ferdinand von Hochstetter was to describe him soon after as 'a blind . . . decrepit old man who was on the very brink of the grave').[1] His followers were also unhappy about the title 'king'. They preferred a traditional term like 'ariki taungaroa'. But other tribes and their spokesmen were insistent and Wiremu Tamehana of Ngati Haua finally persuaded Te Wherowhero to acquiesce to both the position and the title. In 1858 he was 'crowned' by Kingmaker Tamehana with a Maori Bible at Ngaruawahia and he took the name Potatau.[‡]

---

† Auckland was capital of the colony from 1840 to 1865, when the seat of government was transferred to Wellington.
‡ There are various dates given for the final raising-up ceremony. Pei Te Hurinui Jones (1968) says 2 May 1859. Other authorities fix the year at 1858.

The rangatira who were party to the Pukawa decision represented most major tribes: Ngapuhi, Te Arawa, Ngati Porou, Ngati Kahungunu, Taranaki, Whanganui and Ngai Tahu; and what came to be called Te Porotaka Nama Tahi — the 'first circle' of supporters, Waikato, Maniapoto and Hauraki. Some were to say in later years that their spokesmen were not authorised to make the commitments that they did; or that the support of Te Wherowhero was not for posterity but for that time and that place only. Nevertheless, the elevation of Potatau was the most nationally representative gesture that Maori had made since the signing of the Treaty of Waitangi in 1840. 'The union of the tribes [was] demonstrated so that all men might see,' James Cowan wrote, 'and then did Te Heuheu and his fellow chiefs transfer to Potatau all the manatapu of the soil.'[2]

In Waikato, the immediate function of the kingship was specific and practical. It formalised a system of local government that had begun to evolve in the preceding years. Communities set up runanga or councils with local chiefs acting as magistrates with authority to imprison or fine offenders. Over these runanga lay the mana of the King and his council of twelve advisors. At Ngaruawahia, which Potatau had named his capital, there was a 'resident magistrate', an official surveyor, and a newspaper called Te Hokioi.

This system allowed life at village level to be regulated in a manner that the system of national government had been unable to achieve.[†] Not until the close of the 1850s did the colonial Parliament show any interest in recognising Maori initiatives by legalising local magistrates; and by that time the system was working too well for the Kingites to accept recognition of Pakeha supervision, particularly supervision that excluded recognition of the kingship itself. Potatau's followers also sought to pay off all debts to Europeans and to prohibit the further sale of land.

The mana of the King that coordinated this system was not that of Potatau alone. In the eyes of his supporters, the chiefs who had raised him up had made him a repository for their own mana and tapu and for that of their lands. Potatau was now a man of intensified prestige and sacredness. This belief was

---

† When Bishop Selwyn asked if it was safe to leave his bags on the roadside at Maungatautari, he was told yes, nobody stole any more: 'Some . . . for fear of God. Some for fear of the Five Pounds', the local fine for theft. This recollection of Maori posterity is disputed by Sinclair (1961, p. 76) who says 'the Waikato had no more "law" after 1858 than before'. But the Waikato view is perhaps accommodated when he goes on to say that 'despite weaknesses of organisation, however, the attempt [to govern] was profoundly satisfying to the participants'. Just before war broke out in 1863 a parliament was also set up at Ngaruawahia, a forerunner of the one established at Maungakawa in 1892 (see page 24).

to impel people to go to heroic lengths to uphold the kingship and, subsequently, to fight for it. It was also the source of the awe in which the descendants of Potatau — known as the kahui ariki — were to be held; the mana of the King came to be regarded as hereditary.

In 1859 the Austrian geologist Ferdinand von Hochstetter sailed up the Waikato River and recorded observations of the waterway and the territory of the Kingites that lay on either side of it:

> The impression made by the sight of the majestic stream is truly grand. It is only with the Danube or the Rhine that I can compare the mighty river which we had just entered. [It] is the principal river in the North Island. Both as to the length of its course[†] and the quantity of water, it surpasses all the others . . . Its waters roll through the most fertile and most beautiful fields, populated by numerous and most powerful tribes of the Natives, who have taken their name from it . . . There are huge sandbanks piled in front of the mouth of the Waikato upon which the sea breaks in foaming surges . . . [These] prevent the passing in and out of larger vessels [and] are a natural bulwark for the Natives. They look upon the Waikato more than upon any other river of New Zealand as being exclusively their own. Never up to the time of my journey had a boat of European construction been known to float upon the proud Native stream.[3]

The 'fertile and most beautiful fields' that so impressed Hochstetter, and the river itself — all factors in swinging the kingship to Potatau — provided the incentive and the means for an invasion of Waikato. Auckland was swelling with new settlers; government ministers and land purchase officers were determined to acquire the fruitful acreage south of the city; the fact that it was controlled by a movement pledged not to sell land damned the Kingites in the eyes of most Europeans and generated public anger.

Potatau died in June 1860 and was succeeded by his retiring son, Matutaera (who would be known as Tawhiao). Like his father, he was committed to peaceful and cooperative development of the country in partnership with Europeans; his only qualification was that the control of local government within Waikato should remain in Maori hands. His first three years in office were tense. Elected members of Government in Auckland made frequent calls for the forceful suppression of Maori groups who sought to prohibit land sales and whose raison d'être seemed to imply disloyalty to the Crown. In 1863 fighting broke

---

† 425 km.

out in Taranaki after troops were sent there to take possession of the Tatarai-
maka block, whose sale was disputed by a group of Ati Awa owners. Tawhiao
did not favour involvement in the dispute; but some of his Ngati Haua and Ngati
Maniapoto followers did and they crossed into Taranaki to help the Maori
defenders (whose case was upheld by subsequent official investigation).
Governor George Grey, recalled for a second term, seized on this participation,
and on a rumoured threat that a group of Maniapoto were preparing to invade
Auckland. He regarded the combination of circumstances as sufficient excuse
to bring the Kingitanga to heel. On 12 July 1863, Imperial troops led by
Lieutenant-General Duncan Cameron crossed the Mangatawhiri Stream into
Tawhiao's territory. Reluctantly, the Maori King and his supporters found
themselves at war.

In spite of courageous fighting at Rangiriri and Orakau, the Kingite forces
were soundly defeated in nine months.[†] Wiremu Tamehana negotiated his own
peace terms with the Government in 1865. But Tawhiao and his close followers
fled into the bush and steep limestone valleys of Ngati Maniapoto territory,
subsequently known as the King Country.

To punish the so-called rebels and prevent the reformation of the Kingitanga in Waikato, the Government confiscated one-and-a-quarter million acres
of land and opened it for European settlement and agriculture. In Kingite eyes
this action was monstrous in its conception and application: tribes who had ·
remained loyal to the Crown lost land along with those who had not; and the
real rebels, Ngati Maniapoto, lost nothing; the confiscations were revealed as a
ploy. The Government was not interested in justice, as it claimed. Its real
objectives were the dislodging of the Kingitanga and the acquisition of the most
fertile Waikato acreage; both were achieved.[†]

Confiscation was a far greater blow than military defeat; its consequences
were to cripple Waikato for the next sixty years. First, a group of tribes that had
formerly been able to support itself comfortably and to offer hospitality liberally
was now unable even to subsist on land of its own. Secondly, the loss of sites
that were traditionally significant — burial grounds, places of prayer, sites of
centuries of habitation, access to the river itself — created an intense feeling of
deprivation. Waikato people had lost all the places that gave them a sense of

---

[†] It has been estimated that this war and the one in Taranaki took a total of 800 European
lives and 1800 Maori lives (see Grayland 1968).
[‡] Indeed, the ministry had decided that the 'punishment should be measured by the needs of
the Government rather than by the offence of the Natives' (quoted by Andersen and
Petersen, p. 224). Subsequently 314,364 acres were returned to loyalist tribes. The final
total of Waikato land confiscated was 887,808 acres.

history, continuity and identity; and they had lost them to people who neither knew nor cared about the history of the land and who appeared to desecrate it as further punishment.[†] Ironically, the very pain of loss and desecration became the basis for an alternative source of Waikato identify and strength. Maori commentators were to suggest subsequently that if Waikato had not shared the transparently unjust grievance of the confiscation, the Kingitanga and the tribal bonds it cemented would have been unlikely to last beyond the nineteenth century.[4]

For twenty years after the war Tawhiao wandered nomadically through Maniapoto and Taranaki settlements. He made contact with the Taranaki prophets Te Ua Haumene, Te Whiti o Rongomai and Tohu Kakahi (and, through intermediaries, the Hokianga one Aperahama Taonui). From Te Ua he took the name Tawhiao and his own version of the Pai Marire religion, which he called Tariao after the morning star.[†] He absorbed and expressed an Old Testament view of himself as anointed leader of a chosen people wandering in the wilderness, but who would one day be delivered into their inheritance. His sayings most frequently repeated and remembered by his followers were of a millennial character — 'This phase of salvation shall not extend beyond the days of my grandchild, and then we shall emerge reborn'.[5] And, as he wandered and preached, Tawhiao made seasonal homes for himself and his retinue at places like Hikurangi, Te Kumi, Taharoa and Te Kakawa.

The stalemate did not please anybody. Tawhiao had no wish to remain separated from the bulk of his followers. And the Government was unhappy about a section of the country sealed off to Europeans (Pakehas were warned that they would be killed if they crossed the Aukati or King Country boundary, and indeed three men were after 1870). The King Country also served as a sanctuary for other outlaws such as the Ringatu prophet Te Kooti Rikirangi, driven there in May 1872 away from his own following in the Bay of Plenty and East Coast.

By the 1870s the insatiable European appetite for land was strong again, and there were plans for a railway that would eventually link the settlements of the North Island from north to south. To avoid lengthy delays and costly

---

† The extent of Pakeha insensitivity to the history of what was to be their own land was underlined by Sir John Gorst when he returned to Waikato in 1907. He visited Taupiri, 'the once sacred mountain of the Maories [sic], most of the timber seemed to have been cut away, and the base so sacred in former days that no traveller could proceed up the river on that shore . . . was now desecrated by a railway station and cutting, and the screams and smoke of locomotive engines.' (Gorst, 1908, p. 300.)

‡ See Chapters 4 and 10. The expression 'Pai Marire' means 'good and gentle'. It was taken from the ritual chant that ended (in Waikato) 'rire rire hau pai marire'.

detours, it became imperative that the King Country be opened. There was also a recognition among the more perceptive government officers, such as Native Minister Donald McLean and the Resident Magistrate William Gilbert Mair, that Tawhiao was not a threat; he was an excessively modest and moderate man. There was far more to be gained by making an ally of him than by leaving him an outlaw.

And so the Government offered peace terms. Sir George Grey, now Premier of the country he had twice governed, visited the King in May 1878 and, according to Mair's diary, offered him 'lands on the left bank of the Waipa, 500 acres at Ngaruawahia, land in all the townships, further money aid and the right over roads, surveys and land dealings.'[6] Tawhiao and his advisers refused such blandishments because they implied relinquishment of the kingship and precluded complete restoration of their former kingdom.

Then, in July 1881, Tawhiao requested that Mair meet him at Alexandra.[†] The King came forth with 600 of his followers. After the exchange of formal greetings, he motioned Mair to stand back. He 'laid his gun on the ground, an example which was followed by seventy of his people. He then had seventy roasted pigeons and a fantail laid alongside the guns, after which the King told Mair: "This means peace." Picking up the fantail he handed it to Mair and said: "This bird belongs to this land. I have ritually endowed it with all the sacredness I possess. It shall be a talisman of peace for this land." . . . The telegraph flashed the information to all parts of New Zealand.'[7]

After this ceremony Tawhiao led his entourage to all the waahi tapu — the sacred places — that had been taken out of Maori hands. He wept over them. The loss of his captial Ngaruawahia left him feeling especially rootless. And because he was rootless he was restless. He remained itinerant, making his home for months at a time at places like Whatiwhatihoe, Maungatautari and Parawera.

Tawhiao never recovered the support that the King Movement had enjoyed before the war. All Waikato tribes — rebels and loyalists — renewed membership. And other groups treated him with respect when, in 1882, he travelled as far north as Waiomio, and south as Wairarapa and Otaki. As a result of this tour he was persuaded to lead a deputation to England with a petition to the British monarch about Maori land grievances. He sailed from New Zealand early in 1884 accompanied by Major Wiremu Te Wheoro, who had fought with the

---

† Now Pirongia. Tawhiao had made occasional trips over the Aukati border before this: on occasions to meet Mair at Alexandra; and a photograph in the Fergusson family archives is labelled 'Sir James Fergusson [then Governor of New Zealand] meeting King Tawhiao, Ngaruawahia, April 1874' (personal communication, Lord Ballantrae, 11/1/77).

Government in the war and been elected Member of Parliament for Western Maori in 1879,[†] and Patara Te Tuhi, who had been given responsibility for issuing the King's proclamations. (Also in the party were Te Ropiha from Hawke's Bay and Topia Turoa from Whanganui.)

Like non-English British subjects before and after him, Tawhiao assumed that the monarch ruled as well as reigned; that because the New Zealand chiefs had ceded sovereignty to Victoria in return for her protection, that same Queen would now consider their complaints in the light of their treaty with her. His confidence, of course, was misplaced. He was refused an audience with Victoria. Sir John Gorst[‡] introduced the party to the Colonial Office, and the Earl of Derby commended their petition to the New Zealand Government, to whom he referred confidently as 'our fellow Englishmen'.[8] These fellow Englishmen, however, eventually answered Derby's request for observations by concluding that they would least embarrass Her Majesty's Government by saying nothing.[9] Acting legitimately and in good faith, the King was dismissed and returned to New Zealand empty-handed. He did, however, use the occasion to make a clear statement to Derby of how he viewed the Maori kingship in relation to the British monarchy: 'I am called a king, not for the purpose of separation,' he said, 'but in order that the Natives might be united under one race, ever acknowledging the supremacy of the Queen and claiming her protection.'[10]

Back home, Tawhiao's reaction to rebuff was to look for Maori solutions to Maori problems through Maori institutions, and to attempt to do so on a national basis. In 1886 he petitioned the Native Minister John Ballance for the establishment of a Maori Council 'for all the chiefs of this Island'.[11] When this produced no result, he set up his own Kauhanganui or House of Assembly at Maungakawa in 1892. It was chaired by the Tumuaki (President) Tana Te Waharoa, son of Wiremu Tamehana and second Kingmaker, and all tribes of the North Island were invited to attend. In fact, participation was confined largely to the Waikato, Maniapoto and Hauraki people already committed to the kingship. At the inaugural meeting, Tawhiao emphasised his attitude to Europeans: 'All Pakeha-Maori, Pakeha storekeepers, blacksmiths and carpenters are my people.'[12] (It was a tolerant view that was to contrast with those expressed later in the same assembly by the second Tumuaki and third Kingmaker, Tupu Taingakawa; the statement was also cited forty years later to justify a Kingitanga alliance with the New Zealand Labour Party.)

Tawhiao's parliament occupied itself with a discussion of proceedings in the national Parliament, interpretations of the Treaty of Waitangi, the confiscation

---

† Te Wheoro lost his seat while he was abroad.
‡ Resident Magistrate and Civil Commissioner in Waikato 1861–63. See page 67.

issue, conditions for land sales, and mundane matters such as forbidding cruelty to animals. Its deliberations, recommendations and petitions (a major one on Maori land in 1895, for example) were consistently ignored by Parliament and public servants, except as a butt for jokes and scorn.

Tawhiao's other major innovation within the organisation of the King Movement was the establishment of poukai — annual visits by the King to Kingitanga marae. They arose out of the need for Waikato men to scatter in search of seasonal work. Tawhiao conceived poukai as a means of drawing people back to their home marae at least once a year on a fixed day, when he would visit them. A secondary motive was the setting aside of one day in the year when 'the widowed, the orphaned and the poor' of each district would be fed and entertained by those who were more fortunate.[13] In subsequent years the poukai evolved into the regular basis for consultation between the Kingitanga leadership and its followers; and into a system of collecting 'tributes' or financial contributions towards the movement's expenses and the upkeep of local marae.

In 1894 Tawhiao began to transfer the remains of his ancestors and relatives from burial places in confiscated territories to Taupiri Mountain, which he designated the major Waikato cemetery.[†] Then he travelled to Parawera where, on 26 August, he died suddenly after a game of cards with friends. His tangi lasted almost a month and his body was carried slowly through Waikato to Taupiri. There, with bands playing funeral marches, rifles firing salutes and dynamite exploding on the hillside, he was buried in front of 4000 followers and mourners on 24 September.[‡]

Tawhiao had been unsuccessful in his large objectives. His appeal to the Crown for the return of Waikato lands — and with them a re-establishment of cultural roots, economic security and family life — had failed; so had his attempt to revive morale and self-reliance through a Maori parliament. And yet it was Tawhiao's memory — his goals and his sayings — that were to dominate Waikato thinking for the next century and determine the objectives of three subsequent generations of leaders. Their tactics were to be different, but their vision was Tawhiao's.

While Tawhiao was being mourned his oldest son Mahuta succeeded to the kingship. In words that were to be quoted as characterising his term of office, Mahuta said over his father's body: 'Depart with all your heritage. And leave me

---

† His injunction in this instance was: 'Gather all our dead together at Taupiri so that when I pronounce the day of salvation they will all hear.'
‡ According to kahui ariki traditions, the body was later exhumed and re-interred elsewhere on Taupiri to forestall interference with the remains.

to fashion a new heritage in your wake.'[14] He was 'crowned' by Tana Te Waharoa with the Bible that the first Kingmaker had placed on the heads of his father and grandfather.

Mahuta was more settled than Tawhiao had been. He had married Te Marae, daughter of the fighting chief Amuketi killed at Rangiriri, and had had four sons: Te Rata, Taipu, Tumate and Tonga (and later a fifth, Te Rauangaanga). Since childhood he had lived at Hukanui near Waahi Pa, across the Waikato River from Huntly. From the beginning of his kingship he took an interest in politics and was prepared to experiment with contact with the national Parliament. In 1896 he successfully sponsored a Ngati Te Ata relative, Henare Kaihau, for the Western Maori electorate. And from the late 1890s, with Kaihau acting as intermediary, Mahuta was in regular contact with Prime Minister Richard John Seddon and Native Affairs Minister James Carroll.[†]

He was also an advocate of accommodation between Maori and Pakeha. 'It has always been a desire of my heart to speak in friendship with the Pakeha people who at one time lived in love and peace with my father and grandfather,' he told a group of European mourners after Tawhiao's death. 'At this time there is nothing that should divide us.'[15] Seddon, sensing and taking advantage of the King's goodwill and naivety, set out to woo him with the Liberal Government's programme of opening up more Maori land to European small farmers. The Prime Minister came to Waahi in 1898 and again in 1903, and he corresponded with Mahuta in between. In 1902 he invited the King to Wellington as a member of the Legislative Council (Upper House) and to sit on the Executive Council as 'Minister representing the Maori race'. Carroll, the only Maori in cabinet, opposed this gesture;[16] but Seddon's weight, as usual, was decisive.

The invitation generated perplexity in Waikato. In an argument that was to be repeated in later years,[‡] some elders saw it as an attempt to tame the Kingitanga, to slot it into a Pakeha-controlled pigeonhole. Others argued that it was an honour and a measure of recognition by the Pakeha Government of the mana of the King.[17] In fact it was neither of those things. Seddon simply wanted access to more Waikato land and knew he was most likely to get it with Mahuta's cooperation.

---

† Carroll had entered Parliament in 1887 as the Member for Eastern Maori. In 1893 he was elected to the Waiapu seat (European); he became the first Maori cabinet minister in 1896, and subsequently the first Maori to be knighted and the first to serve as acting-Prime Minister.
‡ In 1937 when Te Puea was offered a CBE, and in 1968 when Te Atairangikaahu was made a DBE.

At Waahi, in the course of a hui to discuss Maori land:
(front) Prime Minister Richard Seddon and King Mahuta;
(rear) Tupu Taingakawa, Henare Kaihau and James Carroll. ATL

Mahuta accepted the positions offered. According to Apirana Ngata, Ngati Maniapoto were so incensed that they came to Government House in Auckland for the swearing-in in May 1903 and sang a derisive song at Henare Kaihau, who they blamed for the appointment.[18] Mahuta entrusted the kingship for the next five years to his younger brother Te Wherowhero while he moved between Waahi and the capital. A colleague of the time, F. M. B. Fisher, noted that the King was not a good mixer in Wellington (unlike the gregarious Kaihau), and that he was most uncomfortable in Parliament and at Executive Council meetings.[19]

Throughout Mahuta's years of office the state of Waikato was one of continuous depression, economic and social. And the basic factor was land: lack of it in the case of families and tribes who had suffered most from the confiscations; and an inability to make it productive in the case of owners. Seddon kept pressure on Mahuta to release further acreage for sale and windfalls of income made the proposition attractive in the short term. A series of well-attended meetings at Waahi between 1907 and 1911 discussed the related questions of local self-government within the King Movement and the disposal of land by sale and lease. The latter was frequently seen as a way of financing the former. (Waikato had declined to set up councils under Parliament's Maori Councils Act of 1900 to supervise tribal affairs, health and sanitation. It saw them as a potential threat to the mana of the King.) These meetings also tried to initiate schemes for the development of unproductive land; but they always foundered because of the Government's refusal to lend money to Maori for this purpose. The Liberals wanted Maori land in production, but in Pakeha hands.

To his credit, Mahuta tried to keep up the pressure. He told the Legislative Council in 1906 that 'it was not sufficient merely to open up Maori lands for European settlement. Parliament should pass a law which would enable the Maori to work his lands.'[20] The Liberals' policy, however, was just that — to open up more and more land on a 'state tenantry' basis for the settlement of 'industrious yeomen' who would become efficient farmers, contributors to the wealth of the nation, and entrenched supporters of the Government who had created them. 'Prices were high, New Zealand credit was good,' one commentator noted. 'Money was cheap and available for any purpose except for the rehabilitation of the Maori race.'[21]

The consequence was that the majority of Maori in Waikato were unable to work, and where they did they drifted from job to job. 'You find them working as labourers and as flaxmill hands,' wrote Pomare in 1907. 'Many of them are extremely poor and live in miserable hovels.'[22] Hone Patene told a 1905 Royal Commission on church schools that his whole hapu were 'digging gum and made nothing at it; they were badly off and drank and wasted their money.'[23] Even in the ranks of the kahui ariki at Waahi morale was low. Te Uira Te Heuheu, daughter of Te Heuheu Tukino, came to live in Waikato in 1913. She was 'staggered' by social conditions. 'There was much drinking, especially among the men. There seemed to be no sense of direction as far as policy was concerned and life just drifted by.'[24]

Health, too, in Waikato was particularly bad. In most Maori communities there, life was a miserable recurrence of typhoid epidemics interspersed with bouts of influenza, measles and whooping cough. This was partly a result of social conditions and partly of the refusal to set up supervisory councils and appoint sanitary inspectors under the Maori Councils Act. There were few doctors in Waikato who would attend Maori patients, no hospitals to admit them and no preventative health measures. (Only four doctors in Waikato received payment from the Native Affairs Department in 1906 for seeing Maori patients; the nearest hospitals were in Auckland and Hamilton but they rarely took Maori and did not want to. Judge H.F. Edgar, of the Native Department, wrote in 1906: 'The hospitals, notably Auckland, are very unsympathetic regarding the admission of Maoris for treatment, their principal argument being that the Maoris pay but little towards the upkeep of the hospital [through rates].'[25])

Disease, therefore, especially typhoid and tuberculosis, was believed to take a heavier toll in Waikato than in other districts, and one that was not even recorded (Maori deaths were not then notifiable as were European ones). The Auckland District Health Officer was concerned about this state of affairs, but only because of its implications for Pakeha communities. He wrote in 1911:

'A recent outbreak of typhoid among Europeans in the Waikato district is attributed to Maoris polluting a stream, and it is said that many in the pah (at Te Hoe near Taupiri) have died. We have no means of knowing how far this is true . . . there is no Maori Council for this district . . . As matters stand, the Native race is a menace to the wellbeing of the European.'[26]

In addition there were few schools in Waikato and consequently no Maori leaders or potential leaders with a European education beyond the most elementary level. Families who had fought in the war and suffered confiscation were bitter and did not want schools; those who did were denied them because of the attitude of the conservatives.[27] Henare Kaihau in 1905 estimated that there were 2000 school-age children in Waikato, of whom only a handful were actually at school. The tribes had no educated mediators — no Apirana Ngatas, Maui Pomares or Peter Bucks — to lead them into the twentieth century. And they were resentful when outsiders tried to assume this role.[28]

This, then, was the kingdom over which Mahuta presided at the turn of the century, and which his niece Te Puea Herangi was to inherit. It was a sad contrast to the one described by Hochstetter and bequeathed to Tawhiao forty years before. Nor was there the substantial Maori support for the kingship beyond Waikato that Tawhiao had initially enjoyed. The 1863 war and subsequent exile of King Movement leaders had re-defined earlier loyalties. The first circle of tribes, of course, remained committed. And another wider circle, while not paying the formal allegiance of earlier years, retained a special and sympathetic relationship with the movement — Taranaki, Ngati Ranginui and Ngaiterangi of the Bay of Plenty, Ngati Tuwharetoa, the Ngati Pikiao section of Te Arawa and Ngati Whatua of Auckland. Beyond this, Kingite spokesmen met with other tribes at hui outside Waikato, such as those held at Parewanui in Rangitikei; and occasionally non-Kingites like Tuhoe participated in sittings of the King's parliament. But there was virtually no formal contact with Ngapuhi in the north, Ngati Porou and Ngati Kahungunu on the East Coast, and the people of the far south.

To the non-adherents Mahuta was, perhaps, a rangatira. But he was little more. By the time Te Puea Herangi moved to the front rank of the Kingitanga it was not only struggling to win acceptance from Europeans; it had to re-establish its role in the eyes of former Maori supporters.

1

Early years

Te Puea Herangi was born at Whatiwhatihoe on the northern boundary of the King Country in November 1883 [1] to a union not then legitimised. Her mother Tiahuia, daughter of King Tawhiao, was an ariki; her father, Te Tahuna Herangi, a half-Pakeha commoner rejected by Tiahuia's family as unsuitable for marriage. The story of the parents' courtship is instructive — it reveals a kind of behaviour that Te Puea grew up to favour, emulate, and eventually to reject when she herself was cast as the figure of family authority.

It was customary for the kahui ariki to arrange marriages. This was not solely to preserve genealogical equality or 'purity', although that was often the justification. It was far more a way of creating or strengthening useful alliances among families and tribes.† This in turn strengthened the structure of Maori social groupings and the authority of their leaders. The object and frequent result was to allow family heads to combine effectively for joint projects and in this fashion to retain Maori control of Maori affairs.

Consideration had been given to Tiahuia's prospects for this reason. In addition, Waikato people had cause to care more about her than about other female members of her family. She was Tawhiao's eldest child by his senior wife, Hera. She was not beautiful, as Tahuna described her, [2] but she was intelligent, strong-willed, and full of energy — features that made her seem larger than her below-average height. More importantly, she was regarded as an inheritor of much of Tawhiao's atuatanga or spiritual qualities. [3] Her penetrating eyes suggested esoteric knowledge, and her quick brain and articulateness seemed to confirm it. With these factors in mind and a view to

---

† The arranged marriage that perhaps best illustrated these objectives was that between Kati, the younger brother of Te Wherowhero, and Matire Toha, niece of Hongi Hika. This union in 1824 consolidated the truce between Waikato and Ngapuhi.

Tawhiao, second Maori King and grandfather of Te Puea Herangi. ATL

strengthening his position in a territory that had fought with the Government in the war, Tawhiao had betrothed Tiahuia to a Ngati Mahuta relative named Tuteao.

The considered plan came undone in 1873. Tawhiao, still confined to the King Country, was visiting Otewa near Te Kuiti. His lieutenants engaged a local boy to look after the horses. After he had secured them for the night, Tahuna came into the meeting house, lay down on his sleeping mat and began to sing a Rarotongan waiata to himself. Solitary performances were not welcomed at Maori gatherings. The older people heard him and told the boy to stand and sing for the whole house. Shy and confused, he would not. Tiahuia was drawn to the banter and she ordered him to sing. This time he did. After the audience had finished applauding, the girl brought her blanket over to Tahuna and announced she was going to sleep with him that night. 'I was frightened of her,' he said seventy years later. 'I knew she was too high for me. Besides, at this time I had not known women.' [4] He was then eighteen years old, Tiahuia about sixteen.

Te Puea's mother Tiahuia.
Turongo House

Te Tahuna Herangi, father of Te Puea.
Ngeungeu Zister

Te Tahuna was the third son of William Nicoll Searancke, a surveyor and draughtsman who had come to New Zealand in 1842. Contrary to allegations that sought to explain Te Puea's wartime activities, he was not German.[†] His family had lived in Hertfordshire for at least four generations and had produced a crop of English brewers, soldiers, lawyers and clergymen; his father had lost an arm serving under Nelson at Copenhagen. William was the eighth child and claimed that he had been educated at Eton.[‡] He trained as a surveyor. He arrived in New Zealand on the *Brougham* when he was twenty-six years old. Work as a draughtsman for the New Zealand Company affected his eyesight and he moved to Te Kopua in the Waipa district in the early 1850s. Like many of his compatriots in similar circumstances, he took a Maori wife. When it became apparent that this woman could not conceive, her family substituted a

[†] Although for some reason W.N. Searancke and his father were both in Germany at the time the former applied for passage to New Zealand. (F.J. Searancke to Directors of N.Z. Company, PRO document CO 208/18, XN/01722).
[‡] One of Searancke's daughters gave this information to Ramsden, and it is apparently confirmed in Norris, p. 5. The Eton College archivist, however, was unable to find the name in the relevant college registers (private communication, 15/11/76).

niece so that the Pakeha husband might know the joys of fatherhood. This too was customary.

Searancke had three sons and a daughter by the second wife, Hariata Rangitaupa of the Ngati Ngawaero hapu of Ngati Maniapoto. They were educated at a Wesleyan mission school at Te Kopua. When the Waikato war appeared imminent, Searancke considered his life in danger and took refuge in Auckland. In 1865 he returned to the Waikato as a Resident Magistrate and with an English wife. Not only did he seek no further contact with his Maori family, he appeared to reverse his former loyalties; in the 1860s and 1870s he reported constantly to the Native Minister Donald McLean on the condition of Waikato Maori. In 1867, for example, he described them as 'lazy, sulky, discontented and half-starved to boot'.[5] He died in Hamilton in 1904 after fathering a family of three daughters by his third wife.

His son Te Tahuna has been described as handsome in a rugged kind of way.[6] He was tall, far taller[†] than most Maori men. His skin was light coloured. He was strong, practically inclined, and had a true singing voice that sounded rasping when he spoke. He was also a religious man who had retained the Methodist faith throughout the anti-European years of the Waikato war and its aftermath.

Although he clearly had no genealogical or political claim to Tiahuia, the liaison did not at first worry Tawhiao and the family. Tiahuia had taken men before. It was all part of conventional and necessary pre-marital experience that made subsequent fidelity more likely. What became a problem was that the sight and sound of Tahuna that had first led to Tiahuia's claim on him evolved into a fierce love that made her determined to keep him. And, for a time, she did. Tawhiao confronted her after some months. He forbade her to see Tahuna and she refused to obey him. And so Tahuna was sent away from the King Country in the hope that once he was out of sight Tiahuia would lose her obsession for him. She did not.

Tahuna went to Nelson and stayed there several years. He even took a Maori wife there. Eventually he returned to the King Country to visit his relatives, imagining that Tiahuia would have forgotten him. When he passed through the pa where she was staying, he found a group of bare-footed women on the marae learning how to waltz. As he stopped to watch them, two of Tiahuia's women came up behind him, covered him with a blanket, and led him to her bed. From that time they remained together in spite of family disapproval.[7]

---

† Over two metres.

Tawhiao refused to acknowledge the marriage for seven more years,[8] although Tiahuia and Tahuna remained in his entourage until he went to England in 1884. Of the senior members of the immediate family, only Tiahuia's brother Mahuta stayed loyal to her (and Tahuna became one of his councillors after Tawhiao's death in 1894). Meanwhile the couple had had three children: Hera born in 1880, Te Puea in 1883 and Tamati. They moved from Whatiwhatihoe to Pukekawa in 1884 and from there to Mercer.

It could not have been easy for someone with a strong sense of family to hold out so long against her own clan. Tiahuia did so because she believed her choice was right for her and that Tawhiao would come to accept it. In this she had the support of the Mercer and the Ngati Tipa people of the Waikato Heads, who built a strong personal following around her that was to become the nucleus of Te Puea's later popularity.† (It was not unusual for different tribes, while acknowledging the supremacy of the King, to have a favourite among the kahui ariki whom they would regard as their immediate leader.[9]) Meanwhile Tahuna had become more confident as a result of living with Tiahuia, even to the point where some people described him as arrogant.[10] He had taken to wearing a huia feather in his hair, a mark of hereditary chieftainship to which members of the kahui ariki felt he was not entitled; this further delayed their acceptance of him.[11]

Finally Tawhiao relented. Tiahuia's behaviour was exceptional; but it was also determined and consistent. What led to tribal acceptance and the status of marriage,‡ according to one of Te Puea's confidants, was the spectacle of three 'illegitimate' children in the kahui ariki ranks and the prospect of more; worse, there was the possibility that Tiahuia might leave Waikato with Tahuna to escape further reproach. And so, before the birth of the fourth child, Wanakore, the relationship was formalised. There were two further children, Te Ngaehe and Te Atarua.* Apart from brief trips away with Tawhiao, Te Tahuna and Tiahuia remained near Mercer for most of Te Puea's early childhood. After Tiahuia's death the family moved for a short time to the Waipa district and Moehake, and then returned to Mercer.[12]

The name Te Puea means 'the rise to the surface' and accounts about its origin in this case differ. The most likely is that which Te Puea herself gave

---

† This group initiated the 'whitebait tribute' by which commercial buyers from Maori fishermen paid a tax that went towards expenses for Kingitanga functions. Te Puea was to revive the practice.

‡ 'Maori' or customary marriage was recognised in New Zealand law if it had the public sanction of family and tribe.

* Tamati died young; Te Ngaehe and Te Atarua in young adulthood; Wanakore in April 1951; and Hera, the eldest, outlived Te Puea.

Judge Acheson: 'Mahuta had a son . . . and exultantly cried "Puea ahau i te ao!" which means "My name will now be known to the world." . . . But the baby died. My mother gave birth to me. I was named Te Puea.'[13] Among her family, however, she was nicknamed Kirihaehae — the incised skin — in commemoration of a minor operation undergone by her uncle Tawera, the first performed on a member of the kahui ariki. Over the years this name was contracted to the more appealing form of Kiri.

Earlier writers such as Acheson and Ramsden tidied Te Puea's character into a neat package of attributes inherited separately from each parent (mystic and poetic faculties from the Maori side, organisational skills and application from the 'German'). Such an approach is more pat than credible. Nor does it explain why, with almost identical hereditary and environmental factors, her brothers and sisters escaped some of the same traits.

Nevertheless it is tempting to relate much of her behaviour to examples set by the parents, particularly as she often stressed how much she came to be influenced by Tiahuia after the latter's death. Like her mother, Te Puea displayed qualities — some human, some peculiarly Maori — that have tended to lie dormant through the kahui ariki line and assert themselves avatar-like in females of different generations.

There was a streak of imperiousness, an air of disdainful command presence, that impelled some people to give these indulged women exactly what they asked for and others to despise them. Tawhiao's cousin Te Paea[14] had it, as did Tiahuia, Te Puea's first-cousin Piupiu and, later, her grand-niece Piki and her second cousin Te Marae Mahuta. This characteristic alternated with a playfulness that was part wilfulness and part genuine affection for family and favourites. It showed itself in a determination to direct the course of games without consultation, and it led to elaborate and sometimes cruel practical jokes. Always, it assumed a blind loyalty for the sake of friendship or, in adult life, for the esprit de corps of the Kingitanga.

In addition to such behaviour — or, perhaps, arising out of it — Te Puea was credited with the Maori qualities of tapu and mana in heightened proportions. The first gave her a degree of exalted untouchability in the eyes of her non-ariki followers; the second an ability to project an aura of wehi or almost palpable prestige. In most members of the kahui ariki these qualities remained latent — they could be claimed or activated when someone assumed a leadership role. In others like Tiahuia and Mahuta, they were apparent at once and the role tended to assume them. Te Puea was one of the latter, her brothers and sisters were not.

Old people were free to spend considerable time with children in the kind of communities in which Te Puea grew up. Indeed, they spent more time with children than did parents, who were preoccupied with the tasks of day-to-day livelihood. They constantly reminded Te Puea that she was a grand-daughter of King Tawhiao. They encouraged her to dominate other children and even adults. They were amused when she did. It was Tiahuia, ripened by the experiences of a similar childhood, who pulled her up. The crisis came one day when Te Puea saw a stick that she wanted lying on the ground and asked an older boy to bring it to her. The boy refused. So Te Puea picked it up and began to lash him about the legs until he was bleeding and crying.[15] Tiahuia sent for Te Puea and Hera and asked about this incident. In particular she asked her second daughter why she, as a child, was ordering people about.

'I said it was because I had been reminded that I was a member of the nobility,' Te Puea wrote later.[16] 'All other people were my social inferiors. At that moment Tiahuia drew out a stick and began to hit me. Somebody rushed forward to intervene but she stopped him. Then she said to all of her children: "Listen to me. You are no better than those you have been beating. You are all equal in rank. It is only because of their agreement that you have been elevated in status so that you can be called people of consequence. So it is for you to honour these people, whether you consider them greater or lesser than you. If they are cold, give them clothing. When they are sick, look after them. It is only through the people as a whole that you will be called somebody of note. But if you have to blow your own trumpet because of this, you are worthless." ' †

In later years, Te Puea showed far more awareness of other people's sensibilities. But she still expected to dominate and direct the course of relationships and activities, and those who grew up around her allowed her to. They remembered her as impetuous and demonstrative. 'She always got her way,' Ngeungeu Beamish said of days in Mercer.[17] 'No one questioned her.' And her reward for closeness was physical:

'If you were near her, her arms would fly out when she saw you and she'd grab you and make a fuss of you. She always got excited by the sight of her relatives and friends. She used to tease me by creeping up behind me and miaowing. That was because my name sounded like "miaow, miaow". We

† This statement was to influence Te Puea profoundly. She frequently recalled it (see Acheson and Ramsden) as the basis for her concepts of leadership and service. This account in her own words comes from the notes she prepared at Waiuku on 15 April 1934 for her evidence to the Royal Commission investigating A.T. Ngata and given on 28 April.

tried to nickname her back, "Ihu Parahe" — flat nose. But she wouldn't have it so it didn't stick.

'Even if she didn't actually know people she'd call out hello to them, Pakeha boys and the like. It didn't even matter if they were rough — she was more likely to call out to them if they were rough. And she'd nearly always win people over. It finished up that they'd do practically anything to win favour from that beautiful, beautiful girl.'

She was beautiful, certainly. So were all the Herangi children at an early age. Te Puea had features that it became fashionable to describe as a pleasing result of racial blending: clear, olive skin; a wide and sensual mouth; a flattened nose; and, most dramatically, large, clear and slightly hooded eyes that suggested depths of knowledge on her side and an ability to enter people's minds on the other.

From her father, the so-called European or German side, Te Puea was credited with an unusual ability for organisation and hard work. More likely, the source of these qualities was the fastidiousness she observed in both parents. Tiahuia was obsessively orderly in housekeeping, maintenance of grounds and property and in dress. She would not relax until obvious things were done and the example of her doing them seemed to have a shaming effect on others and persuaded them to help.[18] Photographs of the Herangi children from this period show them groomed and neatly dressed, which was not solely attributable to the occasion of having a picture taken (they were also photographed with other people who did not take such obvious care). These things were unusual for the time and the social climate in which Te Puea grew up. Other members of the kahui ariki, it was noted, did not then place so much importance on orderliness.[19]

Te Puea retained these concerns throughout her life, particularly a fetish for tidiness and a feeling for style in clothes. She enjoyed dressing up for occasions as much as she enjoyed deliberately dressing 'down' when her sack-cloth working clothes (also aesthetically pleasing in a gipsy fashion) seemed to Pakeha to be incongruous with her rank. In younger days, the dress sense also got out of control at times. Her father, who took her to buy clothes while she was at school in Auckland, was persuaded that she had to have a wide-brimmed hat with plumes of ostrich feathers. She wore this back to school and was sent home to remove it.[20]

Her father too, while not as forceful as Tiahuia, was as meticulous about detail. He enjoyed farming and home maintenance, and he liked to keep complete sets of tools and household utensils. He also looked after these tools with excessive care and was unwilling to lend them. This gave him a reputation among other men of being something of an old woman.[21]

The four children seated in front are Herangis: Wanakore, Te Puea, Te Atarua, Tamati. Behind are Tuhi Hira and Te Ranga Poutapu. Turongo House

Apart from her mother and tribal elders generally, Te Puea remembered respecting only two other particular people in childhood: Tawhiao, from a distance; and Mahuta as a result of intimate association. Physically, Tawhiao was an unimpressive man — he had a turned eye; he was short and shambled as he walked; he wore cast-off European clothing; he was asthmatic; and he had a fondness for alcohol. But spiritually he was a charged person. He personified all the qualities of ihi, mana and tapu that the Kingitanga had brought the kahui ariki. His ohaoha or sayings were received with the reverence given to divine revelation, studied closely and continued to guide the King Movement for decades after his death. He was regarded as a medium between the spiritual and the physical worlds. And he had one arresting personal characteristic — his full facial moko.

Like all Waikato children, Te Puea was brought up to hold this grandfather in awe. The first time she remembered encountering him she knew immediately who he was. Tiahuia had taken her to the pa at Mercer when she was six years old. As she was playing marbles with a group of children, she saw a pair of European boots at ground level next to her. Few Tainui Maori wore footwear at this time. Then she heard constricted and heavy breathing. She began to run her eyes up the body until they reached the cross-eyed, tattooed face. Everything she had heard about the man who was now looking at her fondly made her so frightened that she got to her feet and ran away.[22]

With Mahuta it was different. She knew him as 'Uncle' and was aware that

Mahuta, third Maori King and
uncle of Te Puea. Turongo House

Mahuta's wife Te Marae.
Ngeungeu Zister

her mother was his favourite sister, the only person to whom he would defer
without question.[23] He too was a short man and his clothes usually looked ill-
fitting. His drooping moustache gave him a Mediterranean appearance. What
always impressed people most about him was his eyes, which were penetrating
and attentive.[24] Like Tiahuia he was believed to have inherited much of his
father's atuatanga. He too was regarded as a medium and his quasi-biblical
sayings, thought to be portentous and prophetic, were recalled and recited on
Waikato marae. Mahuta was more thoroughly versed than any other member
of his family in Tainui history, chant and song, and he often composed waiata
for special occasions. It was he, more than any other person, who gave Te Puea
an interest in these things.

Te Puea had shown promise from early childhood. Great things were
expected of her because, it was felt, great things had been given her. In addition
to her kahui ariki status, she displayed intelligence and leadership qualities.
Consequently, with Tiahuia's approval, elders had taken her aside and tried to
imbue her with a sense of responsibility to the Kingitanga and a knowledge of
ritual and procedure that would enable her to take a leading role in its activities.
But only Mahuta was able to persuade her to learn with undivided attention.

Most of her Maori education, she was to say later,[25] was from him, 'and it was all in Maori'. On occasion he locked himself in a room with her so that she had no option but to remain with him. If she fell asleep he rapped her awake with a stick. This was one of the few parts of her upbringing that she never rebelled against — this and her father reading to her at night from his Maori Bible which, she said, she came to know thoroughly and to enjoy.[26]

Both parents had strong views on formal education and ones that were at variance with those generally held in Waikato. Tawhiao, Te Puea recalled, forbade Waikato children to go to school in case they should 'weaken' by following Pakeha thoughts and fashions.[27] Further, there was a belief that Maori who went to government or church schools 'came back with European ideas as to how they could best fleece their own people'[28] (and the behaviour of some licensed interpreters and Native Land Court clerks, who wrested land and heirlooms from the uncomprehending, seemed to confirm this fear). There were few enough schools in Waikato anyway. According to evidence given to a Royal Commission on Maori church schools in 1905, only one government school had been provided for the whole of the Waipa district between Whatawhata and Huntly. Waikato's lack of interest was used as an excuse for not providing schools, and those children who did want to go often found it difficult. Consequently, few Waikato children received formal education and this more than any other factor impeded Maori acceptance of Pakeha institutions in the area for several generations.

Tiahuia, however, again disagreed with her father.[29] She felt strongly that a Pakeha education was necessary to equip her children to cope with the world as they would grow up to find it. And Tahuna valued his own literacy; his views were preserved in his evidence to the 1905 Royal Commission. He lamented that so many Waikato children were receiving no education. 'The majority of children in the Waikato are running at large; there might be about 500 not attending school. In the Waipa there are quite 300 from Ngaruawahia to Whatawhata . . . they should be taught trades and callings.' He also noted that, although St Stephen's School in Auckland was financed from Waikato Maori trust funds, no Waikato children had gone there in twenty years.

Tahuna emphasised his determination to get his own children educated. He told the commission he had tried to get his sons into St Stephen's and a daughter (Te Atarua) into Queen Victoria School. But they were not accepted on the ground that 'they do not take children of rank like mine — that I was in a position to pay for them'. In fact he was not. His children's rank, derived he said from Tiahuia, was not commensurate with his income. 'I thought if I sent them vegetables and produce of that kind they would meet the case, and I wrote offering to do so.' His offers, however, were refused.[30]

Te Puea was enrolled at Mercer Primary School on 6 May 1895, the year after Tawhiao's death. At the time the family lived at Pukekawa and she had to walk the distance there and back each school day for fourteen months. After school, she liked to 'sit at the feet of the elders and listen as they talked . . . the tribal knowledge of the old people was prized by everyone. Merely by sitting still and keeping my ears and eyes open, I quickly came to appreciate the wisdom and kindliness of the old folk . . . I came to realise that man is a queer mixture of greatness and commonplace.'[31]

In July 1896, Tiahuia sent Te Puea to Mangere Bridge School in Auckland. She stayed with a cousin, a Mrs Wati who lived near the school and helped to look after Mangere Pa.[32] The roll at this school was heavily Maori and Tiahuia felt her gifted daughter was not being extended. So, after a year at Mangere and a visit home, Te Puea was despatched to Melmerly College, Parnell[†] where 'I had to speak nothing but English'.[33] She was accompanied by Ngeungeu Beamish's older sister Maata, and they boarded at the home of a part-Maori family named Mackie, who treated them well but also made them do gardening and chores around the house. This last obligation annoyed Mahuta, who considered it demeaning for women of rank.[34]

As a consequence of almost three years of European schooling, Te Puea's subsequent command of spoken English and written Maori was good. The experience also encouraged her to adopt later the 'un-Maori' practices of keeping accounts, writing voluminous letters to friends and associates, and making daily entries in a journal. All these habits were foreign to her Maori upbringing, which encouraged communication and transmission of information orally. Her written English, however, her grasp of spelling and construction, remained weak. It was a source of frequent regret to her in later years that she had not remained longer at school to become proficient in this too.[35]

In Maori matters she was unshakeably confident and competent. Her prodigious memory and strong musical sense had absorbed all she learned from Mahuta and other tribal teachers who had taken an interest in her. From early adulthood she was regarded as an authority — albeit an initially non-practising one — on Tainui history, chant, kawa, song and song movements.

In April 1898 Tiahuia died suddenly[‡] and Te Puea, now aged fifteen, was recalled from school in Auckland. Not long afterwards her elder sister Hera married Tungia Te Ao and moved south to Otaki. Te Puea found herself, she

---

[†] It was not Queen Victoria School, as suggested in some accounts of Te Puea's life.

[‡] Te Tahuna subsequently lived for many years at Pirongia before coming to Turangawaewae late in his life, where he died on 7 August 1944 at the age of eighty-eight.

said later, 'head of the tribe. I was greatly supported and they were greatly proud of me. Not the whole of Waikato . . . but those living at Mangatawhiri' (the name most frequently used for the Maori settlement at Mercer until it was known later as Te Paina).[36]

Te Puea in her late teens was beautiful, headstrong and popular, and suddenly without restraining influences (Mahuta was living at Hukanui near Waahi and from 1903 was attending meetings of the Executive and Legislative Councils in Wellington). She was also suffering from the 'family curse' of tuberculosis. She launched into a phase of excessive smoking and drinking and frenetic sexual activity[†] that was heightened by an awareness of the disease eating her lungs. There were times in her late teens when she was frightfully ill — weak, coughing and haemorrhaging. The conviction that she would not live long (shared by her family) drove her to further bouts of excess in the periods of remission. She intended to live what little life she had left to the full.

Her confident sensuality and recklessness seemed to seek and attract the same qualities in men. The animus that possessed and drove her sought physical contact and expression. A photograph from this period shows a wide-mouthed, bare-shouldered woman, hair down, reclining with a feather cloak draped loosely about her. It is a portrait with some of the qualities of Goya's Maja paintings. It suggests an alluring woman who is physically available and wants to be wanted. And wanted she was. At hui, according to Michael Rotohiko Jones, she had only to point her finger at a man and she got him.[37] Tai Mitchell of Arawa met her for the first time during this period. He was working as a surveyor near Mercer and he and his party were invited to Mangatawhiri to sample what was then known as Waikato hospitality.

'She was a very handsome girl indeed. That was the first occasion I was to observe a peculiar Waikato custom that was then popular. Te Puea, chanting a ngeri and followed by her girls, approached us with a teapot in her hands. The teapot was filled with neat whisky. Te Puea paused before each guest. When my turn came I refused to drink. Te Puea, who was furious with me, insisted. But I had promised my future wife that I would not touch liquor and I was equally strong-minded . . . There were few men who would have wished to withstand her — Te Puea was very attractive indeed.'[38]

---

† In adolescent days there had been a suspicion of a relationship with her cousin, Te Rata. But it was a subterfuge. Te Rata persuaded Te Puea to join him under his blanket at a hui, to general approval, but only to allay suspicion so that he could invite another girl there later in the night (Ramsden, Notes after a visit to Waikato, January 1932. R.P.).

Te Puea in her early twenties, the reckless years. ATL

Some of her early relationships were accepted by the kahui ariki, unwillingly but resignedly, and achieved the status of customary marriage — those with Tom Paikea of Tangirau and Paraire Herewini of Takapu, for example. The marriage to Herewini in particular was regarded as one of promise. His family was related to Potatau on his father's side, and Major Te Wheoro, who had accompanied Tawhiao to England, was his uncle. Paraire himself was identified as a future leader of the Kingitanga[†] and one for whom Te Puea would be a valuable partner. But it did not last. Te Puea had continuous arguments with his mother who lived with them in the cottage Paraire had built at Takapu, and who was as strong-willed as the younger woman (she was also an East Coaster who lacked ariki status and local acceptance). Te Puea simply left the house one morning after a particularly intense fight and walked to Waahi. She never went back.

None of these early liaisons lasted long. After bouts of passionate infatuation they degenerated into petty and often drunken bickering. Te Puea was still

---

† Which he became. After the death of Patara Te Tuhi he took the position of King Movement scribe and was responsible for issuing many of the panui and proclamations of Te Rata and his successor Koroki. He died as one of Waikato's most senior elders in 1970.

wracked with tuberculosis and this drove her back to drink. She felt little remorse at the time but in later years was to repent of those days with almost evangelical testimonies. And she was to go to considerable lengths to preserve girls in her care from similar experiences. She told Judge Acheson in 1940 (in an idiom that probably owes more to Acheson's presentation than to Te Puea's delivery):

'I was too young to know what I wanted. The wise words of my mother ceased to sound in my ears. I dropped my father's bible studies . . . They encouraged me to give speeches at tribal gatherings. I was carried away by these things. I became thoroughly spoilt and headstrong . . . I loved. Love gnawed at my breast. Its whirling power threatened to make . . . my mind [blank] . . . Tribal approval. Tribal disapproval.'[39] And, in a letter to Merenia Ramsden: 'I am not a clean woman, Merenia. I have been through a life in my younger days which, when I look back, makes me hang my head in shame. I have brought up sixty young girls and I watched them to see that they didn't follow my footsteps. Some got away with it — it is the way of the world.'[40]

Potentially the most destructive of these relationships was one with a European named Roy Clements Seccombe, then of Mangere. Seccombe belonged to an established Auckland family. His grandfather Richard Seccombe, son of a Devonshire squire, had come to New Zealand in 1840 and established what was reputed to be the country's first brewery. Later he set up Lion Brewery in Khyber Pass Road, Auckland. The grandson was dark-haired, good looking in a raffish kind of way and had a jesting sense of humour. According to his relatives,[41] his only direct contribution to the family business was that he was alcoholic. This condition, along with his propensity for gambling, had given him the reputation of being the black sheep of the family — a status he seemed to enjoy.

Te Puea was one year older than Seccombe. She appears to have met him in Mangere when she was staying with the Wati family or with a woman named Te Aorere, who kept a house for Mahuta at the foot of Mount Mangere. She was attracted to him physically,[42] by his pursuit of drinking and horse racing, and by his initial ability to pay for these things (his mother, Lily Seccombe, kept her two sons supplied with family money). Seccombe's relatives and Te Puea's confidants believed the couple had married legally. But there is no record of such a formality. Certainly she lived with him for a year at Mangere in about 1910, and she occasionally took him to Waikato for regattas and races. Ngeungeu Beamish remembered seeing them together on the balcony of the

Delta Hotel at Ngaruawahia and hearing her Maori grandparents express disappointment and strong disapproval.[†]

The disapproval was general throughout the kahui ariki and Waikato. Te Puea had become involved to the extent where she was prepared to renounce her Maoriness and reject the responsibilities that her family had given her. A final confrontation with Mahuta changed that.[‡] But even after the relationship was terminated, Te Puea was dogged for some years by Seccombe and his mother trying to obtain land from her as a form of settlement.[43] [*]

Te Puea's capacity for intense but short-lived relationships did not end with Seccombe. Within a year of reconciliation with her family, another attack of haemorrhaging resulted in her being sent south to recuperate at Tokaanu on the shore of Lake Taupo. There she renewed acquaintance with Te Tahi Iwikau of Tuwharetoa, whom she had met previously at Waikato hui. Physically, he was an appealing man — handsome like most of the male Te Heuheus (he was a nephew of the paramount chief Te Heuheu Tukino) and although not tall, he had an exceptionally upright bearing. Unusually for a Maori, he was freckled.[44]

Te Uira Te Heuheu, Tahi's cousin, recalled seeing them together at Tokaanu in 1912:

'Te Puea then smiled at me that wonderful smile of hers. She was an exceedingly pretty woman, and dressed in the height of the then fashion. I can remember . . . the large picture hat that she wore. She had all the accessories of a well-dressed woman . . . I later copied . . . her dress. But it was her eyes that impressed more than anything else. Father and Mother later took Tahi and Te Puea around the lake to various marae.'[45]

The trip around Lake Taupo was to familiarise Tuwharetoa with an arranged marriage. Te Tahi was a great-grandson of Te Heuheu Iwikau who had been offered the Maori kingship ahead of Potatau. Although Waikato had traditionally frowned on kahui ariki marriages outside the tribal district, it was generally acknowledged that Ngati Tuwharetoa were closely connected to

---

† Roy Seccombe apparently left unfinished business in Ngaruawahia. When his cousin Thomas Thorn Seccombe checked into the same hotel soon after the beginning of World War One, the local constable burst into his room as he was washing and twisted his bare arm behind his back. Then he released him saying, 'No, you're not Roy Seccombe. You haven't got a tattoo.'

‡ See Chapter 2.

* Seccombe eventually served in World War One, became a freezing worker when his inheritance was exhausted, and finally died in Auckland in December 1938.

Tainui and that the Te Heuheu family was genealogically compatible with the kahui ariki.[†]

Genealogically, perhaps, but not necessarily in other respects. Te Tahi was interested in the organising work Te Puea had just begun, and he helped her on the dairy farm she was looking after at Raungawari near Pukekawa, across the river from Mercer.[46] But they had savage arguments. According to a close acquaintance of the time, Te Puea encouraged Tahi to have relationships with other women. Then she would abuse him for doing so. He was insecure among a strange tribe and was often made to feel an outsider.[47] To compensate for these things he drank heavily and argued back. Among the insults Te Puea remembered their trading were the reasons Potatau was chosen as King: Te Puea claimed it was because Te Heuheu was not good enough; and Tahi answered it was only because Te Heuheu had condescended to give Potatau the title.[48]

One night in 1916 Te Tahi came home drunk and pulled Te Puea out of bed. He beat her savagely and began to strangle her. 'I believe he would have choked me had the people not pulled him off,' Te Puea said later.[49] The incident led to lengthy tribal discussion at Mangatawhiri and Waahi, and as a result Te Tahi was sent back to Tuwharetoa.[‡] It was intolerable to Waikato that an outsider should physically assault a member of the kahui ariki.[50]

To her intense regret Te Puea had been unable to have a child of her own with Te Tahi or in previous relationships. To compensate for this she had begun to collect homeless children.[*] And she and Tahi had taken a young relative, Papi Pokaia, into their home. When Tahi returned to his own people he took Papi with him and remarried. Years afterwards, when he died unexpectedly, Te Puea was to follow him to Tuwharetoa to find the girl and bring her back to Waikato.[**]

After Te Tahi, Te Puea showed no further interest in physical relationships. She had become wholly involved in her political and organisational work for Waikato. To the kahui ariki and people of Waikato, however, particularly to Mahuta's widow Te Marae, it was unthinkable that a woman in her position should be without a male partner. She had by then achieved a position of pre-eminence in the Kingitanga that she was to hold for life. It was desirable that

---

† Te Uira Te Heuheu married Taipu, one of Mahuta's sons, in 1913.
‡ In a letter to J. Lundon, defence counsel for the Tuhoe prophet Rua Kenana, Te Puea signed her name 'Te Puea Iwikau' in July 1916 (Judith Binney, personal communication, 24/8/79).
* See Chapter 3.
** Te Puea never conceived, a fact which must be attributed to her condition in view of the many men with whom she associated.

she should have a husband who would be strong — but in an entirely supportive and non-competitive way — and perhaps capable of giving her children.

And so in 1922, after lengthy family discussion, Te Marae selected Rawiri Katipa (also known as Rewi and Dave, and later as Tumokai).† He seemed ideal. He was tall and muscular with regular features and later to be described as 'a god-like boy'.[51] Although he had had no formal education, he was an energetic and gifted manual worker with considerable mechanical skill. He was totally loyal to those he regarded as being in authority, and committed to carrying out the responsibilities they gave him. He was also twenty-one years old.

Te Marae discussed it with Katipa's older sister and then with Te Puea. As a general proposal, a marriage had been talked about for years. This time, it was specific. 'I didn't want him,' Te Puea said. 'I knew he was too young for me'[52] (she was then thirty-eight). But she accepted because there appeared to be general approval among her family, and because she did want a close companion and helper. Tumokai was the last of the participants to be told. He knew Te Puea well, he had already travelled with her and worked with her. But he held her in awe. 'We looked up to the old lady as more of a god than anything else, coming through all the difficulties as she had done then.'[53] But he too agreed. And this partnership that was formally announced in March 1922 lasted the rest of Te Puea's life and, as far as Tumokai was concerned, beyond it.

For Te Puea, it was the first marriage in which there had been no previous physical attraction or contact. Her acceptance of it, and its durability, were evidence of an evolved maturity and certainty of purpose. Energies and emotions that she had formerly expended in private affairs were now invested in tribal work. Her health too had improved; the tuberculosis had receded for a time. She was now dedicated solely to planned action for the betterment of her Waikato people.

---

† Meaning 'the worker' — a nickname given by Te Puea and eventually accepted as his first name.

2

Return
to the river

More than any others in New Zealand, the tribes of the Waikato Valley are a river people. Five centuries of continuous occupation of its banks have embedded the river deep into the group and individual consciousness.

Initially it drew Tainui canoe descendants in from the west coast and hill country for purely practical reasons. It made the process of survival less arduous. There was food in the river and its swamps and tributaries — eel, freshwater crayfish, whitebait, mullet, shellfish, waterfowl and wild vegetables. The waterways provided irrigation for kumara, taro and hue. They offered a network for travel and communication. The river was an inexhaustible source of cleansing, refreshment and recreation. Its curving course and proximity to low hills created easily fortified positions, some of which proved impregnable. With use, the river acquired easy familiarity for the inhabitants; but never contempt. The power of its sluggish flow was awesome — tameable by craft, but unstoppable when winter and spring floods disgorged over banks and inundated homes and gardens.

The river's associations grew and ripened with the history of the inhabitants until memories of heroes and villains, of battles, significant journeys and natural disasters, of settlements erected and destroyed — all became part of the river's story, all were commemorated in names and features along its banks. The life of the river became inseparable from the life of the people, and each took the name of the other.

The water also assumed religious significance. Waikato was addressed in prayer and oratory as a thing with a life and aura of its own; the spirits of the dead were believed to mingle and move with its currents; the people and their characteristics were described in proverb in terms of the river's features; and its stretches and bends were populated with guardians called taniwha who showed themselves and intervened in human affairs when signposts of a supernatural order were needed.[†] The river became a source of spiritual as well as physical cleansing. Whenever Waikato people were sick, uncertain, or about to undertake a journey or new venture, the advice of their priests was always the same: 'Haere ki te wai', go to the water. And at the water they would pat the surface, invoke the ancestors there, and turn in the direction of the rising sun and sprinkle themselves.

More than any other gesture, living alongside the river was an affirmation for Waikato people of who they were and what they were. The river's associations would be reinforced daily by visible characteristics that suggested a pattern of life and activity independent of its course to the sea. Eddies and currents whorled on the surface, sometimes running back on themselves and causing the water to flow upstream along the banks. Branches of waterlogged trees broke the surface and trembled and vibrated. And, particularly in winter, fogs rolled off the water and blanketed the whole valley for days at a time, often during a period of mourning. When these coincided with frosts, it was as if a new ice age had risen out of the earth — grass and thistles stood stiffly, trapped in white crystals that seemed like a death shroud in the dull light, but which sparkled and danced when the sun finally broke through to warm the earth.

Much riverside land had, of course, been lost to Waikato in the confiscations. And with it old habitation sites redolent of bones and memories. But when Tawhiao and his followers emerged from the King Country they showed a preference for resettlement near the river (at Waahi, Pukekawa and Mercer, for example), and whenever possible they bought back land along the banks, particularly between Rangiriri and Huntly.[1] Many of the kupapa tribes and families who had not fought the Crown and hence had had land returned, grafted themselves to the Kingitanga after Tawhiao's reappearance and offered homes for the disinherited, to whom they were related closely (the Ngati Tamaoho people around Pukekawa, for example, and Waata Kukutai's Ngati Tipa between Tuakau and the Waikato Heads).

Te Puea had lived close to the river from infancy, particularly near Mercer. She used its launch and barge transport in the lower reaches and took part in the annual canoe regattas at Mercer and Ngaruawahia. But from 1910, as a result of a decisive encounter with Mahuta, she began a conscientious occupation of the river bank that was to last initially for nearly twenty years and finally for the last fifteen years of her life.

---

† The expression 'taniwha' is used literally to refer to these mythical creatures, and metaphorically to refer to chiefs, as in the proverb, 'Waikato taniwharau, he piko he taniwha' — Waikato, river of one hundred bends and on every one of them a taniwha or powerful chief.

In 1910, Te Puea was apparently still living with Seccombe at Mangere.† She was temporarily rejected by her family because of this relationship and, initially, she was prepared to brazen out a period of ostracism as her mother had done. Eventually, however, at least two pressures began to undercut her determination. Seccombe and his mother were trying to persuade her to sign over family land into his name as a mark of her good faith in the relationship. The idea of allowing depleted reserves of inherited land to pass into European title she found distasteful.[2] Secondly, the elderly Waikato people at Mangere Pa, whom she could not avoid seeing frequently, continually advised her to leave Seccombe or at least go home to Waikato to discuss the relationship with Mahuta; if she did not, they said, they would have her taken back forcibly.[3] It was an appeal she must have found difficult to reject persistently. Her upbringing had conditioned her to listen to elders and her natural inclination was to regard such people with fondness. Also, being an affectionate and demonstrative person, she must have missed the daily contact with friends and relatives that she had enjoyed at Mercer. True, she was able to visit there and did so throughout her cohabitation with Seccombe. But such visits were temporary and strained.

It was during one of them that Te Puea met Mahuta unexpectedly in the main street at Mercer.[4] He had returned permanently to Waikato from Wellington after the lapse of his term on the Legislative Council.‡ Although they had not seen a great deal of each other in the previous decade, Te Puea made it clear later that her early affection for him and memories of the time he had spent teaching her were undiminished. Her feelings, then, must have been contradictory: on the one hand the regard that arose from relationship and experience; on the other the determination to make up her mind independently about what she was to do with her life. She was by no means the first person committed to the concept of tribe who nevertheless reacted strongly against the feeling of being owned, and the reality of having the most intimate decisions about her life debated publicly. It was a situation in which the weak could be dominated easily; but it encouraged rebellion in the strong-willed, as it had in Tiahuia.

Mahuta, perhaps already distressed by financial losses and emotional difficulties that were to become public knowledge before the 1911 General Election, was in no mood for courtesies. He was aware of the spiritual qualities that were believed to have passed from Tawhiao to Tiahuia to Te Puea,[5] and of the early

---

† The absence of documentary records for this part of Te Puea's life makes it difficult to establish dates other than by circumstantial evidence.
‡ According to Pei Jones, he resumed the kingship on 21 May 1910 (Jones, 1968, p. 144).

potential she had shown for leadership. And he was worried by an absence of these qualities in the people around him who were assuming leadership roles (the Member of Parliament Henare Kaihau, the Kingmaker Tupu Taingakawa, his own wife Te Marae, and his eldest son Te Rata, who was chronically ill). There was an imminent danger that effective leadership of the Kingitanga would pass outside the kahui ariki. Mahuta, then, felt isolated, in need of support. He was direct.

He asked her how she dared to live with a European and ignore the responsibilities that her family and tribe brought her. 'I stood my ground,' Te Puea said thirty years later, 'and said that I had exercised my rights. He replied that I had thrown aside my duty to the kingship and to the people. I made no answer. He saw that I still intended to defy him . . . he told me that he was moved in the spirit to feel that I was indispensable for the future welfare of Waikato.'[6] Finally, having extracted no concessions from Te Puea, Mahuta resorted to blackmail. He threatened to commit suicide. 'You see that road there?' Te Puea said she did. 'I'm going to lie on it and let that car run over me.'[7] And he moved away from her as if to throw himself in the path of a vehicle coming towards them. Only then did Te Puea appreciate the extent to which her uncle was in extremis. Her reaction was immediate. 'The strife and rage within me ceased. I ran after Mahuta and dragged him back out of danger.'[8]

That was the turning point; Te Puea was persuaded. She went to Auckland, broke with Seccombe and returned to Mercer. 'I hurried back to the tribe, and was received joyfully by the people who had previously shunned me. It was then clear to me that they, like Mahuta, had been moved by forces beyond their [knowledge] to desire me to lead them to a different life.'[9]

There were many reasons why this 'different life' was to be sought in Mercer, or Mangatawhiri, as the Maori part of the settlement was then known. Te Puea had spent most of her early life in the district; the nucleus of the following she had inherited from her mother lived there. Tiahuia had made a point of asking Te Puea to take care of them. 'If I should die,' she had told her daughter, 'you must return to Mangatawhiri. Do not abandon the people there. I want you to die among them.'[10] And the settlement had been a significant one for Tawhiao. He had named it for the stream Te Pou o Mangatawhiri (the pillar of Mangatawhiri) that had marked his northern boundary. So long as people lived there they perpetuated the name as a reminder of the injustice that had followed the crossing of the stream by Imperial troops in 1863.†

---

† After leaving Mangatawhiri Te Puea was to perpetuate this reminder by giving the name TPM to her touring concert party.

Mangatawhiri or Te Paina, as it now came to be called, was in 1910 a small village of around 100 people on the swampy river flat just north of Mercer township. The low-lying site at a point where the river narrowed between two ranges made it particularly vulnerable to flooding. There were no community facilities like a meeting house or dining room. Nevertheless Te Puea settled back there and resumed dairy farming on the western side of the river on 600 acres of land at Raungawari that had been given to her mother by Ngati Tamaoho.[11] When she was not busy on the farm she concentrated on her first major tribal project: calling Tawhiao's elderly followers together at Mangatawhiri to recite tribal history and genealogies so she could begin to write them down. This activity was the origin of what was to become in the 1920s a daily journal of activities.[†] She also revived the whitebait tribute among the tribes of the lower Waikato as a means of raising money towards the costs of Mahuta's hui and poukai.[12 ‡]

Her popularity, however, was not universal. It was confined almost solely to the mixed tribal inhabitants of Mangatawhiri, the Ngati Tamaoho, and the Ngati Tipa of the river mouth. In other places, particularly Waahi,[*] there was resentment at the preference Mahuta had shown for her over other potential leaders and members of the kahui ariki, like his own sons.[13] Her authority had to emerge through several tests before it was to be accepted by more than a small section of Waikato people.

The first test came in 1911 as a result of events in the neighbouring tribal district of Taranaki. There, elders had become dismayed at their inability to obtain compensation for confiscated territory seized by the Crown at the same time as Waikato's, and to resolve complex tenure rights to leased Maori land on the west coast. They had appealed to Parliament, to Prime Minister Joseph Ward, and to Native Minister James Carroll.[14] But they achieved no satisfaction.

---

† The material Te Puea collected at Mangatawhiri seems to have been added to Te Rata's journal, which until 1976 was in the possession of Pei Jones; and to the miscellaneous papers now kept at Turangawaewae Marae, Ngaruawahia.

‡ Alex McKay (interview) has noted: 'She called it moni ika — "fish money". The Ngati Tipa people, from Tuakau to Port Waikato, voluntarily levied themselves one penny for every pound of whitebait sold. And they refused to sell to buyers who went up and down the river unless those buyers paid a licence fee of £2 each. The buyers kept both these sums of money back and once a year their representatives would come to Mangatawhiri and later to Ngaruawahia with two cheques: one for the moni ika made up of the one penny levies; the other for the licence fees.'

* The feeling of tension between Te Puea and the Waahi community was never wholly erased. After Te Puea moved her settlement in 1921, the earlier competitiveness between Waahi and Mangatawhiri then operated between Waahi and Turangawaewae.

At first their petitions were delayed and then a formula, devised by Carroll to cope with leasing arrangements, was rejected by Taranaki on the ground that it would simply perpetuate ambiguities and inequalities.

A consensus evolved that, as things stood, Taranaki could not look to Parliament for solutions. The tribal spokesmen decided to look for a younger and better educated man to enter Parliament and steer their case through the complicated processes of legislation. Their difficulty was that Taranaki was not an electorate. It was a section of the Western Maori seat dominated by Tainui and held by Henare Kaihau for Mahuta and the Kingitanga.

This fact did not discourage Taranaki. There were longstanding links between the two districts. There had been the shared experience of wars in the early 1860s, a limited exchange of fighters, and both had suffered defeat and punishing confiscations. Then, in the mid-sixties, Tawhiao had established warm relations with the Taranaki religious leaders Te Ua Haumene, Te Whiti o Rongomai and Tohu Kakahi. The very name Tawhiao had been given him by Te Ua,[†] and he had taken the Pai Marire faith with him from Taranaki to Waikato. The connection was frequently celebrated in recitation of the proverb: 'You take one handle of the basket and I shall hold the other,' an expression of confidence in progress through cooperation.

At a joint tribal meeting at Parewanui near Bulls in 1911, Taranaki tried out their proposal on Te Rata who, in the company of Taipu and Tupu Taingakawa, was representing Mahuta. Te Rata did not commit Waikato to support Taranaki's campaign. But he asked if there was somebody in Taranaki sufficiently old and prestigious to activate ties between the two peoples. An elder from Ketemarae Pa near Normanby was named, and it was agreed that he should notify Tupu Taingakawa when the prospective candidate was chosen.[15]

A subsequent meeting at Ketemarae asked a Methodist minister Robert Tahupotiki Haddon to accept the candidacy. He declined, saying, 'I can't reverse this collar I am wearing.'[‡] At this point the man who had been appointed the first Maori Medical Officer of Health in 1901, Dr Maui Pomare, arrived and it was probably not by chance.[*] He was invited to accept the nomination and he agreed at once. The elder Hapimana Tauke telegrammed

---

† Previously he had been known as Matutaera; see page 22.
‡ This phrase was to be used against Haddon when he sought the seat after Pomare's death in 1930. He was to become a strong ally of Te Puea's at Ngaruawahia from the early 1930s.
* Newspapers had speculated as early as December 1909 that he would seek parliamentary election (see clipping dated 14 December 1909, in Maori Purposes Fund Board papers, WTU ms 189, folder 172).

Tupu, and Waikato was informed of Pomare's candidacy. The next step was a formal approach to Mahuta for support.

Maui Pomare was at this time a handsome and impressive man. He was thirty-five years old, dressed elegantly, and wore a waxed moustache. Born in Taranaki to parents of Ngati Toa and Ngati Mutunga descent, he had been well educated at St Stephen's School in Auckland, Christchurch Boys High School and Te Aute College. At the last of these, in the company of fellow students and former students like Apirana Ngata and Peter Buck (Te Rangi Hiroa), he became part of a group that was to be called the Young Maori Party. These intelligent, confident and European-educated Maori set themselves the task of bringing their people into more fruitful contact with European practices and institutions. In particular they wanted to lift standards of health and hygiene to halt the sharp population decline that in the late nineteenth century threatened extinction for the Maori.[†] More generally, they viewed Maori survival as linked to partnership with the European and the adoption of European technology. They were also to advocate the extension of literacy and agricultural development schemes into Maori districts.

Pomare became a Seventh-Day Adventist and received further education at the American Medical Missionary College in Michigan and the Battle Creek Sanatorium. He obtained a doctorate in medicine in 1899, and returned to New Zealand to become first medical officer in the Health Department with special responsibility for Maori health. He was an individualist, perhaps to a greater degree than other members of the Young Maori Party group. He and Buck had become disillusioned with the concept of tribe, particularly with the way it had impeded the introduction of European practices in Taranaki. While their terms as medical officers coincided (1905 to 1909), they wrote complementary annual reports for the department and for Parliament outlining what they saw as problems and solutions in Maori health. Buck, for example, had commented in 1906:

'The communism of the past meant industry, training in arms, good physique, the keeping of the law, the sharing of the tribal burden, and the preservation of life. It was a factor in the evolution of the race. The communism of today means indolence, sloth, decay of racial vigour, the

---

† The pre-European Maori population was perhaps as high as 100,000. The 1878 census recorded 43,595, and by 1896 this had slumped to 39,854. The *New Zealand Herald* had noted 'that the native race is dying out in New Zealand there is, of course, no doubt' (17 August 1874).

crushing of individual effort, the spreading of introduced infectious diseases, and the many evils that are petrifying the Maori and preventing his advance.'[16] Pomare added: 'The Maori having been an active race and having always been kept in a state of excitement by wars and the rumour of wars, can now only find vent for his feelings on the racecourse, gambling and billiard-playing, with an occasional bout in the Land Court.'[17]†

Both believed that, in addition to adopting European technology, the Maori had also to adapt to the prospect of individual competition amongst themselves and against Europeans. 'As long as [the Maori] can depend on his communist brother for a meal,' Pomare had said elsewhere, 'so long will you have him lazy.'[18] Pomare's and Buck's own careers were to reflect this competitive, devil-take-the-hindmost view of life. It contrasted with that of community cooperation held by Te Puea.

Pomare had clearly performed well as a medical officer. His purely medical advice was sound and timely, although he was far more effective at communicating it to Pakeha audiences than to Maori. Buck seems to have had more success with his own people. Ultimately, Pomare and Buck felt they were making insufficient progress and their clear, well-argued annual reports spoke of the same difficulties each year. Both felt they were not supported by the department and Parliament as strongly as they should be, and both concluded they could only bring about the necessary policy changes and financial commitment to Maori health from Parliament itself. They decided to seek candidacies to join Ngata in the House of Representatives (Ngata had been elected to the Eastern Maori seat in 1905; Buck took Northern Maori in a by-election in 1909; Carroll, still Native Affairs Minister, held the general seat of Gisborne).

Apart from the Taranaki land claims, therefore, Pomare had additional and substantial personal reasons for seeking national leadership. Once nominated, he threw himself into the campaign with a thoroughness not seen previously in Maori electorates. He had to extract support from eleven major and separate tribal groups. His earliest coup was to win the sponsorship of Te Heuheu Tukino of Tuwharetoa, who had stood as an independent in the four preceding elections. On each occasion Te Heuheu had accumulated the second- or third-highest polls, obtaining over 1300 votes in 1905 and 1908. Provided he could retain this support and Taranaki loyalties remained constant, Pomare needed a

---

†This statement explains in part why Pomare was to welcome World War One and the opportunity for Maori participation with considerable enthusiasm.

swing of just over 500 votes to take the seat (out of a total poll of about 7000 votes). The only way he could hope to accomplish a shift of this magnitude was to secure the whole Taranaki vote and to wrest support from Mahuta's followers in Waikato.

According to Lady Pomare, he spent the first few months campaigning continuously in the southern part of the electorate. He came home dispirited one Saturday night and announced that somebody important had let him down and that he was 'cooked to a turn'. He rested the following day and on the Monday set out for Waikato with a group of Taranaki elders saying as he left, 'I have hopes.'[19] The Pomare who presented himself to Mahuta at Waahi Pa must have been appealing. Apart from his appearance, he was an eloquent and effective orator in Maori and English. Through his Ngati Toa mother, he was of Tainui descent. Nor was he unknown in Waikato. He had passed through in the course of his duties as medical officer, and two years previously had visited Waahi in a futile attempt to set up a Waikato Maori Council.[20] He also had a historical link with Waikato which now, showing an intelligent sense of timing, he proceeded to recall.

Almost 90 years earlier, Mahuta's grandfather Te Wherowhero had been trapped in battle with Ngati Toa and Taranaki tribes at Okoki in Taranaki. Te Rauparaha, an exiled Waikato leader to whom Pomare was related, saved Te Wherowhero's life. According to the Taranaki version of the story Te Wherowhero called out to him: 'E Raha, he aha te koha kia au?' Raha, what is your gift to me? The gift was that Rauparaha enabled Te Wherowhero and the remnants of his force to withdraw safely.†

Pomare's escort at Waahi consisted of ten elders representing Taranaki from Waitara to Patea and led by Pouwhareumu Toi and Marokopa Tahuata. After these had been introduced and spoken for him, Pomare said to the King, 'Mahuta, what is your gift to me?'‡ He was, in the fashion of Maori speech-making, suggesting a debt and asking for its repayment. Mahuta recognised the allusion at once. He asked exactly what Pomare wanted. Pomare said 600 votes.[21] Mahuta, visibly upset, said: 'You don't know what you ask. Am I to be

---

† Details of how this took place differ in Waikato and Taranaki versions. Waikato say it was by Te Wherowhero's defeat of a large number of fighters in single combat; Taranaki claim it was a result of being shown an escape route.

‡ This is Taranaki's version of the allusion and Pomare's of the meeting with Mahuta (confirmed by Lady Pomare in a letter to Eric Ramsden, 19 January 1944). Waikato's is that the words used on both occasions were 'Let the fight be by single combat and between chiefs only.' Te Puea said (letter to J.F. Cody, 7 September 1945) she had not heard that the historical allusion had been made. Pei Jones suggested in a note to the same letter that it may have occurred in conversation rather than across the marae.

true to my friends of today or loyal to my ancestors? Go away, I shall send for you when I have decided.'

To understand the considerations that would have passed through Mahuta's mind at this point, it is necessary to recall the conditions then prevalent in Waikato and to examine the record of the man Mahuta was being asked to abandon, Henare Kaihau.

Waikato Maori in 1911 were poor, without the security of regular employment and income, disease prone, largely uneducated and demoralised.[†] Mahuta's own flirtations with national government and his experiments with Maori local government had produced no visibly beneficial results. The men on whom the King had leaned most heavily for advice and the formulation of strategy had been Tupu Taingakawa and Kaihau. Taingakawa's contribution is discussed elsewhere:[‡] he had a propensity for pushing proposals to extremes and antagonising those with whom he negotiated. And Kaihau, whom Mahuta had invested with enormous discretionary powers and tribal responsibilities, had given the King cause for even greater concern.

Henare Kaihau in 1911, at 127 kg, was a man of immense physical presence and a master of business and political rhetoric. Experience had also shown him to be something of a con man.[*] His eyes had a glazed half-closed look. To his supporters this suggested shrewdness; to others, low cunning; it could equally have been a consequence of dissipation (his appetite for food and alcohol were described as 'gargantuan').[22] His confidence had been growing with parliamentary experience. The former Cabinet Minister F.M.B. Fisher described him as 'extraordinarily good-natured and genial . . . In everything except the language, Kaihau was merging into the Pakeha way of life and doing it with considerable gusto.'[23]

Kaihau saw himself rather than Tupu Taingakawa as executive head of the King Movement. In his many proposals to Parliament and the press for a separate Maori parliament, Kaihau always declared or inferred that he would be its 'premier'.[**] He also had hopes of founding a dynasty of power and money. He built a vast homestead for his family near Waiuku and encouraged

<hr>

† See pages 28 to 30.
‡ See Chapter 3.
* 'Henare Kaihau,' said the *Auckland Star* of 11 June 1910, 'declaimed his speech with much dramatic fervour. He explained that he had not come the day before because the omens were not favourable. As a matter of fact, he missed his train at Pukekohe.'
** 'When asked who would probably occupy the high office, Mr Kaihau modestly admitted that the people wished him to accept it.' (*Dominion*, 31 August 1910)

his children to be interested in politics with a view to taking his place.[24] His wife Maewa also contributed to the family's mana as a composer of popular Maori songs. (Among others, she is credited with writing the words of the internationally favoured farewell song 'Now is the Hour'.)

Kaihau did not form a dynasty, however, and his reputation did not survive his career. He has been described by journalist and historian Eric Ramsden as 'Mahuta's evil genius'[25] and 'the real power behind the throne'.[26] For a time he was both these things. Mahuta's highly spiritual and other-worldly character made him particularly vulnerable to manipulation by someone as assertive and apparently worldly wise as Kaihau. The Member of Parliament's oratory about separate Maori institutions was forceful, his proposals for financing them through land sales persuasive, and his suggestions for generating additional income from private investment sounded plausible.

It was Kaihau who spearheaded the Liberal Government's policy of land acquisition in Waikato, although he continued to stand for Parliament as a Reform candidate.[†] During his parliamentary term, Maori land was alienated at the rate of 185,000 acres a year, much of it in Waikato (the 1910 land conference at Waahi, for example, discussed the disposal of 600,000 acres). Frequently, he benefited personally from these transactions, a fact which resulted in charges of corruption being laid against him in Parliament.

Mahuta, as a result of litigation through the Native Land Court, had succeeded in having some blocks of land that should not have been taken in the confiscations returned to Waikato in his name. He was persuaded by Kaihau to allow money collected in trust funds from the sale and lease of this and other territories to be banked in Auckland under Kaihau's name.[27] Other funds Kaihau took directly from Mahuta and invested in Auckland land companies.[28] In 1911, shortly before Pomare approached him for support, Mahuta had learned that these companies had collapsed and that Kaihau had lost over £50,000 of Kingitanga monies.[29] There was no hope of recovering them.

This came as a severe shock to Mahuta and one that impaired his physical and mental health.[30] The money had been held in his name, but only because the tribes concerned had wanted to protect it with his mana. It seemed a gross betrayal of trust, the last thing Mahuta would have consented to had he had any hint of the outcome.

---

† Kaihau is popularly credited with having been a Seddon follower and a Liberal Party supporter. But according to Sheila McClean (MA thesis on Maori representation), Kaihau stood for Parliament as a Reform candidate in 1905 and 1908, and as an Independent in 1911.

This was bad enough. But it was not the full tally of Kaihau's alleged crimes. He was accused in addition of retaining trust fund payments for use on his own property and for building up his own estate.[31] And he was suspected of securing income from land in Auckland held originally in Potatau's name and subsequently leased to the Crown. These payments should have been coming to Mahuta (Te Puea was to try to have this matter investigated by Raumoa Balneavis, Apirana Ngata's secretary, when she visited Wellington in August 1928). In Parliament, Kaihau was found to have accepted bribes from constituents and this led to a reprimand from the Speaker and to Opposition leader Massey calling for an abolition of Maori seats.[32] And he had been criticised for persistent absenteeism.[33]

Even if Pomare had decided not to contest Western Maori in 1911, it is doubtful that Kaihau could have survived the accumulation of grievances building up against him. Another term in Parliament would have been one of increasing attacks from his colleagues on one side (Ngata was later to refer to him as 'a crook')[34] and his constituents on the other. Pomare's request presented Mahuta with, if not a solution to growing difficulties, at least to way of halting a downward slide.

According to Te Uira Te Heuheu,[35] Mahuta also had an intensely personal reason to brood about Kaihau's duplicity. The King's wife, Te Marae, had been publicly accused of an earlier and adulterous relationship with Kaihau. Mahuta heard the alleged accusation and believed it. It contributed to his severe depression and from this time on he had lived apart from Marae. She in turn refused to go to him to discuss the matter, though she was urged to do so by everybody close to her.†

For all these reasons, Mahuta found himself disposed to support Pomare. The major obstacle was one of protocol. Kaihau was his candidate, encouraged by him to stand in 1896 and supported by his patronage from that time. If he were to change candidates publicly, even as a result of severe provocation from Kaihau, the King's mana would suffer still further. Instead, Mahuta apparently thought of Te Puea and her new determination to stay with the Waikato people

---

† Pei Jones, who had not heard of this accusation, described it as 'preposterous' (personal communication, 25/10/75). 'I am rather inclined to think that the story must have been retailed to Te Uira by someone who knew that [she] was having a rather miserable time with Te Marae and . . . there was a feeling of grudge in it.' Te Marae had told Te Uira, however, that the story was true (Te Uira Te Heuheu to Eric Ramsden, Ngaruawahia, 4 November 1944). Other Waikato informants have drawn attention to the fact that members of the Kaihau family were among the Kingitanga's most energetic and loyal supporters in the 1970s.

and to work for him. The political development offered both a way out of a procedural difficulty and a test of Te Puea's loyalty and leadership qualities.

After three days of consideration, Mahuta sent for Pomare and the Taranaki party, who had been accommodated at Waahi. 'The only help I can give you,' he is reported to have said, 'is to tell you to see my niece. She holds the key to the Waikato door. If she uses the key and opens the door, you will be fortunate.'[36] And so Pomare's group trekked down the river to Mangatawhiri, accompanied by two Waikato elders carrying Mahuta's message for Te Puea. One of them was Mahau Kaihau, Henare's older brother;[37] this in itself was an indication of Mahuta's wish to change loyalties.

Te Puea was not at Maungatawhiri and had to be sent for from the Raungawari farm. At the settlement, she was given the message: 'The King approves Maui Pomare as a Member of Parliament for the Western Maori electorate. Maui has made a pledge that though I and others failed, he will persuade the Government to hold an inquiry into the confiscation of Maori lands in the Waikato, Taranaki and elsewhere.'[38]

While this last promise was an additional reason for favouring Pomare,[†] the request nevertheless astonished Te Puea.[39] She had not been previously entrusted with a specific commission from Mahuta; she knew Kaihau had been a powerful advisor and the King's major channel to Sir James Carroll and the Government; she knew Te Marae was one of Kaihau's strongest allies; and there were family links between Kaihau and the kahui ariki (common ancestors four generations back and, more recently, a marriage of Tawhiao's cousin to a Kaihau). The presence of Kaihau's brother was almost sufficient to lay her doubts. She asked Pomare what he would do as elected representative for Waikato. Then, 'after hearing what he had to say, I decided to support him.'[40]

There appear to be no detailed and first-hand accounts of how and to what extent Te Puea campaigned for Pomare. She wrote simply that, with the Waikato elders Mahau Kaihau and Te Ruihana, she 'conducted Maui Pomare and the Taranaki elders through the Waikato'.[41]

According to Tumokai Katipa, they visited only the communities of the lower Waikato River: Mangatawhiri, Tauranganui and Port Waikato. This is probable — these were the people who already knew Te Puea and supported her and among whom she could expect to be influential. Also, it was possible for a popular leader to swing dozens of votes in such communities. Because of widespread illiteracy, Maori voting was by declaration to a returning officer

---

† And it was Pomare's appearance of being constantly about to fulfil this promise that kept Te Rata and most of Waikato loyal to him in later years, in spite of other provocations.

(and prior to 1910 it had been by show of hands). This made it difficult for individuals and families to conceal their choices from one another. In places where a degree of tribal cohesion and loyalty to traditional leadership survived, it was possible for individuals to affect the voting patterns of whole communities.[†]

Te Puea's followers were none the less shocked when she appeared to be setting a candidate up against the King's member.[42] They asked her how she justified this. She replied on each occasion: 'You've seen what Henare's done to Mahuta. And yet you would still vote for him?'[43] And she reiterated: 'This is the man Mahuta has chosen.'[44] For most people, nevertheless, the campaign raised puzzling and painful conflicts of loyalty. Mahuta himself took no part.

The result was that Pomare won by 565 votes (2464 to Kaihau's 1899).[‡] He had stolen from Kaihau almost exactly the number he had calculated he would need. Polling place figures told their own story. At Hukanui (dominated by Te Marae) and at Kaihau's own tribal strongholds, his count remained commensurate with that of the 1908 election. But at Waahi (where Te Puea had some support) and more especially at the lower river polling places of Te Paina (Mercer) and Tauranganui, his votes fell at the same rate as Pomare acquired them. An additional blow for Kaihau had been the candidacy of his old adversary Tupu Taingakawa who had polled 581 votes, many of them from Ngati Haua people who had previously supported the sitting member.[45]

Te Puea was as surprised as nearly everybody else — and she became intensely anxious. In spite of the fact that she had been following Mahuta's instructions, she felt sure she would be chastised: by Kaihau, by the rest of Waikato, and possibly even by Mahuta himself to save his face (and with whom she had not even discussed the campaign directly). She was certain there would be consequences and she determined to face them immediately. She went to Waahi the day the results were announced.[46]

She found the marae in an uproar. People had come in from all over Waikato to hear the figures read out and listen to subsequent tribal discussion. As Te Puea walked through the gates she was met with shouts of derision and abuse, and she believed her life might be in danger. She walked through the crowd, none the less, and straight over to Mahuta who was sitting against the

---

† Ngata was to say later that this system of voting had produced representation that was 'more or less the result of tribal influences' (NZPD, 1937, Vol. 249, p. 816).
‡ Although he had stood as an independent, Pomare voted with the Reform Party in the first parliamentary session following the election to put the Liberal Government out of office for the first time in twenty years. He remained a Reform member and was initially given the innocuous cabinet post of Minister in Charge of the Cook Islands.

trunk of a pear tree alongside the meeting house. He said nothing. She lay down beside him and waited.[47]

Kaihau stood on the marae and blamed her bitterly for conceiving and executing his defeat. He accused her of deceit and disloyalty. He was followed by Te Marae who echoed his anger and condemnation.[48] While the stream of invective continued, Te Puea looked at Mahuta to see what effect it was having on him. The King was wearing his favourite old kiekie straw sun hat. As Te Puea watched him, he pulled the brim over his face. There was a split between the brim and the crown of the hat through which she could see his eyes. Very deliberately, he winked at her.[49] Then he said, 'Don't be frightened of your uncle. He's the last person that would harm you.'[50]

The speeches finished and Kaihau walked off the marae with his family.[†] Then Mahuta got to his feet. Instantly, there was total silence. He began by saying he was pleased with the results and pleased with Te Puea. He turned towards his niece and said, 'I am now somebody because of you. My word to you now is that you should gather people together at Mangatawhiri.' Te Puea called out that there was no meeting house there. Mahuta said: 'Your ancestors didn't need meeting houses for their discussions. The sky was their roof.' Then Te Puea said there was not enough food at Mangatawhiri to feed a large crowd of people. Mahuta, replying to this, pulled open the front of his shirt and exposed his belly and slapped it saying, 'I'll be food, food, food. Even if the whole country should eat me I'll never be consumed.'[‡] Then he spun round and appeared to lose control of himself, confirming that he was not well. But up to that point he had spoken lucidly and unequivocally.[51]

Te Puea returned to Mangatawhiri, vindicated and confirmed as Mahuta's chief organiser. Shortly afterwards the King sent her his vest pocket watch. It was made of gold and engraved on the back with her name and the year (by this time, 1912).[*] Over the following months people began to drift to

---

† Kaihau made one further and unsuccessful attempt to enter Parliament in 1919 when he polled only 215 votes, relegating his candidacy to a minor one. He died on 20 May 1920.

‡ This speech came to be regarded by Waikato as being of crucial importance. It was Mahuta's public delegation of authority to Te Puea that validated what she had done and what she was to do subsequently, and it was the first suggestion that leadership initiatives should come from anywhere other than Waahi and Mahuta's immediate family. It was a formal and public confirmation of a mission that the King had previously communicated to Te Puea privately. This version of the speech is from Tumokai Katipa, based on Te Puea's account of it to him.

* According to Pei Jones (personal communication, 11/9/75), this action was 'a symbolic bestowal of the leadership role'. Te Puea gave the same watch to him in 1937.

Mangatawhiri as a kind of sanctuary. Most of them were elderly and landless, and Te Puea made them welcome and found homes for them.[52]

Throughout 1912 Mahuta became noticeably more depressed and withdrawn. He frequently shut himself into his house at Hukanui to drink and he remained estranged from Te Marae. It is probable that he was further distressed by his wife's continuing loyalty to Kaihau; and by the fact that the former Member of Parliament persuaded the King's eldest son, Te Rata, to invest money in land agencies in Auckland that he had established as an alternative career.[53] Though his behaviour in public continued to be erratic, Mahuta's followers still listened attentively to him when he did speak and sifted his words for significance.

On 6 November he attended the poukai at Tauranganui, close to where the Waikato disgorges into the sea. His message to the people there was this: 'Listen to me, my ancestors. Heaven is now open to me and I am about to depart. I shall be away, and then I shall return. If your house is not in order by the time I return, then I shall never come back. My father is in the Trinity — in the Father, the Son and the Holy Ghost. If you become weary, pray to me and I shall see to your well-being.'[54]

Late in the afternoon of 9 November, the Waikato River offered its last recorded sighting of a congregation of taniwha. A group of children playing on the eastern bank at Mangatawhiri saw a disturbance like wind ripples coming towards the settlement from the seaward end of the river. But there was no wind and the rest of the water was calm. They ran back to the houses and called the adults who were there, mainly elderly men too old or sick to work. These came to the edge of the river and watched in silence as the creatures advanced upstream breaking the surface of the water with their backs and fins. Those that were close enough to the bank to be recognised included shark, stingray, and snapper, huge old men snapper.[55] A message was sent to Te Puea at Raungawari and the community gathered and waited restlessly. The following day word came from Hukanui that Mahuta, physically and mentally spent, had died at the age of fifty-seven.

3

Consolidation

Mahuta's death left Te Puea in an uncomfortable position. Te Rata was to be King. But, as his father had recognised, he remained a sickly man. He had been an invalid from childhood and as an adult he suffered from rheumatism, arthritis and heart disease.[1] He was also a shy man, easily dominated. Rather than assume leadership on positions of controversy or public responsibility, as Mahuta had done even though he found it distasteful, Te Rata preferred quiet discussions about tribal history or being alone to write in his journal (he had received a primary education).[2]

The Kingitanga historian Eric Ramsden was to say of him later that he appeared to be 'an ineffective ruler.[†] He hid himself away in Waahi . . . and seldom or never appeared among Pakehas. Occasionally . . . he did go to Auckland for the races, but no one appeared to be aware that Te Rata was even in the city. He never attempted to cut any figure . . . and never uttered any of the defiant challenges in defence of his people that other Waikato rulers were known to have done.'[3] He married Te Uranga of Ngati Koroki and had two sons, Koroki and Tonga.

To Te Puea and her supporters it was clear that Mahuta had intended her to be Te Rata's protector and organiser and she behaved accordingly. But to other leaders of the Kingitanga, particularly to the Waahi section of the kahui ariki, the position was by no means clear. They saw a leadership vacuum. And there were two candidates to fill it, the King's mother Te Marae and the Tumuaki or Kingmaker Tupu Taingakawa.

---

† Ramsden did not recognise that the mana of the kingship derived from the office rather than the office holder. This distinguished the position from others of Maori leadership, and it made it likely that the movement would continue to function regardless of the calibre of the incumbent king.

Te Marae was a dominating woman. She had an upright bearing, a beauty that was almost fierce, and a penetrating stare. Those who knew her invariably described her as an 'old fashioned' Maori, disciplined, of visibly rangatira status.[4] Unlike many of the kahui ariki she believed implicitly that those born of aristocratic stock had a moral responsibility to lead well, to live exemplary lives, to take care of their appearance. Te Uira Te Heuheu said she was also capable of being a kindly woman and more than anybody else she was responsible for the younger woman's adoption of Maori manners that she had lost through her European education. 'She showed me the nobility and dignity of her own simple way of living.'[5]

Nevertheless only the strongest of personalities could stand up to Marae in conflict. There is ample evidence that Mahuta feared her and felt he was unable to control her. In particular, he had viewed her as Kaihau's ally and felt that their combined initiatives had undermined his own position. She was also an admirer and supporter of Tupu Taingakawa. Had it not been for the coincidence of Mahuta's death with Te Puea's emergence, Marae would almost certainly have assumed the dominating role in the King Movement, pulling the leadership reins together in a coalition that would probably have included Kaihau and Taingakawa.[†] She did not like Te Puea, nor did she accept at first the role that Mahuta had cast her in.[6] According to Piri Poutapu, she went to Taingakawa to discuss ways of limiting Te Puea's influence.

Tupu Taingakawa was an ambitious, energetic and obsessive man who did not know the meaning of the word compromise. He was short and bullet-like in stature. The second son of Wiremu Tamehana, he was the leader of Ngati Haua and had inherited the title of Kingmaker on the death of his older brother. And he took it seriously. He believed the Tumuaki was an institutional part of the kingship, that he shared and upheld the mana of the King, and that in some senses he preceded and was senior to the King because 'you couldn't have a king without a kingmaker'.[7][‡]

More important than those inherited considerations, however, Taingakawa had enjoyed a long period at the centre of the movement and, being forceful and articulate, had increased his presence and weight in a cumulative fashion. He had dominated the Kauhanganui parliaments from the 1890s as 'president' or 'premier'. He had also taken a specialist's interest in the terms of the Treaty of Waitangi and the question of land confiscations. Both issues he debated at length and lost no opportunity to berate Pakeha listeners about them in person

---

† So long as Te Puea had a voice in King Movement affairs, however, she was determined that Kaihau would not be forgiven for the misfortunes that had destroyed Mahuta.
‡ This view persisted among Ngati Haua leaders in 1976.

when they came his way, and also by letter and petition. The frequency and manner in which he pursued such matters alarmed Sir John Gorst,[†] particularly when Taingakawa spoke of taking Maori grievances to the Imperial Government in London.[8]

It was characteristic of Taingakawa that in 1911, liking neither major candidate for the Western Maori seat and still smarting over the cursory dismissal by Parliament in 1909 of his major land petition, he decided to stand for Parliament himself (an act that ensured Pomare's election). The only votes he picked up were those of his own tribal loyalists.

There was a clear difference in emphasis between Taingakawa and other Kingitanga leaders of the turn of the century. He advocated a hard line on the raupatu issue — immediate return of confiscated lands — and he was in favour of Waikato and Maori tribes generally governing themselves as far as possible without reference to Pakeha institutions. All this at a time when Mahuta had been trying to steer the Kingitanga into contact with political parties and the Government and exploring generally gradualist policies. Taingakawa claimed in 1900 that a group of Kingite supporters had seceded from the movement under his leadership (they were almost all Ngati Haua), and from that time there were frequent reports of his holding meetings in opposition to those at Waahi.[‡]

After the death of Mahuta, Taingakawa was to make one final lunge for control of the Kingitanga. He established a new Kauhanganui at Rukumoana near Morrinsville, invited tribes from Waikato and throughout the country to make use of it under his leadership, and he erected a huge monument to Mahuta to suggest that this place was now the repository of the former King's mana (it was a bronze statue cast in Italy and erected on a huge marble base). His objective was nothing less than the transference of the movement's nerve centre from Waahi to Ngati Haua territory.[9] In the event, he was thwarted by Te Puea — the axis shifted first to Mangatawhiri and then to Turangawaewae.

In the meantime, however, there was Mahuta's funeral. It was an occasion for pause and reassessment. It marked the end, for a time, of Waikato's

---

† Gorst had been a Resident Magistrate and Civil Commissioner in Waikato from 1861 to 1863. He had been favourably impressed by some Maori leaders, and had impressed Waikato in turn as an intelligent and fair man. He revisited New Zealand in 1906 and 1907 after a tumultuous and ultimately disappointing career in English politics that had included being part of the leadership of the Conservative and Liberal Parties.

‡ The *New Zealand Herald* reported (11/6/1910): 'As a result of his meeting with Sir Joseph Ward, King Mahuta has sent Messers P. Kirkwood and W.T. Hughes to Matangi, where a rival meeting is being held by the followers of Tupu Taingakawa, with the object of laying Maori grievances before King George and the British Parliament. Mahuta is anxious that no action should be taken in this direction until the question has been again before the New Zealand Parliament.'

experiment in cooperation with the European Parliament. It also exposed the variety of attitudes for and against the Kingitanga that were then current.

When Tawhiao died, there had been little doubt among the supporting tribes that the kingship should continue. And at the time of his accession, none at all — all the original reasons for establishing the office had still been valid. At Mahuta's death the situation was clearly different. The land wars had been fought and lost; Maori customary law was everywhere being eroded by European law; the settler Government was maintaining peace throughout the country; Maori opinion was represented through the four Maori seats in the national Parliament; and Maori land continued to be alienated in a fashion that most Europeans and many Maori leaders thought inevitable and desirable.

Perhaps the most significant new ingredient in the assessment of the kingship in 1912 was that, as a result of Mahuta's earlier cooperative policies, many people outside Waikato felt entitled to a say in the future of the institution. And they viewed it in the light of what they felt about the future of the Maori race in general. Pakeha leaders of both major political parties saw the future of the races as one of assimilation that would ultimately erase distinctively Maori features; educated Maori leaders in Parliament saw it as one of integration, in which the Maori would adapt things of use and value from the Pakeha world and abandon what they regarded as retrograde features from the Maori inheritance. To Carroll, Ngata and Buck, the Maori kingship came into the last category.[10] They were not members of the original 'first circle' of supporters. They saw the institution itself and the title of Maori King as unnecessarily divisive and backward looking. For this reason, Carroll went to the funeral prepared to act as thin end of the blade of execution.

The new Reform Government's view was quite clear. As one commentator has put it, 'the Pakeha interpretation of the origins of the kingitanga . . . stressing themes of Maori separatism, aggression and rebellion, defined public attitudes and dictated official policy.'[11] Because most Europeans believed the King Movement was subversive and separatist in its origins, it followed that its continued existence was a threat to social order and policies of assimilation. Acceptance of the validity of the kingship would mean an acceptance of its claims — Pakeha responsibility for the war of 1863, the obligation to pay compensation, and the desirability of two races in New Zealand continuing to exist separately alongside each other.[12] These views were completely unpalatable to the Reform Party, its Prime Minister William Massey and its Native Minister William Herries.

For these reasons Government and Maori representatives combined to try to persuade Waikato to drop the title 'king' in the hope that collapse of the institution would follow. They were possibly encouraged by the prospect of a weak incumbent in the person of Te Rata. The representative of the Under-secretary of Native Affairs was to attend the funeral with the instruction that 'no notice be taken of the kingship element'.[13] And Carroll, no longer Native Affairs Minister but still the Maori member with the greatest mana, argued for the replacement of the expression 'king' by the Polynesian term 'ariki'. In particular he reasoned that the former title belonged to the Pakeha, who viewed its use by the Maori with disfavour.[14] Te Heuheu Tukino, whose grandfather had passed the original title to Potatau, supported Carroll. These were the heavyweights.

The Kingitanga spokesman was Tupu Taingakawa. He too was unequivocal: Waikato had not wanted the title King; but other tribes had placed both these things on Waikato and they had been protected as a sacred trust — the more so since blood had been spilled to preserve them. 'Now,' he concluded, 'we consider the name King tapu and will not agree to discarding it.'[15] Carroll replied petulantly and provocatively: 'This thing you persist in wearing as a head covering will perish. But so be it, you keep that which will perish: let me perform work that concerns the people of the land.'[16] †

Carroll's proposal was rejected by the tribes of 'te porotaka nama tahi' (the first circle of adherents, Waikato, Maniapoto, Raukawa and Hauraki), and Taingakawa anointed Te Rata on 24 November 1912. The ceremony took place alongside Mahuta's body and employed the same Bible that had been used to elevate Potatau and Mahuta. The funeral took place the same day. In deference to Te Marae's strong wishes, Mahuta was not interred on Taupiri according to Tawhiao's instruction. He was laid in a tomb built outside his home at Hukanui.‡

Te Puea appears to have remained in the background at Mahuta's tangi, regarding it as the prerogative of the widow and the movement's male spokesmen to set the terms of debate. Immediately afterwards, she returned to Mangatawhiri and threw herself into building up the facilities at the pa itself, now referred to as 'Te Paina'. First she dismantled a disused Ngati Tamaoho hall on the western bank, bound the timber together, and had it floated across the river.[17] On the Mangatawhiri side it was reassembled under the direction of the Ngati Whawhakia elder Hori Paki and it became the community's first meeting house.† This done, Paki and the elderly men who made up most of the pa's male population then built a dining hall.

---

† The same arguments for and against the title were heard over fifty years later at the funeral of Mahuta's grandson, Koroki. The kingship then showed no sign of perishing.
‡ His body was carried to Taupiri under Te Puea's direction in 1941. See Chapter 10.
* Hori Paki was to become Waikato's longest-serving worker. He actively supported Tawhiao, Mahuta, Te Rata, Koroki and finally Queen Te Atairangikaahu, whom one of his grandsons married. He died in 1972 at the age of 106.

While construction was proceeding slowly, Te Puea moved back and forth between the settlement and the farm at Raungawari that she was still working with Te Tahi Iwikau (she remained married to him until 1916). In the evenings she continued to encourage the old people to recite tribal history and sing Tainui songs. She kept stressing to them that the community was undergoing a period of preparation for the day when Te Paina would be capable of hosting major Kingitanga functions.[18]

Te Puea was by no means popular throughout Waikato. Piri Poutapu remembered that many people were still suspicious of her intentions at this time and jealous of the favour she had won from Mahuta. Her following was still local, still drawn largely from the lower river settlements. And in 1913 she was to increase its size and intensify its loyalty as a result of a severe outbreak of smallpox.

The largest smallpox epidemic recorded in New Zealand was first detected in Whangarei in May 1913. It had been carried to the country by a Mormon missionary from Arizona whose chosen vocation was to win Maori converts. His illness was more contagious than his faith. Most of those who contracted the disease from him were Maori, and constant movements to hui and Maori Land Court sittings over the next month ensured that the outbreak spread over the Auckland province before it was identified and checked by vaccination.

According to the Auckland District Health Officer there were 1777 Maori cases and 111 European ones; there were also fifty-five Maori deaths.[†] But he went on to say that the departmental record 'by no means gives a complete return of the cases since the greater part of the outbreak was among Maoris, and in consequence only about a quarter of the cases were seen by my medical men and reported.'[19] The outbreak lasted just over a year, the last cases being notified in April 1914.

Waikato, along with Auckland City, Marsden and Kaipara counties, Thames and the Bay of Plenty, was among the areas hardest hit. No separate figures were recorded for the disease there and, as the district health officer noted, most cases were in Maori communities and not seen by doctors.

The disease was a most unpleasant experience for those who caught it or were associated with cases, even when it did not lead to death. It brought several weeks of influenza-type symptoms, aching muscles, and pitting and scabbing of the face, back and other parts of the body. According to the cases reported, it affected mainly people in the twenty to thirty age group.[20]

---

† The outbreak among Maori was considered so severe that Peter Buck left Parliament while it was sitting to return to his electorate and help with vaccinations.

At first the outbreak was thought to be chicken pox. Once it was established that it was more serious, Te Puea committed herself full time to coping with the epidemic at Te Paina and the lower river settlements.[21] She built open-air shelters thatched with nikau, placed the infected cases there away from their families, and saw that they were nursed and fed until they recovered.

The physical magnitude of the task was bad enough, although she was assisted by her sister Hera. It was made more considerable, however, by other factors. There was still a widespread belief in Waikato that sickness was caused by spiritual factors, by chinks in the armour of personal tapu brought about through a hara or offence against some deity, or by makutu. Such convictions frequently led to a resignation to illness as something inevitable rather than something that could be cured; or to a preference for tohunga treatment instead of medical care (which could be quite inappropriate when, for example, it involved immersing a pneumonia patient in cold water).

Te Puea was the first Waikato leader to accept and preach that identifiable Pakeha-introduced diseases could be cured by Pakeha medical treatment.[†] But she accepted her people's fears about treatment in Pakeha institutions. Maori patients were reticent to leave the security of friends and family for a frighteningly unfamiliar and impersonal hospital environment. Hospitals in turn were most unwilling to accept Maori patients (at this time there was only one hospital in Waikato, in Hamilton).[‡] When they did, it was usually in extremis; and if the patient died there as a consequence of receiving treatment too late, Maori fears were reinforced.

Te Puea's solution was an anticipation of community health services — she attempted to establish Maori hospitals within Maori settlements so that patients could be separated from those they might infect, but without being removed from their home community or a Maori environment.[22] They would be treated in proximity to their families and, even if they were attended by Pakeha doctors (there were only three Maori graduates in medicine in the early years of the twentieth century), they could at least be nursed by Maori. It was this concept that led Te Puea in the late 1920s and in the early 1940s to try hard to set up a purely Maori hospital in Ngaruawahia. She hoped even to have Maori doctors in attendance. She was to be defeated, however, by public health authorities.

---

† Although the precedent had been set by Te Puea's uncle Tawera when he accepted treatment for an inflammation the year she was born. There were other disorders that she did not put into this category, however: see Chapter 10.
‡ See page 29.

In 1913, the most she could achieve was the rows of makeshift, open-air shelters for patients, and nursing care by herself, Hera and other women from Te Paina who were unaffected by the disease. Te Puea said of that period: 'I found that Maori people were dying by the riverside. We could get no nurses for them.[†] I had very little money so all my sister and I could do was to make a camp from nikau palms . . . [and] we nursed as many as possible back to health.'[23]

While medical facilities were apparently not supplied to Te Paina, the settlement like other infected communities was placed under quarantine. There were restrictions on the movement of Maori to prevent further contamination and once they were declared, Te Puea's efforts had to be confined to her own community. Piri Poutapu was then living at Mangatawhiri under her care. 'We were isolated to keep us away from the Pakeha. But we didn't mind. We went down to the river and stayed there. We had to exist on Maori food and there was plenty of it around at the time — pigeon, eel, fish in the river. The river was clean then and all the food that came out of it was healthy. The only things we really missed were flour and butter and sugar and tea. No one brought these things to us.'[24]

It is part of the published mythology of Te Puea's life that she began to mother orphaned children at this time.[25] The alleged numbers of these 'smallpox orphans' varied from forty-five[26] to 246.[27] But those who lived with her during the epidemic say this was not correct. According to Tumokai Katipa, after she had begun nursing people at Te Paina nobody died there. 'She put up the shelters, she looked after them — but nobody died.'[28] The deaths occurred in other settlements further down the river. Katipa believed later writers confused this period with the influenza epidemic[†] when they quoted Te Puea on the subject of her orphans, and that they confused 'orphans' with the large number of children Te Puea was responsible for at Te Paina but had not actually taken into her own home.[29]

As the epidemic tailed off, Waikato became engaged in a debate that exposed some of the earlier rifts in the King Movement. Mahuta and Tupu Taingakawa had disagreed strongly and publicly over whether the Kingites should mount another appeal about the injustice of the Waikato confiscations to the Crown and the British Parliament. Taingakawa, in his dogged pursuit of arguments that tended to be valid but beside the point, believed they should; Mahuta felt the only realistic course was to continue negotiations with the New Zealand

---

† The first Native Health Nurse appointed to Waikato, Miss Ella Cooke, did not go there until later that year.
‡ See Chapter 5.

Parliament, particularly in the light of the futility of Tawhiao's earlier pilgrimage.[30]

With Mahuta dead and Te Puea not yet in a position of ascendency, Taingakawa was able to effect one more major policy decision. Drawing on his extensive powers of oratory and fantasy, he persuaded Te Rata, Te Marae and a majority of Waikato that justice would be achieved if a further delegation went to England to petition the Crown to revoke the confiscations as a breach of the Treaty of Waitangi. He, of course, would be an essential member of such a delegation.[†] An inter-tribal meeting in Raglan in 1913 agreed that all Kingitanga adherents would contribute a shilling a head to build up a travelling fund; and Te Marae sold family land to make up the cost of a fare for four to England.[31] On 11 April 1914, the delegation sailed from Auckland in the steamship *Niagara*. It was made up of Te Rata, Tupu Taingakawa, Mita Karaka and Hori Tiro Paora (the last two acting as secretaries and interpreters).

They arrived in London late in May and booked into the Hotel Metropole. Those who saw them there were impressed favourably and surprisedly, as if the party had been expected to behave in an uncouth fashion. A journalist cabled back to New Zealand: 'Te Rata and his companions are arrayed in London suits of the best cut — morning coats and silk hats; and they look a thoroughly creditable and well-conducted party, attracting no unwelcome attention, and behaving themselves, as behoves the dignity of chiefs. The hotel attendants speak highly of their bearing.'[32]

The hotel attendants may have been the only hosts to express approval of the visit. For the rest, the party was an embarrassment as Tawhiao's group had been thirty years before. Tupu Taingakawa had told Waikato that Sir John Gorst had recommended such a mission when he re-visited New Zealand in 1907.[‡] Now, in England, Gorst made it clear he had done no such thing.[33] This was a particular blow to Te Rata who had been relying more than anything else on Gorst's sympathetic assistance. Gorst, who was ill when the party arrived, initially declined to see them. When he did, the most that this former confidant of Benjamin Disraeli and Lord Randolph Churchill could manage was a letter for Taingakawa to give to an organisation called 'the Aboriginal Protection Society', a contact that apparently produced no results. They also visited the New Zealand High Commissioner, Sir Thomas Mackenzie, who undertook to try to arrange an audience at Buckingham Palace provided nothing embarrassing was

---

† One of the few dissenters from the decision, still flexing some political muscle, was Henare Kaihau (clipping, Turongo House collection, 22 May 1914).
‡ This was simply not true. In his book *New Zealand Revisited*, Gorst states he advised against the visit (p. 308).

The Kingitanga delegation in London, 1914: (from left) Mita Karaka, Tupu Taingakawa, King Te Rata and Hori Tiro Paora. Tupu's position and posture indicate that he saw himself as leader of the group.

Turongo House

raised;[34] the Colonial Secretary (briefly); and a man named Andrews who engaged a lawyer for them to draw up an elaborate document entitled 'Maori Rights', for which they were charged £500.

Finally, on 4 June, the party was received by King George V and Queen Mary. For the first time Maori royalty came face to face with a reigning British monarch (a gesture that was not to be repeated for another forty years). Te Rata laid cloaks and Maori weapons at the King's feet[35] to symbolise his acknowledgement of the mana of the British Crown and a rejection of the wars of the past. And that was all. Nobody else wanted to see them, and the most that the Colonial Secretary's office could promise was that their claims would be referred back to the New Zealand Government.[36] They sailed for New Zealand on 10 August.

The whole episode had been another one of misunderstanding, embarrassment and futility. For this, Tupu Taingakawa had to accept much of the blame, particularly for misleading the delegation about Sir John Gorst's advice. The only visible and continuing consequence of the journey was that the London lawyer sent further bills for his consultation and for the preparation of the illuminated document on parchment paper.[37]

Six days before the party left London hostilities were declared between Britain and Germany. Under interpretations of constitutional law then current, all colonies in the Empire were now at war.

Te Puea's response to the challenge she faced from Tupu Taingakawa and Te Marae was to consolidate loyalties at Te Paina, extend its facilities, and prepare it for use as a ceremonial centre for Te Rata. Her first opportunity to organise a major hui came while Te Rata was still overseas; and it provoked a clash with Te Marae and the members of the kahui ariki based in Waahi.

Te Puea conceived the idea that Waikato should welcome Te Rata home at Te Paina. The proposal was canvassed and debated throughout 1914 on most major marae, and it was a mark of Te Puea's growing influence that it was accepted at first with enthusiasm. Then, other people who felt they stood to lose by having the spotlight taken off them had second thoughts. As a result of politicking by Tupu Taingakawa's wife, with the encouragement of Waahi leaders, it was decided to hold the function at Waahi instead.[38] But Te Puea was not beaten. Displaying an imagination and an initiative that was to enable her frequently to out-manoeuvre opponents, she cabled Te Rata at Sydney and told him he was invited to attend a welcoming function at Te Paina. He, delighted and ignorant of other suggestions, cabled back giving full approval. Te Puea now had the mana of the King as a blessing on her proposal and the Waahi faction was forced to back down.

The hui was held late in September 1914. Te Puea remembered it especially for the fact that the owners of Orakei Marae in Auckland had just been persuaded to sell large portions of their land;[39] the women came to Te Paina in fur coats and hats with ostrich feathers. As preparations for the King's arrival were nearing completion, Michael Rotohiko Jones (who had just left Wesley College in Auckland) [†] arrived at the marae with his uncle Tutahanga, who was campaigning for Maui Pomare's re-election.

My uncle told me that the main reason we were calling there was so I could be introduced to my distant cousin, who I had heard of then as 'Princess' Te Puea.[‡] I was a young fellow, nineteen. I had visions of a fairytale princess dressed in courtly robes and was very anxious to see her.

We went to the meeting house first and my uncle said, 'Where's Kiri?' And they said in the dining room. So we went there, but they said, 'Oh no, she's out the back cooking.' I was surprised at that, to find a princess in the kitchen. Out there we found a circle of women sitting on an earth floor peeling potatoes and Te Puea was among them, wearing a sack-cloth apron. That was my first sight of her.

That night, after Te Rata's party had arrived, they were given a big reception in what was then the Mercer Town Hall by the mayor and Pakeha citizens. Straight after there was a ball. Te Puea insisted I go in her party and even provided me with a young lady. This time, as we paraded through the hall, she was in a full-length, dark-red dress made of velvet, and had a kerchief tied around her brow. She looked every inch the princess I'd imagined her to be.[49]

After the hui Te Puea accompanied Te Rata to his home at Waahi where she had to face the anger of members of the family who lived there. As she was

---

[†] Michael Rotohiko Jones and his younger brother Pei Te Hurinui were to become two of Te Puea's most influential advisors and spokesmen from the 1930s. In particular, she was to lean on them heavily for matters requiring expertise in the Pakeha world; she called them affectionately 'those bloody hurai', a reference to the fact that their natural father, Daniel Lewis, was Jewish.

[‡] This seems to be the earliest reference to Te Puea as 'princess'. The title, of course, was purely honorific. It is not a Polynesian one, nor was it formally adopted as a term within the institution of the Kingitanga like the title 'kingi'. It was merely a popular attempt to describe Te Puea's standing within the movement in an equivalent European term. It came to be more favoured by Pakeha than Maori after she was discovered by the press in the 1920s, except in cases where Maori spokesmen were attempting to impress her status on a European audience. Te Puea herself preferred to be called simply 'Te Puea'; or, by those who were related or were close friends, 'Kiri'.

Te Puea (top) and her sister Te Atarua at Te Paina, shortly before the outbreak of World War One. Ngeungeu Zister

often to do in subsequent years, she simply brazened it out until the opposition wilted: 'I always had a room in a certain house at Waahi. My things were there and it was always kept for me. When I arrived I found Taipu there. He was very angry with me for taking Rata to Mangatawhiri. He was black in the face . . . He was in my room purposely. However, I had my kai as if nothing was wrong and kept to the room. And he left.'[41]

The outbreak of war in Europe had no immediate effect on Waikato. The question of enlistment was discussed at hui, but the unanimous opinion was that no King Movement supporter should serve overseas (this was also the decision of the Kauhanganui in July 1915).[42] When Te Rata returned from England he was asked if Maori soldiers should not sail in a contingent to support his friend King George. He gave what was to become his standard reply: 'Waiho ma he hiahia,' leave it to individual choice. If Maoris wished to enlist, they could. But no one should be forced to.[43]

The neutrality of the movement's leaders was more apparent than real, however — its purpose was to make harassment by the authorities and prosecution under wartime regulations more difficult. In fact, away from Pakeha hearing, Te Rata, Te Puea and Tupu Taingakawa all actively discouraged Waikato enlistment. And recruitment figures showed their success (there were no Waikato volunteers in the first two native contingents that sailed for Europe in February and September 1915).

They based their position primarily on Tawhiao's often quoted speech to Resident Magistrate William Gilbert Mair. As he emerged at Alexandra from his confinement on 12 August 1881, the King had said: 'Listen, listen, the sky above, the earth below, and all the people assembled here. The killing of men must stop, the destruction of land must stop. I shall bury my patu in the earth and it shall not rise again.' He turned to Major Mair. 'As for your weapons of slaughter, return them to people who are weary of them. Waikato, lie down. Do not allow blood to flow from this time on. War shall not come to this island. It has been outlawed. Any man who starts a war in this country shall pay for it.'[†]

Being of a highly tapu nature like all of Tawhiao's remembered sayings, this statement was taken literally by Waikato. It was an injunction never again to fight (which Waikato had not done); and it was a prophetic assurance that no matter what happened in Europe, the war would not spread to New Zealand.

There was another factor: the outstanding grievance of the confiscations. 'They tell us to fight for king and country,' Te Puea was fond of saying at the time, referring to a recruitment poster. 'Well, that's all right. We've got a king. But we haven't got a country. That's been taken off us. Let them give us back our land and then maybe we'll think about it again.'[44] It was also ironical, as a member of the kahui ariki has written since, that fighting for king and country (their king and their country) was the very crime for which Waikato had been punished fifty years before. 'If it was wrong then, what made it right now?'[45]

So Waikato adopted the attitude that the war did not and would not touch them. It was a Pakeha fight among Pakeha nations and they were best left to it. But Waikato was not to be left to its own position. In spite of the fact that successive New Zealand governments had refused every petition and request for assistance that the King Movement had lodged, Parliament was to decide that the movement owed allegiance to the country as a whole in time of national crisis. And the weapon conceived to extract that allegiance forcibly or punish Waikato for the crime of separatism was the selective imposition of conscription.

---

† This version of Tawhiao's statement is Te Puea's own and was repeated by her to Peter Fraser at Parliament in July 1942. It was printed and distributed in an undated issue of *Te Paki o Matariki* the same year and differs slightly from the version in the official minutes. Translation by Mick Jones.

4

Conscription
and Pai Marire

The origin of the Waikato anti-conscription campaign lay in a decision in Wellington to over-commit Maori troops to the war in Europe. The decision was taken in Wellington by the Member of Parliament Te Puea had helped to elect, Maui Pomare, and the Native Contingent Committee, of which he was chairman. (Other members were the incumbents of the Maori seats and Sir James Carroll; Pomare's chairmanship arose from his being the only Maori in the coalition war cabinet.)

At the time of the outbreak of hostilities the Imperial Government had opposed the idea of native peoples fighting in a war among Europeans. Their loyalties might prove suspect; they might even turn on their colonial masters; they might have to be treated as the equals of European soldiers in circumstances where this could become an embarrassment.[†] But the decision to deploy Indian troops along the Suez Canal in mid-1914 changed that. Once Pomare, Carroll, Ngata, Buck, Tau Henare and Taare Parata saw that other non-white members of the Empire were allowed to participate, they were determined that a Maori contingent should go to the combat zones and take its share of fighting and casualties.

They argued strenuously and eventually successfully against the policy that Maori troops should be given garrison duties only. Their efforts also ensured

---

† The Administrator of Samoa cabled the New Zealand Government in October 1914 that he did not want Maori sent there, partly because they would have to be treated as if they were white, and this would have an upsetting effect on the Samoan population (see O'Connor, p. 51).

that the contingent was allowed to retain its own identity and operate as an independent unit known originally as the 'Pioneer' and subsequently (from October 1917) as the 'Maori Battalion'. Provision was made within the battalion for platoon groupings along regional and tribal lines.

Peter Buck, as Member for Northern Maori, was one of the first to argue for a Maori combat role. He was also one of the first to volunteer for service and he sailed with the first contingent. He was later appointed second in command of the Pioneer Battalion. His despatches from the front line to the Native Contingent Committee frequently fired members' enthusiasm for the Maori war effort, at times when events at home could have caused it to flag.[†]

For Pomare in particular it was a matter of racial pride that the Maori soldier should stand alongside others of the British Empire. He was to write with great satisfaction of the war's effect on 'the position of the Maori as a social and political entity in the life of New Zealand. Our people's voluntary service . . . gave a new and glorious tradition to the story of the Maori race. It gave the crowning touch to the sense of citizenship in the British Commonwealth; it satisfied in the one fitting fashion the intense desire of the Maori to prove to the world that he was the equal of the pakeha in the fullest sense — physically, mentally and spiritually. The rush of the Maori to offer his life in the nation's service not only gave proof that his hereditary fighting temper was as strong as ever at the call of danger; it enabled him to exhibit the supreme qualities of citizenship; a larger patriotism than mere clanship; endurance, valour and self-sacrifice in the highest degree . . . Henceforth he was the racial peer of any man on earth.'[1] The 'larger patriotism than mere clanship' referred to another step that Pomare hoped the Maori would take along the path of evolution — that of overcoming the effects of tribalism. For groups like Waikato, the sense of tribe was the strongest source of identity and inspiration; in Pomare's eyes it was a debilitating handicap.

Pomare, and to a lesser extent Carroll and Buck, frequently displayed insecurity about their Maori background. Their major way of coping with this was to excel in so-called Pakeha activities — education, professional skills,

---

† Of the action at Gallipoli Buck was to say: 'My heart thrilled at the sound of my mother tongue resounding up the slopes of Sari Bair. The Maoris had passed through their baptism of fire with courage and dash surpassed by none and had proved themselves worthy of their ancestry.' (Condliffe, p. 132). He was also impressed by the organisation of the war effort as evidence of a high degree of sophistication. He quoted one Maori volunteer as saying, 'Yet some of the Maoris ask for mana motuhake, the right to govern themselves. Let them travel with the Expeditionary Force and they will never open their mouths again.' (Ibid, p. 126) Significantly, perhaps, the expression 'mana motuhake' was a favourite of Tawhiao's.

Parliamentary debate, English prose, pursuit of fashionable standards of dress and behaviour. Buck and Pomare in particular seemed often to apologise for their Maoriness.[†] They saw it as something with which they had necessarily started out, but which they wanted to blend into the wider world of European culture and attainment; and they hoped to be accepted by Europeans for their ability to do so. (Ngata was somewhat different. He showed himself to be far less compromising in asserting his Maoriness, especially late in his public career. Although he had mastered European literacy and politics, his approach was one of trying to bend the system to incorporate Maori ways of doing things. He was also unapologetic about tribalism and used the reality of it to give impetus to his projects, particularly the land schemes.)

One can only sympathise with these turn-of-the-century parliamentarians. They were bridge people. They trained and emerged as leaders at a time when the earlier evangelically humanitarian themes of colonisation had given way to settler greed and racism that were often explicit and brutal. In order to win acceptance for their people and themselves as Maori, they had first to win acceptance as Pakeha — they had to show that they were not only as capable as Europeans, but more so. This was the impulse that drove Carroll, Ngata, Buck and Pomare, and they succeeded. It is the major reason why — in Pakeha eyes — the quality of Maori representation was so high during their terms of office and so disappointing subsequently.

The Maori members' near-fanaticism about Maori war participation must be viewed in the light of these broader attitudes, as must their frequent inability to win full acceptance from their own people at the community level.[‡] The 'rush of the Maori to offer his life in the nation's service', of which Pomare spoke, was far more apparent among his committee than among his people. After the first contingent of 505 men had sailed for Egypt in February 1915, the Native Contingent Committee found it impossible to meet agreed quotas for reinforcement (150 men every four weeks). Ngata, characteristically more bluntly honest than his colleagues, acknowledged that early promises about the Maori willingness to fight were 'all wind and words'.[2] Second and third drafts sailed in September 1915 and February 1916; but of the last only 111 out of 314 were Maori. The largest part were Niue Islanders and Rarotongans who posed special difficulties when they were transplanted into a European climate.[3]

---

† Buck, for example, speaking of the 'less advanced culture' of the Maori as he accepted his honorary doctorate from Yale University in 1951 (Condliffe, p. 227).
‡ In *Vikings of the Sunrise* Buck referred to his being 'horribly conscious that I was talking to my own people like a foreigner' (Buck, 1938, p. 261).

From May 1916 only two drafts swollen by Rarotongans reached the fixed rate of reinforcement. The later ones failed to reach half that number.[4]

While Maori servicemen distinguished themselves in combat in Gallipoli and in sapper duties on the battlefields of the Western Front, there was no disguising the fact that recruitment was steadily drying up, that initial enthusiasm had not been sustained. And that which had been accomplished had placed the load disproportionately on certain areas (especially Arawa, Ngata's East Coast and Ngapuhi of the north). Recruitment was especially low in Taranaki and Maniapoto, and non-existent in Waikato. Embarrassingly, these areas were part of the voluble chairman Pomare's electorate.

By June 1915, Defence Minister James Allen was writing to the New Zealand forces commander Sir Alexander Godley that 'whether we shall be able to keep the Maori reinforcements is difficult to say, as the Maoris seem to have a disposition not to serve led by some of their chiefs who are beginning to feel sore over the land question.'[5] And, trying to shame the non-combatants, he wrote to a Te Kuiti correspondent the same month in terms that echoed Pomare's: 'I understood the native chiefs in New Zealand were also anxious to stand alongside of their pakeha brothers in the defence of the country of their forefathers and in defence of the great British Empire.'[6]

While the parliamentarians were activating the Maori traditions of Tumatauenga, god of war, Te Puea was reinforcing those of Tawhiao, prophet of peace. And Waikato's refusal to serve became a growing embarrassment to Pomare, the Maori members and the Government. But not to Te Puea. In addition to the confiscation grievance and Tawhiao's pacifist injunctions there was another factor that distinguished Waikato's attitude from that of the Maori MPs. Although its livelihood depended to some extent on acceptance by the Pakeha majority, its sense of identity in no way did. The system had given nothing when Waikato asked; why should Waikato give anything when the system made demands? Te Puea's approach to Maori-Pakeha relations, particularly of the kind that involved conflict, was to let the mountain come to Mohammed. And come, eventually, it did.

The first case that drew the attention of the authorities to Waikato's attitude towards military service was the desertion of a recruit in Auckland. He was arrested at Taupiri and made a statement to the police that he had changed his mind about service because his parents were opposed to enlistment. After leaving camp, he said, he had gone to King Te Rata's house at Waahi. 'Rata told me that if I did not want to go, to sign my name in his Book and he would carry on in the matter.' He was also told to stay in the pa and not to resist arrest.[7] As a result of the police report on this incident, the Officer Commanding the

Auckland Military District, Col. G.W.H. Patterson, urged the army to prosecute Te Rata. But higher authorities doubted that such a case would succeed because the Maori contingent was then a voluntary unit.[8]

The next case was Tonga Mahuta, the King's brother, who consistently refused to report for territorial training. He was first fined for this in 1914, and then the outbreak of war disrupted the scheme. In February 1916 the army decided to prosecute a small number of the fifty or sixty men from Waahi eligible for training who had refused to comply with instructions. The group was to be selected on the basis of family prominence and education. Previous experience had shown that the attempted prosecution of uneducated Maoris 'had resulted in a great deal of trouble with the interpreters and often resulted in the dismissal of the case.'[9]

Tonga Mahuta was first prosecuted in January 1916. But because his lawyer announced that a satisfactory scheme for training territorials in Huntly was imminent, the magistrate imposed only the lightest of fines, five shillings. No training was subsequently performed. Further prosecutions followed in April 1916, April 1917, January 1918 and June 1918. The matter was not resolved until Tonga's call-up in the conscription ballot of August 1918 made the territorial training issue irrelevant.

That the Kingites associated this training with war service was made clear to the Officer Commanding No. 4 Group (Hamilton), Major E.H. Northcroft. Northcroft visited Waahi on 26 June 1916. The hui then in progress stressed concern that a member of the kahui ariki was being subjected to pressure by the authorities. 'If this bond is not taken off him it is . . . hurtful to the feelings of his mother and to the whole tribe on account of the said Tonga Mahuta Tawhiao Potatau Te Wherowhero being one of our Royal Family.'[10] This last point was an issue of great sensitivity that was to be raised subsequently by Kingitanga spokesmen: that while European VIPs were exempted from provisions of the law that were incompatible with the responsibilities or the dignity of their office, Maori leaders were not.

By this time the failure of the Native Contingent Committee to meet reinforcement quotas had brought Waikato's refusal to enlist to the attention of the Government. Defence Minister Allen made a personal visit to Waahi on 24 November 1916, the day of Te Rata's annual coronation anniversary hui. Te Rata, however, was not present. And there were few men of military age to be seen.[11] An *Auckland Star* reporter made it clear that he considered the hui demonstrated how low the Maori kingship had fallen. There was no sign of the fighting spirit of Potatau and Tawhiao, but merely 'an effeminate, ease-loving buffoonery which delights in tinsel, in the blare of a make believe brass band, and the enervating pleasure of the dance hall.' A banner 'flaunted brazenly in the breeze like a patchwork quilt, and symbolised those of Rata's young men who slouched about with hands in pockets, and cigarettes in mouth, in striking contrast to the well set up, alert and drilled company of young fighting men from Narrow Neck.'[12]

Allen addressed the gathering in emotive terms. He exhorted them 'to save New Zealand from the fate of Belgium, and their women from being the sport of German bayonets. He appealed to Waikato pride. Surely they did not want to be the only Maoris to whom it was necessary to apply conscription. "If you fail now you and your tribes can never rest in honour in the days that are to come." In reply Tupu Taingakawa admitted that his people were holding back because they were aggrieved and had been since 1861, but the question of recruiting had no more to do with him than with the King. The attitude of them both was that if the young men wished to go they could and he was willing now to repeat this publicly in Allen's presence.'[13]

It was apparently the failure to achieve anything at this meeting that convinced Allen that conscription would have to be applied to Waikato. He wrote to Sir Alexander Godley in December 1916, 'I'm afraid it will take pressure, not talk, to bring them in.'[14]

In the middle of the same year, while conscription for the whole country was being debated in Parliament, Pomare made it clear that he wanted it applied to Maori: 'Sir, the Maoris won their spurs on the fields of Gallipoli, fields which have been made sacred not only to the Pakeha but to the Maoris by spilling blood there. That blood cries out to us for utu, and utu they shall have: and if by conscription utu is to be extracted, then, Sir, let it be conscription.'[15]

It was left to Tau Henare, who had replaced Buck in the Northern Maori seat, to act as a voice for Pomare's recalcitrant constituents. 'In a brief speech, which he refused to deliver in English, he linked Waikato and Taranaki reluctance to volunteer to the confiscated lands.' He also made the highly sensible suggestion that it would be an incentive for service to give confiscated lands not already settled to Maori returned soldiers.[16] Ngata too, in later years, was to speak sympathetically of Waikato's position and liken it to that of the Irish, 'not rebels but an oppressed minority attempting to protect themselves from the illegitimate demands of the colonising power.'[17]

At first, in August 1916, the Military Services Act did impose conscription on Pakeha only. The dismal failure of the Native Contingent Committee to meet their reinforcement quotas, however, led to the extension of the Act to Maori in mid-1917. But it was to one group of Maori only. The record of the imposition of conscription on Waikato can only be described as shameful. It validated all the worst Maori fears about Pakeha duplicity. In particular, it confirmed that while the Maori was called upon to obey the law to the letter, Pakeha authority had the power simply to change the law when it proved convenient to do so.

First, on 26 June 1917, an extension of the Military Services Act was gazetted in terms that applied conscription to all Maori. But communications from the Minister of Defence made it clear that its application was to be on Waikato alone. (He wrote on 18 February 1918 assuring Nau Paraone Kawiti of Ngapuhi that only Waikato was involved and he hoped 'you will assist me in ensuring that the Waikatos take their fair share in helping to protect our Country and King in this time of National peril.'[18])

In the event, the law was applied to the 'Waikato-Maniapoto Land District' being the only legal territorial definition the Government could devise that embraced Waikato tribes. It raised another inequality, however. It meant that Maniapoto was included in the measures even though its rate of enlistment was higher than that of Pomare's own Taranaki people.[19] According to Eric Ramsden,[20] Maniapoto had, on a population basis, supplied six times the number of recruits that Taranaki had. It also raised a further red herring as an explanation for why the Government was taking the step: some Maori now felt that Pomare was using his influence to extract revenge for the defeats Taranaki had suffered at the hands of Waikato-Maniapoto in the nineteenth century.[21]

Secondly the Government decided (with the apparent agreement of the Maori members) to compile a ballot register using the 'completely confidential' information collected in the 1916 census — a clear violation of law.[22] At first the census enumerators were to be used as registrars (because their 'integrity', meaning 'silence', could be relied upon); and then it was decided to give this job to the police because of the assumed extensiveness of their local knowledge. The procedure then was to allow a short time, ostensibly for Maori to register under the Act (regulations were gazetted on 14 February 1918, and enrolment was to be completed by 20 February, giving six days). In fact, Maori were not expected to register at all and the time was to be used by the police to amend and extend the confidential census information for the ballot, giving particular attention to spelling of names, marital status, and so forth.[23]

The result was utter confusion. The police understood neither the nature nor the point of these machinations. Official instructions and recruiting posters made it clear they were to accept enrolments; 'unofficial' advice told them it did not matter. Eventually they asked for an extension of time to 20 March to complete the rolls and this was granted by somebody else who did not appreciate the new rules of the game. The secretary of the recruiting board was exasperated: 'The Constables apparently have not the faintest conception of what they are supposed to do. It does not matter a scrap if the Natives do not come to register. They were never expected to do so.'[24]

Further confusion arose from the fact that in some key areas the Government Statistician's information was useless. In Huntly, where jurisdiction included Waahi, a constable reported that most men eligible for the first division call-up were not even on the roll with which he had been provided. In the same town there were only six registrations, all Ngapuhi from North Auckland. The *Huntly Press* blamed the situation on the Government's failure to force Tonga Mahuta to train. 'The average Maori,' it editorialised, 'has now imbibed the idea that he is above the Government and some think they are above any power on earth.'[25]

While all this was going on an atmosphere approaching panic was building up among some Maori groups, and in areas where Europeans felt vulnerable to reprisals. The Maori Ladies' Committee of Ngongotaha urged Cabinet to cut off old age pensions for King Movement supporters; large, restive gatherings were called at Waahi and Rukumoana to discuss tactics as the deadline for the close of enrolment approached; and Mr J.C. Jack of the Kawhia Rifle Club wrote to the Minister of Defence about the danger of imminent rebellion along the Waikato coastline:

> The natives are much under the influence of their elders who seldom leave their settlements, and who have no conception of the power behind their white neighbours. They see only an alien race, inferior to them in numbers and at the present time inferior in collective physique . . . The history of subject coloured races, the world over, proves that they are practically sure to revolt at some time, whether well governed or not, and their chance of success or failure seems to weigh little with them . . . Should conscription be enforced with these people, (as it decidedly should be) they would probably take to the bush, and be a menace to every man, woman and child.

Jack's solution was the establishment of rifle clubs in small settlements and the distribution of rifles to every white settler. This would, he assured Allen, have a wondrous effect on the coloured mind.[26]

Matters simmered uneasily, nobody being quite sure what would happen. On Pomare's advice, the Government and police expected only passive resistance from Waikato in the event of a confrontation: the same words of Tawhiao that forbade them to take up arms for their country abroad also excluded the possibility that they would fight physically for their honour at home.

The next act of official duplicity took place on 6 May 1918. Gazetted notices of those who had been called up in the first division were withheld, and personal notifications were posted to those balloted in plain envelopes instead of ones marked OHMS, as required by regulations. (Legislation defined those eligible to serve in the first division as 'unmarried men between seventeen and thirty years of age.'[27]) By 20 May the Maori Medical Board was ready to interview those ordered to report for examination. As expected, few appeared. Of the thirty-one people balloted in Huntly only six reported and these were apparently all employees of the Pukemiro coal mines and therefore eligible for exemption.[28]

Meanwhile, Te Puea had assumed leadership of the anti-conscriptionists. Although she had frequently spoken out against participation in the war from the time it began, she did not become involved full-time with the issue until Te Rata's coronation hui in November 1917 (exactly one year after James Allen appealed to Waikato at Waahi). This time the hui was held at Te Paina. Te Rata was ill, as he seemed to be more often than not, and Te Puea was responsible for all the arrangements. It was the kind of function she had dreamed of holding at the pa in the days when it had been run down and poorly equipped.

'It was a very big day. Many visitors. Tai Mitchell was there, also Mita Taupopoki [both from Te Arawa] and people from Taranaki, Wairarapa, even Kaipara.'[29] Te Puea initially declined an invitation to attend the session that discussed the imminent prospect of conscription. As far as she was concerned, Waikato had little left to fight for; and she still preferred to leave formal marae debate to male spokesmen. But the meeting sent for her at a point of deadlock. Some people were still completely opposed to service, some were wavering because of conscription, and visitors were urging Waikato to fall into line with the rest of the country. They asked for Te Puea's opinion. She gave it by singing a song she had just composed, later to be popularised as *The Song of Te Puea*. It said, in part, 'Stand firm, Rata, at the pillar of Waikato, look to the west and hear the groaning of the seas far out on the coast as I sing my song of sorrow.'[30] It was a lament emphasising the disinheritance of the people of the west (Waikato), and advising Te Rata and his followers not to compromise in the face of this injustice. It was interpreted by the meeting for what it was: a refusal to participate in military service.[†] After she had finished, the hui

---

[†] Throughout 1917 and 1918, particularly when the anti-conscription campaign was fully under way, Te Puea composed many laments, action songs and hakas about the war. These contributed to her growing reputation as a medium between the spiritual and secular worlds, and their performance was an important ingredient in sustaining Waikato morale.

reaffirmed a policy of opposition to enlistment and conscription, and asked Te Puea to shelter those who might be balloted at Te Paina.[31]

Waikato felt exceedingly vulnerable at this time. With the course of the war they had come to be regarded by Pakeha neighbours as seditious traitors, even German sympathisers. Employers who had previously offered seasonal work withdrew it. 'We were most unpopular everywhere,' Te Puea said. 'And we were very poor. The people . . . looked to me . . . With others I cut flax and took it to the mill. With the money we got bags of flour and sugar. That is how we fed the people.'[32]

With the announcement of enrolment dates for the ballot in February 1918, Te Puea sent word to all Waikato and Maniapoto men of conscriptional age to join her at Te Paina if they had not done so already. Tae Tapara of Maniapoto had taken refuge with others in the rugged limestone hills behind Marakopa. They planned to live in caves as outlaws. Te Puea's message to him was, 'You and the others who are hiding are to come here. If we are to die, let us all die together.'[33]

As the Medical Board began its hearings in May and the names and numbers of defaulters became apparent, the group of fugitives at Te Paina grew. They filled in the time of waiting as best they could. 'The old people occupied themselves with waiatas and chants,' Te Puea remembered, 'while the younger ones made love — even in the daytime. At the time I had a boat on the Waikato River. It went from place to place collecting food.' Other people 'played football and rounders. There was nothing else to do. The meetings in the hall were packed. We managed somehow to have kai every day.'[34]

The *Huntly Press* was incensed by the spectacle of so many people openly flouting the law. It called for stern Government measures. 'They are so involved with a sense of their own position (which they consider much above that of their white brother) and the mana of their Kingi Te Rata that they really believe they are in a position to win the day — they believe the Government dares not enforce the law on them.'[35]

Law enforcement was, however, on the way. Pomare's advice to Allen on 7 June was that the gathering was merely waiting to be taken to jail. 'Send one or two policemen at the very most,' he said, 'and do not make any demonstration . . . There is plenty of time for that later if they resist.'[36]

There was no resistance. The party of constables that arrived at Te Paina on 11 July 1918 was expected and welcomed by a huge crowd. 'They were received by Maori girls, some of them playing brass band instruments, and escorted to a bench reserved for them in the meeting house.'[37] The leader of the party, a Sergeant Waterman, waited till the hall filled with people and then he got to his feet and spoke first. He spoke slowly and clearly, in the manner of a constable in the execution of his duty:[†]

'We have come here in accordance with the instructions of the Government,' he told an attentive audience. 'We have come to apprehend the men whose names have appeared in the papers as having been balloted. On account of the severity of the fighting in Europe, King George of England has asked the Government of New Zealand to assist in the war with all its men who owe allegiance to the Crown in New Zealand. Therefore we have come to take charge of these men. We also have warrants for all men included in the ballot . . . The Germans are seeking to subdue the whole world . . . his laws are not as good as the laws of England . . . If you were under the laws of the Germans you would be in a bad plight indeed . . . We look to you, Te Puea, to help us to identify the men whose names I will read from this list. Although I would like it better if the men themselves would come forward as I read out their names.'

The sergeant sat down and waited. Te Puea rose to reply, first greeting the people present and the police party in traditionally courteous terms. Then she said to Sergeant Waterman, 'These people are mine. My voice is their voice . . . I will not agree to my children going to shed blood. Though your words be strong, you will not move me to help you. The young men who have been balloted will not go . . . You can fight your own fight until the end.'[38]

When she had finished the police read a list of names and, as expected, nobody stepped forward. So the local constables waded into the sitting crowd and began to arrest those present whose names they believed were on the list. They made several mistakes as a result of incorrect identification and inaccurate information. Te Puea's future husband, sixteen-year-old Rawiri Katipa, was mistaken for his elder brother. Another arrested was a sixty-year-old grandfather named Anu. None of the seven men taken cooperated and each had to be lifted and carried to waiting cars.

The most tense moment came when the police moved towards Te Rata's youngest brother, Te Rauangaanga, then also only sixteen. The girls sitting in front of him spread out the King's personal flag, as if to protect him. The constables stepped over this and picked up Rau and a great sigh went through

---

[†] The following quotations are from an anonymous manuscript prepared by somebody present for submission to the *New Zealand Herald* 'so that they would know the works of the Government towards the Maori people. However, it came under the notice of the Government and this report would not be allowed for publication.' The manuscript is in a minute book with notes of Kingitanga meetings between 1905 and 1918. These extracts were copied by Eric Ramsden on 27 August 1947 at the home of Mr Tio Rene of Takapuwahia, Porirua, in whose possession the minute book was then held.

the meeting. Te Uira Te Heuheu said later that 'if Te Puea had but raised her little finger there would have been bloodshed.'[39] Instead, she walked up and down in front of the rows of sitting people with a switch in her hand, murmuring that they must remain calm and quiet. As Te Rauangaanga was carried out she called to him: 'Be patient. Let the spirit of your father and also the spirit of your ancestors be with you. God bless you.'[40]

The police paused before moving off with the prisoners and Te Puea spoke to them once more: 'Return to your Government and tell them what I have said. I am not afraid of the law or anything else excepting the God of my ancestors . . . I will not allow any violence or blood to flow through my fingers . . . Go in peace and goodbye.' Sergeant Waterman thanked Te Puea and the crowd for behaving peacefully, and said he would return. He hoped that next time people would see their way clear to assist him.[41] Then the prisoners were taken by car to Mercer Railway Station and by train to Auckland, where they agreed to walk peacefully to the army training camp at Narrow Neck.

Te Puea began an angry exchange of telegrams with Pomare in which she told him to 'laugh from your exalted position at my people who are being imprisoned like slaves in accordance with the works of the Pakeha. Leave it to God to judge us.'[42] Pomare replied: 'Young lady, be moderate in your language. Like a rangatira, permit the youth to go . . . There is no laughter in me but I am deeply concerned for you.'[43]

The police returned twice more to Mangatawhiri before the end of June. 'They searched the pa for guns,' Te Puea said. 'Of course we had no guns. All they found were the people at play . . . Some of the girls and boys were in the houses making love when the police looked in.' Again, the resistance of those arrested was passive. 'One of them was enormously fat. He just lay on the ground. The police had much difficulty in carrying him to the motor car. Of course no one would help them. We had to laugh, despite our tears.'[44]

Because of the inadequacy of information held by the police, the application of these penal provisions of the Military Service Act continued to be inconsistent and incorrect. Men were taken in mistake for their fathers or brothers, some were over age, some under, some married with children. Some had names that had not even been called in the ballot but they did not object to being taken because they liked the idea of a trip to Auckland, where they had to be released. Of the twenty-seven Waikato men arrested in June, only sixteen were eligible and medically fit.[†] Only one of these showed an initial interest in

---

† This was according to army records (O'Connor, p. 77). In fact, at least two of these sixteen were under-age and therefore not eligible.

service. Te Rauangaanga was specially cultivated by Pomare and Major H. Peacock. Eventually, after being offered a variety of enticements including a commission, he was persuaded to train. He also agreed to sign a letter asking Waikato to stop resisting the law and another to Te Rata saying how well he was being treated.[45]

But for those who continued to refuse to cooperate, life in detention became very unpleasant. Tae Tapara, acting under instructions from his father, had been one of those arrested in June. 'We were taken to Narrow Neck Camp where we were medically examined and passed as fit for overseas service,' he wrote 26 years later. 'Thus began our affliction . . .

> After refusing to wear the uniform of the soldiers we were given our first military punishment. For 40 hours we received only bread and water. Once again we were asked to clothe ourselves in military uniform and once again we refused. This time the punishment was . . . two weeks on bread and water. For the third time we were advised . . . and for the third time we said no. Our punishment this time was no blankets to sleep under. The next day we were paraded in front of 1000 soldiers or more. For the last time we were asked: 'Do you still refuse to put on the uniform of the soldier?' Again we answered yes . . . our verdict . . . was two years' goal in Mount Eden Prison with hard labour. For eight months we served our sentence.[46]

In an effort to change Waikato policy and regain control of a situation that was increasingly embarrassing and farcical, Pomare showed great courage by visiting the anti-conscriptionist headquarters, apparently in the winter of 1918.† He was advised to take a police escort but refused, and was accompanied only by his old political ally and mentor, Te Heuheu Tukino.[47]

The Waikato River was in flood and most of the open ground at Mangatawhiri was under water. There was only one piece of dry land on the marae and there Pomare and Te Heuheu sat while their male hosts, stripped to the

---

† The exact date of this visit does not appear to have been recorded. It is probable that it was between the end of June and the beginning of August 1918: the anti-conscriptionists were gathered at Mangatawhiri; Lady Pomare noted that it was in the 'middle of winter' (letter to Eric Ramsden, 19 January 1944); Pomare's speech appeared to refer to matters raised in his exchange of telegrams with Te Puea in mid-June; and the vehemence of Waikato's reaction suggests some of their men had already been taken. It is possible that the visit occurred the previous year, 1917. Te Puea was adamant that it took place at Mangatawhiri, but gave the year as 1917. On the same occasion, however, she also thought the arrests had taken place in 1917, which they had not.

waist and standing knee-deep in the water, insulted them with abusive haka prepared for the occasion. At intervals the performers turned away from the visitors and exposed their buttocks, the whakapohane or ultimate gesture of contempt in Maori terms. According to Lady Pomare this went on for about three hours.[48]

The climax came when a group of female poi dancers replaced the men. One of the women came forward to within feet of Pomare. Te Puea said she had no idea what was about to happen, the incident was not planned. She 'had no pants on, only the piupiu. She pulled back the latter and exposed her person to Pomare and Te Heuheu, and worked it in such a way that I had never seen before . . . like a concertina. Te Heuheu stared straight at her, the tears pouring down his cheeks. But Pomare opened his umbrella and attempted to shield himself from the woman. That shows the difference between those two men. A rangatira is always able to face anything . . . She kept calling out what was the use of her private parts if Pomare was going to take away her husband. In fact, by that she spoke for all the women with husbands and sweethearts.'[49]

After this performance Pomare thanked Waikato. Offering an interpretation of his behaviour that differed from Te Puea's, he said he had always known he was a rangatira 'but not the truly big rangatira they made him that day'.[50] Then he appealed to Waikato to reverse its position. He argued that Tawhiao's words had banished all warfare overseas, away from New Zealand. In order to keep it there, he said, the Maori had to fight in Europe. Finally, and perhaps most inappropriately, Pomare called upon Waikato to take up arms as Christians. This came too late. The anti-conscriptionists were already practising another faith, and one which Pomare associated with the old days of primitiveness and barbarism.

From the time Te Puea had taken control of the campaign, there had been a strong feeling among her followers that she herself was being led by the spirit of Tawhiao.[51] Tumokai Katipa put it this way: 'Tawhiao's words were there, alive, floating in the air around us all. Then they chose her to settle on, to carry them out.'[52] The feeling that a mantle had fallen on her shoulders was intensified by Te Puea's appearance of walking round in a dream, as if being continually inspired and directed by forces outside herself. She described herself as being 'possessed'.[53] And Te Uira Te Heuheu remembered that 'she did not seem as if she was on this earth at all. She completely transfixed [us] . . . It was the expression in her eyes.'[54] It was also the kind of experience out of which religions are born.

The belief in possession consolidated Te Puea's powers of leadership at the time and after the campaign. And they were enhanced still further by an incident that took place on one of the first nights that the anti-conscriptionists were gathered at Te Paina. It was seven o'clock in the evening. Dinner had been eaten, the scraps cleared away and the cooking utensils washed. Te Puea rang the bell on the verandah of the hall to summon everybody inside for a whaikorero to discuss organisation and tactics. Tumokai Katipa was sitting in the hall alongside his mother:

> It was getting dark in there. We only had two kerosene lamps hanging from the roof in the centre so that the light flickered on some people's faces and others were in deep shadow. We were all uncertain, frightened, not knowing what was going to happen to us.
>
> Then Te Puea stood by the door and said it was time to begin. 'But first,' she said, 'we must karakia. Is there somebody here who will lead?' She expected a person to stand up. But do you know there wasn't. There was absolute silence. All the Christian churches had deserted us then because they thought we were breaking the law. They didn't want to get caught with us or go to prison with us.
>
> And then this old kaumatua from Manukorihi in Taranaki stood up. He was there with some of his people who also didn't want to fight because their land had been taken. And he reminded Te Puea of the saying of Tawhiao: 'I have taken my faith from the base of the mountain, and I have laid it back there. In time of difficulty you will find it there.' Now Tawhiao had said that before he died. He was referring to his bringing Pai Marire from Taranaki, from Te Ua Haumene. He did it because the Pakeha churches had fought with the soldiers in the war. But once he said he'd laid it back there, that was it. The people stopped doing that karakia. They hadn't done it since. And Mahuta had allowed the Christian churches to come back in.
>
> But now this kaumatua was saying, 'Here is your time of difficulty, now is the time to take this faith up again from the base of the mountain.' And Te Puea said, 'Yes, you're right.' And at that moment two Waikato elders, Hoani Taurea and Te Hira, stood and started up their chant, one leading and the other answering. 'Rire rire pai marire.' And there was a roar all round the hall as the older people there from Tawhiao's time joined in. And they all remembered Tawhiao and those days with him, and the tears were rolling down their cheeks as they chanted.
>
> I didn't know what was happening. I looked at my mother and she was crying too, crying and chanting. So I asked her what was going on. And she just whacked me to keep me quiet till it was over. But later on she explained to me.[55]

Te Puea accepted wholly the suggestion that it was time to uplift Tawhiao's old religion. It had an obvious ability to raise and sustain morale, to recall the days of wandering in righteous exile with the old king and relate the uncertain present to a continuous history. But in addition to this, it seemed to Te Puea to be part of her own spiritual evolution and that of Waikato as a whole. From that night she held Pai Marire prayer sessions every morning and evening at seven o'clock. It was a routine that lasted till the day she died.[†] And the prayers — which were chanted and were a mixture of Old Testament scripture, appeals to ancestors and Maori gods, and invocations to stars — sustained the resistance movement.

'They made us unshakeable,' Piri Poutapu said. 'Those prayers incorporated Maori things that the Pakeha churches had no place for, appeals to spirits and forces they didn't know about, ways to make sick people well again.[‡] Every time we said them we knew our ancestors were right there with us and we were all right.'[56]

Arrests continued into August 1918 as further ballots were drawn. On 24 August, forty-four men were taken, including Tonga Mahuta and Wanokore Herangi, Te Puea's brother (who was then the father of seven children and had not in fact been balloted). On this occasion, to the surprise of the police party, Tonga called on everybody there who had been named to accompany him to camp. Those who did far exceeded the number of names called out and added to police confusion. Of this new intake thirty-four refused to take the uniform and were sentenced to twenty-one days' detention. One of them was Here Mokena aged twenty-two:

[At first] we were not treated unkindly. But when we refused to do any work at all, we were treated with considerable severity . . . We were made to sleep on the bare boards with only two blankets. There was neither mattress nor pillow. We all felt the cold severely. Most of the time we were hungry because we were given only bread, and little enough of that, and water. We became covered in lice and used to pass the time away by having races with the kutus . . . Men who had been in prison told us that ordinary prisoners were treated better than we were because they at least had the usual comforts.

Te Puea brought us food but it never reached us. She used to come and sit outside the prison. When we went out to mimi we could see her there.

---

† Her followers from that time who were still alive in the 1970s continued the practice.
‡ Te Puea's part in the return of Pai Marire led to a belief on the part of her followers that she could cure sickness. This aspect of Pai Marire in Waikato and a fuller account of its other beliefs can be found in Chapter 10.

Just to get a glimpse of her we would invent an excuse to go to the whare mimi. The fact that she was there gave us . . . heart to continue.[57]

Mokena and his companions did not understand the procedures that were being unleashed on them. And because they did not, the punitive measures did not produce the intended results. After being subjected to what the army called 'detention' and 'dietary punishments', they were court-martialled in small groups from September onwards. The authorities hoped each time that the spectacle of one group being punished would cause the next to relent. It did not. Among the measures considered for the further punishment of defaulters were shipping them overseas to the front and depriving them of all civil liberties for ten years.[58]

Te Puea too was under investigation. Her leadership had been reported in the press. And there were widespread rumours among Europeans in Waikato that she was a German supporter. Once it became known that her grand-father's name was Searancke, the matter was explained satisfactorily for many people; they did not have to look further for motivation and explanation. This is not easy to document — many of the people who retailed this accusation were later embarrassed by it. But as late as 1944 Lady Miria Pomare, echoing the prejudices of her husband, was still talking about 'the German element' in Waikato.[59] And some informants went to considerable trouble during the preparation of this book to produce evidence that Te Puea was German and therefore untrustworthy in wartime.†

In fact, of course, the Searanckes had been at least four generations removed from possible German habitation — six generations by Te Puea's time. She, however, then knowing nothing of her Pakeha antecedents, was not in a position to deny allegations about her pedigree. She simply said, 'What if I am German? So is the British Royal Family. In fact I am neither pro-German nor anti-British. I am simply pro-Maori.'[60]

No legal action could be taken, of course, on the basis of Te Puea's genealogy. But the Officer Commanding the Auckland Military District, Col. G.W.H. Patterson, believed 'the so-called Princess Puea of Mercer' could be prosecuted under war regulations for inciting her men not to enlist. In September 1918 he prepared a scheme by which further arrests would be

---

† Cf letters from G.G.R. Brown, Te Awamutu, 20/3/75; J. Durrien, Auckland, 15/3/75; K. Allott, Auckland, 13/3/75; and M. S. Stacpoole, Auckland, undated: These refer to Te Puea variously as 'a half-caste German', 'daughter of a German judge', and 'daughter of a German drover'. The spelling of the surname is given as 'Sirrank' and 'Serank', all of which is, perhaps, an indication of the reliability of wartime rumour.

contrived at Mangatawhiri in a manner that would goad her into making anti-conscription statements in front of reliable witnesses. The scheme was overturned by army headquarters in Wellington on the ground that an unsuccessful prosecution would only raise Te Puea's prestige.[61]

Te Puea must also have been given some credit by the authorities for the fact that the whole Waikato campaign had been non-violent. Under less confident and less restraining leadership, the arrests could have led to fighting and bloodshed. When an earlier opponent of enlistment, Rua Kenana, had failed to respond to a charge of sedition in 1916, a party of sixty police had stormed his Urewera stronghold. Two Maori were killed and four constables wounded in the resulting exchange of rifle fire.†

The war's end on 11 November 1918 left a nightmarish tangle of loose ends and unpunished offences. There had been four ballots in which a total of 552 men had been called up. From these, seventy-four had finally agreed to go to camp; 111 had been imprisoned; and 100 warrants waiting to be executed were still in the hands of the police (the balance of the total had not been eligible). Some details were dealt with quickly. Those training were sent home and the outstanding warrants were cancelled by Cabinet order.[62] But the cases of defaulters were more difficult to resolve. They were considered by a Religious Objectors Advisory Board, set up to advise the Minister of Defence on exemptions. By March 1919, the board had decided to recommend special treatment for the Waikato Maori offenders:

> We found that none of the Maoris who appeared before us objected to Military Service on 'bona fide religious grounds', but nevertheless we are of opinion that these cases merit your most earnest attention, with a view to deciding whether these men should in equity be longer detained in prison. We consider it extremely doubtful whether they are fully conscious of the nature of their offence, and whether they understand or appreciate the reason for the further punishment they are to suffer by the deprivation of civil rights, if their names appear on the Military Defaulters list. The following quotation from a reply given by one of the Maoris . . . appears fairly to represent the Maori Objectors' point of view:— 'At the Treaty of Waitangi we signed to make peace and they put a Bible in our hands. They have now taken the Bible away and put a sword into our hands and wish to make us

---

† Te Puea expressed sympathy for Rua's stand, and for him after his subsequent conviction. In July 1916 she wrote to the prophet and to his defence counsel Jerry Lundon, inviting Rua 'and his tribe' to visit her at Mangatawhiri (Judith Binney, personal communication, 24/8/79).

fight.' We found that the work and conduct of the Maori Objectors while in prison had been exemplary in practically all cases.[63]

Against the advice of the military, Cabinet decided on 20 May 1919 to release all Maori prisoners. The decision was never made public because of the Government's wider determination not to treat other defaulters 'leniently'.[64]

For Waikato, the conclusion of the affair seemed a victorious one: none of their conscripts had been sent overseas; Te Puea had stood up to Pakeha authority, devised tactics to confound it, and apparently been successful. Those who returned from custody and from training at Narrow Neck received a tumultuous welcome at Mangatawhiri. 'We did everything we possibly could for them,' Te Puea said, '. . . to show our appreciation of their bravery and control.'[65] But not all did return. Four died of influenza and their bodies were not returned to Waikato for burial, a source of anguish and resentment.[†] And those who did come back brought the infection with them, with devastating consequences.

Te Puea's claim to leadership in Waikato had been established by her rank and personal qualities, and confirmed politically by Mahuta's selection of her for special duties, including a campaign on behalf of Pomare. Now, ironically, a campaign against Pomare[‡] had demonstrated beyond doubt her ability to bring people together, to organise their living activities on a large scale, to control them on occasions of tension, and to articulate their feelings to themselves and to outside authority. She had made herself known dramatically to Maori in Waikato who had not previously been aware of her; and she had come to the attention of Pakeha authorities in Auckland and Wellington.

Even more significant than these things, however, the revival of Pai Marire in association with her leadership seemed in Waikato eyes to provide a spiritual endorsement of her ascendancy. From this point her former political rivals in the King Movement were eclipsed (apart from sparks generated briefly by her uncle Haunui, her cousin Piupiu and Tupu Taingakawa from Ratana ranks in the 1920s). From 1918, the story of Te Puea and the story of Kingitanga are synonymous.

---

† They were Te Apa, Kikiri, Tame Tahi and Rupene (interview Piri Poutapu, also Eric Ramsden notes, RP).

‡ From the imposition of conscription until the rise of the Ratana Movement in politics in the early 1920s, Te Puea was sworn to unseat Pomare. She regretted her part in his election, and felt he had betrayed Waikato. Te Rata remained loyal to him, however, until the MP's death in 1930. The King felt obliged to support Pomare as the Kingitanga member because of Mahuta's selection of him in that role, and because Pomare had promised to establish a commission of inquiry into the confiscations (a promise finally fulfilled in 1925).

5

Turangawaewae: Preparations

Feelings of elation in Waikato at the conclusion of combat were short-lived. As had happened so often in the past, the white man's peace proved more devastating than his war. An epidemic of influenza that affected 720 million people worldwide and took over 20 million lives reached New Zealand in July 1918.

The first wave, although widespread, produced few fatalities. The second, from late October to December, was virulent and killed over 6700 people (more than a third of the New Zealand casualties in the war). A Royal Commission investigating the outbreak concluded there was 'a strong presumption' that the later strain had been introduced by the arrival at Auckland on 12 October of the S.S. *Niagara*, the same ship that had taken Te Rata to London. On board were Prime Minister William Massey and Finance Minister Joseph Ward.[1] As a result of their presence the ship was not subjected to quarantine regulations then in force for infected vessels.†

The stronger strain spread rapidly through military camps and Armistice celebrations. The experience of earlier epidemics‡ was confirmed when

---

† The *Niagara* contamination theory was the most comforting explanation for the outbreak in New Zealand. A more disquieting view was that which produced evidence of a simultaneous eruption of the severe strain in all parts of the globe, including ships that had been at sea continuously for three weeks. Indeed, some of the more virulent cases appear to have been developing in New Zealand before the *Niagara* docked. Nor was it to be the destiny of the *Niagara* to sail off into historic obscurity: she was mined by the Germans off the New Zealand coast on 19 June 1940, and sank with a cargo of gold bullion worth more than £2½ million.

‡ In 1826, 1838, 1844, 1853, 1887 and 1890 to 1894.

Polynesians displayed far less immunity to the disease than Europeans. In consequence their population was reduced dramatically. In addition to physical vulnerability, Maori settlements also exhibited the very features that authorities warned were most likely to spread the infection: 'overcrowding', 'thronging', 'poor ventilation', 'inadequate water supplies and sanitary facilities', 'alcoholic excess' and 'fright'. The greater Polynesian disposition for respiratory ailments and heart disease intensified the vulnerability since most influenza deaths resulted from an aggravation of such conditions.[2] Maori communities also had few of the supplies recommended for use preventatively and to alleviate distress after the onset of symptoms ('liquid soda chlorinate gargles, face masks, prophylactic vaccination and good nourishing food').

The consequence of all these factors was a devastating Maori death toll and death rate never accurately determined. Buck, noting that the estimate of Maori deaths was well below that which actually occurred, called the epidemic 'the severest setback the race has received since the fighting days of Hongi Hika. Influenza in three months caused more casualties to the Maoris than the campaigns in Gallipoli, France and Belgium.'[3]

For official purposes the number of Maori deaths registered was estimated at 1130 or a rate of 226 per 10,000 of population — over four-and-a-half times greater than that of Europeans. This was bad enough. But the actual total must have been far higher since Maori deaths were still not notified.[†] Many Maori communities never saw a medical officer during the outbreak and were not asked for an estimate of fatalities.[‡] Some of them were almost annihilated (a Pakeha visitor to the Ati Awa settlement at the headwaters of the Waitara River in Taranaki counted 140 people there before the epidemic and less than fifty afterwards).[4] The full extent of official negligence in Maori health was concealed. Of 111 witnesses who gave evidence to the subsequent Royal Commission, for example, not one was Maori.

There was another factor that intensified the social consequences of the epidemic even further. Previous outbreaks had taken their heaviest toll

---

† The Maori Births and Deaths Regulations of 1913 provided for such notification but they were not enforced. According to the Registrar-General in 1976, Maori registrations of death were 'few and far between until after the Second World War' (private communication, 7/9/76).

‡ At the time of the outbreak there were no Maori Medical Officers. The estimated toll of the epidemic moved consciences in the Department of Health and in 1920 a Division of Maori Hygiene was created with Peter Buck as its first director.

among the elderly and, to a lesser extent, the very young. This one, on the figures recorded, was most virulent among young adults and people in their prime. The greatest number of deaths occurred in the twenty to forty age group, with those aged thirty to thirty-five being hit hardest. This meant that in the aftermath, whole communities found themselves without mothers and fathers, primary wage earners and active leaders. A vacuum was created that placed a greater burden on adolescence and middle-age.

Te Paina appears to have been as badly hit as any Maori settlement. The outbreak reached its peak there in the third week of November 1918, a week after the Waikato conscripts in training had returned from Narrow Neck.[5] Tumokai Katipa estimated that in a community of about 100 people, only three adults in the vulnerable age group remained unaffected, of whom he was one.[†] The infection lasted about three weeks and for this time community life came to a halt. Whole families were laid up at the same time; the worst cases lay dying while others struggled from their beds to find water and perform daily necessities.

The symptoms were an unpleasantly intensified form of those produced by conventional influenza: high fever, increased pulse, mottling of the skin, headache, pains in the chest and limbs, shortness of breath, often bubbling sounds in the chest caused by a bloody froth, vomiting, diarrhoea, and what was described in official reports as 'dirty tongue and foul breath'.[6] This last was remembered unofficially as 'a burning of the mouth that left the throat and tongue dry except for a black discharge.'[7]

Tumokai Katipa could remember no outside doctors visiting the settlement with assistance, no one recording the names of the dead, and a great deal of contradictory advice. 'The one doctor who was at Mercer couldn't do much and didn't even try. Nobody knew what they should be doing. One person told us not to drink water and we believed it for a while. Then one of the ones who was ill went mad and jumped into the river and drank quite frantically. He got better. Others, my sister among them, were crying out for water, their mouths all burnt. And we didn't give them any. And they died. We just didn't know what we should have done.'[8]

Te Puea, although ill herself, again set about caring for the sick as best she could. There were no open-air shelters this time, the rate of infection was too high. Most people stayed in their homes. She rose from her sick bed

---

† Such a degree of infection was not unusual. Of the Maori who remained at Narrow Neck in November, the official report noted, 'practically all were affected in the second wave'. (AJHR, 1919, H31, p. 29)

each day and prepared boiled water and food for distribution to those families whose members were all sick. She tried to organise clean water for washing, but this was difficult — almost everybody had become sluggish and unresponsive.[9]

'We just lived from day to day in a kind of daze,' said Tumokai. 'It didn't seem real. It got so that people hardly knew what was happening and didn't care. We just took things as they came, that was all.'[10]

Taking things as they came included coping with death continuously for a fortnight. Of the 200-odd people there, Tumokai estimated that about fifty died.[†] One of the unaffected men was busy every day building makeshift coffins. Tumokai's major job was to ferry corpses upriver in Te Puea's launch to Taupiri for burial.

> I used to leave at about six o'clock in the morning when it was just getting light. We'd load the bodies of people who had died in the night on to the boat, which was about twenty feet long and had an old standard engine. There was no time for relatives to mourn. Most of them couldn't anyway. Then off we'd go, two of us, chugging up the river through the fog. I tell you, it was eerie. We often thought we saw things and heard things to do with the spirits of those people.
>
> We'd get to Taupiri, unload the bodies, bury them in wide graves and then return to Mangatawhiri by about four in the afternoon. Sometimes we had to turn around and go straight back with some more. Each time we got there, hello — somebody else dead. This went on for two weeks. I lost a lot of my family: one of my sisters and my two brothers-in-law. People were just dying everywhere. In some ways, you know, it was harder to be the ones who went on living.[11]

In the aftermath the Te Paina community was numbed. As people recovered, long tangi were held for the mass dead, without the bodies. Then, in December, Te Puea visited all the settlements between Mangatawhiri and the Waikato Heads and gathered up children orphaned in the epidemic — just over 100 of them — and elderly people who no longer

---

† Te Puea's younger sister Te Atarua also died in the epidemic at Otorohanga on 12 November. The number of adults able to vote at Te Paina in the 1919 general election was thirty-nine, compared with eighty-one in the two previous elections.

had relatives to look after them. It was a spectacular extension of the project she had begun six years before of making Mangatawhiri a home for the homeless, and a fulfilment of her mother's wishes.

She could not and did not take all the children into her own home, although she did have two or three there at a time. She made the whole community at Te Paina responsible for them and placed them with the surviving adults. She would make a point of seeing each of them every day, supervising mass sittings in the settlement's dining hall, and being entirely responsible for their education. It was the same group she was later to take with her to Ngaruawahia, and most of its members were from families she had already known and who had looked to her for protection since Tiahuia's death.

By the beginning of 1919 Waikato was sorely in need of a morale booster. It came in March with the long-awaited opening of Te Rata's Kauhanganui or Parliament House in Ngaruawahia. The planning for this building had been carried on for a decade. Mahuta had set aside £600 for it. He intended it to be a partial fulfilment of Tawhiao's wish that the movement should re-establish headquarters at Ngaruawahia,[†] and partly a forum (away from Tupu Taingakawa's Ngati Haua-dominated parliament) where Maori policy could be clarified and consolidated before presentation to the national Parliament.[12]

The site in Ngaruawahia township was purchased before Mahuta's death. But the first application to build was rejected by the Town Board.[13] Ngati Rereahu, a subtribe of Ngati Maniapoto, took up the project again late in the war and asked Te Puea to help. 'I sent out notices to the tribes of Waikato, Hauraki, Taranaki, Maniapoto and Rangitikei to collect money,' Te Puea said of her first fund-raising campaign. 'A pound for each male and female member. That money was gathered and it amounted to £1800. The remainder was made up by Ngati Rereahu and an outside tribe, Ngati Kohatu of Kaipara.'[14]

The building was made of brick and stucco, very much like a conventional European house on the outside, but with a carved gable at the front. It was opened on 18 March with a function that was reported fully by the Pakeha press. There were about 2000 Maori present, many from other districts. As usual, Te Rata was unable to attend because of ill health. But

---

† See page xx.

Turangawaewae House, Ngaruawahia: built as a Maori parliament. ATL

Maui Pomare was present.[†] The *Weekly News* noted that the project was the result of a prophecy by Potatau, but it had only become practicable 'through the efforts of Princess Te Puia [sic], a cousin of the present "king".'[‡]

'The excitement became intense as the time for opening the ornamented doors approached. The pois began to swing and the onlookers repeated welcome songs in unison as the three Maori princesses, Te Puia [sic], Uira and Piupiu,* all relations of the "king", were led to the ornamented doors. At once the various chiefs advanced into the council hall, or "throne room" as it is known by the natives. They were followed by several wahines uttering plaintive cries.'

What the *Weekly News* did not report was that the three 'princesses', led by Te Puea, had shortly before rolled up their sleeves and cleaned out the

---

† There is no indication published that he suffered further indignities at Waikato hands that day as a result of conscription, although Te Puea was to abuse him in public the following year.

‡ It was customary for the Pakeha press until Koroki's accession to the kingship in 1933 to place the expression 'king' in inverted commas. Understandably, Waikato found this offensive. Strangely enough the expression 'princess' was rarely written this way although it could have been with far more justification since it was not a recognised Maori title. This *Weekly News* report, while well intentioned, succeeds in mis-spelling almost all the names of Maori participants at the function.

* Te Uira Te Heuheu and Piupiu, a first cousin of Te Puea's (daughter of Te Wherowhero, Mahuta's younger brother).

drains behind the house with their bare hands after the pipes had become hopelessly clogged with human excrement.[15] It was typical of Te Puea that she did not suggest somebody else perform the highly unpleasant task but simply began herself knowing that others would help. Also unreported, she had sung a song of lament for Waikato defaulters still in Mt Eden 'crushing stones' as a punishment for 'upholding the mana of the king'.[16]

The *Weekly News* went on to describe the throne room: 'At the western end is the "royal" chair raised on a dais, draped with gorgeous feather and flax mats . . . On either side are stools, that on the right for the use of the native "premier", Tupu Tangahawa [sic], that on the left for one of Rata's leading chiefs. There is no other furniture in the room, the custom being for the lower natives to sit upon . . . the floor.'[17]

In the event, the Parliament House (Turangawaewae House, as it came to be called) was rarely used. It was too close to European housing to be suitable for hui; the desire for a Maori parliament waned dramatically in the early 1920s as Tupu Taingakawa turned his attention to the new Ratana Movement; and Te Puea's own Turangawaewae Marae became the nerve centre for the movement and the fulfilment of Tawhiao's prophecy about Ngaruawahia. During World War Two Te Puea converted the building into a health clinic. After the war it became the first headquarters of the Tainui Trust Board.

The most important feature of the report of the opening of the house was the emphasis it gave (albeit attributed to the wrong person) to the 'turangawaewae' prophecy. In 1881, after he had emerged from exile and laid his arms before Major Mair, Tawhiao had made a sentimental journey through Waikato to visit the places of most significance to him, now largely inaccessible to Maori occupation because of the confiscations. At Ngaruawahia, abandoned in 1863 when Cameron defeated the king's force at Rangiriri, Tawhiao paused before the tomb of his father Potatau and wept. Then he said to his followers, speaking slowly and distinctly: 'Alexandra will be a symbol of my strength of character, Cambridge a washbowl of my sorrow, and Ngaruawahia my turangawaewae.'[18]

The expression 'turangawaewae' provides the key to understanding Te Puea's behaviour and her obsession for reciting Tawhiao's sayings. It has rarely been fully explained to non-Maori;[†] it is perhaps difficult to explain. The concept has no precise equivalent in English. It is conventionally

---

† I have heard well-intentioned guides say to confused visitors at Turangawaewae Marae: 'Of course the name means footstool,' as if that were sufficient to explain its significance.

translated by the archaic biblical term 'footstool'. More recently, it has been conveyed as 'a place to stand'.[19] Literally, it means 'a place where one puts one's feet'. But it has connotations of birthright, of ancestral continuity, of a place to which a person really belongs, of roots that are the source of identity and consequently the origin of the right to speak and behave as a Maori. For most older Maori, their turangawaewae is the place where they were born if that place has long-standing Maori significance; or it is the marae with which their family (traced through either parent) has been longest associated. Not having a turangawaewae is, in terms of recent tradition, tantamount to not having Maori credentials, not having the right to speak on a marae.†

When Tawhiao called Ngaruawahia his turangawaewae, therefore, he was doing far more than turn an oratorical phrase. He was referring to Waikato's intimate association with that place, to the fact that his father had been confirmed in the kingship there, and to his own childhood and long residence there. More important, perhaps, he was suggesting that the loss of Ngaruawahia symbolised and contained all the connotations of Waikato's defeat — loss of livelihood, identity, morale and self-respect. His followers took the saying one step further and interpolated that until Ngaruawahia was re-established by Maori occupation, that loss of mana would not be recovered.

By the time Te Puea had begun to work towards a settlement at Ngaruawahia, therefore, her preoccupation had become just that: trying to re-establish the mana of the Kingitanga; or, as she frequently put it, 'to make Waikato a people again'.[20] There were many concrete ways in which she was to set about this — model settlements, helping people become economically self-reliant through farming, building new meeting houses, obtaining Pakeha recognition of the movement. But to her the fundamental step — the one that had to precede all others to make what she was doing auspicious and spiritually valid — was the creation of a pa at Ngaruawahia.‡ And when she used the name Turangawaewae she was using an expression that for Waikato people was pregnant with feelings of disinheritance from the past and hope for the future. It had the force that 'Erin go bragh' had for the Irish.

---

† The expression was probably not pre-European, although the concept was; 'turangawaewae' acquired a wide currency in the Maori language only after Te Puea's establishment of the marae of the same name.
‡ Here Ngata's subsequent comparison of Waikato to the Irish is relevant. The establishment of Turangawaewae Marae was an act as necessary for Waikato's self-respect as the transference of authority from Westminster to Dublin was for that of the Irish.

There were other sayings of Tawhiao relevant to Te Puea's objective. She spoke of sanctifying a further statement that the old king had made just before his death calling on Waikato to make 'a permanent home for itself at Ngaruawahia for the security of future generations'.[21] And, on another occasion, he was reported to have said: 'My people shall fall, but when their darkness is greatest there shall arise a woman from my loins who shall lead them to a better life.'[22]

These prophecies weighed on Te Puea's mind. And they were a source of power for her, particularly after the revival of Pai Marire when she had come to be seen as someone 'possessed' by Tawhiao, as a living fulfilment of some of his millennial promises. Her other obvious source of strength was the group of young people she had gathered about her from the influenza epidemic — too many to support easily at Te Paina, but a loyal and potent source of labour and stamina for a project that could capture their imagination.

The land on which Potatau and Tawhiao had actually lived in Ngaruawahia was unsuitable and unavailable for settlement. It was now a public reserve at the junction of the Waikato and Waipa Rivers, close to an area thickly populated by Europeans. Since Mahuta's time elders had been looking for an alternative site. From the time the war finished, Te Puea had been waiting only for the purchase of such a site to move to Ngaruawahia; and this took place in 1920.

The Ngati Rareahu fund-raising committee under the leadership of Te Rata's advisor John Ormsby had decided to investigate a double section of ten acres. It was on the east bank of the river, opposite Ngaruawahia township. The site was in poor condition, however — it had housed the armed constabulary's stables immediately after the Waikato war, and had then been used over a long period as the town's unofficial rubbish tip. By 1920 it was covered with decaying refuse and a tangle of scrub. Nevertheless, it was available. It also had an ingredient of traditional significance; it was the site of the spring from which Tawhiao had drawn drinking water when he lived on the west bank. And it was alongside the river and in full view of it.

Tribal discussion at the Parliament House in 1920 considered the site and authorised Ormsby and his committee to buy it. Te Puea approached the same tribes who had contributed to the Kauhanganui, and again the money was raised. But this time there was a price to pay for public deliberation. A Ngaruawahia bootmaker named William Dunstan heard about the plan, located the absentee owner in Auckland before the committee was able to do so, and bought the property with a deposit of £100 and a mortgage of £200. He then refused to sell it to the committee for less than £1500, a figure they were obliged to accept. Consequently, he made a profit of £1200 almost overnight.[23] For Waikato, it was another instruction in the Pakeha way of doing business.

Before Te Puea could make final preparations for moving to the site, one further issue engaged Waikato's attention: the visit of the Prince of Wales to New Zealand in April 1920.

In spite of the Kingitanga's quarrels with successive New Zealand governments, one theme had remained constant in their activities: loyalty to the British Crown. It had been articulated again and again at marae functions;[24] it had been demonstrated by Tawhiao's and Te Rata's trips to England. In 1920 Waikato decided that the most appropriate way they could demonstrate it again, in the face of persistent Pakeha suspicion of their intentions and commitment, was to invite the Prince to stop at Ngaruawahia so they could pay respects to him at the Parliament House.[25] Te Rata lodged this request with the Government through Pomare and was soundly slapped down. The Prince was to be welcomed by all Maori people at a single function at Rotorua on 27 April, he was told. If Waikato had anything they wished to demonstrate, they must do so there.[26]

It was an insensitive response and probably originated with Massey and Pakeha members of Cabinet rather than Pomare (although the Member for Western Maori was in favour of diminishing tribalism and did have reason to feel vindictive towards Waikato). Waikato felt insulted. If they were to welcome the Prince it had to be with their own feet on their own ground. There was no way they would traipse to the territory of their traditional adversaries, Te Arawa. 'To do so,' Te Puea said, 'would be like making the mayor of Auckland go to Wellington to welcome somebody on behalf of Auckland.'[27] Te Puea met Pomare accidentally at Frankton Junction early in the year and berated him with this argument. 'Who are you to control Waikato?' she concluded, shouting at him. 'If the old people were still alive you would not dare to put your foot there.'[28] The issue may not have been of great importance for Pomare; wherever the welcome was held, he as the only Maori Cabinet minister was guaranteed a place of prominence.

The precedent for Maori receptions for royalty at Rotorua had been established in June 1901 with a function there for the Duke and Duchess of Cornwall. Mahuta had been invited to attend but refused for the same reasons Waikato advanced years later. The logic of the Rotorua arrangement was apparent only to the tour organisers and the Rotorua people themselves: the Arawa people were already experienced at offering 'Maori' entertainment for visitors (they had been doing so since the 1870s); it had become known as the Maori part of the tourist circuit; and there was in addition a diverting thermal area to be viewed close by; therefore, let the Natives come together and perform their rituals of welcome there.

If government policies of the 1960s had displayed a divide and rule mentality, this one exhibited a policy of unite and rule. It took no account of tribal feeling which, in spite of Pomare's jibes about 'mere clanship', was far stronger than Maori race feeling. It also took no account of anti-Arawa feeling which was strong for reasons other than traditional tribal antagonism. In particular, Waikato was scornful of the 'penny-diving' mentality in Rotorua which, they felt, led the Arawa to prostitute their Maoriness for the sake of tourist money. Most tribes, however, faced with the Arawa reception or nothing, went along with it. Waikato was to stand aloof on its own.

Aloof but hopeful. Right to the day itself, Te Rata believed the Government would change its mind; or that the Prince would change it for them — with a naive belief in the good faith of royalty and its mythical power to overturn the decisions of governments, Te Rata was confident that the Prince would be moved to change this one on account of the Maori King's meeting with his father in 1914.[†]

And so on the morning of 27 April 1920, as the train carrying the Prince from Auckland to Rotorua was about to pass, Te Rata stood on Ngaruawahia station with a retinue of elders and a karanga party; the Parliament House was stocked with food; hundreds of Kingite supporters milled about the entrance to watch Maori royalty re-establish its links with English royalty. The train, of course, passed straight through. There was not even a pause. And Waikato felt humiliated.[29] Loyalty was demanded of them by the New Zealand Government, but that same Government denied them the opportunity to express it.

There was a sequel, however. The following day, 28 April, Tupu Tainga-kawa met the Prince of Wales privately at the Grand Hotel in Rotorua. With what one assumes must have been Te Rata's approval, the Kingmaker presented the royal visitor with two patu pounamu. One, from Tainui as a whole, was an ancient patu that had belonged to Potatau, first Maori King.

---

† This gesture had a further sequel eighty years later when Mohammed Al Fayed, owner of Harrods, sold by auction in New York many of the items he had acquired by purchasing the Duchess of Windsor's estate in Paris. Among those items were two patu pounamu, believed to be those given to her late husband when he was Prince of Wales. Tainui attempted unsuccessfully to halt the sale of the taonga. The matter was resolved when the items were purchased for Te Papa Tongarewa, the Museum of New Zealand.

This was passed to the Prince with the handle pointing towards the donor, an indication that, according to Maori protocol, the gift should eventually be returned to Tainui. The second, a ceremonial weapon of more recent vintage, was handed over on behalf of Ngati Haua with the handle pointing towards the Prince, an indication that it was to belong to him and his descendants. Maui Pomare, standing at the Prince's side throughout the ceremony, is presumed to have explained the significance of the gifts and the manner in which they were given.

By the middle of 1921 Te Puea was ready to shift to the new kainga site, now known as Turangawaewae. Part of the Te Paina community was prepared. They knew of Tawhiao's whakatauki, and they had heard tribal discussion authorising Te Puea to establish a settlement. It had also become obvious that Te Paina was not after all a suitable site for the swelling population of homeless people Te Puea had been accumulating. In particular, it was a miserable and vulnerable place in winter — the river narrowed there and frequently overflowed into the low-lying and swampy ground on which the settlement had been built. In spite of Mangatawhiri's traditional significance, therefore, the younger inhabitants looked forward to something more suitable.[30] But they had no idea how it was to come about, how a whole community was to be uplifted from one place and transplanted in another.

Te Puea made her first move early in August. She gathered the whole community into the hall and announced that 170 of them were to shift that month. She also identified who they were. 'I'm taking you away from these wet flats,' she said that night. 'I have no idea how we shall survive — much of it depends on how we work and how the Pakeha at Ngaruawahia treat us. We may find it easier to die here than to live there. But we have to go. And we are going to build a marae there that will be suitable for everybody throughout the country; a marae that, one day, people will visit from all over the world. And we're going to do it for Waikato and for our king.' Then she repeated Tawhiao's whakatauki about his turangawaewae and said it was the guarantee of their success.[31]

On 11 August, Te Rata executed a deed of trust. It declared that the site of Turangawaewae, purchased in his name, was 'for the use of the members of his tribe, and of all people who shall fully acknowledge his chieftainship or that of his successors.' It was to be a papakainga 'for use without charge of the homeless'.[32]

6

Turangawaewae: The long march

On the morning of 11 August 1921, the sun was unusually bright and warm for winter. It was, Te Puea said, a day of hope.[1] Caesar Roose of the Roose Shipping Company in Mercer towed a 15-metre barge to the riverbank at Te Paina. Into its ample hold (4.5 metres wide, 1.2 metres deep) the Turangawaewae migrants began to load their possessions and the equipment they needed to clear the site at Ngaruawahia.

'It may have been a day of hope in Te Puea's mind,' said Piri Poutapu, 'but everybody was crying. It was like the feeling our ancestors must have had when they left Hawaiki — families were being divided, friends were being left behind. We were going on a journey from the known to the unknown. We were leaving a place that had so much history for us, the home where most of us had grown up, played, made friends, fallen in love, and been taught everything we knew. I was only fifteen at the time. But I cried freely along with the old people.'[2]

Not everybody came. It was Te Puea's intention that a group remain at Te Paina as a support base — to provide food, employment and other resources that might be lacking in Ngaruawahia. So after the barge had been loaded, there were formal speeches and farewells on the marae in front of the hall. Then the first group climbed into the barge on top of their gear and a steamer pulled them off the bank and up-river late in the afternoon. They left Mangatawhiri to the sound of poroporoaki across the water. Upstream, they stopped at Horohoro for the night and reached Ngaruawahia the following morning.

Over the first month Te Puea established 170 people of all ages on the new site. She wanted, she told them, to take a large family, not simply a band of young workers.[3] Those who made this early trek bore family names that were to be identified with life at the new pa for the next eight decades: Katipa, Poutapu, Kukutai, Muru, Pinga, Tapara, Matatahi, Enoka, Kawiti, Taupiri, Irirangi, Hauauru, Hiwinui, Haggie, Tahapehi, Kirkwood, and of course Herangi.

What they saw when they reached Turangawaewae greatly increased their misery and their desire to return to Te Paina. 'We tried to sustain ourselves with this vision of the marae we were going to establish for Tawhiao and Te Rata and Te Puea,' said Piri Poutapu. 'But oh dear — it was difficult to hold on to that vision once we got there.'

> On the flat where we landed, below a steep bank, it was swampy, water-laden. And covered with gorse and blackberry and all the kinds of scrub you can imagine. That's what we had to live amongst. Then there was the bank behind, also covered in scrub, and then the piece at the top where the marae itself was to be. That too was a tangle of scrub. There were high gum trees where we wanted to put the main buildings and a great hole where Te Puea said the courtyard of the marae was to go. We just couldn't see it then. We didn't like it at all.[4]

In the early weeks the elderly people were taken at night to sleep in the Parliament House on the 'Pakeha side' of the river. But Piri Poutapu, Tumokai Katipa and the younger workers remained on the site.

> First thing we had to do was clear a space for our homes. We did that on the swampy flat, right alongside the river. The water was all right then, no pollution. We could use it for washing, drinking and cooking. So we put up a makeshift kitchen to shelter the food and prepare meals in. It had a punga frame and an iron roof which we'd brought from Mangatawhiri. Next to that, in the shade of the willows on the water's edge, we put storage cupboards.
>
> All the food we had at that stage was Maori food. We took eel, carp and mullet from the river, we'd brought potatoes from Mangatawhiri. Once we'd got established we used to go into the bush to get bush food. The range just above Ngaruawahia is called Hakarimata — raw feast. And it was just that. We took kingfern, nikau, tara, mamaku, ti — all of it edible on the inside. And of course there were pigeons — no restrictions on them in those days.[†] And Te Puea's launch, with Tumokai driving it,

---

† There *were* laws against the killing of native birds – but Tainui were unaware of them at this time.

would bring down more supplies we'd built up at Mangatawhiri — tea, flour, sugar.

Once food was taken care of we cleared a space for the sleeping quarters. We pulled out the scrub and dug narrow drains to run the water off the flat and into the river. The ground was shaky at first, trembled as we walked on it. But it got hard after we'd made the drains and the sun had been on it for a while. Then we pitched our houses right next to the drains.

The 'houses' were made from tents and sacks — mostly sacks — grain bags split lengthways, opened out and then sewn together in larger sheets. We'd have a manuka frame and drape two flies over it, then a rack: that made one storey. Then under the rack some more sack walls hanging down and room to sleep and store things. We didn't feel so bad after a while as things took shape. We just got stuck in. There was so much to do we didn't have time to think.[5]

Once sleeping and eating quarters were up, Te Puea had planned to send out all able-bodied men and women to find work in and around Ngaruawahia. This would raise money for additional food (especially meat and soup bones) and for the large community buildings, of which a meeting house and dining room were the priorities. It was at this point that the settlers encountered strong hostility from the citizens of Ngaruawahia. The latter did not want a Maori pa on their doorstep; they considered it would be an eyesore and a health hazard; in particular, they did not want Te Puea because of what they had regarded as her disloyal behaviour during the war.[6] 'The Pakehas of Ngaruawahia would not give us employment,' Te Puea said later. The reason was what she chose to call their 'hatred of the Maori'.[7]

After weeks of pestering local land owners and conducting reconnaissance trips around the district, Te Puea finally persuaded some farmers to give her workers what she termed 'the lowliest forms of employment'.[8] They got contracts to cut gorse, manuka and blackberry. This work was available only because nobody else wanted it, and her men did it at ridiculously cheap rates because the alternative was no work at all and a return to Mangatawhiri. They also went out hawking for clothes. And, for the women, there was gum.

Much of the peat swamp around Ngaruawahia had been kauri forest in prehistoric times. The peat preserved both the timber and the gum from these old stands. Until the depression of the 1930s there was a considerable market for the gum in Europe where it was used in the manufacture of varnish and linoleum. Extracting it, however, was difficult and painstaking work. Large areas of damp, wood-strewn earth had to be dug over or probed with spears, and there was no guarantee of finding the material. Most likely areas in Waikato had already been well worked by Dalmatian diggers.

'We asked if we could work land where gum had already been found,' Te Puea wrote. 'This was eventually granted, but we had to pay for the right to do so. In some cases we had to cut scrub first before we were allowed to look for gum. Each Saturday it would be sold to a commercial buyer and we generally received five shillings for the week's work. I kept saving this until we had three pounds. Then I was able to buy materials for the first houses for the elderly . . . After that the farmers discontinued letting us use the gum land. We were only allowed to look for it if we first dragged out large trees from the swamp for them to use as posts. At this stage, I was sure we were doomed.'[9]

Nevertheless by the end of the first year about a dozen permanent houses were up among the sack-cloth shelters. The first building had been the Ahurewa,[†] a miniature house built to protect the tapu relics in Te Puea's care and to act as a focal point for the tapu and mauri of the site. (The objects included the bone chisels with which Tawhiao had been tattooed. They were removed in 1938 and placed inside the gable of Turongo House.)[‡] The shrine was framed at the front by carvings from the nineteenth-century canoe *Taheretikitiki*, which had last been used to ferry Richard John Seddon from Huntly to Waahi for one of his meetings with Mahuta.

The early houses were made almost entirely of indigenous materials to keep costs low. The frames were lashed manuka poles or ponga, the walls and ceilings made from tied raupo, and the roofs thatched nikau branches. Pressed earth floors were swept daily and sprinkled with water and pumice sand from the river. Where the buildings were large enough for partitions, these were made from opened grain sacks.[10]

It was the appearance of houses that seemed to give the disgruntled residents of Ngaruawahia the excuse they had been waiting for to take action: the dwellings were proof that the settlement was to be permanent; and they were clearly sub-standard. A group of ratepayers went to the borough council* and demanded an official inspection of the pa. The council

---

† The name Ahurewa is a common Polynesian one to denote a site of religious significance.
‡ Contrary to a reference in Phillipps 1955, p. 209, the Ahurewa at Turangawaewae never contained bones.
* Ngaruawahia had become a borough in 1920.

arranged this with the Health Department and an inspector arrived one morning at Turangawaewae without warning. Te Puea' was delighted. 'We are poor, certainly,' she told him. 'But we are also clean.' The inspector looked in every building on the site and finally told Te Puea that, under regulations then applying, everything was in order. He went further and said the standard of cleanliness and hygiene was higher than that in many European homes across the river.[11]

While Te Puea took the inspection in good heart (probably because it left her one up), the manner in which it had been originated and sprung on her hardened her feelings against the Pakeha residents of Ngaruawahia. She was to describe herself as 'pro-Maori rather than anti-Pakeha' in the 1940s.[12] But in the early 1920s there is no doubt that she was simply anti-Pakeha, and with good cause. The accumulation of events that had shaped her life up till that time gave her little reason to hope that Pakeha would even understand what she was doing let alone cooperate with her. They had precipitated a war with her people and then crippled them permanently by taking Waikato land; her own Pakeha grandfather had abandoned his Maori family apparently without qualms and had not recognised his descendants subsequently, even when he had an opportunity to do so; they had turned the full weight of the law against Waikato for conscientious objection to conscription; they had refused to allow a demonstration of loyalty to visiting royalty; and finally, they seemed to be raising every obstacle possible to prevent her doing what ostensibly Maori were being encouraged to do: set up a model, well-behaved community. This last course was certainly one that appealed to Europeans in the Waikato. But they preferred it to be done out of sight.[†]

The sight of Turangawaewae was, however, increasingly obtrusive. On Christmas Day 1921 the first hui was held there and it attracted not only Waikato and Maniapoto well-wishers, but also supporters from Auckland and Hauraki.[13] Te Puea's community was now established and functioning: it was able to shelter its own inhabitants and offer hospitality to guests.

Early in the New Year of 1922, Te Puea and Tumokai agreed to marry in the wake of family discussion.[‡] They decided the pa was sufficiently self-reliant for them to have a brief honeymoon.[14] It was the first holiday Te

---

† Te Puea was amused rather than vindictive when, twenty years later, some of the same residents who had tried to sabotage the establishment of the settlement went to great lengths to try to obtain invitations for functions there in honour of visiting VIPs.
‡ Later, for official purposes, Te Puea was to give 3 March 1922 as the wedding date, the day they began living together at the pa as husband and wife.

Tumokai Katipa and Te Puea head off from Turangawaewae
on honeymoon, 1922. Turongo House

Puea had taken in ten years (there had been trips to other districts for hui,
but these always involved social obligations and unrelieved contact with
hundreds of people). They slipped away from Turangawaewae quietly,
Tumokai on his motorbike, Te Puea in the sidecar.

The first stop was at Te Kawau near Mokau, where they stayed with
Ihakara Wharemaru;† then they went on to New Plymouth and finally
Parihaka on the slopes of Taranaki Mountain. This last place had special
significance for them — it was the area in which Tawhiao had made contact
with Pai Marire, and where he had sent a Te Kaumarua or group of twelve
supporters to cement Tainui links with Taranaki.

---

† Here Te Puea made contact with Ihakara's daughter Heeni, who knew the visitors must be
important because her parents laid out 'that rarest Pakeha delicacy, tinned fruit'. Although
Heeni was warned not to bother the guests, Te Puea said (typically) as soon as she saw the
small girl: 'Come over here and sit with me.' It was the beginning of a long friendship.
Heeni came to Turangawaewae in the 1940s as a Methodist deaconess. By the end of Te
Puea's life she was one of the closest female friends.

Although the break was short it affected Te Puea deeply. She was shocked at the amount of drinking she saw at Parihaka and the social difficulties this caused. The experience helped shape her later policy of banning alcohol from Waikato marae. And it was her first opportunity to investigate the extent to which support for the Ratana Movement had spread.[†] It was not only strong in Taranaki, it had even won over pockets of King Movement followers among Tainui Wetere's Maniapoto people, with whom she had discussions at Mokau (and where she learnt that her cousin Piupiu had offered herself to Ratana as a Kingitanga leader who would draw Te Rata into the Movement). In Te Puea's mind, Ratana was an undistinguished charlatan and a usurper of traditional loyalties: she viewed him as a threat to Te Rata's leadership and told the Maniapoto people sharply that they could not serve two masters. She returned from the holiday physically rested, but angry.

Back home her 'children' welcomed her tumultuously as though she had been away years, not weeks.[‡] Te Puea was surprised and moved.[15] At this time, physically the most difficult for the community, they were fiercely loyal, even when she was driving and punishing them. Piri Poutapu was one who had been with her almost from birth. Although not literally orphaned, he had been in the sense that Te Puea had wanted him more than his natural parents. The later arrivals frequently looked to him as their spokesman. He remembered:

She was hard on us in those early days at the pa. Really hard. We had to do exactly what we were told. We had to do it even if we didn't know how. We found out about jobs on the job. And she had it organised so that there was something for everybody to do — cleaning, clearing, scavenging for food, outside contracts, cooking. She was always spreading the load, always thinking about how things could be kept going in the times she wasn't going to be there.

---

† The movement had begun in 1918 when Tahupotiki Wiremu Ratana had a vision on his family farm near Wanganui in which he was told that the Maori were the chosen people, and he was to be the 'Mangai' or mouthpiece of God. He attracted widespread and interdenominational religious support through his initial mission of faith-healing. By 1922 he had decided that the movement should enter politics and in the General Election of that year his eldest son, Tokouru Ratana, surprised all observers (and alarmed Te Puea) by coming to within 800 votes of unseating Maui Pomare in Western Maori; Pomare obtained 3855 votes, Ratana 3037.

‡ In her written communications in the 1920s and 1930s Te Puea most often referred to the Turangawaewae community as her 'children'.

We had to eat exactly what was put in front of us: soup, bones, puha, bread, eel. If anybody left anything — crusts or fat — then crack over the hand with a stick; and there was nothing for that person next time round. But we loved her like a mother. We knew there was always a reason for this sort of treatment. Because she was looking after us. She had a big load on her shoulders and she had to share it round. It was all part of our teaching. That's how we learned to survive. She was always thinking of what individuals could do for the people as a whole, and making us think that way too.

Then there were the times we'd get very close to her. At the pa or out on tour, she'd sometimes gather us all round her and tell us stories. Often the history of our people, jokes about things that had happened to us, the work ahead of her, her plans for each one of us. That's how I learned that I was to do building and carving, Dave [Tumoaki] was to do the cropping, Rangitaua [Tapara] to look after singing and the marae, and so on. It was all planned. In the evenings, when we were together like this, she'd teach us songs and haka doing all the actions herself. She could really be fun — flashing her eyes and rolling them. We'd all laugh. We loved her in those moments too.

Te Puea's maternal instinct was enormous and apparently insatiable. She could move from an encounter with adults that left her angry, and then be softened immediately by the sight of one of her children. She simply loved them — loved watching them, talking to them, fondling them, scolding them, sitting with them by the river telling them stories. More than anything else they were her source of renewal when she was tired or dispirited, and of confirmation that what she was doing was worthwhile. They rewarded her with affection and loyalty. Poutapu recounted:

We all hated the times when we were away from her. Once my uncle took me to Huntly and kept me there; and she came and got me and put me on a train. Another time I was with my parents, my real parents in Cambridge, and they weren't going to let me come back. She wrote to them and said: 'Send back my son or I'll come and get him myself.' She kept tabs on all of us.

Then there was the time she sent me to Pirongia in 1922 because her father had asked for help on his farm. He asked for me. He was getting too old to manage some of the work. I was supposed to go back to the pa when I'd finished but he wouldn't let me. When Te Puea saw him she'd say, 'How's Bill getting on?' And he'd say, 'Fine. He doesn't want to come back.' It was a lie. I thought she hadn't sent for me because she didn't want me any more. Te Puea waited and waited and finally knew something was wrong. So she got on her horse and rode from Ngaruawahia to Pirongia.

I was rabbiting with a mate. The horse had to come through this paddock with a lot of gorse in it and we saw this lady when she was about a mile off. Well, we couldn't tell it was Te Puea. She was in riding gear. But we saw the head of the horse above the gorse and when it got closer we knew that horse. It was Major, Te Puea's stallion. So from half-a-mile away we started to run to her through the gorse. And we ran and ran and when we reached her we grabbed her by the feet and hugged her and hugged her. We told her about the rough time we'd been having. And she said, 'You're coming back with me.' And she took me straight back to Turangawaewae.

Yes, We loved her and she loved us. I'd have done anything for her then.[16]

At times during 1922 the availability of work at Ngaruawahia seemed to improve dramatically. There were periodic contracts for flax cutting, bush clearing, road construction and potato sowing and harvesting. These brought in enough money for Te Puea to feed the community and to dismantle the old Ngati Tomaoho hall at Mangatawhiri and ship it up-river to the new site. Here it was used as a dining room and assembly hall and named Kimikimi (to seek) to commemorate the need to go out to look for work. An additional building called Te Kauta (the cookhouse) was built shortly after.

In spite of the more frequent jobs, however, Te Puea still felt insecure. She wanted a source of income that was more predictable and able to be controlled by her own workers; and one that was more in keeping with their Maori identity. So it was that when Pei Jones first visited the pa as an officer of the Native Land Court in the winter of 1922, he found her training her first concert party inside Te Kauta. The building was 'a crude raupo-walled combined cooking house and sleeping quarters, about forty-five feet long. Though presenting a somewhat primitive exterior, it was scrupulously clean inside; beds were neatly arranged at one end, and well-scrubbed tables, a cupboard and a number of chairs were arranged at the opposite end.'

Te Puea had decided that, each night after the completion of their manual work, the younger members of the community would learn action songs and haka. Some of these things, particularly the words and actions of the poi songs, she would teach herself. But for the haka training she had recalled an elderly Waikato expert called Te Nguha Huirama from Tuwharetoa. Pei watched the old man at work with the group and found him a hard taskmaster. He insisted on heads being erect, bodies 'stately', fingers that did not drop 'like boneless appendages'. Poorer performers were sent to the back row.

> Te Puea sat with her back to a log fire at the kitchen end of the whare. The rows of performers had been so arranged that from where she sat she could see most of them. Now and then she interposed to press home a point . . . in Te Nguha's talk. She was happy. There was, at times, a faraway look in her eyes. Perhaps, already, she was looking into the future . . .
>
> Very good progress was made by the time supper was served. The boiled pork bones and puha and the potatoes cooked in their jackets in the hot embers and ashes were simply delicious. Midnight had come and gone, and it was three in the morning when I returned to my hotel.[17]

By December Te Puea had decided that a group of 44 was ready to perform publicly. She borrowed as many Maori costumes as she could, sewed others herself, and bought a second-hand set of blazers and white trousers for a group within the group that was to play non-Maori music on string instruments (called 'The Band'). Then she named the troupe Te Pou o Mangatawhiri after the stream north of Mercer to dramatise yet again the memory of the war and confiscation. 'I am going to keep reminding the Pakeha of these things,' she said, 'until we get compensation for what was stolen.'[18] The name was shortened to TPM.

The first concerts were given in December at Ngaruawahia and Tuakau. The Ngaruawahia venture cleared £4 overnight, immediately justifying the venture in Te Puea's eyes. But she discovered it was impossible to repeat the performance more than once or twice a year in such a small town. So she decided to take the group on tour.

Early in 1923, swags on their backs, the TPM set out to travel round the outskirts of Waikato by public transport and on foot. They continued the tour through the main centres of Kingitanga supporters and finished up in Auckland. In the smaller centres, they found much goodwill but little money. 'The people in the Maori communities were no better off than we were,' Tumokai Katipa remembered. 'The houses they lived in were of a low standard with raupo walls and dirt floors. But these people supported us as fully as they could. They sheltered us, fed us and paid to come to our concerts. It was out of sympathy for Te Puea.'[19]

Te Pou o Mangatawhiri troupe on tour for the first time,
December 1922. Turongo House

By the time the group reached Auckland, Te Puea noted, the members
had improved greatly with experience.[20] And she had been able to bank
£100. She decided to try a two-night stand at the Auckland Town Hall. It was
not a success — the cost of hire accounted for almost all the takings. But
they cleared sufficient to head north to the Kaipara district, to Woodhill,
Helensville, Dargaville, Warkworth, Whangarei; and finally as far away as
Kawakawa, Kaikohe and Kohukohu on the Hokianga Harbour.

The *Northern Advocate* described the Whangarei concert in terms that
indicated the variety of the programme and that were typical of press
reaction throughout the tour:

The concert . . . was really first-rate . . . It includes men's haka parties,
women's pois and Hawaiian hula dances, and a dozen little Maori maids,
whose charming dancing was one of the most popular features of the
show. There was a fine string band consisting of steel guitars, mandolins,
mandolas, banjos and the popular Hawaiian ukeleles. The stage was set
as a typical pa, and the use of pungas [sic] and nikau in the decorative
effect gave the whole performance a pleasing harmony . . .

Braves, wahines and piccaninnies, the whole party sing and dance
with that naturalness that gives a good Maori display its unique charm .
. . Born to be musical, they all kept perfect time in their movements and
in their singing, while many a choir of Europeans might envy the skilful
blending of their voices and instruments.[21]

Behind the facade, however, the group was not as slick as performances suggested. Often members had to walk 50 km at a time, leaving one venue at eight in the morning and arriving at the next only in time to perform (on one occasion, for example, they walked from Kaipara Flat to Warkworth and back). This avoided cutting into the money that had been saved. Towards the end of the tour soles were worn off shoes and replaced with cardboard, and shirts were disintegrating and mended only at the front so they could be covered by a jacket and held with a tie. Frequently, the whole party had to sleep outside under trees and hedges, in swamps, and once in stationary railway carriages. They often went without meals. When they did eat, it was as cheaply as possible — fish heads, bone soup, and wild vegetables that they found growing along the roadside.[22]

By July the temperature had dropped and the weather was unpleasant. Money was still coming in from concerts; but the group was frequently tired, cold and wet, and morale was slipping. Te Puea decided it was time to return to Turangawaewae. In over three months of continuous touring and performing the TPM had saved £900, the largest sum the community at Turangawaewae had ever had at its disposal. With it, during the remainder of 1923, a larger combined kitchen-dining room was built. It was opened on Christmas Day and, like its predecessor, named Kimikimi.

These early concerts had consequences that went beyond the immediate aim of raising money. First, in spite of hardships, they were immensely uplifting for the morale of the group who travelled. These young adults and children developed a spirit of coordination and cooperation that spilled over into other and subsequent projects. Their feeling of camaraderie had a musical expression — a Maori musical expression — that they were able to share with non-performing members of the community.

Secondly they were responsible for a resurgence of interest in Maori music and action songs in many of the Maori districts they visited. 'Up to the time when Te Puea organised this party,' Pei Jones has noted, 'the haka had practically become a thing of the past in Waikato and most other parts of the West Coast of the North Island. Following on her tour . . . a revival took place.'[23] The whole concept of entertaining and fund-raising by Maori concert was foreign in most parts of the country until this time, except in the Arawa territory around Rotorua † where the practice had been carried on from the 1870s and 1880s, largely to service the tourist trade attracted by

† And Ngata was to claim later that Te Puea's group 'can do these things more pleasingly than the loud-voiced tourist-hardened Arawa maidens' (letter to Buck, 4 January 1929).

'The Band', a sub-group of the TPM. Members include Tumokai Katipa (middle row, left) and Tae Tapara (middle row, right). Turongo House

thermal activity.[24] It has also been claimed that the TPM was the first group to popularise stringed instrument backing for Maori songs.[25]

Thirdly, the tours brought the names Ngaruawahia and Turangawaewae before a wide public for the first time. In the case of Maori communities, they introduced them to Te Puea's 'band of gypsies' and established relationships that became the basis for cooperative tribal ventures in the future.

The effects were not all beneficial, however. To some onlookers, Maori and Pakeha, the TPM were simply 'the sideshow people', a source of amusement and contempt. This attitude prevailed in Ngaruawahia early in 1924 and the lack of work became so acute that Te Puea was forced to return for a time to Mangatawhiri with some of the younger members of the community to work there in the quarries and the flax mill.[26] But Turangawaewae did not have to be abandoned. Now the older people were able to live there in dignity and comfort and keep the settlement open.

The next two years were difficult ones of consolidation and expansion. In addition to the building projects, Te Puea also conceived and supervised the landscaping. Large quantities of earth had to be moved to fill the hollows in the upper part of the site. A marae proper and lawns were laid out and bordered with flower beds. Although electricity was not then supplied to the district, the pa had lighting at night. Tumokai set up first a steam generator,

A TPM member demonstrates action song gestures and pukana. Turongo House

which had to be tended constantly, and then an oil-fired one which he converted from an engine discarded by the borough council.[†] But money was always short and Te Puea enforced economies rigidly. Nothing was wasted. Flour bags and sugar sacks, for example, were always kept, boiled and made into clothes. Sacks were still used for room partitions; and, for people who kept pets, the sacks were dipped in concrete and made into animal shelters.[27]

From June 1925 the TPM went on tour again to raise money for a sleeping house large enough to accommodate guests at major hui, to be called Pare Waikato. This time they visited Hauraki, the Bay of Plenty, and south Waikato; then they went further south to Taumarunui, Taupo, Wanganui, Raetahi, Taihape, Rangitikei, Manawatu and Foxton; and finally Wanganui again then up through Taranaki to Waitara and home to Ngaruawahia.[28]

It was on this tour that Te Puea had her only personal encounter with T.W. Ratana, whom she now regarded as the arch enemy of the Kingitanga. It was brief, and it illustrated Te Puea's capacity for quick thinking that almost always wrong-footed her rivals. While they were performing in the Rangitikei district close to Ratana Pa, Te Puea and the female members of TPM were given a large room in which to change for an evening concert. They were doing this when a girl brought a message in: Ratana was outside and wished to see her urgently. Te Puea told everybody in the room to take off their clothes. They did so and waited. Ratana, unaccustomed to being kept waiting, became impatient. He pulled open the door and walked in to confront Te Puea. His eyes only left the ground once, however. Faced by a roomful of naked women he was nonplussed. He backed out, closed the door, and left the settlement immediately. Te Puea, who retained an uncompromising blind spot about the prophet and his movement until the 1940s, was pleased with this outcome. She saw no point in talking to the man.[29]

The date for the opening of Pare Waikato had been set for 18 March 1927. And Te Puea was determined there should be no postponement, even when things began to go wrong in the frenzy of final preparations. Members of the pa on a roading contract worked with such speed that they finished ahead of schedule and the borough council did not have enough money available to pay them; so Te Puea sent them off flax-cutting.[30] A visiting

---

† When Ngaruawahia and the pa were attached to the national grid in the 1930s Te Puea donated the oil-fired generator to her friends in Te Kao, Northland.

carver was working so slowly and — Te Puea believed — so poorly on the front of the house that Te Puea dismissed him.[31][†] Finally, the day before the opening, the porch boards were still not laid and nobody could be spared for the job; a pregnant woman named Te Kahurangi arose from her confinement, worked until midnight laying and nailing down planks, and had her child at two a.m. (one of the first to be born at the pa); at dawn the next morning she was swimming in the river with the rest of the community.[32]

Until the middle of 1927 there were few references to Kingitanga activities in the country's metropolitan papers except for rare occasions like the deaths of Kings, functions attended by Members of Parliament, or meetings involving conflict. Nothing of Te Puea's work at Turangawaewae had been reported other than in concert reviews. When the movement was mentioned, it was usually in patronising or ridiculing terms, and the title King was still placed in inverted commas.[‡] Few Europeans outside Ngaruawahia knew about Turangawaewae and even those who did had little idea of its functions and objectives.

All this was to change dramatically as a result of the curiosity of an Auckland journalist. In August 1927, Eric Ramsden was twenty-nine years old. He worked for *The Sun* newspaper* and knew little about Maori affairs. Talking to a Government Land Purchase Officer named W.E. Goffe, however, he heard about Te Puea and her pa. He suggested to his editor Percy Crisp that he go to Turangawaewae with a photographer to compile a major feature on Te Puea. Crisp agreed. The new paper's circulation was not strong and he was looking for ways of building it with colour material not carried by other Auckland publications. The story of a fairytale Maori princess on their doorstep sounded appealing.[33] So Ramsden wrote several times to Te Puea asking if he could visit the pa and interview her. Eventually she said yes; but only because she was 'fed up with the continual requests of that Pakeha — I agreed to put a quick end to them.'[34]

To Te Puea the idea that publicity could help her objectives was novel. Ramsden had great difficulty persuading her to have her photograph taken. Again, she relented because it seemed the easiest way to remove a

---

† It has been said (Phillipps p. 201) that Te Puea completed the carving herself. According to those who lived at the pa at the time, however, this was not true. (Interview, Alex McKay.)
‡ Up to this time the only journalist Te Puea knew and respected for his knowledge of Maori language and objective accounts of the wars of the 1860s was James Cowan (see letter to Eric Ramsden, 2/4/43. R.P.).
* Established in 1927 and incorporated into the *Auckland Star* in 1930.

Tumokai performs with a taiaha in front of the Ahurewa at Turangawaewae. Turongo House

nuisance. The result of the visit was a full-page feature with illustrations published in *The Sun* on 10 September.

It is written in the effusive style that Ramsden came to adopt as a matter of habit when he discussed Maori things. Women became 'wahines', girls 'maidens'; men were 'braves', 'stalwarts', 'rangatiras of the old school'; Te Puea herself was 'a princess of Maoriland' in whose veins flowed 'the bluest of Maori blue blood'. Like well-intentioned Europeans before and after him, he was reacting to a general ignorance of non-European cultures by affecting a florid prose that hung a gauze of romance around Maori activities and attempted to invest them with epic and mystical qualities. He came quickly to appreciate the journalistic appeal of such neglected subject matter presented in this fashion, and he virtually cornered the newspaper market for Kingitanga material throughout the remainder of his working life. Apart from these personal considerations, however, Ramsden also recognised the need for the Kingitanga and its leaders to make themselves intelligible to a Pakeha audience, something they had not succeeded in doing up to this time. He was the first to persuade Te Puea of this necessity, and he was most willing to act as an intermediary.

The first photograph in *The Sun* feature showed Te Puea looking more pudgy than she had done at any other time in her life. Temporarily, she was completely free from illness and had put on considerable weight. She was wearing 'the familiar silk handkerchief' around her head and across her shoulders had 'a handsome Milanese floral shawl'. She was content. She had much to show Ramsden for the seven years (to the month) on the formerly blackberry-covered site:

> Ngaruawahia pa is a model of cleanliness. Everything has its place. The native women see that it is kept in the spick and span order directed by the Princess. There is a general tidy-up both night and morning. Any Maori who shows signs of falling from grace is ridiculed into line with the others. There must be no fighting in the pa. Neither must any native bring drink within its confines . . .
>
> Each hutment has its own little garden. The whares are carefully spaced from one another. Visitors are housed in the capacious and well-ventilated meeting house [Pare Waikato], part of the carving for which the Princess did herself [sic]. The big recreation hall is electrically lighted. The fittings were installed by the Maori boys, who likewise operate the engine . . .
>
> Work is in progress on a plot of land on which eight tennis courts will be laid out. There is already a sports ground available. A billiards room is likewise part of the equipment of this modern pa. There is no necessity for the young Maori to wander into the village in search of diversion.

Ramsden, always one to be impressed by gracious and mannered living, found that the food and its presentation departed from the stereotype of Maori eating.[†] 'Though I sat on a mat beside my hostess it was difficult to

---

† Which had been well expressed, if iniquitously so, in an editorial in the *New Zealand Observer*, 6 October 1917. The Maori, the *Observer* noted, becomes 'repeatedly drunk and offensive to sight and smell, and rude in speech . . . He fills restaurants side by side with clean people and may be seen with his hands full of fish gabbling loudly.'

imagine that one was not lunching at a first-class hotel. The lobster mayonnaise was served from a cut-glass bowl. The pork and fowl, both cooked in the open at the hangi, had a flavour, though, that no French chef could impart. Then there were trifles and meringues, bread cooked in the earth, and we drank King Tawhiao's spring water.'[35]

The elegance of the food preparation was no accident. As part of her determination only to entertain visitors if she could do so memorably, Te Puea had summoned to her pa her old family friend of Mercer days, Ngeungeu Beamish. Miss Beamish had been educated in a Pakeha environment. She had completed secondary schooling in Auckland at Miss Baston's College, a 'finishing school for ladies', and then worked for the Department of Native Affairs in Wellington. She was proud of her Maori background (she was a grand-niece of Major Te Wheoro); but, like her friend Pomare, she believed that what they regarded as 'the best features of Maori life' should be grafted as quickly as possible on to European style of living and behaviour.[36]

Te Puea did not accept this view, but she was happy to make use of the expertise it had given Miss Beamish. To her, Ngeungeu seemed very much of a 'lady' and she wanted her to teach the girls at the pa how to make Pakeha food (salads, trifles, Spanish cream, cakes, even cucumber sandwiches), and the etiquette for serving it.[†] Over the next decade, as other tribes came into contact with these dishes at Turangawaewae, their popularity spread and they became as accepted a part of Maori kai at hui as sea eggs and rotten corn. Meanwhile Ngeungeu and Alex McKay[‡] were to act as Te Puea's 'social secretaries', deal with her correspondence with Europeans and advise her on protocol for Pakeha-type functions.

Such advice was needed very soon after Ramsden's first visit. *The Sun* feature aroused widespread interest. It increased the volume of Pakeha visitors to the pa and introduced a wide number of other people to its existence so that when Te Puea approached them on subsequent fund-raising ventures they were already approvingly aware of who she was and

---

[†] The first experiments with jelly at the pa attracted more than the usual number of guests and produced consternation because 'no matter how much you cut it up it doesn't die, it just keeps on trembling' (interview Tumokai Katipa).

[‡] McKay, who had run away from his parents' home in Pembrokeshire at the age of 16 to work for his great-uncle in Waikato, had developed a close relationship with Te Puea after she had taken him to the Raglan poukai in 1919. He worked on dairy and sheep farms in Waikato and, for a time, in Huntly coal mines. He gave much of his free time to Kingitanga activities and their organisation and came to be known as Areka.

what she was doing. Te Puea very quickly became conscious of this and appreciative.[†]

Late in 1927 Te Puea came to Auckland to show Ramsden a letter from Government House in Wellington. It said the Governor-General, Sir Charles Fergusson, had read the story in *The Sun* and would like to visit Turanga-waewae to see for himself what had been done there.[37] Te Puea was uncertain about the proposal. She welcomed the recognition it implied; but she was not sure she could guarantee a friendly reception (while the British Crown was generally respected among Tainui there was still considerable resentment against New Zealand figures of authority because of the confiscation and the imposition of conscription); nor was she confident that the resources of the pa were adequate to support a function of the magnitude that she felt the occasion merited.

The possibility of embarrassing incidents was not merely hypothetical. There had been no formal vice-regal contact with Tainui Maori since Lord Ranfurly had visited Mahuta at Waahi shortly after the turn of the century (although some Maori had attended a function at Ngaruawahia for his successor Lord Plunket). And, when Sir Charles Fergusson's father, Sir James, had visited Ngaruawahia as Governor in April 1874,[‡] a chief had stripped off his blanket in front of him and shouted: 'You have slain my people and taken my land. Naked I came and naked I go. Here, take my garments too.'[38]

Ramsden believed the opportunity was too precious to be allowed to pass. He persuaded Te Puea to issue an invitation to the Governor-General and his wife, Lady Alice Fergusson (who had an additional interest in Te Puea's work because of her foundation the previous year of the New Zealand League of Mothers, and because her father, Lord Glasgow, had visited Ngaruawahia as Governor in 1894). The Government House letter, Ramsden told Te Puea, was 'an olive branch'.[39] It would lead to further fruitful contact between Turangawaewae and Pakeha authority.

---

† She was to say in 1934 that Ramsden's articles had 'broadcast our activities to the country as a whole and people discovered that [Turangawaewae] was a worthy venture. And so we received the support of the Pakeha, including the Government and wealthy people'. (Waiuku notes for Royal Commission evidence, M.J.P.)

‡ Eric Ramsden, after conversation with Te Puea, identified this incident with Sir James' visit. The year 1874 comes from Sir Charles Fergusson's diary entry for 30 April 1928; and the Fergusson family have a photograph taken there in 'April 1874'. Another researcher, Angus Ross, states he has been unable to find corroborative evidence for the visit (personal communications from Lord Ballantrae, 21/9/76 and 11/1/77).

The event itself on 30 April 1928[†] was a qualified success. The number present was small and Te Rata refused to attend; but the King's brothers Tumate and Tonga Mahuta represented him and reported back favourably. Everybody who did attend was most favourably impressed by the Fergussons' transparent interest in the pa and their kindness, which put people at their ease rapidly. Sir Charles was reported in the *Auckland Star* as saying he would 'do all in his power to help Te Puea and her people. In the South Island he had seen a beautiful English rose — the emblem of love — growing round a fine old totara. He liked to think of the Maori and Pakeha growing up together in that way.'[40][‡] In his diary entry for the day the Governor-General described the reception as 'a good show' and hoped the visit would improve Maori-Pakeha relations. Te Puea was confident as a result of the visit of her ability to retain the vice-regal contact and, according to Ramsden,[41] Te Rata did not subsequently challenge her authority on matters of ceremony.

This function also strengthened Te Puea's hand in dealing with Pakeha visitors to the pa. She now insisted with more assurance that they show a degree of deference towards the institution of the Maori kingship, as the Fergussons had done and were to do on a subsequent visit in 1929. Having established that Te Rata's office was worthy of attention, she was then determined that it should also attract respect. She may have been gratified that Europeans were coming in increasing numbers to look at Turanga-waewae, but she became progressively more severe about protocol — not for her own aggrandisement but for the mana of the kingship. She told Ramsden with relish the story of a 1927 visit.

A well-dressed Pakeha woman walked straight through the main gate of the pa and over to where Te Puea was digging a drain.

'Can I see the Queen?' she said. 'I want to look around.'

Te Puea, in sack-cloth work clothes, stopped digging and looked at her. 'The Queen? What Queen?' she said. 'The only Queen I know of is the wife of the King and she's at Huntly.'

'Well,' said the woman, 'the Princess then. She'll do.'

Te Puea was becoming progressively more annoyed at the off-handedness. 'I don't know about any Princess,' she said. 'But would you

---

[†] According to Ramsden the visit took place on 16 May. But Sir Charles Fergusson's diary makes it clear it was on 30 April.

[‡] Which prompted one quick-witted kuia, not convinced of the merit of the relationship, to call out: 'Yes. We know about the English rose. It strangles the Maori plant.'

come to see a European Princess without introduction or formality and ask to be taken around her house?' No, admitted the woman, she would not. 'Well,' said Te Puea, 'it's the same for the Maori.'[42] And she went on with her digging.[†]

By 1928 Te Puea had reason to feel satisfied. She had established her model village and it had taken root — it functioned with a life of its own. While the lack of guaranteed employment was still a source of anxiety, the inhabitants of Turangawaewae were more secure and contented than they had been before. There was more time for leisure than in earlier days. Te Puea was turning with joy to less frenetic tasks, like showing young mothers (many of the orphans of the earlier days) how to massage babies to open their chests and strengthen their muscles.[43] A first generation of inhabitants was being born at Turangawaewae just as the oldest settlers were beginning to die.

In addition, with the encouragement of Ngeungeu Beamish, Alex McKay and Eric Ramsden, the Kingitanga was beginning to seek and achieve a degree of acceptance from European institutions. Not only had Te Puea consolidated earlier plans, she had set the course for a change of direction that would take her and the Kingitanga into far more extensive contact with other tribes and an association with future governments. In fifteen years she had become the dominating figure in Tainui Maori affairs; through her efforts to extend Turangawaewae facilities even further over the next year, she was to become a national figure. And it was the Mahinarangi project that brought her this wider attention.

---

† This story and apocryphal variations of it are still popular at Turangawaewae. Te Puea and her followers enjoyed both the surprise that Europeans showed at finding a person of rank in work clothes, and the necessity to remind Pakeha about protocol and courtesy. It was small revenge for the number of times the Maori had been slapped down for ostensibly the same reason. The struggle to win the protection of protocol for members of the kahui ariki continued. Twenty-eight years later Piri Poutapu was to write to author Dick Scott, who had sent King Koroki a complementary copy of *The Parihaka Story*: 'You cannot ask your Queen to go canvassing your books if you were to write the history of your own people. So in fairness to King Koroki you should treat him the same way. After all, the Pakeha people taught us proper manners.' (Poutapu to Scott, 12/2/55.)

7

An end to isolation

The meeting house Mahinarangi was conceived as a hospital. When Eric Ramsden visited Turangawaewae in the late 1920s, standards of health in Waikato were little better than they had been twenty years earlier.[†] The pa itself was a model of sanitation and cleanliness. But other settlements had poor sanitary facilities or none at all; living quarters were crowded, unventilated and frequently dirty; the perennial nightmares of typhoid and tuberculosis were undiminished. In addition, Waikato people were still reluctant to accept medical care or hospital treatment.[1]

Other than by preaching and example, Te Puea could do little about uplifting conditions in other Maori settlements. She could, however, influence attitudes to hospitalisation. 'I felt Waikato should have a small hospital of its own. Our patients could stay there, Maori nurses could take care of them, and doctors could come to them.'[2] It would be an application of European medical care in a reassuringly Maori environment. Maori rules of tapu would be observed, for they were not incompatible with Pakeha practices. 'To wash the head . . . in the same utensil as the rest of the body is abhorrent to [the Maori woman],' Te Puea told Ramsden. 'Neither will she permit male and female clothing to be washed together.'[3]

Te Puea also feared that a repetition of the smallpox or influenza epidemics would again catch her people unprepared.[4] She now knew about

---

† In 1929 a dysentery epidemic killed an estimated two percent of the Waikato Maori population. Seven years later, the newly appointed Medical Officer of Health in Hamilton, Dr H.B. Turbott, was to say that in health matters Waikato Maori were 'very backward compared with those of other areas' (*New Zealand Herald*, 12/9/36).

and encouraged vaccination; she was aware of the principles of preventative medicine. All that Turangawaewae lacked was a place for treatment permanently available — and one that she did not want to be open to Tainui people alone but to any Maori who might be afflicted by illness.[5]

This decision made, the next task was to find money. Labouring and contract work were usually sufficient to meet the everyday needs of the pa. But Te Puea knew of only one way to raise large sums of money quickly. She decided to go on tour again with the TPM, and to tap a relatively wealthy section of the Maori people that she had not yet visited: Hawke's Bay and the East Coast of the North Island.

'The immediate reason for our going to the East Coast was that we had been invited there by Paora Hapi of Nuhaka,' Te Puea wrote.[6] Hapi was a Mormon to whom Te Puea had previously offered the facilities of Turanga-waewae for a church hui. In return, he suggested a TPM tour on which the Mormons would host the group in communities where church membership was strong. But Te Puea wanted to go further afield. 'I remembered this man Ngata,' she recalled. 'I had heard how he was supporting Maori activities. It occurred to me that he might be sympathetic to our cause and help us when we arrived in his territory.'[7] So Te Puea wrote to Apirana Ngata in September 1927 and outlined her plans.

At this point something needs to be said about Waikato–East Coast relations. In 1927 they had been virtually non-existent for over sixty years, since the wars and the skirmishes of the 1860s. In the wake of these disturbances the Ngati Porou people of the Coast had taken a different path from Waikato to cope with what Ngata called 'conditions imposed by the Pakeha'.[8] Each tribe regarded the other with some suspicion and a degree of jealousy.

First, and most fundamentally, Ngati Porou had remained loyal to the Crown during the land wars. They had refused an offer of the Maori kingship ('Hikurangi is a mountain that does not travel,' Te Kani a Takirau had said). And they had regarded Waikato as rebels in the war of 1863.[9] This feeling was intensified when Tawhiao sheltered Te Kooti Rikirangi, the guerilla fighter whom Ngati Porou troops had been pursuing without success. After the war, they gave no recognition to the kingship. They not only claimed it did not represent them, they asserted that it was not even a Maori institution (as late as 1938 Ngata spoke of East Coast attitudes as 'not dictated by any regard for . . . the kingship, which is not a Maori idea'[10]).

As a result of these views, Waikato and Ngati Porou patterns of relating to the Crown and to Europeans had diverged widely after the 1860s. Ngati

Porou had favoured accommodation with the Pakeha system from its own position of strength (unlike Waikato, it retained its land). While it kept the Maori language and upheld Maori values, it embraced the Anglican Church, Pakeha education and participation in the political system. The existence of Te Aute College from the 1850s had had a profound effect on the tone of leadership on the Coast — it began a process that was to culminate in the formation of the Young Maori Party at the turn of the century. University graduates like Ngata and Dr Tutere Wi Repa seemed to enjoy their ability to take on the Pakeha at his own games. Waikato by contrast seemed backward to them and Wi Repa expressed contempt for the Kingites' policy of sullen isolation from the inter-cultural contact that Ngati Porou found beneficial, even exhilarating.[†]

A crop of East Coasters emerged as leaders straddling Maori and Pakeha worlds through participation in the public service (Raumoa Balneavis, for example) and ordination in the Anglican Church (Rewiti Kohere and Hakaraia Pahewa). In the North Island, only the Arawa people had opened themselves up to association with the Pakeha to the same extent, and they without the same degree of conspicuous success. Other tribes had produced individual leaders of outstanding capacity (Kahungunu's Carroll, Taranaki's Buck and Pomare). But Ngati Porou had reason to believe that they, as a group, had led the Maori into the twentieth century.[‡]

As the East Coast strode along a path of integration and acquisition of European skills and technology, Waikato had largely festered and brooded in depression and isolation. The only asset Waikato had that Ngati Porou did not, perhaps, was a greater degree of cohesion that arose from shared resentment and absolute loyalty to the Kingitanga. Their missions had been Wesleyan as well as Anglican, and these had tended to be less intent on 'civilising' the Maori. They had not gained access to St Stephen's School in Auckland, even though this had been financed in part by Waikato trust funds, and leaders like Te Tahuna Herangi had tried hard to have Waikato children admitted. They had no university graduates to build a consciousness-

---

† See, for example, Tutere Wi Repa's letters to Eric Ramsden, R.P.

‡ Ngata was to question whether this course had been wholly beneficial. He wrote to Buck in 1929: 'I rather think that in moments of introspection you and I . . . must acknowledge that our hearts are not with this policy of imposing pakeha culture-forms on our people. Our recent activities would indicate a contrary determination to preserve the old culture forms as the foundations on which to reconstruct Maori life and hopes.' (Ngata to Buck, 1 August 1929. R.P.) In some respects Waikato was to exhibit some purely Maori strengths that Ngati Porou had lost, particularly (after Ngata's death) the ability to act as a tribe with some coherence.

raising path of precedent into professional competition with the Pakeha. By the late 1920s only one Waikato Maori had received any university education: Te Puea's first cousin Tukere Te Anga (his mother was one of Tahuna's sisters); but he had not graduated and until 1929 worked with the Department of Native Affairs in Wanganui; subsequently he came to Waikato as Maori Welfare Officer and was given a house at Turangawaewae by Te Puea.[†]

These were some of the factors that had steered Ngati Porou and Waikato away from each other. And the divergence had been intensified in the minds of some East Coast leaders by the Kingitanga's refusal to participate in the country's war effort in 1914–1918. But there were links that offered precedents for contact. Both tribes shared common ancestors through Mahinarangi (a coast woman who had married Turongo, a Waikato ancestor of the kings); and there was one of Tawhiao's enigmatic sayings made at Hikurangi in Waikato, 'The taut rope to the East Coast will never be severed' (although until 1927 there was every indication that it had been).

By 1927 the leaders of both tribes had considered reasons for wanting to establish contact and cooperation; on both sides these reasons arose from the pursuit of policies that had been successful enough to inspire optimism, but not enough to allow their completion.

Ngata had been in Parliament for twenty-two years. He was in a position of stronger influence with a Pakeha Minister of Native Affairs (Reform Prime Minister Gordon Coates) than he had been before. Further, there were clearly prospects that he might come to hold this position himself as a result of a change of government or the formation of a coalition between the Liberal and Reform Parties (in the event he was to hold ministerial rank for both reasons). He also had a clearer idea than at any other time in his political career of the kinds of policies needed to lift the Maori people into a position of greater strength in relation to the European without diminishing their Maoriness.

The essence of these policies lay in incorporation schemes that allowed consolidation of Maori land titles scattered by inheritance, and consequent eligibility for loan finance to make improvements that would allow (or increase) production. This would be complemented by a nationwide revival of Maori arts and cultural activities in competitive settings; the building of carved community meeting houses; song and dance competitions; even

---

† He was to act as a highly competent 'spy' for Ngata. His reports on Waikato to the minister are perceptive and well written.

Maori sports meetings — all these aimed at raising the strength and confidence of Maori consciousness while the land schemes would offer income and a means of survival in a rural and communal Maori atmosphere. Gordon Coates had accepted these broad objectives. In 1925 he had set up the long-awaited commission to inquire into the confiscations in Taranaki and Waikato, and earlier a Maori Purposes Fund Board to finance worthy community activities from unclaimed interest earned by Maori land board funds. With Ngata, he was looking for ways of implementing in detail the land development and cultural programmes. They had already concluded that it was necessary to replace as far as possible the leadership of the European-educated elite with that of traditional figures capable of selling new ideas to isolated and conservative communities.[11] In this context, they appear to have discussed the desirability of recruiting Te Puea as an ally before either had actually met her to discuss the proposal. And Ngata's conclusion was that she was 'the powerhouse [of Waikato] . . . and if an object is found on which it may be brought to bear, much good may result.'[12]

In addition, Ngata and Coates were conservatives in the New Zealand political spectrum. They jointly feared the rise of the Labour Party and — even more — the popularity of the Ratana radicals. Ngata regarded the Ratana Movement's pot-pourri of Maoriness, Old Testament theology, faith-healing, and brass band campaigning as 'bizarre',[13] but dangerous. In a short time the movement had almost toppled Pomare and gained a foothold in two other electorates.[†] A considerable part of its political appeal arose from the apparent inability of the major parties to offer anything to the Maori by way of land development and rectification of the confiscation grievances. Now that the system was prepared to deliver some of these goods it became important that a leader with a strong following like Te Puea work with parliamentarians as a buffer against Ratanaism. This conviction of Ngata's had become more urgent with the knowledge that Ratana himself was wooing the King Movement leaders and hoped for a federation embracing both groups.[14]

On her side, Te Puea had reached an impasse in Waikato. She had built her model settlement and it was winning high praise from the Europeans

---

† Tokouru Ratana's strength in Western Maori remained constant at around 3000 votes until he took the seat in 1935; Eruera Tirikatene came within one vote of winning Southern Maori in 1928 and finally did so in 1932; Northern Maori steadily built up a Ratana block into a majority by 1938. In Eastern Maori, however, the Ratana candidate Tiaki Omana was not a serious threat to Ngata until he took the seat with a spectacular increase of support in 1943.

who saw it. But neither Turangawaewae nor Te Puea's role in the Kingitanga were universally accepted by Tainui as a whole; nor was the pa large enough to accommodate inhabitants and visitors on the scale Te Puea hoped for; it still lacked a hospital; and it did not have enough land to provide the community with a farm and gardens.

To secure these additional goals, Te Puea needed more money (and she had milked the immediate and earlier sources dry) and a degree of influence beyond Waikato, possibly in Wellington where Ngata had begun to demonstrate that it was possible to obtain assistance for Maori projects through Parliament and the public service. But she would not consider working through her Member of Parliament, Pomare. She believed he had not produced and would not offer anything of benefit to Waikato because of loyalties to his Pakeha colleagues and his Taranaki constituents. 'She distrusted Pomare,' Ngata was to say later, because he 'tried to interpret the Waikato mind in terms of a Taranaki mentality'; and because of his 'suspicious motive of political advancement [for himself]'.[15]

'I looked around,' Te Puea said of that year, 1927. 'I saw that Tawhiao's words [about Turangawaewae] would not come to fruition. I had to look for more money . . . and the East Coast was the only area we hadn't been to.'[16] She had also broadened her awareness of Maori things to include people outside Waikato, which was one reason why she now wanted to hold larger and more representative hui for the discussion and resolution of Maori issues. '[I wanted] to try to link up all aspects of the Maori people so that they could be more united. And to stop the process by which one tribe was denigrating another.'[17]

This wider feeling was new. It had evolved on the TPM concert tours as she found unexpected reserves of goodwill outside Waikato for her and her community project, and as she enjoyed the attention that hosts showered on her.[18] She had seen for the first time people in other districts wrestling with the same problems of lack of income, lack of confidence, an inability to conserve Maori ways of doing things and difficulties in coping with Pakeha institutions. Increasingly, she was developing a consciousness of Maori as Maori rather than Maori as simply Waikato or Tainui. The feeling was to grow even more in the 1930s into one of solidarity with all coloured and subject peoples ('Is there any God in heaven . . . to protect the poor natives?' she asked Ramsden[19]). This vision was also an extension of Tawhiao's one of kotahitanga for the Maori people that he had preached in vain.

There was one further factor. She too was concerned about the Ratana Movement, although not so much as an obstacle to the welfare of the Maori nationally but as a rebellion within the ranks of the Kingitanga. By 1927

Tupu Taingakawa was no longer a threat to her — although he had accompanied Ratana abroad in 1924, his importance within the Ratana Movement had shrunk to negligibility as his star had faded in the King Movement; without influence in Waikato he was of little value to Ratana.[†] He was to die in 1929.

But Te Puea's uncle Haunui and cousin Piupiu were a different matter. Both, as dominant leaders of the kahui ariki, had large local followings at Waahi and in the King Country. Both continued to sponsor Ratana hui as if they were supported by the Kingitanga as a whole. Te Puea had frequently to repudiate such claims.[20] The rival meetings were more than an embarrassment to her, they were an insult. So long as she continued to dismiss Ratana as a charlatan and view his major objective as seeking to dominate or absorb the Kingitanga, she could only view Waikato membership of the movement as unforgivable disloyalty to herself and Te Rata.

Haunui and Ratana also played upon the feelings of older members of the Kingitanga, those for whom the war of 1863 was a first-hand memory from their childhood. This group, referred to by James Cowan as the 'diehards', wanted no compromises with the Pakeha system and unconditional return of the confiscated land; they distrusted what Te Puea was doing at Turangawaewae and her flirtations with people outside Waikato. The leadership of this group centred on Haunui at Waahi.

Other members of the kahui ariki, especially Tumate and Tonga Mahuta, were slowly being won over to Te Puea's view of things, although by no means uncritically so.[21] The ailing Te Rata, however, was now completely under her influence. By 1927 there was no possibility that he would join the Ratana Movement (and on several occasions he crept out of Waahi disguised to avoid meeting the prophet[22]). More of a worry to Te Puea was what would happen after Te Rata's death, and he was obviously not destined to reach old age. At worst, there was a possibility that Haunui — as Tawhiao's son and a man with fire in his belly — would capture the kingship; at best, he might prove more influential with Te Rata's successor than Te Puea and consequently undo much of her work. Anything, therefore, that strengthened her power, her mana and her own community was highly desirable in Te Puea's eyes.

---

† Tupu's influence in the King Movement had waned as that of Te Puea waxed. With Te Rata's abandonment in the 1920s of the Kauhanganui as an instrument for determining movement policy, there was no longer an activist role for the Kingmaker. His tribe Ngati Haua had few resources of their own to support his crusades and when he died in 1929 there was difficulty raising money for the tangi at Rukumoana Pa.

And so it was a marriage of complementary objectives that took Te Puea to the East Coast and into the orbit of Ngata in 1927. Skilled at activating traditional precedents for what she had already determined to do, Te Puea placated die-hard objections to the tour by saying that she 'also wanted to examine what Tawhiao said at Hikurangi about the Coast . . . [to] look at the philosophy underlying it.'[23]

For some reason Te Puea delayed posting her letter to Ngata. It did not reach him until 1 October, the day she was leaving Turangawaewae. He telegrammed back at once advising her not to come because it was inconvenient for Ngati Porou. But it was too late — Te Puea had already finalised arrangements with the Mormons. Her concert group of twenty-five, travelling more comfortably than they ever had before, drove to Napier in a truck and a car bought on time payments.

Te Puea discovered at Napier that Ngata and his wife Arihia were also there. She and Tumokai went straight to the hotel where he was staying and arrived, as Ngata remembered, covered in dust and asking why Ngati Porou had refused to issue an invitation to the TPM when the group was so close. It was not the first time they had met — Ngata had attended Waikato hui in his earlier days as a Member of Parliament. But they did not know each other at all well. He explained the position to her carefully. First, noting that they were travelling with pots and pans, he said he would prefer them not to come as 'gypsies'; secondly, the timing was inconvenient because of other tribal commitments. He suggested that they carry on with their tour and return to the Coast at Christmas time. Te Puea agreed happily; this was not the refusal she had expected.[24]

From Hawke's Bay the TPM went to Palmerston North and there Te Puea had another encounter that was to prove profoundly influential on her subsequent policies: she met Prime Minister Coates.

Joseph Gordon Coates in 1927 was on the way to becoming a tragic figure in New Zealand political history. Two years earlier, aged forty-seven, he had become one of the country's youngest Prime Ministers at Massey's death; his career seemed full of promise. But he had not acquired the faculties for ingenuity, expediency and concealment that — for most public figures — make politics the art of the possible. He could be open about his feelings to the point of sentimentality and sententiousness; he was frequently honest to the point of brusqueness; he was an awkward public speaker. Lacking both private guile and public charisma, he was to be rejected by the electorate and demoted by his colleagues. During the Great Depression he was abused viciously.

One of Coates' strengths (that Te Puea suggested later was a liability in Pakeha eyes[25]) was that he established an easy rapport with Maori. Unlike most parliamentarians he had grown up close to Maori communities north of Kaipara Harbour and was said to have Maori descendants. He enjoyed the florid character of Maori idiom and he was sensitive to land grievances. A visit to Eru Ihaka's Te Kao settlement in 1925 had shocked him and he described the inhabitants there as 'the poorest people I have seen in my life'.[26] As Minister of Native Affairs, he said he was determined to 'remove old grievances so that economic and social change could proceed,' and to tackle Maori problems 'in a comprehensive way rather than by the piecemeal efforts of the past.'[27]

In Te Puea's eyes Coates was worthy of attention as the man who had established the commission on the confiscations.[†] She also discovered to her surprise and delight that she liked him immensely.[28] He was not the least intimidating, he was easy to talk to. From the day they met she referred to him as 'Gordon' in private and — with a touch of pride — 'the Honourable Coates' in more formal communications. Coates was also impressed by Te Puea. He had already heard from Ngata of her potential for carrying out government land development schemes. When she invited him to visit Turangawaewae early the following year he had no hesitation in accepting; in turn, he invited her to Wellington.

From Palmerston North Te Puea took the TPM to agricultural shows in Wanganui, Stratford and Gisborne. And it was from Gisborne in December that they moved at last into Ngati Porou territory, the path now cleared by Ngata.

The stature of Sir Apirana Turupa Ngata[‡] on the East Coast at this time was nothing short of gigantic. He won elections without serious opposition. He was 'Api', the double university graduate who had succeeded with apparent ease in the Pakeha world and who was able to keep political promises. When he wanted assistance from a Ngati Porou marae he got it simply by asking.[*] In the case of Te Puea's visit, although he was not there to escort her personally, the fact that he had invited her ensured that she was persona grata at every marae from Tolaga Bay northwards, in spite of latent anti-Waikato feeling.

---

† The commission did not report until 1928 when it found the extent of the Waikato confiscation to be unfair, and recommended annual compensation payments of £3000, an offer that was unacceptable to Waikato. See page 249.

† He was knighted in 1927 while in Opposition, a measure of Coates' admiration.

* 'When Api wanted a beef he just asked for a beef and he got it; when Whaia asks for a beef they say, "Get it yourself." ' (Interview Whaia McClutchie, Ruatoria, October 1973.)

'It was at Tolaga Bay,' Te Puea wrote, 'that we began to see real money for the first time. The sun hadn't even set before our place of entertainment was full. Some people missed out on seats. We went from there to Tokomaru Bay and there the money increased again, as did the hospitality.'[29] That was how it continued all the way up the Coast — each community tried to outdo the previous one. Although they were not large in size, the sums they contributed were (£464 in Waiomatatini, £105 from Tokomaru Bay[30]). By Waikato standards this was big money indeed; Te Puea noted that this section of the tour raised £1336 for the hostel.[31] Ngata was to say later: 'That was how Ngati Porou showed their respect for Te Puea.'[32]

Ngata himself arrived from Wellington in time for Christmas and he spent it with Te Puea and the TPM at his home marae of Waiomatatini. There was no entertaining here. They were to regard it, he said, as their home too. And they did; exhausted at this mid-point of the tour, members of the group simply slept and ate. Te Puea was greatly moved by this simple kindness.[33] Later, at Hicks Bay, she extended an invitation to 'the whole of Ngati Porou' to visit Waikato.

Te Puea discussed the name of the proposed meeting house-hospital with Ngata. She told him she favoured that of Potatau, her and Te Rata's great-grandfather. But Ngata said no. The extent of East Coast cooperation meant there could be only one name, he told her: Mahinarangi, the woman who linked Tainui and East Coast genealogies and from whom she and Te Rata were sixteenth-generation descendants.[34]

The tour had consequences beyond the raising of a large sum of money. Ngati Porou were partially disarmed of their anti-Waikato feelings by Te Puea's transparent goodwill and appealing nature. They also approved of the high standard of the TPM performances. For her part, Te Puea saw Ngata's incorporation schemes at work and (partly as a consequence of them) the prosperity and good health of so many of the Coast people. She was surprised at the extent to which they had surrounded themselves with the trappings of European civilisation — books, armchairs, pianos, hot water and telephones, amenities rarely seen in Waikato Maori homes; she suspected at first that they had become Pakeha. But after experiencing their hospitality she was able to say they had 'been Europeanised but the Maori spirit remains'.[35] As a result of what she saw on the Coast, Te Puea was to go out of her way to acquire many of the same amenities for Turanga-waewae over the next ten years.

In mid-January the Waikato party left the Coast. But the tour was not yet finished. The TPM returned home through the Bay of Plenty and into Te

Te Puea at Apirana Ngata's home, Waiomatatini, Christmas 1927; with Captain Pitt, a Ngati Porou returned serviceman, and his daughter. Henare Ngata

Arawa territory where, for the first time, they faced (and survived) the scrutiny of an audience of professional Maori entertainers at Ohinemutu.

On 13 February 1928, Te Puea and the TPM made a triumphal entry at Turangawaewae where they were welcomed by a large crowd of Waikato-Maniapoto. They had been away for more than four months and had travelled nearly 1600 km. But there was little rest over the following six months. The Fergussons visited the marae on 28 April, and on 27 May, Eric

Ramsden arrived with the entrepreneur Philip Hayward to arrange a three-week series of concerts in Auckland, for which the group was to be paid £80 a week (less than they had made in one night at some of their venues on the Coast).

They stayed in Auckland from mid-June until the first week in July. The current issue of the *New Zealand Picturegoer* promoted the concerts among its blurb for Ramon Novarro in *The Student Prince* and Douglas Fairbanks in *The Gaucho*. Te Puea's photograph shared space with that of Mary Pickford, then starring in *My Best Girl*. The TPM was described as 'the biggest Maori troupe ever brought to Auckland', and the 'most talented combination in all Maoriland'.[36]

Meanwhile Gordon Coates had come to Turangawaewae on 28 May, the first Prime Minister to visit a Waikato marae since the Liberals were in office. Te Puea showed him at first hand what she was doing. She also asked him to secure for her ownership of an unused six-acre 'police reserve' just beyond the pa so that she would be able to grow her own vegetables.[37] Coates promised to investigate this and again invited Te Puea to Wellington.

Arrangements for the Wellington visit were finalised in July and on 28 August Te Puea left Turangawaewae with the TPM for a fortnight of performances in the Deluxe Theatre (later named the Embassy). She was forty-three years old and visiting the capital for the first time. Transport and accommodation for the group were organised by the Department of Native Affairs and paid for by the Government. In spite of the concerts, the real purpose of the trip for Te Puea was to test the sincerity of Ngata's and Coates' offers of assistance.[38] They in turn were setting out to prove their goodwill and the advantages of working with the Department of Native Affairs. They went to great lengths to impress her, laying on a variety of functions and entertainments for her and the group: a Parliamentary reception, a visit to the Fergussons at Government House, afternoon tea at the Coates' home, a beach trip, even free tickets to the New Zealand-New South Wales rugby match at Athletic Park.

At Parliament, Te Puea had her last-but-one meeting with Maui Pomare; and a reconciliation. His health had broken down. He was overweight, an ashen colour, and suffering from a number of disorders, including tuberculosis which was to kill him two years later. When he saw Te Puea he was unable to get to his feet. But he beckoned her to sit beside him.

> He looked so ill that my heart went out to him. It was then that, after all those years, he admitted to me that he had been wrong in forcing conscription upon Waikato–Maniapoto. Pomare took my hand, pressed

it against his cheek, and said how happy he was that I had spoken to him. [He] had not forgotten what I had done for him in former years. One of his last acts on leaving for California, where he died two years later, was to send me a farewell telegramme.'[39]†

Later in the week, the Pomares too entertained the Waikato party at their home in Belmont where Te Puea said goodbye to her former adversary.

As Ngata and Coates had intended, the visit opened for Te Puea a source of power she had never previously explored: access to politicians and public servants who could unlock the resources of the State on her behalf. She left the Native Affairs Ministerial Private Secretary Raumoa Balneavis a long list of matters to investigate for her.[40] These items included an inquiry into Kingitanga land titles at Manurewa and Mangere, from which Henare Kaihau was believed to have misappropriated income.[41]

After the visit, Te Puea was to become the department's most voluminous and indefatigable correspondent. She discovered that local authorities and civil servants could be moved by ministerial directive from Wellington. And she exploited her special relationship with Balneavis and (later) Ngata to the full. She asked for favours ranging from increases in pensions for her supporters to the installation of a post box at Turangawaewae.[42] Some of these letters attracted exasperated notes from the officers to whom they were referred, who were not always as sympathetic as the minister and his secretary.‡ And the official correspondence from the Wellington end included solemn acknowledgements for consignments of whitebait.[43] In the 1940s Te Puea was to transfer the same attention to Peter Fraser. Her visible access to such people, and her ability to secure favours as a result was a major and additional source of her future mana in Waikato.

The climax to a busy fortnight was the Prime Minister's reply on behalf of the Government to her request for assistance with the building of Mahinarangi and the purchase of land for farming. 'On 14 September the Honourable Coates invited me to his office. His message to me there was this: "You and your children return to Ngaruawahia. I shall build your house, support it, give money for its construction. I shall also give you 200 acres of

---

† The message read 'E noho ra arohanui (farewell and much love) from Mira and self. Maui Pomare.'
‡ One such note, from Native Affairs Chief Clerk George Shepherd, worried that Te Puea was under the impression that a car supplied by the department for her land department supervisory duties was a personal gift (see note on Te Puea letter to Ngata, 28 May 1931. M.J.P.).

land to be farmed by you and your children, and the money to start this project too. I am going to fulfil all your wishes because of the care you have taken in looking after the orphaned, the widowed and the destitute." [44] What Coates did not say, understandably, was 'because the Government needs the support of a strong traditional leader to launch its land programmes and hold back the threat from Ratana.' But that did not need to be spelled out: Te Puea shared those objectives too. And what Coates had said was true enough and sincere on his part.

Coates arranged to supply Te Puea with timber for the house from the Frankton Railway Timber Mill, and £1000 from public funds towards the cost of construction. He promised a property of about 200 acres close to Ngaruawahia with an advance of £1000 so that Te Puea could 'initiate and carry out cultivation and farming operations for the maintenance of her people and settlement'. Ngata was to visit Waikato to investigate the second part of the agreement. [45] Coates also arranged for a £250 subsidy from the Maori Purposes Fund for a hostel for Waikato workers in Tuakau, provided the local people could raise an equal sum. [†]

Te Puea established one further set of useful contacts in Wellington: she met representatives of the tribes and Maori organisations of the south. They included Hapi Love of Te Ati Awa, Taite Te Tomo (representing Ngati Raukawa, originally a Waikato tribe), and Kingi Tahiwi of Ngati Raukawa, later of Ngati Poneke. The last of these organised reception and farewell functions for the Waikato group. The *Dominion*, reporting the welcome, said that with Te Puea's visit 'the last remnants of antagonism between natives and European populations of New Zealand are consigned to the limbo of forgotten things.' [46] Te Puea addressed both gatherings, noting at the same time that Waikato custom did not allow women to do this. (In fact, she had no hesitation about speaking in public, although she preferred to do it inside halls or meeting houses rather than on a marae proper.)

Home again on 15 September, Te Puea was ecstatic about the success of the trip. 'We have never had such a time,' she wrote to Ramsden. 'The Government certainly put itself out . . . It was also quite a financial success. For the contract at the Deluxe Theatre I received £200.' [47] A fortnight later Ngata arrived from Wellington to drive in the first post for Mahinarangi. Building was under way. For the inhabitants of Turangawaewae, accustomed to long-term plans and delays, events had moved with bewildering speed. [48]

---

† Which they did; later, Te Puea was to make similar hostel arrangements for Waikato workers in Hamilton and Rotorua.

8

Mahinarangi:
A coming together

The General Election of November 1928 shocked Te Puea as much as it surprised the nation's press. The Reform Government was turned out of office for the first time in sixteen years as a result of the Liberal Party (renamed United) joining forces with Labour members. Elderly, ailing Sir Joseph Ward was again Prime Minister.†

Te Puea was bereft. Apart from Ngata, she had no contacts or confidence in the new regime. Writing to Ramsden on 8 December she spoke of Coates as 'our fallen idol'. He was 'our poor premier and friend, the only one the Maori has ever had in the political arena . . . He has tried so hard to help me and my Maori people I will always look upon him as our Prime Minister.'[1] To Coates himself she gave what seemed to her the most likely explanation for his defeat. 'Perhaps it was on account of your love for the Maori people that you have been displaced by your own people.'[2] She repeated an invitation to him to open Mahinarangi on 15 March 1929.

The election aftermath was not entirely without compensation. For the first time since James Carroll was in office, the country had a Maori Minister of Native Affairs. And Te Puea was optimistic that Ngata would be committed to the plans for land and cultural development that he and Coates had outlined to her in Wellington. 'The people should lean on Sir Apirana Ngata,' she told Coates in the idiom she reserved for formal communication, 'for the reason that he is a man whose sense of justice and whose assistance towards his own tribe have been abundantly apparent. The Waikato tribes

---

† He had previously held the office from Seddon's death in 1906 until 1912.

have experienced the invaluable assistance he has rendered them and he is left to put into effect your undertakings.'[3] Less stiffly, she told Ramsden that Ngata 'has been extremely good to me and will see that the Maori get fair play.'[4]

Ngata visited Turangawaewae again on 8 December and Te Puea was able to report the same day: 'The hostel is now under way and by march we hope to have both hostel and tennis courts thoroughly completed[†] . . . Sir Apirana secured me the services of a very competent builder from the East Coast. He thoroughly understands Maori art and architecture, so that relieves me of a fair amount of responsibility.'[5]

Ngata and Te Puea were determined that the cultural section of the opening function would be on such a scale as to impress upon the audience that something memorable was taking place. 'The running of the hakas and poi dances had been left entirely to Apirana and myself. We are going to give them the real thing. Instead of only a dozen in the haka teams there will be dozens, which will make all the difference in the world. The big canoes too have all been done up. Very much painted up and befeathered as in the old days.'[6] This wish to evoke the 'old days' was not simply nostalgia. It was a deliberate attempt to cloak the innovative policy she was launching (contact with the Government and with other tribes) with the appearance of a revival of past glories.[7] It was a way of making radical ideas more acceptable to the cautious element of Tainui opinion.

By January there were 45 people working full time on construction. 'A big gang,' she wrote to Ramsden, 'and plenty of mouths to feed. One bullock and six bags of potatoes at every meal and plenty of trifles with brandy keep them fit and working.'[8] The 'gang' consisted of Richard Wills, the Pakeha builder engaged by Ngata, and a team of Turangawaewae men under his direction. Ngata also provided a group of Arawa carvers to decorate the inside pillars of the hostel and to supervise the outside carving done by an untrained Waikato group. Piri Poutapu showed so much promise on the latter job that Te Puea was to dispatch him later in the year to the carving school at Ohinemutu in Rotorua.[†] Women and girls from the pa did the tukutuku panels and rafter painting under Ngata's direction.

The shape of the building was that of the conventional meeting house because Te Puea believed a Maori hospital would not be acceptable to

---

† The opening hui was timed to coincide with the national Maori tennis championships.
‡ He subsequently returned and established the Turangawaewae Carving School, which was still functioning after his death in 1975.

Building the meeting house Mahinarangi, 1929. *Auckland Museum*

patients unless it presented a familiar and comforting appearance.[9] But modifications to traditional design allowed for nursing requirements: windows were placed between the wall panels, for example, to admit light and ventilation; and there were no poles to block a central aisle — the support posts were placed either side of the ridge pole.

Official support for the project was sustained down to details. Raumoa Balneavis arrived early in the year to view progress and Alex McKay (working at the pa in his spare time) showed him that the carving tools were blunt. Three weeks later three new sets of tools were sent from Wellington, purchased from the Maori Purposes Fund. 'Te Puea was wild,' McKay remembered. 'She didn't want any more charity and told me to send them back. But I didn't. I explained to her it was unclaimed Waikato money that paid for those tools. It was the first time we had drawn on the fund apart from the money for the Tuakau hostel.'[10] Salaries for the Arawa carvers were drawn from the same source.

In earlier years the construction of important buildings was said to be surrounded by happenings interpreted as being of a supernatural nature. They served to remind onlookers that what they were building had a mauri (a life-force) of its own; and that the process was tapu. Mahinarangi was viewed in this light and one incident seen by all the outside workers did much to spread beyond Turangawaewae itself an acceptance of the importance of the building.

Tumokai was one of the witnesses: 'We had just put the ridgepole in place. Somebody said, "Quick, look at the river." So we did. It was very rough on the surface in one place, as though it was being stirred about. We

Apirana Ngata leads his Ngati Porou party on to Turangawaewae for the opening of Mahinarangi, March 1929. The earlier house Kimikimi can be seen in the background. Turongo House

watched for a while and then went back to work, paying little attention. But not long after we saw a log floating on the surface. To our surprise it was floating upstream, against the current. We were puzzled and couldn't understand how this could be. Then the log simply disappeared. To my mind it was a sign that we were being watched and blessed by our ancestors.'[11]

In Ngaruawahia township, cynicism about the project that bordered on racism was rife. A joke popular at the time suggested that Mahinarangi stood roofless for some weeks because once it was covered there was to be no more alcohol allowed inside the pa.[12] In fact, Te Puea had forbidden consumption of alcohol within Turangawaewae from the time of its establishment.

The building was completed in time for the opening hui. And from 11 March to 22 March 1929, the Turangawaewae community was host to what Ngata called 'the most historic assembly of tribes since the Maori wars of the sixties'.[13] Over 6000 people representing every tribe in New Zealand attended. Ngata himself brought 1000 East Coast supporters, responding to Te Puea's invitation of a year before.

Two features of the gathering distinguished it from others held previously in Waikato and elsewhere. First, Ngata took full advantage of the representativeness of the participants. For over a week he centred marae discussion on the broad question of how the Maori could best adapt to sharing the kind of life offered by European society. Individual topics considered included social welfare, land development, the future of Maori language, arts and crafts. His justification for structuring debate was that, as new minister, he wanted opinion from the grass roots. In fact, he was preparing a cross-section of his people for the programmes he had already selected and which he was to introduce over the next six years.

The other feature that drew favourable comment was the large number of extensive haka and poi displays organised by Ngata and Te Puea. Pei Jones noted that they were 'high class performances. The tribal groups . . . were well trained, and a number of their parties had over 200 performers.'[14]

Maori visitors previously unfamiliar with Te Puea's ways of doing things had plenty of opportunity to learn during the course of the hui; and in their learning her reputation grew. On the day of the Mahinarangi opening, Te Puea was up at dawn collecting rubbish from the lawns and the marae proper; Te Aritana Pitama of Ngai Tahu was astonished that 'a woman of such rank and prestige should perform that menial duty'.[15] Later in the morning, while speeches were in progress, a Waikato conservative got to his feet and began to berate Ngata; Te Puea signalled to one of her boys to ring the lunch bell early and cut the speaker off. And the morning Sir Charles Fergusson arrived, she intercepted a case of champagne that had been ordered for lunch; 'You can't let a man of his rank drink water,' she was told; Te Puea said that if the Governor was a rangatira he would be satisfied with whatever he was offered; the champagne was drunk at the roadside outside the pa.[16]

Ngati Porou again outstripped other tribes with donations. Indeed, on view as they were before a national audience, it became a matter of tribal mana to do so, a form of Maori one-upmanship. Ngata spoke later of how he moved among his tribal leaders to see how much each proposed to give and noted to his satisfaction that the total would be several hundred pounds. But Wi Potae of Tokomaru Bay said nothing and his nose was twitching, which his friends recognised as a sign of anger. 'At last he spoke, expressing strong disapproval of the sum in hand, recalled the whakapapa involved and the close relationship of the kahui ariki with the Coast. Then he took out his cheque book and wrote a cheque for £100. Materoa [Reedy] and the others followed his example. In a few moments £1100 was in hand.'[17]† That day

---

† The magnitude of East Coast donations to Mahinarangi became an embarrassment. When Ngata flourished them at her in later years, Te Puea was to speak of trying to pay the money back so that there would be no indebtedness.

a total of £1441 was handed to Te Puea as visitors' contributions towards the cost of the house.

After the week of preliminary discussions, three opening ceremonies were conducted for Mahinarangi. The first Maori kawa ritual was performed on 17 March in front of the visiting tribes. The beam of the house was stepped over by Te Mare, eldest daughter of Te Heuheu Tukino (and sister of Te Uira). Following this, the carved tekoteko figure of Potatau on the front pillar was to be unveiled by Ngata's wife Arihia, a gesture of appreciation by Te Puea for Ngati Porou assistance. Then the name of the figure was to be pronounced by the officiating priest, Tutanekai of Te Arawa.

As Lady Ngata stepped forward, however, there were audible grumblings from the ranks of Waikato elders: 'Why should she do this? Why not somebody from Waikato?'[18] That was the beginning of an embarrassing scene. Pei Jones was watching: 'Lady Ngata made several tugs without result on the cord which covered the tiki. [I] was asked by Tumate . . . to climb up on the roof and assist in the unveiling. On examining the position of the six-inch nail to which the unveiling cord was tied, I could not see anything preventing the nail coming free and I called down to Lady Ngata to give another tug. She made several more tugs, still without results, and it was then I freed the nail with a slight finger pull on the cord . . . Such a hitch, of course, is a serious matter in all Maori ritual . . . and is viewed as ominous of ill-luck or evil.'[19] In the confusion, Tutanekai forgot to name the tekoteko and a second kawa ceremony was performed at dawn the following day.

On 18 March, Gordon Coates performed the official 'Pakeha opening'. Before unlocking the door, he complimented Te Puea before a crowd of 5000 people 'and said he would do all in his power to place Maori aims above political controversy. The Maoris, who had brains and physique equal to the Pakehas, were now walking the road leading to prosperity and self dependence,' the former Prime Minister concluded.[20]

In her own major speech to the hui, delivered in a quiet voice that had everybody silent and straining to hear, Te Puea saluted Ngata as the instigator of whatever progress the Maori people had made. 'You found Waikato dejected; now they are hopeful,' she said. 'Pull down the barriers erected in other days . . . From this day on it is my earnest prayer that we will all draw closer together in love, one for another — let this be our kotahitanga.' As she finished speaking the TPM came out behind her singing one of Te Puea's own compositions, Ko Te Rima Tenei, which began: 'I have wandered aimless for five years. Now at last a dream is coming true.'[21]

The hui was not an unqualified success. Te Rata, again, had been too ill to attend. And there was a tragic aftermath that undercut some of the goodwill arising from the establishment of Waikato-East Coast relations. On 8 April Makarini Ngata, Apirana's eldest son and heir apparent to the leadership of the family, died of acute dysentery contracted at the function; ten days later Lady Arihia died as a result of having nursed her son.[†] In some Waikato minds the deaths were a consequence of Arihia's being asked to unveil the tekoteko; they had been presaged in her inability to remove the cloak. The incident intensified fears among the elderly about the wisdom of Te Puea's new policy of outside contact and cooperation. Conservative opinion on the Coast was that Arihia and Makarini had been makutu'd by Waikato. This alleged act would never be forgiven or forgotten by some Ngati Porou (and when Te Rata's successor Koroki visited the Coast nine years later he was spat upon by somebody who recalled the incident).

Between Te Puea and Ngata the bereavements produced an ambiguity of feeling that at times almost destroyed their relationship. When Ngata was in extremis in later years — angry or intensely depressed — he too was to blame Waikato for causing the deaths. (At the opening of Raukawa meeting house in Otaki on 12 March 1936, for example, Ngata replied to a Waikato refusal to allow Koroki to enter the house under a carving of a woman with her thighs open: 'This is not the first time the Waikatos have aimed a blow at me; my wife and son died after the opening of Mahinarangi.')[22]

There was a further disappointment. Some time between March 1929 and the end of that year, 'the authorities'[‡] intervened and refused Te Puea permission to use Mahinarangi as a hospital. Times had changed from the days of makeshift shelters on the riverbank. Although Waikato health in general was not much better in 1929 than it had been in the previous decade, there was now a much stronger element of public control. Private hospitals had to be licensed, and to be licensed they had to meet criteria that Mahinarangi in its homely fashion could not. It was bitterly ironical to Te Puea that the alternative to first-class hospital facilities had to be no facilities. 'It was my turn to cry then,' she said. 'I had set my heart on a hospital.'[23] The unwillingness on the part of Waikatos to use Pakeha

---

† Accidents of this kind suggest that there may have been justification for the then government policy that overseas VIPs (such as royalty) were not to eat at Maori functions. According to Waikato, the Ngatas' infection was traced to watermelon from a Chinese market garden.

‡ The expression 'authorities' is Te Puea's own (see Roberts, p. 322). I assume she referred to the Health Department, but am unable to find a record of the decision. A newspaper story about the TPM tour of the East Coast, however, stated that the hospital project 'has the endorsement and support of the professional men of the Waikato district' (undated clipping, T.H.C.).

institutions persisted; and the public health authorities for their part did not try seriously to alter this situation. And so for another decade most Waikato Maori who needed hospital attention failed to receive it.†

Mahinarangi remained the focal point for Turangawaewae, however. It stood at the head of the marae proper. All major ceremonies were to be conducted in front of its porch and the bodies of leaders were to lie there in state before burial. Instead of becoming a hospital, the building was used as a reception hall, the major venue for the shelter and entertainment of distinguished visitors, and a museum for the relics of the Kingitanga that Te Puea considered appropriate for display. The interior was subsequently furnished in the style of a European living-room.‡ On rare occasions people were also invited to sleep there, but the bulk of visitors were to be accommodated in tents and other buildings on the marae.

The unfortunate sequels were not sufficient to turn back the clock, however; nor to erase the precedents that the Mahinarangi function had established. Waikato had held its first national hui; representatives from every tribe in the country had made their way to Turangawaewae. For a whole week abrasive and parochial topics like the injustice of the con-fiscations and the place of the kahui ariki in Maori life had been put aside in favour of a discussion of wider Maori problems and goals. And in addition to the Maori participants, the audience to these discussions had included at various times the Governor-General, a former Prime Minister, a future Prime Minister, the Minister of Native Affairs, senior officials of the Native Affairs Department and the Native Land Court, the Health Department's Director of Maori Hygiene and the first Maori bishop, F.A. Bennett of Te Arawa. The Labour Party representative was an intense Scotsman who pursued an active interest in Maori affairs from the time of the hui, Peter Fraser.

Te Puea had demonstrated to a broad section of New Zealand that they could come together fruitfully and without antagonism on a Waikato marae (and one of the purely practical advantages of Turangawaewae that she was conscious of from this time was that, unlike most Maori gathering places of traditional significance, its proximity to the main trunk railway line made it easily accessible).

She had also given Waikato a taste of the benefits to be gained by

---

† A change in attitude on the part of hospital authorities was apparent only after the appointment of Dr H.B. Turbott as Medical Officer of Health in Hamilton in 1936.
‡ Furnishings and fittings for Mahinarangi and (later) the companion house Turongo were paid for from the moni ika — the whitebait tribute; the floor covering in the meeting house was referred to subsequently as 'the whitebait carpet'.

initiating careful, controlled relationships with people and institutions outside the Kingitanga. In particular, she had shown them a group — Ngati Porou — who had sought economic security through participation in Pakeha systems of education and administration. And there was the miracle of Mahinarangi itself, raised from nothing in a matter of months as a result of outside help. It stood not simply as a venue capable of drawing together Maori from all over the country, but also as the first house built in Waikato in modern times that displayed to an elaborate degree the living Maori skills of carving and interior decoration. And much of this decoration had been executed in distinctively Waikato themes not seen in the district since the nineteenth century.

Te Puea and Waikato were now — and were to remain — part of the national network of government, public service and inter-tribal consultation; all parties had had an opportunity to view one another at first hand. The realisation of this achievement laid the foundation for the next stage of Waikato development: a return to economic security through farming.

9

Back to the land

On 23 September 1929, surrounded by fifteen of her children, Te Puea knelt by a pile of turned earth at Waipipi near Waiuku. She scooped up soil in both hands and held it up, saying as she did: 'Give us the strength to build what we have come to build, give us your blessing on our work.' The invocation, Pai Marire fashion, was to ancestors; the work the conversion of a block of neglected land into a dairy farm. Thinking of those ancestors, particularly Tawhiao who had been a former owner of the block, Te Puea began to cry. And her workers standing around her with bowed heads wept too.[1]

At one level Te Puea's identification with the land could be described as mystical. Speaking to Judge Acheson in 1939 she said, 'The land is our mother and father. It is the loving parent who nourishes us, sustains us . . . When we die it folds us in its arms.'[2] But she also had a highly practical view. She was fond of quoting the proverb 'with one cultivation a man dies, with two he lives.'[3] In production, land could feed those who worked on it and earn a surplus to support tribal activities. Most important, it could do this in circumstances that allowed Maori to remain in their rural tribal home, close to family marae and sources of culture. It offered a means of retaining a lifestyle that emphasised Maori values, and selecting from a position of strength which aspects of European life the Maori wanted to accept and which to reject.

By contrast the communities of struggling subsistence farmers and displaced seasonal labourers that composed Waikato Maori society in the 1920s were unrelievedly vulnerable to cultural and economic depression. Gordon Coates had said in Parliament in 1928 that many Waikato were 'living on small areas, completely cramped; and they have no real kainga to go to at all. They travel from one end of the country to the other working at flax-mills, roadmaking, draining, and so on; but they have no real home and

Te Puea's love of children is apparent in this photograph with Hoturoa, the Tainui name she gave to Michael Ramsden. Turongo House

very few places where they can get together and settle as a people.'[4] By 1929, with the onset of the Great Depression, many of the itinerant labourers had been forced back to their home settlements where there was no income-producing work and little to sustain them. 'A very large per centage [sic] fills the ranks of the unemployed,' Tukere Te Anga reported. They were 'a menace and a burden to those who are only able to obtain a bare existence [from the land].'[5]

It was because of this vulnerability that Te Puea had asked Coates in 1928 for land close to Turangawaewae and money to lift it into production. Without this resource, Te Puea's work would come to a standstill: she would not be able to obtain final security for the inhabitants of the pa, nor could she extend her programme of Kingitanga activities into other Waikato communities suffering from listlessness and shifting populations.

Many of these other communities were not landless. Outside the con-fiscation area, especially in the west and north-west of the district, the tribes who had been loyalist in the 1860s had retained inherited land. And along the western riverbank between Raungawari and Huntly the kahui ariki held properties that had been gifted to them or bought with Mahuta's money by Hori Paki after the turn of the century. The problem for people on these properties was the perennial one: little of the land was in production, most of it was overgrown to the point where considerable expenditure of money and energy was needed to clear it; and up to the late 1920s no government had been prepared to make loan finance available to Maori owners for this purpose.

There was a further factor that influenced Te Puea. She believed strongly that working on the land was in itself a healthy way of life. 'Think of the fresh air and the clean living,' she wrote to Ramsden. 'On a farm when one is busy there is not time for mischief. All one's time is occupied with work. What is more, one is one's own boss.'[6] She had enjoyed the time spent between 1910 and 1920 working on the farm at Raungawari; the period of hard physical labour there had apparently driven her tuberculosis into remission and improved her general health. She believed in the dignity of manual labour.[7] And another proverb she quoted frequently to her workers was: 'Food gathered by others merely tickles the throat, that grown by one's own effort provides satisfaction.'[8]†

---

† Te Puea believed the most worthy features of Maori thought and values were contained in traditional proverbs; she regarded it as a parental responsibility to make her orphans familiar with them as part of their Maori eduction.

Coates' and Ngata's plans for Maori land development had shown Te Puea a way to re-establish Waikato Maori on the land with renewed access to all these advantages (they had farmed on a large scale prior to the war of 1863). The relevant legislation was passed in November 1929. The Native Land Amendment and Native Land Claims Adjustment Act authorised the Minister of Native Affairs to advance money for 'the better settlement and more effective utilisation of Native Land . . . and the encouragement of Natives in the promotion of agricultural pursuits and of efforts of industry and self-help.'[9] The Minister was empowered to gazette land for development with or without the owners' consent, charge it with expenditure, and advance up to three-fifths of its value in loans. The loans would be allocated through local Native Land Boards, who would also be responsible for administering the scheme. The money would allow clearing and development and would be paid for from subsequent agricultural production. In cases where Maori non-owners carried out the development, they too would be paid and given an option to lease or buy the land when it became debt-free.

This legislation was a major innovation in New Zealand public life. It was the first time Parliament had agreed to make money available for this purpose to Maori owners (although Europeans could be advanced loans of up to ninety percent of the estimated value of their properties). It was the measure for which leaders like Mahuta and Ngata had been calling since the early years of the century. Its passage in 1929 was due largely to the sympathy and personal efforts of Coates and Ngata. But one commentator has suggested that a further reason was the strong fear that the Maori would become a major financial burden on the tax-payer, particularly in time of depression. 'A small expense incurred in 1929 would save the Government from any future large-scale outlays for unemployed Maori,' William Worger has written.[10] In addition, Ngata's scheme offered a means by which insolvent Maori owners could settle outstanding debts for rates and survey charges, 'an issue which antagonised all Pakeha ratepayers'.[11]

To Te Puea's disappointment, Ngata was unable to secure land under the scheme close to Turangawaewae as Coates had originally promised. He offered her a 200-acre block at Horohoro near Rotorua, which she turned down because it was outside Waikato. Then Te Puea heard through her sister Hera† that the owners of blocks at Onewhero and at Waipipi near

---

† Hera had first married Tungia Te Ao of Otaki; on his death she married his father, Hema Te Ao; when Hema joined Ratana in the early 1920s Hera returned to Waikato, married Whetu Kingi, and lived near Waiuku.

Waiuku in the north-west corner of Waikato were interested in the scheme. The 284-acre Waipipi block was under threat of seizure by the Franklin County Council for non-payment of rates. Te Puea persuaded Ngata to gazette both areas and, with the consent of the owners, she decided to work at Waipipi.[12]

On 19 September 1929, she left Turangawaewae in the hands of the community's elders. Although she was to return there regularly, especially for the organisation of hui, she did not live there again continuously for another ten years, when she was able to buy a farm adjacent to the pa. She took with her to Waipipi fifteen of her children, initially all able-bodied adults under thirty-five. They were to sleep at Tahuna Pa until houses were built at Waipipi itself; then they were to be joined by dependents.

The group worked under the direction of Patrick Barry, appointed Pakeha supervisor under the terms of the scheme's legislation. From the first day members threw themselves into the job. The men collected timber and began to build dwellings; the women, led by Te Puea, cut gorse, blackberry and akeake, and collected kauri gum turned up by the plough.[13] Six of the males went on to the official pay-roll at six shillings a day. One sent his share back to Turangawaewae for his wife and children; the rest supported the fifteen members of the work party. These wages were used, Te Puea noted, to buy 'food, petrol, working clothes, medicine and cigarettes'. It was a commonly-agreed, cooperative arrangement. 'We were all of one accord.'[14] Barry, of course, was paid separately and travelled back and forth each day from Waiuku.

By 10 October a communal sleeping house and a building for cooking and eating had been completed and the workers moved on to the Waipipi site. The project's single tractor, looked after by Tumokai, had begun to plough. Te Puea recorded the daily routine (and quoted it from her diary five years later to the Royal Commission on Native Affairs):

> Two of the girls would get up at four in the morning to . . . cook breakfast and heat the water for washing. Then all the rest would get up at five o'clock. At six we began work and did not stop until seven each night . . . When it rained, the children's clothes dried on their backs because they did not want to stop for anything . . . [At night] we were impatient for daybreak so that work could continue.[15]

Their progress was such that, to Ngata's mind, it thoroughly justified the concept and practicality of the scheme. In less than three months they had cleared and ploughed 280 acres. The Minister believed it was a better result than a comparable group of Pakeha workers could have achieved.[16] In Parliament, he was to describe the performance as 'an illustration of the working-bee or ohu operating under an energetic hereditary chieftainess who spared neither herself nor her people in the sphere of productive effort.'[17] As an immediate gesture of appreciation he arranged for the group to be paid a bonus and given a fortnight's holiday.[18]

In December Ngata persuaded Te Puea to move to the adjacent Tahuna block with twenty-one workers (she left six at Waipipi, initially to disc and harrow the land and subsequently to milk the dairy herd established there). Tahuna was a problem. It belonged to the descendants of Henare Kaihau, although Te Puea believed Kaihau had only held it in trust for Tawhiao. Since the politician's death in 1919 it had deteriorated rapidly. The family had been unable to pay rates and they had refused an opportunity to work the land themselves under Ngata's scheme.[19] Ngata told Te Puea she was the only person who was capable of clearing the land within the funds available, and consequently of saving it from European ownership.

He also held out an attractive prospect: 'If you can satisfy the Government's requirement within ten years [that is, get the land into production and clear the debt], you will be able to lease the land for the following thirty years. If the owners wish to sell, you will have first right of purchase. If they want the land back, they will have to pay you for improvements.'[20]

Te Puea did not finally agree to the proposal until she was approached the same month by a group of Tahuna Pa residents who were anxious about the prospect of the land being taken by the council. At that point she moved on to the 300-acre block and she began work there on 2 January 1930. It was a situation that contained seeds of future conflict. The Kaihaus had not forgiven Te Puea for unseating their father from Parliament twenty years before; Henare's widow Maewa was still living at Tahuna, as was his sister. Te Puea noted: 'We worked until eight at night. I waited in vain for the people to whom this land belonged to come and help us clear it, but none came. I also asked Kaihau's daughters to come and cook for us so that we could all be free to work. But they didn't come.'[21] The Tahuna residents were not enamoured with the ohu concept.

Nor were the Kaihaus the only people to hesitate about involvement in the scheme. Te Puea's early and wholehearted acceptance was far from signalling the acceptance of Tainui people as a whole. Among the elderly in 1930, there was still strong suspicion of involvement with a government whose predecessors had appeared to persecute the Kingitanga. This suspicion had increased rather than diminished with the building of Mahinarangi. That was believed in die-hard circles simply to have brought the enemy closer. This section of Waikato opinion had dubbed Te Puea 'Mrs Kawanatanga' — Mrs Government. The term was more insulting than the English translation suggests; it implied that she had sold herself and Waikato — prostituted both — for government money. Few people dared use the expression to her face. It was not simply that she was a person of rank and mana, but also that her quick wit and devastating tongue always got the better of an adversary in a verbal exchange (which was a reason Ramsden was keen to see her in Parliament).

One person who took the risk was Te Wharua Herewini. It was ill-judged. His family had marched with and been paid by the Imperial troops at the battle of Rangiriri, which had inflicted the first defeat on Tawhiao and his followers in 1863. As Te Puea and Tumokai walked on to Waahi Marae for a hui, Herewini threw himself on the ground in front of them and began to whine at Te Puea. 'Mrs Kawanatanga, Mrs Kawanatanga, gimmee gimmee gimmee some.' 'What are you talking about?' Te Puea asked him. 'Come on,' the old man said. 'You've made lots of money. You've sold yourself and Waikato to the Government. Now give me some.' 'What?' said Te Puea. 'Has all your Rangiriri money run out?' And that ended the exchange.[22]

It was not until Te Rata and his brothers Tumate, Tonga and Te Rauangaanga entered the scheme in 1931 and 1932 that die-hard objections were finally laid.[†] As Tukere Te Anga had warned Ngata in 1929, 'with the older folk, all land matters . . . are wrapped up in the King Movement. Nothing is done to or with their lands on their own initiative, but every act must be sanctioned by the King, for in their point of view, all lands are voluntarily vested in [him].'[23] When the King took no initiative, it was impossible for individuals — even Te Puea — to persuade Waikato as a whole to act; once Te Rata was in the scheme, however, it went ahead in leaps. Ngata reported to Buck in March 1932 that Waikato were 'throwing blocks into the scheme faster than we can take them'.[24]

Even when doubts lingered, Te Rata was to persist in trying to change opponents' minds. He and Tonga made trips to Kawhia in February and March 1932 until owners there agreed to place land under the scheme; at another meeting at Tahuna in March, Te Rata advised his people to 'go into the scheme and . . . not to sleep but to follow [Te Puea's] way of working.'[25] By 1933 the King and his brothers were working 600 acres among them and

---

† Land vested in Mahuta's name had been divided among his sons at his death, an action that was to cause some controversy in later years, but which enabled each son to build up and support a personal following from his own property.

when Te Rata died late that year, Ngata described him as 'the greatest champion of land settlement among the tribes'.[26] He had become this as a result of Te Puea's example and encouragement.

When Eric Ramsden visited Te Puea at Tahuna in January 1932,[†] she was the salaried supervisor for three projects in the immediate area embracing nearly 5000 acres and supporting several hundred people. (Barry, the Pakeha supervisor, had been dismissed by Ngata in 1930.) The workers had brought in their dependants as the scheme progressed. At Tahuna itself, where Te Puea lived in a house built by Tumokai, there were six families including 35 children. Her other blocks were Waipipi and Onewhero, each with their own communities, and the latter included Opuatia, Koheroa and Waikarakia.

Ramsden was impressed at how comfortably everybody on the scheme was living through the Depression; but at the same time at how cheaply everything had been done. Some of the houses, including Te Puea's, were made of timber. Others had dirt floors, raupo walls and corrugated iron roofs. 'They were well lighted and ventilated. Each hut is about 20 feet by 14 feet, and the cost has not exceeded 10 or 11 pounds,' he noted. The main reason for the economies was that 'the people have built their own . . . No European carpenters or architects. All the work . . . is done by the Maoris — also draining and the laying of water pipes. They erected their own windmills and some of them dug their own wells, using the services of water diviners.'[27]

Because only a small percentage of the workers were being paid, the community spent as little as possible on food. One of the reasons Te Puea had chosen to go to Tahuna was its proximity to the sea and seafood.[28] She was constantly supplementing groceries and meat with fish, shellfish, eel, and wild and home-grown vegetables. 'The cost for . . . food and groceries at each settlement . . . is considerably under five pounds a month,' Ramsden wrote. Twice a month four pig's heads and eight soup bones for each settlement were brought from Auckland as delicacies.[29]

Te Puea was always looking for ways to bring in additional money for other essentials. 'I send the wives and children to pick ferns,' she told Ramsden. 'The ferns are sent to Auckland for sale. With the money we buy old clothes. Sometimes I get four sacks . . . at a time. I make the women wash them in hot water. When the clothes are dry I show them how to patch

† Ramsden had been working for the *Sydney Morning Herald* since 1929 and was not to return to New Zealand permanently until 1942, when he moved to Christchurch.

Te Puea and her friend Eric Ramsden. Turongo House

all the holes, also how to press them. Later on, when the people get on their feet, they can buy satin and silk if they like, also a castle in which to entertain.'[30] And, on another occasion, 'I have made many pairs of pants for the small boys out of sugar bags. They are very warm.'[31]†

Resources were always stretched at this time. But Te Puea never hesitated to offer hospitality to other people displaced by the Depression

† Te Puea's energy and powers of improvisation were to rebound on her. When she asked the Government for relief work in Waikato in 1934, she was told that the Maori did not need such assistance as much as the Pakeha (Te Puea to Eric Ramsden, 11/8/34. R.P.). The Member of Parliament for Western Maori (who had succeeded Pomare in 1930), Taite Te Tomo, went so far as to state that the Maori could get by on half a loaf of bread in circumstances where the European needed a whole one. From that time on he was known in Waikato as 'Half-a-Loaf Te Tomo' (interview Pei Jones).

(which had been one of the factors leading to abrasion with Patrick Barry, the first supervisor). While she was dictating letters to Ramsden at Tahuna, a European walked past the open front door. 'A few minutes later Te Puea rose and left the room. She came back and we resumed our work. Some time afterwards I had occasion to enter the main portion of the house for some typing paper. Seated at the table in the kitchen I saw the Pakeha who had passed the door. I spoke to him. The man was hungry and obviously thirsty. "I only asked for a little water," he said. "And see what these people have given me? . . . They are very generous. Surely they must be wealthy Maoris?" "No," I replied, "they are anything but" . . . "Well," he said, "I would never have been treated like this by Europeans." ' Later Te Puea took the man further on his way to Waiuku in the car with which Ngata had provided her for her supervisory duties (she travelled each day among the scheme's settlements).[32]

The success of the scheme — the fact that it enabled Maori to subsist with dignity and even comfort during Depression years and established security of work and income for the future — never failed to astonish Te Puea. It was a constant source of gratitude. And most of that gratitude she directed at Ngata who, in her eyes, had made possible the impossible. The Minister was, she told Ramsden, 'a wonderful man: he is the only Maori member in the house who has ever done real good for the Maori. Let us hope he will live long to lead the people to a better way of living.'[33] And to Ngata himself she wrote: 'Thanks and appreciation . . . generosity has been showered on me.'[34] Her letters to him from 1929 to 1934 are full of affection and respect. Their differences and minor mutual irritations arising from tribal loyalties and the aftermath of the Mahinarangi opening[†] were submerged in the knowledge that each needed the other; and that mutual need generated feelings of commitment and love. She addressed him as 'e Pa' — father — and signed her letters 'from your daughter' or 'from your sister'; he signed his 'from your loving parent' and 'from your father'.[35]

Ngata used Te Puea's success to entice other tribes into the scheme. In talks all round the country and in the reception of deputations at his office in Parliament he frequently recommended doubtful leaders from other districts to visit Waikato and see the benefits for themselves. Many did so. He also persuaded Te Puea and Tumokai to go into Arawa territory from 1932 to 1936 to work on the Tikitere block near Rotorua. The major purpose was to demonstrate to the locals that hard work on unpromising land could

† See page 152.

Tumokai and Te Puea outside their home on the land development
scheme at Tahuna near Waiuku. Turongo House

produce spectacularly successful results.[36] Tumokai went there permanently from 1932, while Te Puea moved between there and the Waikato schemes where, until 1935, she remained a supervisor.

In addition, Ngata sent Cabinet colleagues like Prime Minister George Forbes[†] and Industries and Commerce Minister Robert Masters to inspect Te Puea's model projects and sample her charm and hospitality. Forbes visited Tahuna in September 1932 and, according to Te Puea, 'could not believe that we had accomplished so much . . . It was, he said, a lesson to the Pakeha people.' She noted too that Europeans in Waiuku were 'jealous' that he had gone to see Maori but not Pakeha.[37] The Prime Minister also visited her early in 1934 at Tikitere. There she sat him on a benzine tin (there was no other furniture in the project huts), gave him a cup of tea, and persuaded him to overrule a supervisor's order that had forbidden her girls to collect and sell gum they found as they cleared gorse.[38]

The scheme had its conflicts and strains, however. The most fundamental one was probably inevitable. It arose from differences in the concept of the scheme. Maori — including Ngata and Te Puea — saw it as a way of enabling Maori to retain a communal life based on Maori values; public servants and parliamentarians viewed it far more as a way of teaching Maori to farm in a business-like fashion so they would not be a drain on the public purse,[39] and of ensuring that land was exploited for primary production as efficiently as possible.[40] To these latter people, Ngata's operation of the schemes had resulted in expenditure that was extravagant and wasteful.[41]

In addition, Ngata's methods of administration came under increasing fire from the press, the public service, and eventually his own colleagues. He had a self-confessed distaste for 'red tape'. He described his term of office as 'signified by the adoption of expedients that cut across service regulations . . . [and] all regulations that do not fit the case of Maori tribes cultivating their lands in the manner best suited to their genius and under leaders of their own kin and blood. The regulations were never framed for such circumstances.'[42] So, frequently, he did not keep conventional records of instructions, conversations and minor expenditure; he relied more heavily on the telephone than on the stenographer; he used his discretion to make and unmake appointments outside public service procedures. Although a

---

† Forbes had become Prime Minister on Ward's death in 1930 and from 1931 led a Coalition Government of United and Reform members. Labour became the official Opposition.

Te Puea entertains Australian visitors in front of one of the land development houses built from timber and raupo in order to conserve money. ATL

minister in a Pakeha government, he sought to function in a manner he regarded as appropriate for Maori circumstances. And this resulted in his downfall.

Political dissatisfaction with Ngata's administration led to an investigation of his department in 1934 by the Royal Commission on Native Affairs; and the commission's report led to his resignation in December of that year. The Minister was found guilty of irregularities in expenditure and negligence in administration; but no major scandals were unearthed.[43] His land development projects up to 1934 had involved the expenditure of just over £500,000, most of which was recoverable.[44] But as William Worger has pointed out, £7 million had been written off on the soldier settlement scheme in 1929 without anything verging on the outcry that greeted Ngata's record as revealed by the Royal Commission. (Labour's Robert Semple, for example, said the commission's report revealed 'one of the worst specimens of abuse of political power, of maladministration, and the misappropriation of public funds, and the greatest betrayal of trust ever reported to this House or any other Parliament in the British Empire.'[45]) It was unfortunate for Ngata that the investigation occurred at a time when the Opposition was in full cry and seizing any stick with which to beat the Government. There is evidence that some Labour spokesmen later regretted their handling of the affair.[46]

One matter on which the commission found Ngata negligent was his dismissal in 1930 of Te Puea's supervisor, Patrick Barry. Barry and Te Puea had had a progressively abrasive and deteriorating relationship. Her evidence to the commission records a long list of disagreements that culminated in Te Puea walking off the Tahuna scheme on 5 November 1930 because Barry had given a gorse-cutting contract to European workers instead of to her own.[47] She returned to Ngaruawahia and rang Ngata; Ngata suspended Barry from the scheme and he was subsequently sacked by the Public Service Commissioner. The Minister had no hesitation about his action. He reported to the Public Accounts Committee that in any conflict between Te Puea and a supervisor, 'I have no doubt that she would have won.' It was up to the supervisor to fit in with the local community, he said; otherwise the scheme would not work.[48]

In his own evidence to the commission, Barry took the view that he was trying to run the scheme on sound business lines while Te Puea was trying to turn it into a welfare operation. The commission accepted this analysis and said, with justification, that the two concepts were incompatible in terms of controlling legislation. If they were to be reconciled, it would have to be under some form of administration.

Such a conclusion, however, is beside the point. The specific evidence laid before the commission, most of it detailed and dated from Te Puea's diary, shows that the sources of conflict only rarely involved the concepts defined by Barry.† Most often they were matters of administration (failing to reimburse Maori workers for legitimate expenses); professional judgment (whether swampland should be ploughed, where to lay fence lines);

---

† Te Puea gave meticulously detailed evidence to the commission in Auckland for 1¾ hours on 28 April 1934. She said the members 'were very good to me'. The official record of her evidence is missing from the commission files in the National Archives; but her hand-written notes prepared at Waiuku (Tahuna) survived in the Mick Jones papers (see notes on sources).

discipline (whether workers should be allowed to smoke on the job or offer visitors cups of tea); and simply personality clashes. The evidence suggests most strongly that Barry was temperamentally unsuited to work with a group of other workers who already had close-knit loyalties.

Where the concepts of business venture versus welfare project did arise, Barry showed himself to be confusingly inconsistent. He was willing to use voluntary labour where it cut costs (as in the case of accepting fence posts from the Tuakau people in 1929); but he was inflexible about not allowing such helpers to be fed from project funds.[49]

It is difficult to avoid the conclusion that commission members latched on to the Barry/Te Puea dispute as an illustration of their theme that Maori social objectives were incompatible with legislative and public service procedures. Apart from appearing unfair in retrospect as a general conclusion, it was also not a conclusion applicable to Barry's performance. Another supervisor with more sympathy and flexibility could probably have worked compatibly with Te Puea; and as Ngata himself believed, the scheme was most likely to proceed smoothly with Te Puea herself as supervisor and he appointed her accordingly.

The commission's report and Ngata's resignation shocked Maori opinion. Both were seen as the result of an attack on the Maori people as a whole. This conclusion seemed justified by comments like that of the Member of Parliament for Wellington Suburbs, R. A. Wright, who said that a 'native' should never again become Minister of Native Affairs.[50] Te Puea told Ramsden that Pakeha had turned against Ngata and it was a miracle that he was not driven insane.[51]

Ngata's demise did not mean the scuttling of the land development projects, however. On the contrary, they were extended and consolidated by subsequent governments and Ministers of Native (later 'Maori') Affairs. No witnesses before the 1934 commission believed that the schemes would not be an economic success. In 1936 the new Labour Government was to spend £200,000 on it, twice as much as allocated in any one year of Ngata's term of office. And the number of people dependent on the scheme rose in the same period from under 11,000 to nearly 18,000.[52] The total acreage gazetted in Waikato-Maniapoto territory alone in 1936 was 44,456.[53] Labour not only forgot the vicious attacks it launched on the concept of the scheme in 1934; a later Minister of Native Affairs, Frank Langstone, was to speak as if his party alone was responsible for its conception and success.[54]

Te Puea's enthusiasm waxed and waned almost daily according to her moods, her health, and the way she felt she was being treated by politicians and public servants. But her fundamental attitude remained one of optimism.[55] 'I would prefer that the sweat of my brow should fall on my own lands than the lands of strangers,' she told Ramsden. 'The people are kept from idleness and drink. It has given them fresh heart to face life under these new conditions, and I feel that a new day has dawned for Waikato.'[56]

Her subsequent regrets were that wages on the scheme did not rise as fast as she believed they should;[57] and that after a decade of hard labour she lost the Tahuna block to the Kaihaus. As she had feared they would, the family simply bided their time until the agreed ten-year period of development was completed. Then they refused to allow Te Puea the forty-two-year lease that she sought. Instead, she received a mere £1100 for improvements and was forced to vacate the house and property in November 1940.[58] She and Tumokai were fiercely embittered by the decision, worked out by lawyers for the respective parties and the Native Land Court. The single consoling factor was that the same month, November 1940, she was able to buy the Paterson property at Ngaruawahia for £7000.[59] This allowed her to fulfil her earlier dream of farming alongside Turangawaewae and providing work and food for its inhabitants.[†] Participants in the earlier project became (like Tae and Rangitaua Tapara) owners of their own farms, obtained leases on the blocks of other owners, or moved on to entirely new developments.

More than anything else, Ngata's scheme had illustrated the complementary character — symbiotic, even — of two forms of Maori leadership. There had to be a Ngata in the House to take an overall view of what was good for his people and to acquire sufficient expertise to bend the European-based system of legislation and administration towards Maori needs. On the other hand, kotahitanga remained an ideal: tribalism was the reality. Ngata exercised little influence on community life outside Ngati Porou. He needed leaders of local and regional standing like Te Puea — partly so he could sell and consequently implement his projects; and partly to convince Cabinet colleagues and an army of cautious and sometimes obstructive civil servants that what was desirable for the Maori was also practicable. Te Puea, and her performance within her own projects, constituted a shop window with which other Maori were enticed into the scheme and European systems of authority persuaded to support them.

† See page 223.

10

Tohunga and parsons

Land development work was interrupted by Te Rata's death on 1 October 1933. Te Puea was distraught. 'God! how I miss him . . . He was the only one that I loved and worked for,' she wrote to Ramsden. 'Because he was my King, a King in name only, a King with a broken Kingdom, and I was his only support. We were such real friends. There was nothing between us. We knew each other's thoughts, each other's secrets. Now it is all over.'[1]

Her grief was especially acute because she had not been with him at the end. Te Rata had called for her at midnight the previous night. But there were no telephone lines open from Waahi. It was nine o'clock in the morning before Te Puea received the message at Rotorua. Then, Tumokai discovered, there was not enough petrol in the car to get them to Waikato. It was Sunday and he had to drive nineteen miles before he found a pump. By the time they left it was midday, and 2 p.m. when they reached Huntly.

'I could see that there was something wrong. I saw all the women on the ground: they were holding their hands to their heads and rolling about.' Te Rata had died at 12.30. 'His last word was for me. He kept calling me and asking all the time. At the last moment he just closed his eyes.'[2]

In the inter-tribal discussion that followed, Te Puea's name was proposed for the kingship.[3] But she would have none of it. It was partly a distaste for women in figurehead positions, and partly because she believed she had received a sign that Koroki, Te Rata's eldest son, was the rightful heir to the title.

At first she had had strong reservations about Koroki. He was young (twenty-four years old), shy and weak. His younger brother Tonga had been regarded as a far more promising candidate for leadership. But he had been sent to Wesley College at Paerata and had died there. Te Rata's brother Tumate was a possibility, as was Tawhiao's son, Haunui. But Haunui's candidacy was anathema to Te Puea because of his Ratana connection. While she was worrying over these considerations she had a dream: 'Te Rata came to me with a child in his hand.[†] I could not see the child's face. The child wanted to cling to Te Rata. But Te Rata urged him towards me. I knew what he meant . . . Koroki was to be the next King.'[4]

The dream decided the question. The next morning she overruled Koroki's own reservations (he had told her he was not fit for the job and that Waikato had 'no land to support a king'[5]) and she presented him to the deliberating elders at the tangi as the only direct descendant of all four previous Kings and therefore the only candidate.[6] Then she took charge: 'I have dressed the boy from head to foot to fit him for his place . . . I have settled all his father's accounts, including electric light and telephone, so that he will have a clean start. I have also banked £100 for him.'[7]

Te Puea's intervention carried the day. From the time of conscription and the return of Pai Marire she had been looked to by her followers as a vehicle for communication from the world of spirits. Part of this reputation as seer rested on her appearance. One of the expressions most frequently used to describe her was that she had 'tohunga eyes'.[8] Judge Acheson wrote about their 'mystical quality. At times one gains the impression of unfathomed depths. At others of [heights] as yet unscaled.'[9]

It was more than appearance, however. Te Puea's beliefs arose from a cosmology that was especially that of the pre-European Maori, but which was infused with other deities, especially the God of the Bible, and which was articulated through Pai Marire concepts and rituals. These beliefs were not the subjects of metaphysical speculation; for Te Puea and her followers they were reinforced by daily experiences. And the most dramatic of these involved communication with the dead, evidence of a mauri or life-force in places and things, matakite or second-sight, and ways of curing some forms of sickness.

The basis for these beliefs is perhaps best understood by a consideration of documented events that illustrate them. While the occasions quoted are separated in years, they are closely related as expressions of what was for her a connected view of life.

The first involves a group of incidents that occurred in February 1929 when Te Puea and Tumokai were on holiday at Ahipara in Northland. Because of

---

† In Ramsden's first draft of this account he wrote that it was Mahuta who led Koroki. A correction in Te Puea's handwriting changed this to Te Rata.

Te Puea and Tumokai and two of their girls, Papi Pokaia and
Tungia Te Ao, en route for a holiday in North Auckland. Turongo House

their proximity to Te Rerenga Wairua[†] — the Leaping-Off Place of Spirits —
they decided to make a trip to this waahi tapu that every Maori had heard
about from childhood. They went by car with Te Puea's cousin, Tukere Te
Anga, her adopted daughter Papi, her niece Tungia, and a Ngapuhi guide
from Te Paki Station. It was a clear, hot afternoon and the party was excited.
The area was regarded as the most tapu in the country because of the
traditional belief that the spirits of the Maori dead converged there.

They left the car at Pandora Camp and walked to the cape, which zigzags
into the sea in a series of three diminishing crests. Te Puea began to recite her
Pai Marire chants as they came down the first hill (called 'Herangi' in early
Ngapuhi traditions); this was, she said, to 'open up the channels'.[10] She and
Tumokai were at first surprised and then disturbed that the Ngapuhi guide
showed no respect for the mauri of the place. When he reached the ledge
below the pohutukawa roots down which the spirits were believed to slide, he
prised oysters off the rocks and began to eat them. Te Puea meanwhile had
made the rest of the party leave food and tobacco some distance away.

---

† The most commonly used Maori name for Cape Reinga, a little east of the northernmost
part of the North Island; in Maori mythology the spirits of the dead converge at this point to
pass from terrestrial life to the Underworld by sliding down a pohutukawa root into a
seaweed-covered hole called Maurianuku.

On the rocks they examined Maurianuku, the hole that was reputed to swallow the spirits into the Underworld. The tide was low and they were able to stand right on the brim, looking down into a mass of kelp tentacles. Te Puea felt uneasy after several minutes and returned to the bank above. The others followed except for Tumokai, who went on staring into the hole as if hypnotised. The water level dropped suddenly and Te Puea had a premonition of tragedy; she screamed to Tumokai who turned away from the hole and began to walk towards them. As he did, a breaker rose out of the sea and swept over the ledge at chest height. The kelp came with it and tangled around Tumokai's legs, almost dragging him into the hole as the sea fell away. He reached the bank as a second wave, even larger, swept the ledge. He was convinced afterwards that he would have been carried into the sea had Te Puea not called out.

Nor was that an end to difficulties. A fog that rolled out of the spring Te Waiora-a-Tane enveloped them on their way back to Pandora Camp and they lost their way. By the time it lifted the sun had set and the guide — who knew the area 'like the back of his hand' — became lost a second time. Finally, unable to speak and with eyes wide with shock, he appeared to become paralysed. Te Puea took his arm and it was she who guided the group back to the camp in the dark, although she had never been there before that day.[11]

Six years later, in 1935 and 1936, Te Puea's health was deteriorating rapidly. She collapsed on several occasions and was bedridden for weeks at a time, usually in an enclosed porch-bedroom made up for her at the front of Kimikimi Hall. Her tuberculosis had reappeared; she had bouts of coughing and three bad haemorrhages; her heart was behaving erratically; and her weight had dropped to seven stone by August 1936. She seemed to be wasting away. Almost overnight, her hair had turned grey. Everybody who saw her believed that she was dying, as did Te Puea herself. 'I do not think I will last long,' she told Ramsden. 'But I will never tell [Tumokai] . . . there is so much to do.'[12]

In mid-1936 Dr Douglas Martin sent her to the Mater Misericordiae Hospital in Auckland for X-rays. One lung had enormous cavities, the other was infected. Dr E. B. Gunson, relating his examination to the information supplied by Dr Martin, sent her back to Ngaruawahia with instructions that she was to rest completely.[13] Before leaving Auckland, however, Te Puea insisted on having a series of formal photographic portraits taken 'for her tangi'.[14] She returned to Turangawaewae in preference to Tahuna because she believed the end was near. At the pa her health continued to decline.

The crisis came on 26 July. Late in the day she collapsed again and then fell into a heavy sleep that seemed like a coma. Momo Ewe, one of her orphans who now kept house for her and nursed her, was convinced she was close to death. Alex McKay was highly alarmed by the fact that she could not be roused and sent for Dr Martin. After four hours of unconsciousness she woke up suddenly and Martin examined her. 'He was dumbfounded. He said that her heart was 100 percent better and that the lung was better than two months ago.'[15] She made steady progress from that evening. A week later McKay was able to tell Ramsden: 'She has gone ahead in leaps and bounds. She eats wonderfully and sleeps from 10 p.m. to 7 a.m. without waking. I will some day tell you the cause of the recovery. I could not tell the doctor, he could only see the results.'[16]

The 'cause' of the recovery, as Te Puea related it to McKay and Tumokai, was that Mahuta and Tiahuia had come to her while she slept, told her she was not ready to die, and shared their spiritual strength with her. She woke with a conviction that she would recover completely (having believed for the previous twelve months that she was dying).[17] Apart from a temporary setback the following October, her progress was steady. A year later McKay was able to say, 'she is very well and continues to put on weight, almost 11 stone now.'[18] Subsequent X-rays showed a change that Dr Martin considered 'miraculous . . . the TB was completely dormant. There were still enormous cavities but they'd dried.'[19]†

In January 1941, Te Puea and Koroki decided to complete a task that Tawhiao had begun, that of reinterring all the remains of the kahui ariki on Taupiri Mountain. It involved shifting two sets of bones: those of Mahuta, contained in a vault at Hukanui in deference to Te Marae's wishes; and of a sixteen-year-old son of Tawhiao named Maungatautari who had been buried at Tapapa in 1884.‡

The case of Mahuta presented no difficulties other than obtaining Health Department permission for the exhumation. That of Maungatautari turned out to be more complicated because the Ngati Tukorehe people at Tapapa Pa who were the guardians of the body refused to give it up. The person most likely to be able to change their mind was Te Puea.

---

† When Dr Margaret McDowall examined Te Puea and had her X-rayed in 1951 she was unable to find any trace of tuberculosis.
‡ This identification of the body comes from Te Puea's diary entry for 25/1/41. In a letter to Ramsden, however (2/2/41), she refers to a child of Potatau.

On 25 January she drove to Hamilton with Tumokai and Peha Wharakura. She went straight to the office of Bunny Woodhams, manager of the department store H. and J. Court Ltd. From there she rang the Health Department to find out if her application to move the bodies had been approved. It had not; the office was still waiting for word from Wellington. So Te Puea had Woodhams place a call to Prime Minister Peter Fraser, who told her to go ahead.[20]

Before she left Court's, Te Puea asked Woodhams for a box. 'A box?' he said. 'What do you mean "a box"?' 'A box to put the bones in, silly.' Te Puea told him. Woodhams assumed she meant a coffin and was about to call Eric Scrimshaw, a local undertaker. But Te Puea stopped him. She only wanted one of the small Chinese camphorwood chests that the store sold for dowry boxes. With one of these strapped to the back of the car, the party headed for Tapapa where a resentful crowd was assembling to put up a fight.

The pa was the last before the Waikato boundary with Te Arawa territory and lay below the Mamaku hills.[†] The meeting house was filled with people by the time Te Puea arrived. After formal welcomes, the local spokesman Karauria Winika and Paora Te Iwiatua Te Karetai (Harry Paul) told Te Puea that the tribe was adamant: the bones were not to be moved. Winika said 'we had no right whatever to come and take the body of the boy from them because Tawhiao had left him there.[‡] They looked upon that body, he said, as their mana: it was tapu and rangatiratanga, and the only opportunity they had of keeping in touch with the Kingitanga. I felt sorry for them. It was a difficult situation. We had to be very diplomatic. It was not until four o'clock the next morning that they gave in.'[21]

The Tapapa people relented eventually because Te Puea changed her tactics. Peha told her they would never give in and he sympathised with their feelings. And so Te Puea, as she often did at a point of impasse or crisis, got to her feet and spoke herself. She said that in fact she did not want Maungatautari's bones alone, her wish was to see that all Waikato remains were transferred to Taupiri; Maungatautari's were just the first. At this point the Ngati Tukorehe audience, in consternation, broke into discussion among themselves. On the other hand, Te Puea continued after several minutes, if they gave up Maungatautari there and then she would drop the claim to the others. Winika agreed at once — he preferred to lose one body than to risk the kahui ariki taking all of them.[22]

---

† It was later moved to the main road to Rotorua, east of Fitzgerald's Glade.
‡ When he had decided to move other kahui ariki remains in 1894.

The participants in the debate slept until late the following day. Then they walked to the adjacent cemetery. 'As we approached,' Te Puea wrote afterwards, 'the rainbow was immediately above it.'[23] It was a good sign; Te Puea regarded it as the deity Uenuku and its appearance an indication of ancestral approval for what was about to happen.† Before entering the burial ground itself, everybody removed cigarettes and matches from their clothing. Among the locals there was disagreement about where the remains were. But Te Puea knew; she walked straight over to a mound surrounded by a shallow trench and said: 'There. You go so far and you'll come across totara bark.'[24] After Peha had led the group in prayers, the local men began to dig. Several feet down they struck rotting totara bark that encased a bundle of bones.‡

After checking with Waahi by telephone, Te Puea and her men headed back for Taupiri at 7.30 in the evening with Maungatautari's remains safely in the camphorwood chest. They arrived after nine o'clock and found a party of old people waiting to receive both bodies. There was still no sign of Mahuta's so she went on to Waahi to see what was happening. When she arrived a group of men stripped to the waist were carrying a lead coffin to the boat landing where the renovated war canoe Te Winika was waiting to carry the bones to Taupiri. From the old wooden coffin, falling to pieces, they also had to transfer walking sticks and hard-knocker hats sealed in the tomb with Mahuta.[25] Te Winika was paddled upstream with the precious cargo.

'That night belonged to us alone,' Te Puea wrote. 'There were at least 300 old men and women waiting to greet him. All Pakeha were fast asleep except two . . .* There were not the usual cries of the tangi, only sobbing. When we got to the top of Taupiri . . . [we] saw the star with the old Maori name Tukaiteuru.** We all felt the presence of the mana: we knew that our

---

† Rainbows had appeared at several points in Te Puea's life when she felt in need of reassurance. See also page 257.

‡ 'How could she know?' Te Uira Manihera asked subsequently when he related this story. 'Because she was guided.' (Interview August 1972.) This was the explanation generally accepted in Waikato. The occasion also had a precedent. Te Puea was told when she was living at Tahuna that a nearby farm contained Maori remains. She sent Alex McKay to the Pakeha owner to seek permission to move them; he knew nothing about them but said yes. Te Puea went to the area in question, about five acres, and zigzagged across it. Then she said to the boys with her, 'Dig here,' which they did; and a body was recovered. She repeated this four times (Alex McKay to Eric Ramsden, 6 August 1953. R.P.).

* They were Health Department officials. Te Puea noted: 'I made them stay to see that everything was conducted properly.'

** One of the stars that Tawhiao had identified as a deity.

tupunas had come back. It was a strange feeling. All the ferns around us seemed like human beings whispering to us. We were not frightened, only sad.'[26]

Mahuta's coffin was lowered into a twelve-foot hole and the box with Maungatautari's bones buried in an additional cavity underneath it. Dawn was breaking by the time the mourners left the mountain. And, Te Puea noted, 'there was Te Uenuku again: the rays of the rainbow covered the top of the hill.'[27]

It is not surprising that, as a result of these kinds of experiences, Te Puea's followers should believe she possessed and attracted spiritual powers. They had seen evidence with their own eyes; and what they saw was consistent with their Pai Marire view of life.

What is more surprising, perhaps, is that Europeans who became intimate friends with her also came to believe — after initial bouts of scepticism — that she was 'charged' in some way. Alex McKay, Judge F. O. V. Acheson, Henry Kelliher[†] and Eric Ramsden — all witnessed things in Te Puea's perception and behaviour that they were unable to explain in conventional terms, and that in some cases unnerved them. Eventually, they fell back on non-Maori explanations. Acheson wrote that Te Puea was 'decidedly psychic';[28] Kelliher that she was 'clairvoyant';[29] McKay that she was able to practise telepathy.[30] Kelliher's opinion grew largely out of Te Puea's visits to his home at Puketutu Island in the Manukau Harbour and her ability to tell him confidently about things that had happened there in the past. McKay has given examples of apparent telepathy that include a day he was gathering pipis with Koroki at Clevedon; Koroki said to him suddenly, 'We have to go back at once, the old lady wants me'; they returned to Ngaruawahia where Te Puea scolded them for being 'a long time in coming'.[31]

In Maori terms, however, Te Puea's experience only served to confirm what she believed as a member of the Pai Marire faith: the Te Rerenga Wairua incidents were a consequence of not acknowledging the mauri of the place; the recovery from illness a result of being able to share in ancestral qualities; the recovery of bones a manifestation of matakite.

The Pai Marire that Te Puea inherited in childhood and revived during World War One was a comfortable amalgamation of Christian and Hebrew

---

† Later Sir Henry Kelliher, the founder and chairman of Dominion Breweries to whom Te Puea went for financial and other advice in the 1940s.

beliefs developed by her grandfather Tawhiao and initially preached by him during his years of confinement to the King Country.[32] On the one hand, it supported the existence of the old Polynesian departmental gods — Tane, Rongo, Te Uenuku and so on. It also expressed a belief in atua, benevolent guardian spirits who took an interest in individuals and looked after their spiritual and physical well-being. In Te Puea's case, the atua was believed to be an owl that appeared and followed her at several crisis points in her life or spoke to her from trees at night with messages about threats, deaths or impending visits.[33] Taniwha in the Waikato and Waipa rivers were also invoked as guardians; as were certain stars which Tawhiao had designated as deities, like Tariao and Tukaiteuru; and deceased relatives and ancestors.

For Waikato, Pai Marire gave these specifically Maori beliefs a form and an expression, and the weight of historical validity. But Tawhiao had also been an assiduous reader and quoter of the Bible. Many of his maxims and proverbs were uplifted wholly from his Maori Bible or were echoed adaptations. He was especially fond of Old Testament verses: he identified personally with sections that confirmed the need for kings and divine approval of kingly authority; and like other nineteenth-century Maori prophets[†] he associated the physical and spiritual disinheritance of his people with the condition of the children of Abraham wandering in the wilderness, oppressed, seeking Messianic liberation.

Whether nineteenth-century Pai Marire adherents believed in a single cosmology that embraced Maori and Judaic-Christian gods is difficult to establish. Te Puea certainly did, and her followers believed Tawhiao had too. From the 1930s she and her Pai Marire elders were fond of saying that there was one god supreme over others: Io in the Maori tradition and Jehova in the Biblical; but they stressed that in addition to the supreme deity there were others and tribal ancestors who operated in subsidiary but none the less influential roles.

The worship of ancestors — the belief that there was no impenetrable barrier between life and death — was the most dominant principle of Pai Marire as practised in Waikato. It taught that death did not close a relationship, it merely transferred a person's spirit from one plane to another; it transformed that person from a living relative or friend into a 'living' tupuna or ancestor. Pai Marire prayers and chants invoked the dead as companions of the living. And Te Puea frequently 'consulted' Tiahuia and

---

† Te Ua Haumene, Aperehama Taonui, Te Kooti Rikirangi, Te Whiti o Rongomai, Tohu Kakahi; and later Tahupotiki Wiremu Ratana.

Mahuta. 'Daily they commune with us and we with them,' she told Judge Acheson.[34] Sometimes the communication was in simple prayer from her to them; at others it was from them to her, most often in dreams or dreamlike experiences. She believed these dead were able to pass on continuing aspects of their personal mauri, mana and tapu and thus strengthen and protect those who prayed to them.

The 'living with death' that was a characteristic of Pai Marire[†] also involved premonition. Sometimes Te Puea's intimations of mortality were wrong, particularly those anticipating her own death in the mid-1930s. But more often, according to her followers, they were correct.[35] She frequently felt and followed impulses to visit people within days of their death.[‡] The premonition that caused her most pain — and to which she alluded most often — was that she and Tumokai would lose Pirihia Katipa, their favourite adopted child in the 1930s.

At the time they had two girls living with them as daughters: Tipi Marokopa Tahuata from Taranaki,[*] and Pirihia whom they had taken in at birth. Pirihia charmed everybody as she grew up. Ramsden first made notes about her after a visit from Australia in 1934. He described her as 'a merry dark-eyed child, with black tresses almost to her waist . . . [She] prattled to me in Maori. When I did not answer sufficiently quickly, she would thump me with her small fists.'[36] Te Puea indulged her and allowed her to travel in the back seat of the car wrapped in a rug. But she was Tumokai's child more than anybody else's. He described her simply as 'my mate'. She would take his lunch to him on the farm most days; then she would often tell him to stop work because he looked tired, and to take her swimming instead.[37]

Te Puea's first hint of anxiety about Pirihia came in a letter to Ramsden in August 1933, when the child was three years old. A Pakeha woman who claimed to be a fortune teller had visited her at Rotorua. 'One thing she told me that distressed me very much — she said that a little girl I love is going to die . . . I wonder if Pirihia is meant? When I told Davy[**] about [it] he was

---

† It was also a characteristic of Maori life generally. As a consequence of poor health, the life expectancy for Maori was considerably lower than that for Europeans in New Zealand. The Maori death rate per 1000 of population in 1935 was 19.29, while that for the Pakeha was 8.22 (H.B. Turbott, Medical Officer of Health, Hamilton). Consequently death of people who had not reached old age was a reality that Maori had to cope with more frequently than Europeans.
‡ For example, visits to Te Awamutu in 1933 (see Te Puea to Ramsden, 8/8/33); and Rotorua in 1934 (Te Puea to Ramsden, 3/3/34) R.P.
* Subsequently to marry Te Puea's nephew Tamati Herangi.
** Tumokai; Te Puea frequently referred to him as Dave or Davy.

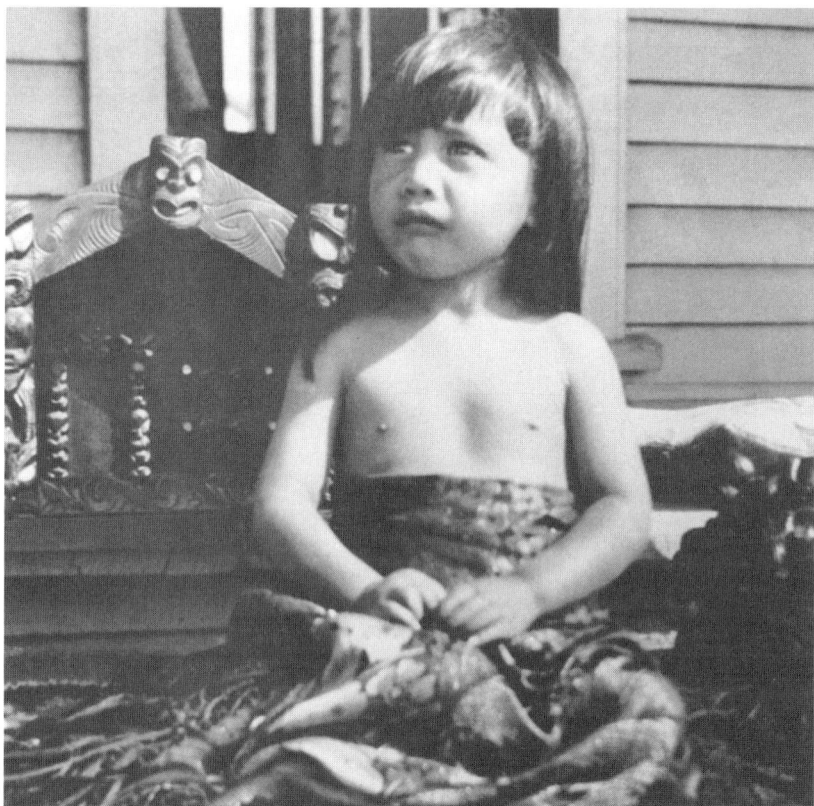

Pirihia Katipa, Te Puea and Tumokai's favourite adopted daughter. Turongo House

so upset that he nearly left his work. He cried all night. In his sleep I still heard him sobbing. He loves this little girl as if she were his own child.'[38]

The hints continued through the 1930s. It was almost as if Te Puea and Tumokai believed the child was too perfect to be allowed to live. Then in August 1939, exactly six years after the first premonition, the fear became concrete. 'Pirihia is very ill. The doctor has given up all hope for her. I took her to Hamilton Hospital to be X-rayed: they found that both lungs were covered with matakohe . . .[†] The tears are in [Tumokai's] eyes every time he goes to work.'[39]

On the evening of 20 September, the child was in bed at Ngaruawahia farm and she called suddenly to Tumokai. When he went to her she said, 'E Papa, karakia.' Thinking that she wanted to go over her Sunday School

---

† Tuberculosis.

prayers, he fetched his Methodist prayerbook. But she waved it away. 'No,' she said. 'Karakia Maori.' So Tumokai began to recite Pai Marire chants for her, holding her hand as he did so. After a few minutes the hand went limp and she died.[40]

Ramsden visited New Zealand five months later. He met Te Puea at a Maori home in Onehunga, Auckland, where she involved him in the mourning that she always carried out for a year after the death of somebody close. When she met friends she had not seen since the bereavement, she would tangi before proceeding to any other topic of conversation or business. On this occasion, the door of the house opened into a darkened hall:

> Te Puea, who had been waiting for me, stood at the head of a procession. I was shocked at her appearance. Suddenly she seemed to have grown old and small . . . I did not expect the tangi that followed. Te Puea began to wail in Maori — not in the karanga or cry appropriate to such an occasion. It was more like the cry of a stricken animal . . . I could distinguish the words . . . 'enter into the house of death' . . . Te Puea stepped forward and pressed my nose in the hongi . . . She threw an arm round my neck . . . and she began to moan . . . All the time she called upon little Pirihia. Dave stood in the background, silently weeping . . . Gradually the sobs ceased and finally she released me.[41]

There was a strong belief among Te Puea's Maori followers that she could cure some forms of illness and physical disorders and this too arose from Pai Marire practices. It was partly because she was a member of the kahui ariki, whose intensified mana and tapu were thought to confer more than conventional power over physical things. (Tukere Te Anga referred to the Pai Marire ritual of curing and healing through reciting the names of the kings as 'a form of tohungaism peculiar . . . to Waikato'.[42]) The faculty for healing was also one for which Te Puea acquired a reputation during the anti-conscription campaign in 1918. Defaulters like Tae Tapara testified that they had invoked her name while they were ill in prison, and that she had come to them in dreams; they claimed to be cured as a result of this.[43]

Te Puea acknowledged the belief in such powers. 'Many people draw about me thinking that just the sight of me will make them well. I can cure them, but I cannot cure myself.'[44] She based her 'cures' on discovering people's hara or faults that had weakened their protective shield of personal tapu; then she would have them confess those faults; finally she would sprinkle them with cold water while she recited the names of Potatau, Tawhiao, Mahuta and Te Rata.[45] 'She used to question them,' Tumokai said

Te Puea, head bound in one of her characteristic white scarves, displays what her followers customarily referred to as her 'tohunga look'. Te Uira Manihera

of the hundreds of people who came to their home over the years. 'Ask them, "Have you done this? Have you done that?" When she was satisfied that she'd found the hara, she made sure it all came out. Then she'd sprinkle them and pray over them.'[46]

Her reputed successes included relief of headaches and depression, knitting broken bones and, in one case, restoring sight to a boy who was brought to her blind (this last was in 1939; Tumokai said he came from Moehake and was brought to Te Puea by his grandfather, an elder named Kohi).[47] Sometimes patients came from as far away as the East Coast or the South Island.[48]

Most of these illnesses were of a 'Maori' kind. Te Puea felt they were likely to be consequences of wrongdoing and subsequent guilty consciences. Her questions and prayers were ways of bringing people to terms with their consciences and relieving guilt and hence anxiety. She distinguished these cases (of which the most extreme were psychiatric, and frightened her) from 'Pakeha illnesses' which she knew to be curable with medication and care.

Te Puea was exceedingly reluctant to talk about Pai Marire and Maori spiritual experiences to Pakeha, unless she knew them well. She expected disbelief, even scorn.[49] After outlining for Ramsden the ritual for relieving sickness, she wrote: 'I have never done this or told this to a Pakeha except Areka McKay.'[50] And, on another occasion: 'We do not speak to everyone of such happenings. But they are familiar enough to us. The Pakeha who has no inner knowledge of our life has little patience.'[51] The more widespread interest in psychic phenomena and faith-healing that was to make such experiences a matter for open-minded inquiry did not reach New Zealand in her lifetime.

A further reason for reluctance was Te Puea's fear that she would be accused of 'tohungaism', a term that in European minds carried connotations of charlatanism, irresponsible folk remedies, or the practice of makutu or 'black magic'.[52] Such connotations had been reinforced by the naming and purpose of the Tohunga Suppression Act of 1907, which outlawed bogus and dangerous practices of folk medicine; and by disparaging references in medical reports (including those of Pomare and Buck) to the continuance of 'tohunga' activities.

In the idiom of traditionally oriented Maori communities, however, there were few such connotations. The word had simply come to mean 'practitioner'. Its root meaning had been 'one who is chosen' and the term had been applied to those believed to be selected by sponsoring deities to become proficient in agriculture, carving, fishing, healing, ritual, or some other specialist activity. In the twentieth century it acquired overtones of a sacerdotal nature so that when the word tohunga was used on its own (with suffixes like whakairo or ta-moko), it usually referred to somebody who performed a religious or healing function. The Ringatu Church, for example, called its ministers 'tohunga'.

Te Puea's mind was not closed to the possibility of other people possessing spiritual or healing powers; but neither was she vulnerable to what she called 'humbug' — the theatrical posturing of the charlatan tohunga. In 1935 she allowed a man named Te Huatahi from Waingaro to live at Turangawaewae. He claimed to be a healer and attracted a large following that included Europeans (one Pakeha who came to see him from Hamilton arrived on crutches and walked away unaided[53]). While Te Puea was resting at Ahipara, however, she learnt that food bills at the pa were mounting up disproportionately. And she heard from Alex McKay that the tohunga had taken to excessive drinking, fighting and swearing. So she sent a message to Te Huatahi that he was to leave. He, deciding that his powers were now stronger than those of Te Puea (who was recovering from illness), refused to go. When Te Puea returned she ordered him out personally and he threatened her with floods, famine and pestilence; finally she had to chase him out with a broom.[54]

After the revival of Pai Marire at Mangatawhiri in 1918, Te Puea did not leave the survival of its ritual and belief to chance and personal piety. She personally instructed all her children from infancy.[55] And at seven o'clock every morning and evening a bell was rung to summon all members of the Turangawaewae community not then working to prayer in the whare karakia (a simple wooden hall in the centre of the residential section of the pa; there would be a similar summons at the land development projects under Te Puea's control).

Eric Ramsden left this description of an evening service: 'Silently, the folk . . . enter the house . . . Te Puea always sits near the door. The service is simple enough.' First, an elder rose to lead the chants and the remainder of the congregation took up the refrains ending with the signature phrase 'rire rire hau pai marire'. Then, 'like the Quakers, as the spirit moves a person he or she will stand and recite a karakia.' This might be anyone from the oldest inhabitant to the youngest child, there were no distinctions of age in these circumstances. 'It is soon over. As the worshippers leave the room, Te Puea will scrutinise each face. If a boy or girl hesitates when passing her, she will nod to them to stand aside. Little happens at the pa that does not sooner or later come to Te Puea's ears.'[56]

These services continued at the pa when Te Puea was working at Tahuna or Rotorua on land development, and there was an additional one at midday on Sundays. It was an organised system of worship that was maintained until her death.

Because she had an 'established' religion, Te Puea was reluctant at first to allow the Christian churches a foothold at Turangawaewae; and she still remembered being abandoned in 1918 by other denominations who had not wanted to become involved in an anti-conscription campaign that they regarded as illegal and unpatriotic.[57] Since then, Te Puea also believed, these churches had patronised her and her children in Mercer, Huntly and Ngaruawahia, by offering them old clothes and charity when what she had wanted most at the time was work;[58] she had not enjoyed contributing to a European sense of superiority by providing opportunities for Christians to practise the corporal works of mercy.

These recollections had made her determined to set her community on its own feet, to provide for its spiritual and material needs without the kind of recourse to churches that would allow them to feel she was beholden to them.[59] For the same reasons she was initially hostile to outside attempts to proselytise within the pa. On several occasions in the 1920s and early 1930s she was overtly dismissive of clergy brought up to her for introduction — one of her few violations of what she regarded as the rules of hospitality. The first non-Waikato Methodist minister to preach within the pa, the Rev. Robert Tahupotiki Haddon, was eventually accepted because of his persistence in the face of being ignored,[60] and his willingness to participate in the evening Pai Marire karakia.[61]

The Anglican Church in particular was unpopular at this time among Waikato Maori. Te Puea's views reflected this feeling.[62] Its origin lay primarily in the fact that Bishop George Augustus Selwyn had marched with the Imperial troops during the Waikato war (he had acted as military chaplain); and that he was rumoured to have been at the head of the soldiers who had set fire to the whare karakia at Rangiaowhia on 21 February 1864, a Sabbath day.

In this last action, non-combatants had been burned to death while they were gathered for prayer. Te Puea repeated the story frequently to visitors during the 1920s and 1930s as an example of Pakeha and Christian duplicity.[63] It confirmed the view that Europeans would say and do anything in order to achieve their objective, and that the churches would be allies in the process. The popular way of expressing it was that used by Mahuta in a Legislative Council debate in 1903: 'When the pakeha first came to this Island, the first thing he taught the Maori was Christianity. They made parsons and priests of several members of the Maori race, and they taught these persons to . . . look up and pray; and while they were looking up the pakehas took away our land.'[64]

For a long time the Anglicans seemed to reciprocate Waikato distaste. The church's senior Maori clergyman in the district in the 1930s, Archdeacon Hori Raiti, frequently referred to Waikato as 'a bunch of heathens' because of their practice of Pai Marire.[65] (But when he died in 1941, Te Puea told Ramsden gleefully, 'the heathens paid all the expenses for his tangi'.)[66] The Bishop of Waikato from 1926 to 1950, the Rt Rev. Cecil Arthur Cherrington, was so poorly informed about Maori matters in the 1940s as to tell Ramsden that Te Puea was 'a ghastly old humbug' who was living promiscuously and deceiving her own people.[67] The bishop was also unwilling to allow the first Maori bishop, Frederick Bennett, to visit Waikato marae in an official capacity.[68]†

There were three exceptions to this general policy of standing apart from the churches. Te Puea was well disposed towards the Mormons: they had been protected from local persecution by Mahuta;[69] and she approved of their schemes to inculcate habits of cleanliness and orderliness in Maori communities.[70] On several occasions in the 1920s she made Turanga-waewae available for Mormon hui. And the highly successful TPM tour of the East Coast in 1927 had begun with a Mormon invitation.

Te Puea also looked on the Catholic Church with tolerance. Although its Maori membership in Waikato was not high and it did not proselytise there with great vigour, it included people who were close to her. In Maori circles there were the Te Heuheus and her brother Wanakore.‡ Even more influential, perhaps, Ngeungeu Beamish and Alex McKay were strong Catholics; it was inevitable that her association with them gave Te Puea a favourable view of their denomination and its clergy. She met Bishop Henry William Cleary (who spoke Maori and was Bishop of Auckland from 1910 to 1929); and, when he was working at Tuakau and Huntly, Father Edward Lyons. Alex McKay has noted that she also found the Catholic concepts of

---

† The ill-feeling between Waikato Maori and the Anglican Church was to persist until the early 1960s when it was diminished by discussion and the common goodwill of King Koroki, Bishop J.T. Holland and Canon Wiremu Te Tau Huata. Canon Huata, in the course of his twenty-one years as Anglican Maori Missioner in Waikato, penetrated to the heart of Kingitanga councils — one of the few non-Tainui Maori to do so (he was Ngati Kahungunu).

‡ Te Puea's cousin Taipu had become a Catholic in 1913 to marry Te Uira Te Heuheu; but he did not continue to practise. There is also evidence that Tawhiao was on the verge of being received into the Catholic Church before the Waikato war broke out (see letter from Bishop Pompallier to Matutaera, 21 August 1862; translation in Auckland Public Library).

absolute authority and confession appealing ones; and the latter, of course, was very like her own process of searching for hara or sins.[71]

But by far the most favoured Christian denomination at Turangawaewae was the Methodist Church. 'Waikato always liked them better,' Te Puea told Ramsden in 1933.[72] The Wesleyans had been established in the district since 1834. They had not appeared to be overtly associated with the government side in the war and confiscation. By the 1930s, the greater proportion of Waikato Maori were still at least nominally Methodist (as was Te Puea's father Te Tahuna). Te Puea's own considerable knowledge of Scripture was a result of long night sessions when Tahuna had read the Maori Bible to her.

The Methodists had also retained formal links with the Kingitanga and with successive kings. Each king had been 'crowned' with a Bible that had formerly belonged to a Wesleyan minister; and, after Mahuta had opened Waikato to Christian denominations after Tawhiao's death, the Rev. Moana Roa had been appointed by the church to act as the King's chaplain.[73]

Te Puea's disposition to Methodism was to be strengthened greatly by the development of close personal relationships with Maori and Pakeha clergy. One, her kinsman Hori Kirkwood, she had known all her life and brought to Turangawaewae in its early days. From 1930 there was Robert Tahupotiki Haddon, originally from Taranaki[†] but appointed to Ngarua-wahia as superintendent of the Waikato-Maniapoto circuit (and his placement there by the church was an indication that Turangawaewae was now accepted fully as the centre for Tainui activities). He was senior officiating minister at Te Rata's tangi, and at Koroki's coronation on 8 October 1933. Te Puea came to regard him as one of her elders.

Subsequently comparable friendships developed with Heemi Rihimona, Matene Keepa, Ngapaka Kukutai, Eruera Te Tuhi, Paaki Moke, Arthur John Seamer and George Irvine Laurenson; and with the deaconesses Sisters Heeni Wharemaru, Margaret Nicholls, Irene Hobbs and Frances Clegg, who were all to conduct Sunday Schools at the pa and help with the organisation of hui. Te Puea established a precedent of inviting senior Methodist ministers to stand alongside her at public functions where she was to be a centre of attention. She said it gave her confidence to enjoy the protection of elders who were also men of God.[74] She was to encourage some of her protégés, like Te Uira Manihera and Maharaia Winiata, to pursue vocations as Methodist ministers.

---

† See page 54.

The closest of these relationships was that with the Rev. A.J. Seamer. In Maori eyes, Seamer was one of the last European missionaries to acquire heroic status (in the twentieth century his impact could be compared only with that of the Presbyterian minister John Laughton among Tuhoe). He had come to New Zealand from Australia as a member of the Salvation Army and begun to specialise in Maori work in 1897. After the Salvationists closed their Maori mission he joined the Methodists and was ordained. When Te Puea came to know him in the early 1930s he was General Superintendent of the Home and Maori Mission Department and spoke Maori fluently.

Seamer was a striking figure, a patriarchal one. He was not tall; but he was spare and austere in appearance and habits; and he projected an almost palpable aura of sanctity that impelled some people to refer to him easily as 'Father Seamer', and others like Pei Jones to regard him as sanctimonious. For most of his adult life he suffered from severe arthritis that frequently restricted his movements; characteristically, he rarely complained.

Before meeting Te Puea, Seamer had moved extensively among the major Maori districts in the course of thirty years' work. He was as aware as any European could be of the nature and extent of Maori social difficulties. This awareness led him in the late 1920s to conceive a scheme to unite all major Maori religions and political movements into one great coalition that would lobby in a supra-tribal fashion and command the attention of the Pakeha political system. The two great pillars of this coalition, he hoped, would be the Ratana and King Movements.[75] The prophet T.W. Ratana already favoured such a scheme; but it was to be the one proposition with which Seamer was unable to move Te Puea, because of her fixed opposition to the Ratana movement.

The other scheme close to Seamer's heart — and one that was successful — was the establishment of an army of 'home missionaries'. These men were lay preachers, not theologically trained or ordained, who acted as ministers in rural districts and were entitled to be addressed as 'Reverend' (C.G. Scrimgeour, who was one of them, called them 'parsons on the cheap'[76]). Many Methodist Maori clergy in the 1930s came into this category. Unlike the Native ministers of other denominations, they were not disadvantaged in numbers or status as a result of having fewer qualifications than most of their Pakeha counterparts.[77]

In most matters, Te Puea listened attentively to Seamer's advice. She particularly respected his transparent sincerity and spirituality. He was probably the only man she knew very well to whom she never spoke an angry word; he may also have been the only person of whom she stood in awe. Certainly he was the only one she allowed in later life to touch her head

— in Maori terms, the most tapu part of the body (and not even Tumokai would touch Te Puea's).[78]

Publicly, Te Puea treated religion the way she treated politics: she never identified herself wholly with one group other than Pai Marire (indeed, one of the reasons Tawhiao was said to have brought Pai Marire to Waikato was so that he would then be able to identify with all the religions of his people[79]). Her first loyalty, she always said, was to the Kingitanga.[80] But it is clear from a statement made by Seamer after her death that at some point, perhaps in a moment of crisis, she allowed him to baptise her.†

Seamer's role grew from that of adviser on religious matters to consultant on a variety of social and political issues. In the 1940s he was to involve Te Puea in a campaign to try to keep liquor out of the King Country;‡ and he was to assume a parental role in the education of Piki, Koroki's daughter. The intimacy of Seamer's association with the kahui ariki was a contrast to the more careful relationships that Te Puea had with representatives of other churches.

Seamer reaped the first fruit of this association in November 1934. The occasion was the laying of foundation stones for a new church and parsonage at Kawhia to commemorate the centenary of the Wesleyan mission there. Seamer was keen that the young King Koroki should be recruited to take the leading role in the ceremony. It would be tantamount to a seal of 'official' Maori approval for the Methodists' work in Waikato, and would boost local support for the building of the church and subsequent worship there. It would also draw Koroki out of the shadows of specifically Maori activities and on to a platform of more widely-attended public functions, another of Seamer's objectives.

The invitation had equally consequential implications for Koroki. Previously, no king had played a major part in a denominational and largely Pakeha religious function. Up to this point too he had been bound in the thirteen months since his succession by the decisions of other people. This time, the advice of most of his elders and of his uncle Haunui was against participation. They felt he was being used as an embellishment for a partisan cause and to inflate the mana of particular clergymen. Te Puea

---

† Seamer wrote to Ramsden on 24 April 1953: 'You are quite astray when you state that Te Puea refused baptism . . . but I am not in a position at the moment to give you details.' (R.P.) It is possible that Seamer baptised Te Puea when she sent for him during her final illness (see page 314); but Alex McKay, present at that time, believed that such a baptism never took place.

‡ See page 284.

favoured Koroki's going, because of her friendship with Seamer, but chose not to push the issue. Koroki decided on his own and he decided to attend. He did not announce this intention until the morning of 24 November, the day of the function; and at that point all opposition from his advisers lapsed. Koroki, his wife Te Atairangikaahu and a large party of Waahi elders drove to Kawhia; the King laid the foundation stone for the new church, and Te Atairangikaahu the stone for the parsonage.[4]†

Te Puea had little association with other churches in the 1930s. The Presbyterians, because of agreements on spheres of influence, were not much interested in work among Tainui. Ratana services were forbidden at Turangawaewae. There was a sentimental link between Waikato and the Ringatu Church because of Tawhiao's sharing his exile with the church's founder, Te Kooti Rikirangi; this association grew with the largely Ringatu Ngati Awa tribe in the Bay of Plenty and eventually led to the holding of annual poukai at Te Teko.

By the mid-1930s, the only religion other than Pai Marire that could have been said to have had a place at Turangawaewae was the Methodist Church. But Catholics and Anglicans participated in hui and tangi; and the ground was laid for what was to become in the 1940s a declared policy of religious toleration.

† Te Puea opened the completed church on 14 March 1935. Construction and interior decoration had been done by Turangawaewae workers and carvers, and Tawhiao's Te Paki o Matariki crest was worked into the front of the pulpit by carver — and later singer — Inia Te Wiata.

11

A river culture

The most dramatic event at Te Rata's tangi in October 1933 had been the collapse at the King's graveside of Harry Holland, leader of the Opposition Labour Party.[†] Holland, unwell, had been warned by Apirana Ngata not to climb Taupiri Mountain for the burial ceremonies on 8 October. His death in these circumstances was regarded by Waikato elders as a payment that would ensure victory for Labour at the next general election.[1]

The immediate result, however, was the first intimate contact between Te Puea and members of the Labour Party caucus (she had met Peter Fraser in 1929). Holland's body rested in state for a time on Waahi Marae, where Te Rata's had lain hours before. Then Te Puea, Tumokai, Haunui, Te Rauangaanga, Pei Jones and a group of elders took the coffin to Wellington for delivery to Holland's parliamentary colleagues. This gesture did not imply political partisanship; if Te Puea's loyalties were committed in any direction it was with Coates' Reform and Ngata's United Parties, because of her special relationship with those men. It was simply a Maori duty that Waikato would have performed for any national leader in the same circumstances.

The Labour Party was greatly moved and presented the Waikato delegation with a letter that read (in part): 'We, the Central Executive and Members of Parliament of the New Zealand Labour Party . . . have learned with great pride and satisfaction of the wonderful demonstration of sorrow and lamentation which your people manifested at Waahi Pa . . . The taking of [our leader] to your hearts . . . has filled us with admiration and humility

---

† Labour had acquired more votes than United or Reform in the 1931 General Election, but the latter parties retained the treasury benches as the Coalition Government. Later, they formed the National Party.

Politicians at the funeral of King Te Rata, Waahi, October 1933. Led by Kepa Ehau of Te Arawa they are (from left) Gordon Coates, Harry Holland, Frank Langstone and Apirana Ngata. Within hours of this photograph being taken, Holland, leader of the Labour Party and Prime Minister in waiting, collapsed and died at Te Rata's graveside on Taupiri mountain. ATL

. . . the classic farewell has stirred the hearts and souls of our people, and will remain for ever with us . . . Your mourning . . . [has] cemented our friendship, and as time runs through the years our regard and respect for your great people will grow and intensify.'[2] Te Puea kept the letter and took its message literally.

The other noteworthy feature of Te Rata's funeral was the virtual absence of discussion about whether the kingship should continue that had wracked his father's tangi twenty years before. 'Much to my surprise,' wrote Pei Jones, 'I found complete agreement that the institution of the kingship was a valuable symbol of unity for the Maori, especially because Potatau's genealogy established kinship links between the holder of the title of Maori King and all the important tribes throughout New Zealand. It was also considered a necessary racial status symbol.'[3] This was a mark of the degree of acceptance that the King Movement had achieved under twenty years of Te Puea's leadership.

The tangi and coronation of Koroki also established Pei Jones of Ngati Maniapoto for the first time as a Kingitanga and therefore a national Maori leader (he was at that time working as officer in charge of the consolidation of land titles and development at the Native Affairs office in Te Kuiti). Jones acted as a mediator between the new King and the deliberating elders, he stood at the King's side throughout the coronation service, and when the crippled Tarapipipi Taingakawa (fourth Kingmaker and son of Tupu, who had died in 1929) had difficulty raising the Bible to Koroki's head, it was Jones who supported his hands. From this time on his special relationships with Koroki, Te Puea and Tumate Mahuta gave him a uniquely influential position within the King Movement as a negotiator among its factions and an occasional spokesman for all of them.[†]

From the beginning of Koroki's kingship Te Puea sought to preserve the position of ascendancy she had consolidated in Te Rata's time. She had taken a preliminary step two years earlier by helping other members of the kahui ariki persuade Koroki to marry her niece Te Atairangikaahu, daughter of Wanakore Herangi. This was in preference to a woman named Te Paea, by whom Koroki had already had a daughter, Julia[‡]. It led to popular references to Te Puea as Koroki's 'aunt', although the blood relationship was slightly more complicated (Koroki being the son of Te Puea's first cousin). She found it necessary to assert her influence at once in the face of attempts by Koroki's uncles — Haunui Tawhiao and Tumate and Tonga Mahuta — to dominate the young King and decided his movements and loyalties. Koroki found himself buffeted by opposing forces, all supposedly united under his mana.

Late in January 1934, Haunui took his acquiescent great-nephew to T. W. Ratana's birthday hui at Ratana Pa. It was a triumph for the Ratanas — for years they had been trying to engineer a coalition of the two movements

---

† Ngata had expressed confidence that Jones would emerge as a national leader. In 1929 he had referred to him in a letter to Buck as a future 'torch-bearer' for Maniapoto (Ngata to Buck, 6/5/29, R.P.).

‡ Te Puea's interference in kahui ariki relationships and marriages extended over a long period. She had arranged for her younger sister Te Atarua to marry Te Rata's brother Tumate before World War One; and at a hui in 1913 she had prevented Te Rata consolidating a relationship with a Tuwharetoa woman (by whom he had already had a son) by throwing away his walking stick and spending all night at the entrance to his tent (Eric Ramsden, notes from Te Puea, February 1940). She was unwilling to allow other members of the family the options she had once enjoyed herself.

under the prophet's leadership. Now the objective seemed on the verge of fulfilment. For the next twelve months Ratana supporters spoke of a 'marriage of the King and the Mangai'.[4]

This interpretation, however, was premature. Te Puea had no intention of allowing her anti-Ratana work of the previous ten years to be undone. She criticised Koroki for accompanying Haunui and then took him to North Auckland for the Treaty of Waitangi anniversary celebrations early in February; she kept him beside her for the whole journey but did not speak to him once.[†] Koroki was greatly embarrassed and his natural shyness intensified.

At Waitangi, however, all wounds healed temporarily. Waikato was united in a display of loyalty to its own King, and to the British monarch in the person of the Governor-General, Lord Bledisloe. They marched on the grounds in impressive style before 8000 people, led by Te Puea and Raukawa Te Heuheu; Koroki and Pei Jones followed the women in feather cloaks. The European public and other Maori groups showed enormous interest. 'The occasion was given historic importance by the presence of the Maori King, Koroki Mahuta, the first of his line to visit the northern people,' a journalist noted.[‡] 'The young King . . . was given a place of honour.'[5] Interest was heightened by the fact that Te Rata had been such a recluse; this function was the first organised by Pakeha that a Maori king had attended as a VIP guest. The apparent acceptance of the kingship reached a climax at a meeting of the Waitangi Trust Board, to which Koroki had been appointed as a representative of the Maori people south of Auckland. Lord Bledisloe pulled out the chairman's seat and said to the King. 'This is really the place for you.'[6]

This meeting marked the beginning of a friendship between Bledisloe and Te Puea and Koroki that was to last beyond the Governor-General's term of office. His acceptance of the title 'King' did much to remove the reticence about using it in government and public service circles. He was also sensitive to Koroki's lack of confidence in public and was one of the few

---

† There were further tussles. In October 1936, for example, Te Puea arrived at the Coronation hui at Waahi to find that Koroki had been instructed by Haunui and Tumate not to appear. To the uncles she said: 'Who do the people come to see? Haunui? Tumate? Me? No. The King.' Then she summoned Koroki. 'If there were no people there would be no need for a king . . . you in turn must honour the people.' (Alex McKay to Eric Ramsden, 17/10/36.) This was the concept of service with which her mother had imbued her. On this occasion Koroki went before the hui.

‡ This was not so: Tawhiao had been welcomed at Waiomio by Maihi Kawiti in 1882.

Raukawa Te Heuheu and Te Puea lead the Waikato party on to the Treaty grounds at Waitangi in February 1934. The youthful King Koroki and Pei Te Hurinui Jones follow them. *Auckland Weekly News*

people who was able to overcome it with banter like: 'Cheer up, King, it is not as bad as all that.'[7]

Te Puea too was attracted by Bledisloe's easy charm; but she was also impressed by his public pronouncements that neither patronised nor romanticised the Maori as many of his predecessors had done.[8] He preferred the expression 'Maori', for example, at a time when most officials continued to say 'Native'. In his speech to accompany the laying of the foundation stone for a meeting house at Waitangi, the Governor-General rejected assimilative policies and appeared to understand the role of institutions such as the Maori kingship. He spoke of a Maori need to 'perpetuate their ancient distinctive nationality, which is in no way inconsistent with their status as free citizens of our great British Empire.'[9] It was a theme that the Kingitanga had been stressing since Tawhiao's visit to London fifty years before, and one that Pakeha authority had been slow to accept.

Te Puea invited Bledisloe to come to Turangawaewae, which he did two months after Waitangi. The visit was an even greater success than that of the Fergussons. Representatives of most Kingitanga supporters attended the hui, including the King and his uncles. Te Puea told Eric Ramsden that afterwards she had felt like grabbing Koroki and dancing on the marae; and she derived some satisfaction from the envious gaze of Ngaruawahia citizens who had tried to displace her community a decade earlier — they were 'jealous because the Governor-General turned down their invitation for afternoon tea at the home of the mayor'.[10]

From this time until his term finished the following year, Bledisloe called at the marae whenever his travels took him through Waikato; they were private visits without attention or ceremony and Te Puea would come from whatever land scheme she had been working on to receive him.[11] As a consequence of the rapport they established, the Governor-General was prepared to use his office to secure favours for Te Puea (such as persuading the Government to donate to the pa the five acres of unused police reserve alongside it;[12] Te Puea immediately sowed it in potatoes).

Te Puea in turn was influenced by Bledisloe's optimism that the Maori could achieve worthwhile objectives by working through the political system; and by his good-humoured belief in tolerance and patience. 'Goodness knows we want the sympathy of the pakeha people and to work in harmony,' she told Ramsden after a visit to Government House in Wellington in July 1934, where she also met the aviatrix Jean Batten. On this occasion she spent three hours with the Bledisloes and reported that they 'were very kind to me'.[13] Afterwards she was dispatched to Parliament Buildings in the Governor-General's chauffeur-driven car, clutching a cheese made for him on his home estate. She enjoyed waving to curious passers-by in Wellington streets. The cheese, intended for use at the pa on a special occasion, did not last long; Tumokai was waiting for her at Ngata's office and had not eaten; he and the minister polished it off quickly with a pocket knife.[14]

The only matter on which Te Puea sought Bledisloe's intercession unsuccessfully was the question of a visit to Turangawaewae by the Duke of Gloucester in January 1935.[15] As on previous occasions, the royal guest was given a national Maori welcome at Rotorua.

Prior to the 1930s Te Puea had given considerable emphasis to the non-material culture of her people — their language, music and oral traditions. She had brought her children up speaking Maori at a time when education policy was discouraging it; at Mercer and Turangawaewae she had sat with them almost daily on the riverbank and taught them Tainui history and songs. The formation of the TPM concert party had been an extension of this education. Although it had set out to raise money, Te Puea also valued it as a means of re-establishing an interest in Maori music and dance forms.

All this had been part of her determination to raise and sustain Waikato morale; she sought to give people confidence in the present and future by drawing from the assurance of a Maori past. Her children had a tradition, they had a history of which they could be proud; all that was necessary was that they be put in touch with this past and learn how to keep it alive.

By the mid-1930s Turangawaewae was functioning more or less independently of her daily presence, the land schemes were operating, her position of influence over Koroki seemed assured. Te Puea could feel she had met the material needs of feeding, clothing and sheltering the people for whom she felt immediate responsibility. She could now turn to more ambitious and more visible cultural projects: the building of a house for Koroki at Turangawaewae; the raising of additional meeting houses throughout Waikato; and the construction of a fleet of canoes that would highlight the tribe's former strength as a people with a river culture and echo the more distant Polynesian tradition of seafaring and exploration.

The building of Mahinarangi and the subsequent dispatch of Piri Poutapu to the Ohinemutu carving school had been an anticipation of this programme. Next to Tumokai, Poutapu was the nearest thing she had to a right-hand man; Judge F.O.V. Acheson called him 'the strongest support to Te Puea on the spiritual and cultural side of her life.'[16] She arranged for him to go to Rotorua in 1929 because she believed that all direct contact with Waikato's earlier carving had been lost.[†] For earlier projects at Turanga-waewae she had relied mainly on the services of itinerant carvers, like Tame Poata of Ngati Porou.[‡] The local tradition had to be re-established.

'Te Puea told me I was to go in search of the culture of our ancestors,' Poutapu remembered. 'And then I had to bring that knowledge and those skills back and share them among the people.' At first he was reluctant to go. He had been married for only three weeks; and he told Te Puea there were people better qualified than he. 'She looked at me and I could see she was wild. She said to me, "Look here, what I say goes. I don't expect you to answer me back." So I shut my mouth. And when I came back after three years I started teaching.'[17]

Poutapu did more than simply teach the mechanics of carving; he also observed the protocols and rituals. As a boy he had learned the religious practices associated with the craft: the chants and offerings to appease Tane for the felling of trees, the imposition of tapu during the carving and construction (prayers, no food, no cigarettes, no women), and the correct disposal of chips. One of his first pupils, Inia Te Wiata, used to speak feelingly not only of his teacher's craftsmanship but also of his spirituality, which encouraged other people to approach the same work in the same manner;[18][*] it set the tone for cultural activities at Turangawaewae. Acheson noted of Poutapu that 'he shuns publicity . . . anything he achieves . . . is humbly credited to his ancestors.'[19]

---

† It had not been, as she discovered seven years later. See page 206. The Ohinemutu school had been established by Ngata in 1927.

‡ Poata also did moko or chin tattooing in Waikato with Te Puea's and Te Rata's encouragement. Earlier, Waikato tattooists like Te Aho Rangi Wharepu, Anaru Maxwell, Kuhukuhu Tamati (a woman) and Ngakau had performed this task. Te Puea herself had refused a chisel tattoo from Anaru after she had watched one being done on her sister Hera (see King 1972). By the 1930s the incidence of moko had diminished and it had taken on the character of a diploma of accomplishment in karanga, powhiri and tangi.

* And which distinguished his work from that of the Ngati Porou carvers Pine and John Taiapa.

Te Puea instructs a group of her children on the riverbank at Turangawaewae.
R.G.H. Manley

This was not sanctimoniousness. The ancestor worship inculcated by Pai Marire had a continuing influence on its adherents. Poutapu believed that, as he carved, his ancestors passed on their mauri and tapu to and through him and into his work. For this reason he would never accept wages, nor would he sell individual items. When Eric Ramsden tried to arrange the purchase of a carved feather box for the artist Augustus John — and stressed that cost would be no object — Poutapu was horrified. 'Surely you . . . realise that we do not carve our ancestors for sale. If you [want] another waka huia I will carve one for you.'[20]

There was a further sense in which carving was considered to represent ancestors: Poutapu consciously re-established an awareness and use of traditional Waikato figures and motifs — especially the sinuous taniwha form that emphasised the mythology of the river — and he visited museums and studied nineteenth-century drawings like those of George French Angas to find those that had been forgotten locally.[21]

The Turangawaewae carving school's first major job had been helping with the construction and decoration of the Kawhia Methodist Church.[†] In 1934 another idea for a carving project took root in Te Puea's mind: Turangawaewae was Koroki's; he had a meeting house there for the reception of visitors; why not also a king's house on the marae, and one that would be elaborately carved and appropriate to the circumstances of an ariki?

She said later that Lord Bledisloe had sowed the idea when he visited the marae in April. Standing in Mahinarangi, by then furnished and carpeted in European fashion, he said to her, 'A drawing room fit for a king.'[22] That set her thinking. What was the point of a drawing room only? Koroki should be able to entertain visitors more extensively, to feed them in a dining room and be able to offer more private sleeping arrangements than were available in community buildings. Most important, he should live on the marae himself in a manner that matched his rank. (She also believed that so long as he remained at Waahi he would continue to be vulnerable to undue influence on the part of his uncles, and of Haunui in particular.[23])

Another factor precipitated a decision. A well-wisher had given her about fifty totara strainer posts, a number far in excess of what she then needed for the Tahuna farming operation. Te Puea took Pei Jones behind the Kimikimi hall and showed him: ' "What other use could they be put to?" Not suspecting what was in her mind I said, "Oh, if they were cut up into suitable lengths you should get a few pounds by selling them as houseblocks." "That's what I thought," ' Te Puea told him. Then she led him to Mahinarangi and told him of her plan to build a house for Koroki alongside it. By Jones' next visit some of the strainer posts, now cut up, had been placed on the site as blocks; others later decorated the new building as carved posts.[24] It was characteristic of her. She never threw anything away; the disposal of excess material often generated a new project simply so that nothing would be wasted.

The difficulty was that Te Puea took the decision, as usual, without consulting Koroki — or, more accurately, what consultation there was took the form of telling him what she had decided to do in his interest and asking him for his approval. He was unhappy about the idea. He liked the Waahi community; he was grateful that he could escape the limelight at Turangawaewae and hide among his family and intimates. Equally important, while he and his uncles accepted the role of Turangawaewae and the need of the Kingitanga for such a public marae, they were not happy

† See page 190.

about moves that would further diminish the importance of Waahi, where the King's annual Coronation hui was still held each October.[†]

It was never easy for Koroki to voice his reservations. He was always far more likely to make them apparent in his behaviour. Further, this project was not one in which Te Puea was prepared to brook dissension. She probably counted on Koroki and Tumate Mahuta changing their attitude once they saw the new house, which was what had eventually happened in the case of Mahinarangi. Her own enthusiasm took wings (when she was seriously ill in 1936, Ngata believed it was only the prospect of completing the house and building a fleet of canoes that kept her alive[25]); she seemed always to need a new project whose fulfilment lay just over the horizon to keep herself and her supporters energised and working towards a goal that excited the imagination.

In April 1935 Te Puea wrote to Ramsden, from Ahipara where she was convalescing, that she had the timber for the house. 'Ngati Tuwharetoa are giving us 15,000 feet. Actually, the cause of my illness was worrying about that house. I want to take Koroki out of the clutches of Ratana's followers.'[26] Ngati Porou also offered to help with carving and tukutuku work, but Te Puea was not happy about this. 'She does not wish to be indebted to Apirana,' McKay told Ramsden. 'He said some very nasty things about [her] at Otaki . . . that Puea had caused enough trouble at other times and practically accused her of the death of Lady Ngata . . . after the opening of Mahinarangi.'[27]

Money for other expenses came from the usual tribal levies. Te Puea issued a copy of the panui and newsletter *Te Paki o Matariki* in May 1935 asking for a donation of 2/6d for every man, woman and child from families supporting the Kingitanga.[28] Later in the year the *New Zealand Herald* published a rumour that Gordon Coates was attempting to buy Maori votes for the forthcoming General Election with a £500 donation to the project. Te Puea wrote back indignantly and described the story as 'malicious'. She explained that timber had come from Tuwharetoa. 'The Waikato people of Waikato Heads and Onewhero have levied 1d per pound on whitebait for two years, which came to £120. Kahupake of Mangere gave £36. Each family that recognised King Koroki has given 2/6d. There have been many

---

† Although the writing was on the wall; the manner in which the hui was run was not to Te Puea's liking, nor was it in line with other Kingitanga activities; Europeans were not welcomed. It was transferred to Turangawaewae in the 1940s, but continued to be organised by Waahi members of the kahui ariki.

promises from Pakeha people but only two [R. C. Knight and Sister Margaret Nicholls] have given. I was even unable to obtain the building subsidy which is granted to Pakehas, so we can honestly claim that this is a Maori house for the Maori King.'[29] As always, her keeping of accounts was meticulous. She was also learning the value of using newspapers to do battle with protagonists and win public support. For an awareness of this weapon she had Ramsden to thank.[†]

The house itself was built by voluntary labour from the pa, led by Tumokai and Poutapu. It was joined to Mahinarangi by a covered walk and for this reason as well as ancestral ones it was decided to name it Turongo (after the Waikato chief who had married Mahinarangi of the East Coast); the two were to be linked in architecture as in life.

The design was Te Puea's and it was strikingly different from anything seen previously. She sought to blend Maori and European styles. There was a carved hexagonal tower with seven (not eight) supporting posts, each representing a major migration canoe; a carved pataka set into the roof for the housing of relics previously held in the Ahurewa; a tukutuku-panelled and elaborately carved dining room (and some of the most impressive carvings were the work of Inia Te Wiata); and a door panel leadlight inset with the King's coat of arms. The dining room was equipped with high quality linen and silverware, there was a sitting room for conferences, bedrooms and a kitchen. All the construction work, with the exception of electric fittings and a little brick-laying, was done by the volunteer work force without payment.

The project also brought Te Puea into contact with two Pakeha who became close friends. B.E. (Bunny) Woodhams, manager of H. and J. Court's department store in Hamilton, supplied the furnishings; and a Health Inspector named T.C. Thompson helped her to improve drainage and sanitation at the pa (and to cope with the new septic tank for the house when it exploded and littered the ground with excrement the day before the opening).

While the concept and functions of Turongo House were of application to Turangawaewae alone, involvement with it did not take Te Puea's attention away from more conventional marae-building activities. It remained her objective throughout the 1930s and 1940s to establish adequate meeting

† She used and was most frequently reported in the *New Zealand Herald* and the *Auckland Star.* Hamilton's *Waikato Times* seemed relatively unaware of her by comparison, and of the Maori renaissance taking place on their doorstep.

houses and cooking and eating facilities on every marae supporting the Kingitanga. Much of this latter activity arose from the land development schemes. Te Puea believed, with Ngata, that once people were settled back on their own land it was necessary to 'put back the mana';[30] and the major way of doing this was to establish or extend marae with attractive and functional buildings. These gave a physical base for community activities, allowed contributing participation in the network of tangihanga and poukai that made up the fabric of the King Movement, and uplifted morale by providing a local and external sign of a culture that was distinctively Maori. And the careful upkeep of such marae, she frequently said, indicated a sense of pride that overlapped into other aspects of life.[31]

Te Puea initiated many of these building programmes from Turangawaewae or during poukai discussion on other marae. She explained to local representatives how to apply for Maori Purpose Fund subsidies and she supported such applications. Sometimes, as in the case of the Paki family marae at Rakaumanga, she actually marked out where buildings should go; at other places, like Tuakau and Te Aomarahi, she dispatched Tumokai and her own workers to assist locals with construction; in cases such as Tauranganui and Whatawhata, the Turangawaewae carving school helped with carving or supervised locals (and her nephew Tamati Herangi, one of Wanakore's sons, was responsible for much of the work done outside Turangawaewae); where marae had to be demolished or removed, like Miria Te Kakara at Raglan (this one under the war emergency regulations), she encouraged their replacement as quickly as possible.†

The result was the construction of about fifteen new major marae buildings in Waikato during Te Puea's period of ascendancy. (In June 1946, for example, Ramsden reported buildings planned or under way at Waahi, Whatawhata, Kawhia, Rukumoana and Tauranganui.) This rate of progress was undercut only by the decline of marae in areas where the population had drifted away (and this process accelerated after World War Two). Te Puea's injunctions and encouragement during her lifetime also resulted in

† The demolition of this meeting house at Raglan, originally built in honour of Te Rata, and the associated shift of a whole Maori community, left a great deal of bitterness. Some Kingitanga spokesmen felt it was typical of the manner in which Maori land was seized by public bodies ahead of more conveniently available European property. Although this fragmented a whole community, the land was never used for the purpose for which it was taken (an emergency landing strip), nor was it returned to the former owners until after a long campaign waged in the 1970s by local kuia Eva Rickard.

the raising of buildings after her death — those at Whatawhata and Mangere, for example; and the huge hall Kimiora at Turangawaewae, opened in 1974, which was an extension of a project she had conceived in the 1940s.

Te Puea was also finding time to turn her attention back to music. The TPM was re-formed in 1935 to raise money for Turongo. Many earlier faces had gone. Most of the original group had married; some had put on weight and Te Puea considered them neither fit nor sufficiently attractive to perform and to please an audience; some too had left the pa. Stars among the new performers included Te Uira Manihera and Inia Te Wiata.

Manihera had been spotted by the Rev. A. J. Seamer as he lolled and sang over a beer keg in Kawhia. Seamer persuaded him to abandon alcohol and join the touring Methodist 'Waiata Choir' (and, eventually, to become a minister). This in turn brought Manihera to Turangawaewae and the attention of Te Puea. He was short, handsome and good humoured. 'We love him,' Te Puea told Ramsden. 'He is a true Ngati Mahuta and a blueblooded Maori. His grandfather [Tuteao] was supposed to have been my mother's husband but she did not love him.'[32] In addition to training Manihera for the TPM, Te Puea made him responsible for performing the wero at the marae.[†]

Te Wiata had also been brought to Turangawaewae in Seamer's choir. Born at Otaki of Ngati Raukawa antecedents, he had a bass voice that the missioner judged to be outstanding and that twenty years later was to bring him to the attention of the world. From the time he settled in Waikato he was awed by Te Puea, and he became one of Piri Poutapu's most promising carving pupils, performing his first work there on the pulpit and panels for the Kawhia church.[33] He and Manihera were taken by Seamer on a tour of Australia in 1935 and they became close friends, Inia nicknamed 'Happy' and Te Uira 'Dave'.[‡]

About this time too Te Puea's imagination became excited by the prospect of reviving canoe building. The importance of the river in Waikato consciousness has been discussed elsewhere.[*] As the former source of sustenance and identity, it had become the most potent symbol that tribal leaders could command. Proverbs like 'Waikato taniwharau, he piko he

---

† A function he was still carrying out forty years later.
‡ On this tour scouts for J.C. Williamsons tried unsuccessfully to lure the nineteen-year-old Te Wiata out of Seamer's company (personal communication, Te Uira Manihera, 12/3/77).
* See page 49.

taniwha' (Waikato river of a hundred bends and on every one a taniwha or powerful chief); and 'Ko Taupiri te maunga, ko Waikato te awa, ko Te Wherowhero te tangata' (Taupiri is the chief mountain, Waikato the river, and Te Wherowhero the overlord) — these were rallying calls, reminders of a stirring past recited to generate confidence in the present and future.

Te Puea had also placed great store by establishing Turangawaewae within sight of the river so that its waters would be a constant and reassuring presence. By the mid-thirties she was conscious that there was only one major way in which she was not making use of the river — Waikato no longer had any large canoes.

In earlier days the canoes had been a means of transporting people, goods and war parties. The Waikato tribes had become highly skilled and drilled in the construction and handling of these craft. By the nineteenth century these skills were more important ceremonially than they were practically. Nothing had moved Te Puea more in her youth than the sight of a team of paddlers ferrying guests from Huntly to Waahi in Mahuta's ornately decorated canoe Taheretikitiki,[34] and then going through its paces and manoeuvres afterwards to salute and entertain the visitors.[35] The impact of this kind of scene — its charisma in the eyes of onlookers — arose from a combination of evocative elements: the length of the three-log craft, the forward arching of its carved prow and feather-tufted antennae, the grace of its stern post and trailing decorations, the synchronised movements of the crew members, their chanting as they dipped paddles, the sharply executed manoeuvres that would cause the craft to pause, shoot forward, turn or reverse. And all this carried out on a river redolent of associations. It was something Te Puea wanted to see again, and wanted a generation who had never known it to see.

By 1936 Taheretikitiki had rotted away, its carvings salvaged and placed on the front of the Ahurewa at Turangawaewae. What was needed, Te Puea decided, was not the creation of another single canoe but the building of a whole fleet representing the craft that had brought the major tribal groups to the country. Alex McKay wrote to Ramsden early in 1936: 'Can you imagine the seven, each manned by descendants of the old seven, come sweeping round the bend to Ngaruawahia?'[36] It was to be more than a project of Waikato dimensions; it was to be an exercise in kotahitanga.

But where were the builders? Te Puea brought the subject up for discussion at each hui she attended that year. After a tangi at Rakaunui near Kawhia, a very elderly man named Ranui Maupakanga got to his feet in the meeting house and said simply: 'I built a canoe for your grandfather Tawhiao.' The claim was not at first accepted. But Te Puea took him aside

At Ahipara in 1936. Turongo House

the following day and, after discussion, she was convinced by what he said. He also had with him two apprentices of earlier years, Ropata Wirihana (already in his seventies) and Rawiri Tamainu, both from Hauturu.[37]

As the next step she salvaged part of an old canoe, Te Winika, that had been buried since 1863. Begun in 1838 on the lower reaches of the river, Te Winika had been completed by Ngati Tipa and Ngati Mahanga carvers in 1845 to be on hand to protect Auckland from the expected Ngapuhi invasion. It was a common sight on the Waikato River for the next eighteen years. After the outbreak of hostilities in 1863, it was dismantled by Gustavus von Tempsky and his Forest Rangers as part of an attempt to neutralise Waikato's use of the river. For seventy-three years the centre hull lay in mud near Port Waikato. Its identity was well known to locals who for some years used the exposed portion as a hurdle for jumping horses.

Te Puea had the hull lifted and brought to Turangawaewae by truck. It was called on to the marae and tangi'd over like the body of a person. Then, under Ranui's direction, two totara trees were selected and felled at Waingaro and taken to the pa to be made into the new fore and aft sections, twenty-four and eighteen feet long. Ranui supervised and Piri Poutapu led the team of carvers doing the adzing. There was a moment of doubt when it came to knitting the hulls. Ranui abandoned his blanket on the ground, shuffled to the fire and pulled a faggot from the embers. Then he went to the hulls and traced the outline for the dovetail joints without measurements. Poutapu made the cuts and the sections fitted perfectly. They were caulked and tied and soaked in water to allow swelling; and Waikato had a major canoe on the water again for the first time in thirty years. It was sixty-six feet long. Three years later Ranui was dead. But by that time Wirihana, Tamainu and Poutapu were able to carry on.[38]

In mid-1936 Te Puea went to Wellington to negotiate assistance for the project. Initially the outlook seemed bright. The new Labour Government[†] was seeking imaginative ways to celebrate the centenary in 1940 of the signing of the Treaty of Waitangi, which had brought New Zealand into the British Empire. The construction of a fleet of canoes to represent the Polynesian migration to New Zealand seemed inspired and, with voluntary Maori labour available, not excessively costly. 'She was in touch with all the

---

† Elected in a landslide in 1935. Haami Tokouru Ratana defeated Taite Te Tomo for Western Maori in the same election and subsequently joined the Labour Government. A King Movement candidate did not hold the seat again until 1969 when it was taken by Koro Tainui Wetere who was a supporter of both the Kingitanga and the Ratana Church.

Ranui Maupakanga, Te Puea's canoe builder from Rakaunui. R.G.H. Manley

heads of the Government and got satisfaction on all points,' McKay reported to Ramsden in June. 'The Minister of Forests, Mr Langstone, has given as much timber as we want . . . from a bush at Mokai, Taupo . . . we will also obtain a grant of £500 towards the cost of canoes . . . from the Maori Purposes Fund.' The Prime Minister and Minister of Native Affairs, Michael Joseph Savage, agreed to visit Turangawaewae the following month.[39]

In October, while Poutapu's team worked on carvings for Te Winika, Tumokai, Wirihana and Tamainu led a team of workers into the bush near Mokai on the North Island's high central plateau. They camped in the Oruanui Forest, four miles in from the nearest road. There they felled three more totara, this time for an 25.6-metre canoe. They observed all the ritual taught by Ranui: Tane was appeased by prayer and offering before the trees came down; first chips were burned, later ones buried; all preliminary shaping was done on the spot; women, food, tobacco and swearing were forbidden in the work area; and the logs were made to kiss their stumps for the last time before being hauled away by tractor.[†]

By early 1937 the project was in serious financial trouble. The logs for the second canoe had been brought by train from Taupo to Ngaruawahia; those for the third were being felled. But in spite of government promises the previous year no money had come forward apart from an unsolicited donation of £25 from Lord Bledisloe in England. 'The Government have done nothing to assist in the construction of the waka,' McKay wrote. 'We understood that the railway freight was to be donated by the Railway Department, and then we received a demand from them for £23, which we paid leaving us with exactly £2 to carry on and feed thirty people.'[40] And, on another occasion: 'The people of New Zealand are so damned apathetic regarding anything Maori. All say "What a grand thing it would be to have canoes for [the] Waitangi centenary", and there they stop. Such people must think that canoes must be of the same species as Topsy — just growed.'[41]

In addition, the men working in the bush had suffered extreme discomfort. They were frequently soaked to the skin and, for one period, were snowbound. Curious onlookers 'desecrated' the sight. Tumokai became ill

---

† As the canoes were being made an Auckland cameraman, R.G.H. (Jim) Manley, shot 20,000 feet of film to record the project and the building of a larger canoe in Northland. His company subsequently went into liquidation and Te Puea bought the film, developed to negative stage, in lieu of debts and to prevent it falling into unsympathetic hands. Thirty years later the New Zealand Broadcasting Corporation transferred the film off dangerous nitrate stock. Eventually it was assembled by the film-maker Merata Mita into a documentary, Mana Waka, first screened in 1990.

Piri Poutapu supervises canoe building at Turangawaewae. R.G.H. Manley

with what Te Puea believed was 'mate Maori' (literally, 'Maori sickness' believed to be caused by spiritual rather than physiological factors).

Nor was money available for the completion of Turongo (Alex McKay estimated £500 was needed) and its opening was delayed for a year. To help meet the costs of both projects, Te Puea took the TPM on a tour of North Auckland in April 1937. But they were turned back to Auckland because of an outbreak of infantile paralysis. There, interest in Maori music seemed to have evaporated. In spite of a public statement of support by the mayor, Sir Ernest Davis,[42] audiences were small and takings low — after five concerts the group's outgoings had exceeded income by £1. In desperation, some members went to work in Mangere market gardens simply to meet the cost of accommodation in the city.

Te Puea was angered by the situation. A newspaper report noted that 'the men who build [the] canoes don't even receive the pay of a relief worker . . . Unless some such encouragement is forthcoming the hope of seeing a fleet of war canoes on the Waitemata in 1940 will fade and vanish.'[43] † In the middle of this struggle the Government confused Te Puea's feelings further by offering her not the financial assistance she was seeking but a CBE in the 1937 King's Birthday Honours List. Alex McKay accepted on her behalf; left alone, given her mood at the time, she would probably have refused it.

The same year A.J. Seamer arranged for the Waiata Choir to undertake a tour of the United Kingdom which would include a royal command performance at Buckingham Palace and one of the first transmissions on British television. The friends who had travelled to Australia two years before, Dave Manihera and Inia Te Wiata, were invited to join the tour.

Manihera had no reservations. He went to Te Puea, asked her permission, and she said yes — his performance would enhance Koroki's and Waikato's mana. Then she blessed him and offered him one of Tawhiao's ear pendants for protection.[44] ‡ 'Go with the blessing of our King and with the pride of our ancestors,' she wrote to him on 3 March. 'Go with the highest ideals in mind for you take with you the name of Waikato and the King Movement. Should you fail or err, then we left behind will suffer the consequences. If you follow an honourable path, then the glory and honour will also be ours.'[45]

Te Wiata's decision was not so easy. He had begun work impressively on the carvings for Turongo; he was also a drawcard attraction for the TPM (his name was the only one singled out for mention on the poster advertising the northern tour). Poutapu was keen that his apprentice should stay at Turangawaewae for the completion of the King's house.

He went to Te Puea for advice but she simply turned the question back on him (as Poutapu described it, one of the ways in which she was 'hard' on people for whom she had high expectations). 'Do what you know your ancestors would want you to do,' she said. That settled it for Te Wiata. There

---

† The Government eventually agreed in 1939 — at the eleventh hour — to pay the canoe workers nineteen shillings a week. But by that time morale was low and most had drifted to other jobs that paid. Only three canoes were completed in Waikato (*Te Winika, Aotea* and *Takitimu*); and one, *Ngatokimatawhaorua*, was built in Kerikeri under the direction of Pita Heperi and Piri Poutapu. The outbreak of war made further government assistance impossible.

‡ Te Puea was the keeper of the kahui ariki taonga or relics. Over the years she developed a custom of giving intimate friends a greenstone ornament to wear if they left Waikato, particularly if they were to travel overseas (and the recipients included Pakeha friends such as the Tuakau police constable Alfred Maiden, Bunny Woodhams when he left New Zealand during World War Two, and Frances Winiata when she accompanied her husband to Edinburgh for his doctoral studies).

Te Uira Manihera and Inia Te Wiata, with Michael Ramsden, in Sydney on tour with the Waiata Choir. Turongo House

214 • Te Puea — A Life

would be other opportunities to sing; there would not be another to carve a king's house.[46] So he stayed and the journey to Europe that was to bring him fame was delayed. Three months later, however, there was some consolation in reaction to his first broadcast made from Auckland while the TPM was trying to raise money there. The *Radio Record* for 7 May reported:

Listeners to the early session of 1ZB on Tuesday night heard a glorious bass voice singing the Negro spiritual *Go Down Moses*. Many could not believe that the soloist was a 22-year-old Maori. Some who took the trouble to telephone the studio manager, Barend Harris . . . insisted it was the voice of Paul Robeson. Barend Harris considers he has made an important find . . . and predicts that the Maori . . . a member of Princess Te Puea's concert party, will become a famous singer.[47]

The *Radio Record* did not really help to lay the path to fame — it omitted to mention the singer's name.

The threads of Te Puea's cultural concerns in the 1930s — the building of carved houses, the revival of canoe traditions, the performance of Maori song and dance — all came together spectacularly at the Turangawaewae Poukai on 18 March 1938. The Governor-General Lord Galway was to cross the river in *Te Winika* and open Turongo House; it was also to be the occasion on which Te Puea was to be invested with a CBE for her services to the Maori people.

The award had exposed dilemmas that were as old as the Kingitanga itself. Did the acceptance of Pakeha honours mean a recognition of the mana of the movement by Pakeha authorities? Or were they simply a means of containing the movement's leaders, trapping them in a net of European protocol? The same queries had been raised when Mahuta was offered his Legislative Council seat in 1902; they had led to Te Puea's rejection of a seat on the same council after an offer had been conveyed by Raumoa Balneavis in 1934.[48]

In the case of the 1937 award, Alex McKay's action had forced Te Puea's hand. McKay had no doubt that she should accept. If his presence at the pa stood for anything it was that the Kingitanga should continue to seek accommodation with the institutions of the majority culture, provided such accommodations recognised the mana of the kingship. In his view the CBE did just that: it was an acknowledgement by the Government that the existence of the Kingitanga and Te Puea's efforts on its behalf worked for the benefit of the Maori people and therefore of the country as a whole. He

Turongo House ready for opening, March 1938. Turongo House

One of the doors of Turongo, displaying Tawhiao's
Te Paki o Matariki coat of arms. Turongo House

Turangawaewae Marae on the day of the Turongo House opening,
18 March 1938. Turongo House

also saw acceptance as the gesture that was most likely to smooth the creases left by some of the recent encounters between the Kingitanga and the Government. He telegrammed Wellington that Te Puea would accept.[†]

Te Puea was not so certain. She was chafed by delays in the Turongo and canoe projects and blamed them on government inaction. She also discussed the matter with Koroki, Haunui and Tumate Mahuta.[49] When she discovered what McKay had done she was angry, but did not overrule him by rescinding the telegram. The fact that it had been sent simply precipitated her decision. She agreed to the acceptance, but with strong reservations.

While she was vain to a degree and enjoyed public attention, she saw her work on behalf of Koroki and the Kingitanga as a duty, a moral imperative; while she performed it she was not so much Te Puea Herangi the individual as an embodiment of the Waikato people carrying out Tawhiao's injunctions.[50] With this view of her role, it was difficult to justify acceptance of an award for it; unless she took it simply as a representative of the people, a first among equals. And this she decided to do.[51]

The day of the investiture went off almost without hitch. The weather was fine. A crowd of 5000 people assembled to watch the Governor-General

---

† In 1977 McKay did not recollect having done this. But he had said in an undated letter to Ramsden in 1937: 'I had an awful job persuading the lady to accept the honour. In fact I wired to the Kawana before she said yes' (Ramsden Papers). Inia Te Wiata's comments on the matter to Ramsden (Diary, 27 February 1947, Ramsden Papers) confirm this account.

and Lady Galway leave Ngaruawahia on board *Te Winika*, cross from the Waipa into the Waikato River, and then move upstream escorted by two smaller canoes to a landing platform below the pa.[†] The completion of this exercise and the later 'sail-pasts' drew cheers and applause from the banks; as Te Puea had anticipated, the spectators found them exhilarating. The fugleman who called the time for the paddlers was the Ngati Whawhakia veteran Hori Paki, by then in his seventies.

Te Puea herself missed the Vice-Regal arrival. She was supervising last-minute details in the kitchen when she was warned that the Governor-General had landed. There was a moment's panic as she changed out of her work clothes in the kitchen. She threw a new skirt over her head, only to find that the waist was too small; she had to fasten it with a safety pin.[52] (She forgot completely about her footwear until the solemn moment when, with head bowed, she walked forward to accept the CBE. Then she saw she was still wearing her slippers with pompoms. Nobody else, however, seemed to notice.[‡])

In addition to Lord and Lady Galway, who were paying their first visit to the pa, the official guests seated on the marae for the formal welcome included the acting-Minister of Native Affairs, Frank Langstone, the Minister of Education, Peter Fraser, the Member for Western Maori, H. T. Ratana

---

† *Te Winika* was used ceremonially for the next thirty-five years. In 1972 it was donated to the Waikato Museum by Dame Te Atairangikaahu.
‡ Apocryphal accounts of this story refer to her wearing working boots. Photographs taken on the day show her to be wearing slippers.

(and this seems to have been the first time that a Ratana leader took an active part in a Turangawaewae function), and Te Puea's old friends deposed from ministerial office, Gordon Coates and Apirana Ngata.

Before he conferred the CBE, the Governor-General defined the qualities Te Puea had displayed to earn it. Straining for superlatives, he spoke of her 'self-sacrificing devotion and stupendous personal efforts', and 'extraordinary capacity for leadership and organisation', and 'a talent for diplomacy in her dealings with other tribes and with leaders among the Pakeha . . . Through her foresight and wise guidance of her people, she made possible the execution of a land development policy among her people and proved their capacity under her leadership to turn idle lands into excellent farms at very little cost.'

Lord Galway could not resist a little paternal lecturing to the audience before him: 'It is a personal responsibility of each one of you to see that the conduct . . . of every man of the race is in every way above reproach. Any failings of the race might lead to a loss of that helpful assistance now being given to you and tends to alienate that sympathetic understanding which is so necessary to further progress.'[53]

It was a foolish, anachronistic statement, one that showed Galway did not have the perception and touch that Bledisloe had displayed. It suggested that while the European had access to New Zealand institutions as of right and regardless of behaviour, the Maori had to earn that right; and that it could be taken away from the whole group by the misbehaviour of individuals. Equally unfortunately, he reverted to the use of the term 'Native'.

Throughout the speech Te Puea had sat on the ground at Koroki's feet, her customary position at hui. When the Governor-General had finished she got to her feet and moved towards the porch of Mahinarangi, flanked by the Rev. Hemana Pokiha of Ngati Pikiao and the Kahungunu chief Waimarama Puhana. The TPM party, the women in their distinctively long piupiu, stood to attention behind her. Te Puea, instead of curtseying to the Governor-General as instructed, bowed and said, 'Tena koe'. As he pinned the insignia on her dress the old women in the crowd began to karanga; when the action was completed the audience broke into cheers. Lord Galway then opened Turongo and sat down to lunch in its dining room.

When it was all over and the Vice-Regal party had gone, Te Puea too left the marae to follow Koroki to 'shout' the workers a keg of beer at the football ground over the road. Round the back of Turongo she found a group waiting for the party. Inia Te Wiata recalled that she pulled the insignia off her dress and let them handle it, saying as she did: 'That's what you boys have earned.'[54]

Te Puea, still in her slippers, steps forward to be awarded the CBE by Lord Galway. Turongo House

Koroki's speech to his workers, in Maori, was one of the few he ever made publicly. And those who heard it were surprised by his fluency and affected by his feeling: 'I hate to think that people believe this house is for me,' he said. 'During its construction and right up to this moment it seemed to me that if it was to be mine, then I was drinking the sweat and blood of you all.' He said also that he was full of appreciation for Te Puea 'because of the great work she has accomplished for the people. It seems to me she has done enough. From now on she should rest . . . I want to keep her in good health so that I can always go to her for encouragement and advice.'[55]

Reports of the speech moved Te Puea to tears. She was even more distressed subsequently, however, by Koroki's refusal to live in the house she had built for him. Although he would stay overnight during the course of meetings and hui, he was most unwilling to give up his privacy and his companions at Waahi. And the Waahi community, understandably, was reluctant to let him go; he was their mana.

Ngata felt the Turongo hui had been a most important one. He detected a 'readjustment of the Waikato attitude towards the New Zealand constitution,' and 'a pleasing note of deference and recognition of the Empire King's representative.' There was also, he said, a readjustment on the part of non-Tainui Maori. 'They were there to pay their respects to the hereditary chief and leader [Koroki] of a very large section of the Maori race and to assist them to the best of their ability.'[56]

There were other functions at Turangawaewae throughout the decade. They included a reception for Queen Salote of Tonga in October 1936 (which led to Te Puea's visiting the Pacific Islands eleven years later);[†] visits by Lord Malcolm Douglas Hamilton and members of the British Empire Games team in April 1938, and in November 1938 by Count Felix von Luckner who left a photograph inscribed: 'To my dear friend Princess Te Puea in admiration from a sailor.' (This last encounter was to feed renewed rumours about alleged German sympathies during World War Two.)

Two memorable events followed close on the Turongo hui. Tumate Mahuta died suddenly on 28 April 1938 and his tangi was held at Turangawaewae, the first there for a senior member of the kahui ariki. A week later his body was ferried downriver by Te Winika for burial on Taupiri. Alex McKay was dejected. Tumate had been heading the Kingitanga's negotiations for government compensation for the confiscation.[‡] 'The pity of it was that he and Te Puea were just beginning to work together [for] Waikato,' McKay told Ramsden. 'I had great hopes for the results of such a combination.'[57]

In May, Koroki took up an invitation issued by Ngata at the Turongo opening and he headed a party of Waikato, Maniapoto, Taranaki and Te Arawa on a visit to the East Coast. It was the first by Waikato since Te Puea's fund-raising ventures of 1928, and the first ever by a Maori king. They visited Tuhoe, Ngati Porou, Rongowhakaata and Kahungunu marae. At Waiomatatini, Tikitiki and Wairoa, the visits coincided with the opening of new meeting houses and Koroki participated in the ceremonials. In case the reception given to him should be taken as support for the Kingitanga, Ngata felt bound to explain to a correspondent:

---

† Te Puea and Salote formed a close relationship. A journalist noted: '[They] possess in common certain instinctive traits; they both have an unshakeable idealism for the destiny of their peoples, a natural unaffected dignity, an unselfish efficiency which always puts the welfare of others before their own comfort, and a keen sense of humour to balance their seriousness of purpose.' (Undated clipping, 1936, Winiata Papers.)

‡ See page 249.

Te Puea (right foreground) watches as Tumate Mahuta's body is taken from Waahi to Taupiri by canoe, May 1938. Turongo House

The East Coast and Wairoa tribes were most respectful and hospitable, but made it quite clear that their attitude was not dictated by any regard for an institution such as the kingship, which was not a Maori idea, but by the undoubted high rank of the visitor, derived from his ancestry, not the least of which was of East Coast origin.[58]

The old statesman was as sensitive to misunderstanding as an ecumenical Protestant fearing accusations of Catholicism.

Certainly this trip, one of the most extensive Koroki ever made, was further evidence of a softening of the attitude of non-Kingitanga tribes towards the kingship. There was no longer a feeling that if they were not actually for it then they had to be against it; Koroki could be welcomed and entertained as an ariki. Earlier, he had led Waikato parties to the more sympathetic territories of Taranaki, Wanganui and Otaki (March 1936); and to Waitara for the opening of the meeting house and the unveiling of Maui Pomare's memorial in June 1936.

Te Puea had carried out all her work in the 1930s while living on, working on and moving among the Waiuku and Tikitere development schemes. She had stayed at Turangawaewae when necessary, but not continuously. By 1938 she was again making a serious effort to find a base — a farm and a home — close to the pa. The Kaihaus had made it clear they would not give her the lease she felt she had been promised (and which she had certainly earned) when the ten-year development period was completed in 1940.

She wrote several times to the Native Affairs Minister, Prime Minister Savage, about alternative arrangements; but without success. The acting-Minister Frank Langstone replied on Savage's behalf: there was no unoccupied Crown Land near Ngaruawahia that could be made available to her; she was not entitled to credit on the strength of the development schemes; and public funds could not be lent for the purchase of privately owned European land near Ngaruawahia.[59] In other words, no help would be forthcoming from the Government.

In the same letter Langstone had the gall to try to distract Te Puea's attention away from her land inquiries by lecturing her on the management of her affairs: 'I suggest that the maintenance of your farm to a high degree of productiveness is of paramount importance and should not be entirely left to the mercies of some of your young men.'[60] This tactic served simply to heighten Te Puea's anger: governments expressed friendship and unreserved approval of what she was trying to do; they offered to help her; but every time she actually asked for that help (it seemed to her), they found reason to refuse. Certainly the breadth of assistance that had been available to her from both government and public service during Ngata's term of office had shrunk; she was not to experience anything like it again until Peter Fraser became Prime Minister and Mick Jones his private secretary. In the meantime, she referred frequently and scathingly in conversation to the letter of goodwill that the Labour Party had sent to Waikato after Harry Holland's death.[61]

By the middle of 1938 the general proposal had become a specific one. A 372-acre farm belonging to the brothers William and Thomas Paterson became available for sale. It was a mere half-mile from Turangawaewae. Te Puea tried to buy the property and its 100-head dairy herd for £7000. But, again, the Government said it was unable to help. 'The increasing calls for the development of idle Native lands, with the consequent heavy expenditure in wages, materials and stock, will severely strain the funds at my disposal,' Langstone wrote to her. 'And as these funds have been set aside specially for the development of idle Native lands, I regret I will be unable to find money for the acquisition of European lands as you suggest.'[62] In disgust, Te Puea took to calling Langstone 'Fish and Chips', a reference to his initials and to his former occupation of managing railway refreshment rooms.[63]

In 1939 the Patersons agreed to let Te Puea buy the property without a deposit and without security, provided she undertook certain improvements first. The farm required a great deal of development to bring it to its full capacity for production. According to Judge Acheson,[†] the owners counted on Te Puea dying before the improvements were completed and the land reverting to them with the value increased.[64] The whole arrangement was obviously unsatisfactory and several of Te Puea's Pakeha admirers, including Acheson, and the lawyers Frederick de la Mare and John Melville, discussed the matter with her. They arranged for Harry Valder, a Hamilton businessman, to lend her the money on fair terms and by November 1940 she held the title. She named the farm the Turangawaewae Estate.[‡] She and Tumokai shifted there, living initially in a caravan attached to a thatched punga-walled cottage. Later they built a permanent house where they remained until Te Puea's death.

Throughout 1939 and 1940 working-bees of volunteers from the pa and further afield cut scrub, cleared drains, dug up kauri logs from the swampy fields for posts and sowed grass. The Chief Surveyor of the Department of Lands, Tipi Ropiha,[*] mapped out boundary lines and paddocks, and brought a group of student workers from the Auckland Teachers College. It was the back-breaking experience of the Waipipi, Tahuna and Tikitere schemes all over again, and Te Puea was now in her late fifties. But the enormous

---

† Frank Oswald Victor Acheson was a Judge of the Native Land Court for the Tai Tokerau (North Auckland) district when Te Puea met him in the mid-1930s. He was a close friend of the Te Heuheu family and became a confidant of Te Puea. His romantic idealisation of the Maori is conveyed in his novel *Plume of the Arawas* (1930), and in his series of articles about Te Puea published in the *New Zealand Mirror* in 1939 and 1940. Europeans who worked with him found him overbearing and insensitive. He was relieved of his judicial appointment in 1941.

‡ Renamed the Te Puea Estate after her death.

* A Ngati Kahungunu, later to become the first Maori to head the Department of Maori Affairs and one of Te Puea's strongest allies in the public service.

incentive was that this time it was for the benefit of herself, Tumokai and Turangawaewae, not absentee owners.

In December 1940 Te Puea could scarcely believe her good fortune. She had a productive farm alongside the pa that helped to provide employment and security for its inhabitants. 'I hardly sleep, thinking if I get up it will all disappear or fade away,' she told Ramsden.[65] Judge Acheson was able to report that the property, previously run down, now bore Te Puea's stamp: the cleanliness and efficiency of the milking shed ensured a 'super-fine' grading for the cream; and every available space within a foot of the concrete yards and the kitchen walls had been crammed with flower beds.[66] Te Puea was indeed at home.

12

War and politics

Ministers in the Labour Government at first found Te Puea a difficult person to deal with. She in turn did not think highly of those she initially saw most often, Prime Minister Savage and Assistant Native Affairs Minister Frank Langstone.[1] She had been especially angered by Savage's decision to take Ratana candidates into the Labour Movement.[2]†

A feature of Te Puea's behaviour Savage found particularly embarrassing was that she took politicians at their word. When they made general statements of intention like, 'If there's anything we can do for you don't hesitate to ask,' then she did not hesitate and she did indeed ask. Labour had been effusive in their expressions of goodwill to the Kingitanga while they were in Opposition. There was, for example, the letter presented to her and Koroki after she had taken Harry Holland's body to Parliament in 1933. It concluded that the Labour Party's and Waikato's mourning had 'commingled our sorrows and cemented our friendship, and as time runs through the years our regard and respect for your great people will grow and intensify.'[3] Te Puea assumed this statement meant that the party would listen sympathetically to her requests and she frequently used it as a lever.

When she visited Wellington in October 1937 for the unveiling of a memorial to Holland, Savage invited her and Pei Jones to his office for a cup of tea. Savage said to Te Puea, 'Now that you're in Wellington, is there anything I can do to mark the visit?' Te Puea put her hand on the Prime Minister's knee and said, 'Yes, there is, and you're going to say yes to it.' Savage shifted in his chair nervously and said, 'Well that depends on what it is.' Te Puea said, 'I want you to make George Shepherd a Judge of the

---

† As late as 1946 Te Puea was referring contemptuously to those who had gone to 'wash Ratana's nono [arse]' (Te Puea to Eric Ramsden, 12/12/46. R.P.).

Native Land Court.'[†] Savage told her the matter would require consideration, but Te Puea said she would not leave his office until he agreed. After some hesitation he did so, and Shepherd's appointment was eventually gazetted in 1940.[4]

(The incident had a sequel. Te Puea had taken for granted that Shepherd would move to Waikato after his appointment; but he remained in Wellington. She then felt she had been used by him to further his career. Her intention had been to use him, but for social rather than private gains. When he arrived at a subsequent function at Turangawaewae she walked up to him and said, 'You've let me down badly, Mr Shepherd.' He was nonplussed. He stammered and said, 'You know my home is in Wellington, Te Puea.' She threw her arms about in front of him and said, 'Yes, I know all about that.' Pei Jones said he had never seen a man as flabbergasted as Judge Shepherd.)[5][‡]

Te Puea's letters in the 1940s show her becoming more cynical and more canny. She began to understand that politicians and public servants said what they did for purposes of the moment — to set the right tone, to put themselves and other people at ease, to win or retain support, not necessarily because they meant what they said. 'Outside Parliament House they are all good men to me,' she wrote to Ramsden. 'Inside . . . it is different. I do not believe them because I have proved that they do not keep their word.'[6]

She was also prone to spontaneous displays of affection that disconcerted some ministers and cut across protocol at public receptions. At the function that followed the unveiling of the Holland memorial, she saw George Forbes and Gordon Coates in the background. 'I left the new ministers and high officers who wanted to talk to me and went to them. Gordon in particular looked so lonely. I sat on the side of the chair and put my arms round him. Then I shook hands with Mr Forbes and said I did not forget his kindness in former years.'[7]

It was not until Fraser became Prime Minister after Savage's death in April 1940 that Te Puea felt she was dealing with an equal and somebody

---

† George Patrick Shepherd had been Chief Clerk in the Department of Native Affairs. He had visited Ngaruawahia and, in a display of less than judicial disinterest, had expressed a strong willingness to help Te Puea and Waikato. She, aware of how useful Judge Acheson had been to the Tai Tokerau people, decided that Shepherd could do similar work in Waikato (she did not get on well with the then judge, C.E. MacCormack).

‡ Shepherd became Secretary of Maori Affairs before his retirement in 1948. Te Puea had little confidence in him after the incident.

whom she believed was trustworthy.[8] He was confident, a man of acute intellect and sharp wit. She also found he had informed himself on Maori affairs to a greater degree than other Labour politicians.[9] (John A. Lee noted that Fraser 'had read far more Maori history than any other member of the Labour party'.)[10] While some people experienced Fraser as a man of frightening calculation and expediency, this was rarely his approach to Maori matters, or to the arts. To him, Maori functions became a source of his increasingly rare excursions into human relations. His former secretary, Mick Jones, has said that in Maori affairs 'Fraser governed with his heart rather than his head. He had never forgotten the experience of the crofters in Scotland.'[11]

By 1940 Te Puea had known Fraser for twelve years and their association had intensified over this period. In February 1939 she had gone to a conference in Rotorua that Fraser was attending as Minister of Education with his wife Janet. She remained in their company for the duration and, at their specific request, stayed several extra days.[12] Fraser for his part judged Te Puea's nature correctly — he knew instinctively when and how to tease her and when she needed to be taken seriously. From the time he became Prime Minister, Te Puea bypassed Langstone, who had assumed the full Native Affairs portfolio, and dealt directly with Fraser. This in turn influenced his decision to take the portfolio himself in 1946, consolidating a Labour precedent that it should be held by Prime Ministers.[13]†

Before Savage died, however, Te Puea had one further dispute with the Government that resulted in Waikato's refusal to attend the national celebrations in 1940, in spite of five years' preoccupation with the centennial canoe fleet. The occasion for the disagreement was the 1938 Social Security legislation. The Act required registration of people over the age of sixteen, a declaration of income, and a tax contribution to the Social Security Fund based on that income. Provision was made for the exemption of the Governor-General, consuls and vice-consuls.

To Te Puea and Waikato the prospect of Koroki having to register at the Post Office or be questioned by taxation officials was one that demeaned his mana. In their eyes his position was unique in New Zealand life. He was not an ordinary wage-earning citizen; his role was an entirely ceremonial one, his income spent almost exclusively on entertaining visitors and supporting Waikato visits to other marae; and there had been little enough of that

---

† Savage too had taken it, but rather half-heartedly; he had delegated most of the responsibility to Langstone.

income. Consequently, Te Puea circulated a petition to the Prime Minister throughout Waikato and among the leaders of other tribes. It asked that Koroki and Te Atairangikaahu be exempted from the Act. Te Puea presented the petition to Savage at a brief meeting on 13 June 1939.[14] It was an action she would not have contemplated ten years earlier. The fact that she even considered an exemption possible was a consequence of progressive acceptance of the King's position by successive Governments and Governors-General, and of her own relations with senior politicians and public servants. In addition to the distasteful negative connotations of the Act, Te Puea also felt exemption would be a positive and formal way in which officialdom could acknowledge Koroki's position.[15] Her expectations, however, were too high. Acceptance of the kingship had not reached the point where such gestures were possible; the Government was not prepared to consider exemptions beyond those specified in the original Act. It felt that one exception would lead to a flood of applications from other quarters, and be seen as a provocation by groups that did not recognise the Maori kingship.

Te Puea argued these points with Cabinet ministers in a series of letters between June and September. 'Through the years we Waikato have been showered by successive Governments with promises and professions of goodwill and the like until we have become almost inured to this sort of thing,' she wrote to Peter Fraser. 'In matters of some moment to us — such as the present one — successive Governments have invariably disappointed us . . . it appears that the Government is determined to relegate King Koroki to some lowly place in the scheme of things.'[16] She also declared Koroki's income (tribal contributions, rents up to £50 per year and portions of cream returns for two farms) and said it was 'barely sufficient to permit of him meeting all the various tribal and other calls made on him.'[17]

She was trying to push the Government too far and too fast. It refused to budge. Ministers replied to each new submission as though the matter had never been open for consideration. Te Puea's verdict to Ramsden was that Koroki had been 'treated like a commoner . . . we have never been treated to such humbug from previous administrations as we have been by this taurekareka Kawanatanga [roguish Government].'[18]

The final slight to bruised sensibilities came in January 1940 when Koroki and Te Puea received circular letters in Fraser's name inviting them to the centenary celebrations at Waitangi on 6 February. These were stamped, not signed, the one to the King addressed simply to 'Koroki Te Rata Mahuta', and in Te Puea's the word 'sir' was scratched out and 'madam' substituted in ink. It was the last in what seemed an avalanche of insults — the refusal to consider the exemption, an unwillingness to settle the raupatu (the confiscation) in spite of the 1928 commission finding in Waikato's favour, a refusal to help with Te Puea's farm purchase, and lack of support for the canoe project. The result was that Waikato decided not to attend the centennial function: there was nothing to celebrate; they did not feel accepted by the Government and the majority culture as an integral part of New Zealand life.

This decision set the cat among the government pigeons. The Labour administration had laid great store in presiding over a public demonstration of national unity and pride. It had devoted considerable attention and money to planning the centennial activities, and was nervous about the possibility of incidents that might suggest something rotten in the state of Aotearoa, particularly cracks in the country's reputation for racial harmony (and Ngata had already given offence in Parliament by suggesting that the Maori had little reason to rise and sing For He's a Jolly Good Fellow to his colonial oppressors).[19]

Frank Langstone wrote a schoolmasterish reply on behalf of the Prime Minister: 'It is only right and proper that the people of New Zealand, both Maori and Pakeha, should combine to celebrate in a fitting way the great charter signed 100 years ago . . . those chiefs and elders who had the foresight and acumen to pierce the veil of the future and sign the Treaty — they knew that they kept the substance while giving Queen Victoria the shadow.'†

The Acting Native Minister went on to take credit for the expenditure of public funds on the land development schemes — something of which he had been bitterly critical in 1935‡ — and accused Maori of being ungrateful for this inclusion in the life of the nation: 'No other country in the world has such a record, yet I regret to say that many of our Maori brethren do not fully appreciate all that has been done for them in a brotherly, loving way.'[20]

The letter failed to woo Waikato. Its tone and lofty claims angered the elders who met with Te Puea to consider it several days before the celebrations. Another from Lord Galway was more conciliatory: 'I had been looking forward to meeting you, as it will be the last opportunity of saying

---

† Ngata, on the other hand, had said the substance had gone to the Queen and the Maori retained the shadow (NZPD, Vol. 254, 1939, p. 724 and following).
‡ In 1935 he had said that money on the schemes 'might as well have been given to children' (NZPD, Vol. 241, 1935, p. 747).

goodbye to the Maori people.'[21][†] But the 'Fish and Chips' letter had set the seal on the decision: Waikato as a group would boycott the centennial.

Ironically, the only member of the tribes who did attend officially, Piri Poutapu, became the centre of a race controversy. He remained at Waitangi to supervise the launching of the 100-foot canoe *Ngatokimatawhaorua*, which he had helped build, and because he believed the anniversary would lay the foundation for racial harmony in New Zealand.[22] In Auckland, as he was returning to Waikato, he stayed a night with R.G.H. Manley; this led to Manley and his wife being evicted from their flat because the landlady, Mrs E.A. Tomlinson, did not allow Maori on her properties.[23]

From the outbreak of World War Two in September 1939 the old accusation of German sympathies was levelled at Te Puea. This was partly a consequence of her behaviour in the past; partly of her own ambivalence; and largely of a public fear of fifth-columnists that reached panic proportions in 1940.

From the past there was the memory of her resistance to enlistment and conscription in World War One. People who had attributed this to German ancestry then — or heard others do so — were only too willing to take up the same allegation. Rumours about the disloyalty of 'that German woman' were rife in European circles in Waikato.[‡] They were fed by the knowledge that Count Felix von Luckner had visited Turangawaewae in 1938 and that he and Te Puea had enjoyed a cordial relationship.[24]

Initially, Te Puea was less than wholehearted about support of the war effort. She still followed Tawhiao's injunction to his followers before Major William Gilbert Mair that forbade them to take up arms. She was also conscious that the injustice of the confiscation had not been settled. 'The blood is not yet dry,' she told those around her, quoting Te Rata.[25] This implied that she was still doubtful whether Waikato had anything to fight for; whether they owed any loyalty to the Government and people of New Zealand.

On 20 September 1939, she wrote a cautious letter to Prime Minister Savage. 'At present it is not quite clear where danger will threaten this Dominion . . . it is not a time for much talk or heroics. It is a time for cool reasoning. The Waikato tribes and all allied tribes endorse the Government's

---

† In fact it was not. Galway was persuaded to come to Turangawaewae for a private goodbye to Koroki and Te Puea on 16 December 1940.
‡ See page 95 for evidence of this allegation persisting into the 1970s.

policy of voluntary enlistments and are prepared to render what help they can for the defences of our country and to assist in the industries of the Dominion.'[26] Implicitly, she was making two points: Waikato would assist in the defence of New Zealand but was unwilling to fight overseas; and she would again oppose the imposition of conscription.†

Privately she was more explicit. 'Waikato are not going to the war,' she wrote to Ramsden in November. 'If any of the young men want to they can. Those that do not wish to go will be able to assist . . . with kai.'[27] Maori Waikato elders, survivors of the 1917 and 1918 anti-conscription campaigns, took an even harder line. When Tonga Mahuta tried to persuade Waikato men to enrol in the Home Guard, the old chief Te Kanawa stood up at Turangawaewae and said they should not take up arms at home or abroad:

> Why should the Maori people guard this island? . . . It is no longer ours. The British evidently do not wish to keep their word as Rangatiras . . . What difference does it make if the Tiamana [Germans] come here? The British have taken our land. They have killed our wives and children. The Treaty of Waitangi is only a delusion to make the Maori people believe that the British people will keep their word of honour.[28]

The feelings of elderly conservatives had been hardened by the fact that the raupatu issue was unresolved, the Social Security tax, and the failure of a Tuwharetoa petition to the Privy Council in 1940 seeking ratification of the Treaty of Waitangi.‡ In turn, Waikato's refusal to attend the Waitangi celebrations had convinced many Europeans that they were disloyal and therefore a threat in time of war.

A further complicating factor seems to have been a confusion in the public mind between the Ratana and King Movements. T.W. Ratana had visited Japan in 1924, accompanied by Tupu Taingakawa; and in 1928 a Japanese bishop, Juji Nakada, had come to Ratana Pa for the opening of the Prophet's temple, which had been designed by a Maniapoto man named Tueka Hetet from ideas conceived in Japan.[29] After the outbreak of war

---

† Conscription had been introduced in July 1940, but for Europeans only.

‡ The Petition arose from Hoani Te Heuheu's attempt to establish that legislation in conflict with the Treaty of Waitangi was ultra vires. He lost a court case against the Aotea District Maori Land Court in 1939 and took an appeal to the Privy Council. Waikato supported this move with petition signatures and with money. Te Puea raised £600 for a lawyer named M.H. Hampson to travel to England to argue the case (Te Puea to Eric Ramsden, 11/7/41. R.P.)

some Ratana did, in fact, express sympathy for the Japanese cause.† But the vast majority remained loyal to New Zealand; Paraire Paikea, the Ratana Member for Northern Maori, was Minister in Charge of the Maori War Effort in the War Cabinet.

Even if there had been some truth in rumours of Ratana-Japanese collusion, people familiar with Maori affairs would have known that the gulf between the two movements made it most unlikely that the Kingitanga would share such feelings. None the less there were suggestions after the Pearl Harbour attack that Te Puea was in league with the Japanese. A former Huntly schoolmistress was to write thirty years later that the influence of Turangawaewae throughout the war had been determinedly anti-British and pro-Japanese.[30]

Accusations assumed such a pitch that they eventually reached Te Puea. She wrote several times to Ramsden in the early war years distressed about them.[31] 'What have I done to deserve such a . . . name?' she asked. 'New Zealand is full of German people. The King of England has more German blood than me.'[32] Ramsden became concerned that the crescendo of slander might destroy all the beneficial effects of twelve years of contact between the Kingitanga and Pakeha institutions. He wrote to the *Auckland Star* from Sydney in 1940:

> It has come to my notice that rumours are in circulation suggesting that Te Puea, being of German origin, possesses Nazi sympathies and that consequently her political attitude has been influenced accordingly. This is not only a malicious and ignorant lie, and most harmful to the reputation of a woman of whom all New Zealanders should be proud, but palpably absurd. The King has no more loyal subject that Te Puea Herangi, ariki-tapairu of Waikato. As to her origin, it is true that her grandfather, once a magistrate in Waikato, was of German stock. But to infer that her mind is influenced because of early family associations is equally ridiculous. Te Puea never met her grandfather.[33]

The rumours did not at first diminish. Public fears were sustained by press reports of fifth-columnists weakening victim countries and promoting military collapse,[34] and the Government was frequently under attack for not

---

† Pei Jones, himself the subject of an investigation, was approached in Hawera by a Security Intelligence Bureau officer for information about the loyalty of members of the Ratana Movement.

taking firmer steps to forestall potential sabotage.[35] The Police Department, which was fully responsible for security investigations up to February 1941, was apparently satisfied that neither Te Puea nor the Kingitanga represented a threat to the nation. But from 1941 their work was extended and duplicated by the Security Intelligence Bureau, set up by Cabinet at the suggestion of the British Government and controlled by an English Army officer with no previous New Zealand experience.[36] This agency did not display the attention to detail and the balances of judgement that had characterised police work; and in mid-1942 it subjected the leadership of the King Movement to a clumsy and unnecessary investigation.

Te Puea learned about the enquiry from two sources. A security officer approached a senior Maori army officer, Rangi Royal, and asked him about the political sympathies of the Jones brothers, Mick and Pei. Royal was amused and immediately rang Mick Jones, who was by that time private secretary to the Minister of Native Affairs; Jones told Te Puea.[37] Then Piri Poutapu was asked about Te Puea's activities by a Raglan County Council official acting, he said, on behalf of the SIB.[38]

Te Puea's response was to seek advice from the Ngaruawahia storekeeper R.C. Knight (who, in Alex McKay's absence for army service had taken over some of the secretarial functions at the pa), and from the Raglan County Council officers K. Wright and H. Wilson. 'With a long discussion they [asked] me to let them handle [the matter] and have a private inquiry before I do anything. So I left it to their wishes.'[39] Eventually, however, she became impatient to end the nerve-wracking business. She rang Fraser, told him what was going on (he appeared not to know) and asked him to 'call the dogs off'.[40] He did so. At the end of that year Te Puea wrote to Ramsden that the Prime Minister had taken a lot of trouble to get to the bottom of the matter and that she was most grateful.[†] She added that she had never thought herself clever enough to be a spy.[41] The following February, apparently as a result of this and other blunders, the SIB was put under police control and its director dismissed and sent back to England.[42]

There had never been any justification for fears about Waikato's loyalty this time. The younger men, two generations removed from Tawhiao's

---

† The contents of a file that appeared to contain the results of this investigation were missing from the National Archives in 1975. It was titled 'Te Puea Herangi and leaders of the Waikato Tribe', Maori Affairs Series 31/53. Archives staff had no idea how the material had come to be removed and instituted a search to ensure that it had not been replaced in the wrong file. A related document in the same folder, a report on Peter Fraser's meeting with Waikato to discuss the war effort, was still in place.

influence, were only too happy to volunteer for overseas service. In July 1940 Te Puea wrote that 300 had gone to camp; two years later, the number had risen to close to 1000.[43] At no stage did Te Puea discourage enlistment. Alex McKay remembered taking two boys to her from the Hopuhopu Camp early in the war. 'They had reservations out of loyalty to their parents' ideas. When we got to Turangawaewae, these boys very correctly made their request to Te Puea that they be allowed to volunteer for service overseas. Te

Te Puea at Turangawaewae with two Waikato volunteer soldiers in the early days of World War Two. Turongo House

Puea said to them: "I'm not going to tell you to go; I'm not going to tell you to stay. If you want to go and you think it's the right thing, then go." One of the boys went.'[44] Among others who volunteered were three members of her own family: Takua ('Darky') Herangi, Monty Searancke and Wini Tukere Te Anga.

When Fraser confronted her with accusations of disloyalty in 1941, Te Puea repeated what she had said in World War One: 'Look, Peter, it's perfectly simple. I'm not anti-Pakeha; I'm not pro-German; I'm pro-Maori.'[45] And pro-Maori meant respecting Tawhiao's pacifist injunction personally, but not interfering in the conscientious decisions of others. It also meant conducting an intensive campaign to support the war effort in non-combative ways.

From the beginning of 1940 Te Puea's letters are crammed with details of fund-raising for the Red Cross (especially from dances, garden parties and selling farm produce), collecting food for army camps (mainly potatoes, pumpkins and shellfish), and dispatching comfort items and clothes to Maori troops overseas. In October 1941 she described a typical week: 'We sent £100 for our Maori Battalion overseas . . . and £200 towards comforts for the battalion, also £100 for the general purposes fund of the Waikato Red Cross.'[46] To help with these activities she was lent service vehicles and a Maori officer returned from overseas, Captain Whetu Werohia, was assigned to her as a driver.[47] At the request of Captain Guy Powles of Army Headquarters† she organised a group of women to make camouflage nets for home defence;[48] and she entertained troops from army camps each Sunday at Turangawaewae. Alex McKay estimated that, over six years, Te Puea was personally responsible for raising between £30,000 and £40,000 towards the war effort.[49]

In spite of this wide and visible range of activities, Peter Fraser still felt that some formal declaration of Waikato's position was necessary.‡ It is probable that the Prime Minister was under pressure from public opinion and his parliamentary colleagues who (apart from Coates and the Maori members) did not know Te Puea well. Consequently Fraser invited her and a group of Waikato leaders to Wellington early in July 1942 to discuss Waikato's war effort. The party included Pei Jones, Roore Edwards, Te Kiri Katipa, Ngapaka Kukutai and Hori Paki. They were accommodated at the

---

† Later Sir Guy Powles, first New Zealand Ombudsman.
‡ Ironically, Fraser himself and one of his ministerial colleagues had been jailed for sedition in 1916 when they opposed conscription.

Midland Hotel at government expense. On the afternoon of 1 July, Fraser welcomed the party at Parliament and thanked its members for their assistance to the country up to that time. Then he said he wanted a statement of where Waikato stood and whether the tribes would be able to increase their contributions to the war effort.[50] Te Puea replied for Waikato the following day. 'I shall do all I can do to help you with everything that I am able to do,' she told Fraser emphatically. But what she was able to do, she was already doing. Waikato had chosen what they felt were the two most appropriate areas of work, caring for the sick and wounded and raising additional food. 'I do not see what other help we can give. We have already fulfilled everything under the headings discussed.' What she was not able to do, she stressed, was to give approval for compulsory service or the idea of war itself. 'If you want to hear from our mouths that we agree to these, then you never will.' And she repeated Tawhiao's statement to Mair at Alexandra. There was much more that the Government could do to help Waikato, however. She referred to the raupatu and the request for Koroki's exemption from the Social Security Act, and asked that she be given more seed potatoes so as to be able to grow more vegetables.[51]

An earlier speaker, Te Kiri Katipa, told the Prime Minister that 'things have changed since the First [World] War because in 1936 Prime Minister Savage promised a settlement of our grievance over the confiscations. Our people will help the war effort . . . [but] I and others of my generation will never forget the wrongs the Pakeha did to our people.' Pei Jones, acting as interpreter, hesitated over this final sentence. But he need not have done. Fraser got to his feet and walked forward to shake Katipa by the hand. 'My word,' he told him, 'you are a man after my own heart. The English people treated my people in the same way as your people were treated. If my people had not been driven off their lands I don't think I'd be here today.'[52] This capacity for identifying with the Maori underdog rather than the Pakeha overlord was one of the features of Fraser's behaviour that won him a high place in Te Puea's estimation.

The major results of the conference were that Waikato felt supported by government approval of the efforts they were making, while officialdom was reassured that the King Movement did not present a subversive threat. Fraser also agreed at last to waive the Social Security provisions for Koroki and Te Atairangikaahu, and said there would be no attempt to conscript Maoris. Subsequently there was no further talk of Waikato disloyalty in official circles; nor was Te Puea impeded in her work by the opinions of die-hard conservatives like Marae Edwards of Kawhia. As an additional measure of assistance, Tonga Mahuta undertook to organise the transfer of Waikato manpower into essential industries, especially the coal mines and freezing works.[53]

Late in 1942 Te Puea extended her programme of entertaining troops to include Americans stationed in New Zealand.[†] There were precedents for this contact. She told Ramsden that Tawhiao had predicted their presence in some of his whakatauki at Hikurangi and Whatiwhatihoe;[54] and when Mahuta was taken aboard the flagship of the American Fleet that visited Auckland in August 1908, he told Admiral Charles Perry that his countrymen would one day come to New Zealand in large numbers.[55]

Her own first encounters with Americans were not happy ones, however. In February 1939 a group of 300 scientists attending a conference in Auckland called at Turangawaewae. One of them, Professor Herbert Gregory, asked if he could take the canoe *Te Winika* back to the United States for museum display: 'As a gift!' Te Puea wrote to Ramsden. 'You can just imagine how I felt . . . I know they do not care for the native people in their own country.'[56] Then she was asked if she would sell the canoe, which she also refused to do. But she said she would build another one for the New York museum if the Americans would secure some land for her near Turangawaewae. She called this arrangement 'a gift for a gift'. The visitors declined and nothing further was heard of the proposal.

Towards the end of 1942 there were more than 29,000 marines stationed in camps around Auckland. These men ranged far afield during their periods of weekend leave and by November there were increasing reports of incidents involving Maori women in places like Rangiriri, Huntly, Ngaruawahia and Cambridge. Te Puea rang Alex McKay early in the month at Waiouru, where he had just been posted as Chief Instructor of the Armoured Training School.[‡]

She asked me to come up to help deal with this problem. I rang the American headquarters at Manurewa from Ngaruawahia and made an appointment for both of us to see the Officer Commanding at 11 a.m. the following day. When we got there we were shown into a side room. Then

---

† By 1944 their number had risen to over 100,000, most of them members of the First and Second Marine Divisions.

‡ He served later with the Expeditionary Force in Egypt, Italy and Japan, and retired from the army with the rank of major.

we waited for one-and-a-half hours. I was boiling. Eventually I said to the aide-de-camp: 'Princess Te Puea made this appointment for eleven o'clock. It is now half-past twelve. When is she going to meet the Officer Commanding?' This officer opened a door and said to someone inside: 'This nigger woman is still waiting for you out here.' I didn't hear the reply. Then he came out and said, 'He won't be long.' Te Puea heard it all. She simply got up and walked out.

On the way back to Ngaruawahia we called in at the various Maori settlements and told them what had happened — Tuakau, Waiuku, Mercer, Rangiriri, Huntly. On the following Monday I was still at Turangawaewae and I took a call from Manurewa. A very irate voice at the other end said, 'Are you aware that I have twenty-seven men in hospital, all assaulted by Maoris?' I said that I wasn't aware of it. But I wasn't surprised. Then the voice said, 'Well, I'd like to see Princess Te Puea.' I told him I thought an appointment could be made and asked him to hold the line, Te Puea said, 'Yes, invite him down.' So I said, 'You're very welcome to come. Would next Sunday suit you?' He said yes and we arranged a meeting for 2.30.

He arrived at Ngaruawahia surrounded by a mass of brass and began lecturing Te Puea straight away. She interrupted him and said, 'Just a minute.' And she told the girls to bring in afternoon tea. He said, 'I haven't come here to have afternoon tea. I've come here to settle this matter of my men being knocked around.' Te Puea said, 'We have an old Maori custom. Before we kill our guests and eat them, we always feed them well.'[57] It was a characteristic performance from Te Puea: she defused the tension with good humour and hospitality. And she suggested that the best way to smooth feelings and prevent future incidents was to bring large groups of marines to Turangawaewae to socialise with Maoris and enjoy their hospitality in controlled circumstances. She said she was also sympathetic about the disorienting effect on the troops of living away from home.[58]

The outcome was entirely satisfactory. On 19 November a trainload of sixty officers (including twelve colonels and eight majors) came to the pa for a day's entertainment. They were taken on tours by Piri Poutapu, fed, treated to TPM performances, and presented with twenty-five ornamented swagger sticks carved by Poutapu's school. Colonel Samuel White wrote to Te Puea the following day that American forces had 'never . . . been received with more warmth or been entertained more lavishly'; he also apologised for the inability of the Officer Commanding, Major-General M.S.

Piri Poutapu escorts American servicemen around Turangawaewae, November 1942. Turongo House

Harmon, to attend because of 'official duties'.[59] For her part, Te Puea was favourably impressed by the Americans' warmth and spontaneity. At first she had thought them 'whaka hihi' [skites], she told Ramsden; but later they were 'tino pai'.[60] There were no further major incidents involving Maori and American troops in the area; and Te Puea continued to entertain parties of marines for the remainder of the war.†

In March 1943 over 400 of them came to Ngaruawahia for the annual regatta, revived by the town and now organised in association with Turanga-waewae. Peter Fraser presented Captain S.D. Jupp with a carved inkstand and a kumete for President Roosevelt. The following year, when she attempted to repeat the function on the same scale, Te Puea was prevented by wartime rationing from obtaining fresh pork. She was indignant: she believed 'poaka' was an essential ingredient at a Maori function. She rang Fraser from the office of Bunny Woodhams (just returned from overseas

---

† It was to thank Te Puea for this hospitality that Vice-President Richard Nixon visited Turangawaewae on 9 November 1953; by that time, however, she had been dead for thirteen months.

service). Woodhams recalled: 'I could hear the Prime Minister at the other end explaining carefully why she couldn't have pork and what the country was doing with it. Most of it was being turned into bacon and ham to be sent to Britain. But she stuck to her guns and said Maori hospitality demanded it. Fraser continued to put his side of the case until Te Puea said finally: "Look, Peter — no pork, no party." She got it of course.'[61]

These wartime regattas and 'garden parties' (as Te Puea liked to call the full day's outdoors entertainment) set a pattern for fund-raising and socialising that was to become a permanent feature of life at Turangawaewae. Te Puea developed networks of contacts through whom she obtained items of food that were often in short supply and equipment (she often rented tents and trestle tables from the Hopuhopu Army Camp, for example).

She was also a perfect hostess, dividing her time between supervising the kitchens and the dining room and caring for her guests. She circulated constantly, but gave sufficient time to each visitor to whom she spoke, to make them feel welcome and important; she excelled at light, bantering conversation. On occasion when she was not immediately recognised, her standing joke was to point to her friend Mihi Thomson — who also wore a white headscarf — and say, 'There, that's the Princess Te Puea.'[62]

She also gave considerable time and attention to training the girls at the pa in the responsibilities of looking after people. She was determined that Turangawaewae would be remembered as a place where visitors felt at home; but she knew a reputation for hospitality could not rest on her efforts alone. She created an army of helpers and hostesses who could deputise for her. 'She kept stressing to us that our job was to make people comfortable there,' Sister Heeni remembered. 'And we did. She also taught us to make visitors feel that it was their presence at a function that made it a success, not our entertaining. We always had to thank them for coming and making the occasion an enjoyable one.'[63]

Putting guests at their ease did not mean issuing them with a licence to take liberties, however. She was quick to stop people when she thought they had gone too far. When the American officer Colonel White kept telling her how beautiful she was and asking her to sit with him, she simply explained that she preferred to wait on her guests. When he persisted, cajolingly, she told him to 'Go to hell'.[64] She also protected her helpers when the attentions of troops became troublesome, but usually in ways that did not involve a guest losing face; by deploying the girls in other parts of the pa, for example.[65]

Te Puea was more politically active in the war years than she had been previously. She was still committed to opposing inroads on the Kingitanga by the Ratana Movement, but her feeling had lost the sharp edge of earlier years. In spite of ill-health, she seemed to have been blessed by a capacity to outlive her opponents: her cousin Piupiu had died before the war; Ratana himself in September 1939; and Haunui — the last major thorn in her flesh — was to follow them in November 1945. There was no longer evidence of a Ratana campaign to take over the Kingitanga. And, even more disarming than the removal of adversaries, she had been drawn into warm relationships with Ratana Members of Parliament, especially Tokouru Ratana (Western Maori) and Paraire Paikea (Northern Maori); both also died before the end of the war.

Pei Jones stood for Parliament on two more occasions in Te Puea's lifetime, the General Election in 1943 and the by-election in 1945 caused by Tokouru Ratana's death (he had stood unsuccessfully in 1930 and 1938 and was to do so again in 1957, 1960, 1963). On each occasion he persuaded Te Puea to support him openly and actively; she issued special editions of *Te Paki o Matariki*, identifying him as the official Kingitanga candidate, and press releases on his behalf.[66] Although he offered himself nominally as an independent, the National Party backed him in 1945 and he was runner-up with 2863 votes to Matiu Ratana's 4663.

The commitment to Pei was personal rather than political, however. Te Puea herself never declared for any one party, although up to the war she had favoured the Nationals because of her earlier associations with Coates and Ngata, now in Parliament under that banner. During the war, however, she was pulled further and further into the orbit of the Labour Party. The relationship with Fraser, although stormy and strained at times, intensified. And on two occasions she was approached by Taranaki elders (Tonga Awhikau, Rangi Marama and Rangi Huna) and asked if she would allow her name to go forward as a Labour nomination.[67] She refused. 'I have no wish for the seat because I cannot understand the Pakeha language or the European way', and, 'Dave came before my eyes . . . I could not leave him.'[68] But she no longer rejected the possibility of a Labour loyalty as she almost certainly would have done before the war.[†]

The proximity to Labour ministers and sympathies was increased when Mick Jones accepted the position of Native Affairs Ministerial Private

---

† In 1949, opposing the nomination of Mrs Iriaka Ratana to the Western Maori seat after the death of her husband Matiu, Te Puea told the *Waikato Times*: 'I did not want a woman to belittle men. It is the tradition of the Tainui canoe . . . that a woman must not jump into the front before the men.' (*Waikato Times*, 30/11/49). It is probable that this is the tactician in her talking; in fact, when she wanted to speak or take a front-line role herself, she rarely hesitated.

Secretary after Raumoa Balneavis died suddenly outside his office in May 1940 (and after holding that position for thirty years).[†] In this capacity and a subsequent one as Maori Liaison Officer, Jones worked with Frank Langstone (who, as manager of Railways' refreshment rooms, had known Jones' father-in-law), H.G.R. Mason and Peter Fraser; and, later still, with E.B. Corbett, Walter Nash and Ralph Hanan. Jones' presence did much to restore Te Puea's faith in the department, something that had waned since Ngata's resignation in 1934. So close did her relationship with Jones and his wife Kahu become that Ramsden was to accuse her in the late 1940s of adopting socialist politics.[69] Her views throughout this time did move markedly closer to Mick's and away from those of Pei, her earlier spokesman.[70]

This shift also involved a drift away from former allies. She told Ramsden in 1942 that she had not seen Ngata for a year and supposed that he had 'forgotten about Waikato'.[71] The following year the Colossus of Maoridom lost his Eastern Maori seat to Tiaki Omana after nearly forty years in Parliament, and the Ratana political hegemony was complete.

Also in 1943, in May, her old friend Gordon Coates died suddenly at his desk in Parliament. Te Puea asked if Waikato could have the body at Turangawaewae for a day; when this proved impossible, she organised a Maori reception for it at St Mary's Church in Parnell, Auckland, then travelled north to Matakohe for the burial. 'It was a real Maori tangi,' she wrote to Ramsden. 'Everybody was in black with greenery on their head, and everybody sobbing. As you say, he was a real friend to Waikato . . . He was also the most rangatira Pakeha I have ever respected.'[72] From this time, apart from Hamilton representative Hilda Ross, Te Puea's friends in Parliament were Labour members.

---

† Because of his commitment to his lucrative Native Agent's business in Hawera, Jones tried to persuade Langstone to take his younger brother Pei for the position. But Pei was unacceptable to Labour because of his National sympathies. Instead, Mick did go to Wellington and Pei took over the business in Hawera for the next five years.

13

Raupatu and other causes

Te Puea interrupted war work in December 1942 to join the fight to keep Orakei Marae in Auckland in Ngati Whatua control. She told Ramsden that, at Koroki's request, she was circulating a petition to Parliament asking that 'the Orakei Maoris be secured in their ancestral home' and their village be 'brought up to present day conditions'.[1] She collected signatures throughout Waikato: on 14 December she took the petition to the Te Awamutu races, and the following day to Kaiaua on the Hauraki Gulf.[2]†

Her interest in Orakei, although active in the last ten years of her life, had been continuous from childhood. The Ngati Whatua tribe had married into the Waiohua people, of Waikato origin, in the eighteenth century; consequently Waikato and Ngati Whatua had frequently undertaken joint ventures as kinsmen. Ngati Whatua had also supported Te Puea's work and attended her hui at Mangatawhiri and Turangawaewae, and some of them had joined her community.

In addition to these connections, Te Puea was moved by the progressive disinheritance of Ngati Whatua. To her, their history seemed to represent that of the Maori people as a whole — only more intensively than in the case of most tribes. They had sold 3000 acres of land to Lieutenant-Governor William Hobson for what became the city of Auckland; then their holdings had shrunk steadily until, by the early 1940s, they occupied a small acreage

---

† The petition, with 3319 signatures, was presented to Parliament on 24 February 1943. It had been signed by all leading members of the kahui ariki except Koroki. It produced no discernible result.

at Okahu Bay alongside Tamaki Drive, from which the Government and Auckland City Council were trying finally to dislodge them.

Their legal position had become tenuous as a result of an inexplicable Native Land Court decision in 1898. This had declared that the trustees of the 700-acre Orakei Block were in fact owners, and that consequently their descendants had freehold titles and the right to sell them. The Crown then set to work to acquire this land and bought all but three acres of it by 1928, including the thirty-nine-acre papakainga area, which the court had twice declared to be 'inalienable'.[†] On the southern margin of the bay was a four-acre site that included the tribe's church and cemetery, given to the Church of England in 1858; the Anglicans had sold this to the Crown in 1926 when legislation was passed to permit the sale of gifted land.

By the early 1940s the community still occupied their three acres and some of the surrounding Crown land. Most of the residents refused to move; they had never recognised the rights of the descendants of the trustees to sell the block, and they argued that the mana of the tribe was vested in the traditional marae site and that its associations could not be transplanted elsewhere. In the meantime the Auckland City Council considered the settlement an eyesore and suggested that because of drainage problems, it was a danger to the health of the wider Auckland community. The council and the Government had launched a concerted effort to have the village evacuated and destroyed and its inhabitants housed on another site.[3]

The proposed resettlement was unjustifiable in Te Puea's eyes. She saw it only as a further example of European rapaciousness. Pakeha had systematically deprived Ngati Whatua of everything that gave the tribe security and identity. Then they abused these Maori for poverty and lack of spirit and used their handicaps as an excuse to plunder them still further.[4] It was also incomprehensible to her that all this should have taken place after the tribe had virtually given away 3000 acres of what became the most valuable real estate in the country.[‡] Was there no end to Pakeha greed?, she asked Ngaruawahia Borough Councillor Bill Eaddy. Finally, the plight of Ngati Whatua was compounded by their lack of effective leadership. It was this last fact that impelled Te Puea to take up the cause.

---

† There were another ten acres on high ground to the east overlooking Okahu Bay, where the community was eventually resettled in the 1950s.

‡ Although an assortment of blankets, trousers, shirts, tobacco, hatchets and other goods to the value of £56 was given to the owners, this was by way of an exchange of gifts. (See Kawharu p. 6)

Eaddy, a service station owner and friend of Te Puea, was also impressed by the merit of the Ngati Whatua case against eviction. He took Te Puea's petition to a meeting of the borough council but received no support. He then gave it to two of his Auckland trade union friends, Pat Potter and Tom Karaka of the Auckland Labourers Union.[5]

Te Puea went to Orakei on 5 April 1954 to talk to the pa's inhabitants and lead them in a general clean-up. Her intention, she told them, was to help renovate the meeting house and build a dining room that could also be used for dances and concerts for fund-raising. While she was there, Potter and a group of trade unionists called on her to discuss ways in which the Auckland Trades Council and sympathetic workers could help preserve the community.

The outcome was a working bee in the first weekend in June in which Te Puea, the Orakei inhabitants and 200 unionists erected a 300-foot palisade fence around the pa. It was made up of a two-foot concrete base surmounted by manuka stakes, with totara posts at eight-foot intervals. Its intention was to hide the alleged 'eyesore', give the residents some privacy, and generally begin the process of upgrading the pa. The timber was donated by a Maori land owner in Waitakere, and the cost of other materials, about £300, was met by the supporting unions. Te Puea was astonished and delighted. 'I could hardly believe it when [the fence] was finished that day. I thought I was dreaming. The next day I came back to make sure it was there. True enough, it was.'[6]

Orakei inhabitants shed tears when Wally Ashton, secretary of the trades council, presented them with a visitors' book for the marae. Te Puea, on their behalf, thanked Pat Potter and all the Pakeha workers. 'For what you have done for our people who needed it most, I do not know how to say often enough "God bless you".'[7] The June issue of *In Print*, a socialist newspaper, carried a photograph of Te Puea waving triumphantly, 'acclaiming' the finished job.†

More than any other issue, Te Puea's views on Orakei strained her relationship with Peter Fraser and at one point almost severed it. To Fraser, the issue was clear-cut: the Crown owned most of the land, Ngati Whatua did not, and their village was unsightly and unhealthy; they would have to be moved. ('The problem could have been solved years ago if orders had

† The exercise gave Te Puea friends in the Communist Party that Peter Fraser felt were unsavoury. Up to the time of her death she kept in touch with party secretary Vic Wilcox.

been given for bulldozers to be used instead of persuasion,' Fraser told Parliament seven years later. He attributed Maori sentiments only to the fact that 'people become attached even to miserable houses'.[8]

Fraser warned Te Puea that if she became involved with the Auckland Trades Council and tried to protect the pa, the police would be sent in and she could end up in prison.[9] 'I told the heads of the trade union but they only smiled and said the Government would not do it because of the coming elections,' she told Ramsden.[10] And to Bill Eaddy the day they put up the pallisades she said she had put on two sets of underwear to keep her warm in jail.[11]

In the event, there were no arrests and some unionists believed this was due entirely to Te Puea's presence.[12] The clean-up of the pa, the concerted action of the Auckland Trades Council and their threat to blacklist any attempt to demolish the pa and rebuild the community elsewhere — all this resulted in a stay of execution. The eviction of the inhabitants and their resettlement on the hill above the old marae site in houses they could rent but not own was not carried out until 1951, the year before Te Puea's death.[†]

Another fruit of Te Puea's wartime work was the first significant progress in lifting standards of Maori health throughout Waikato. The progress began through her association with the Medical Officer of Health in Hamilton, Doctor H.B. Turbott, and one of his inspectors, T.C. Thompson. Te Puea enjoyed the company of both men and they were prepared to put the resources of the department fully behind her efforts to improve sanitation and reduce infectious disease.

The first thing Dr Turbott attacked after his appointment in the mid-1930s was the high typhoid mortality rate (thirty-six times greater for Maori in Waikato than for Europeans). The cause, quite clearly, was the casting of human excrement and the absence of piped or tanked water supplies in Maori communities outside Turangawaewae. Turbott extracted a special vote of £40,000 from Minister of Health, Peter Fraser, to cover the cost of tanks and privies for the four Waikato counties. The next step was to find a way of distributing them and persuading people to use them. Te Puea met both needs. She offered lorries from the Native Affairs land development

---

† Late in 1951 the Orakei meeting house was burned down on government orders. Te Puea, in hospital a few weeks afterwards, asked Hamilton Member of Parliament Hilda Ross to tell the Maori Affairs Minister E.B. Corbett that she could still smell the smoke; she believed firmly that the National Government had resorted to arson to drive Ngati Whatua out (interview Alex McKay).

schemes to deliver the privies and tanks to Maori householders; and she persuaded Turbott to visit all the marae concerned to explain the scheme and ensure local cooperation. It was an apparent success: by 1940, after two years of the scheme's operation, the Maori typhoid mortality rate had dropped to the level of the European rate.[13]

Turbott's second scheme was to reduce the high rate of tuberculosis infection and mortality. He began a house-to-house survey in 1940 to detect sources of infection among Maori families. District nurses conveyed people to hospital for Mantoux tests and X-rays, and specialists there isolated active cases.

'Here we struck trouble,' Turbott recalled. 'Hospital was regarded as a place you went to when you were dying. And there was nowhere to stay in Hamilton if you were Maori and wanted to visit a patient; none of the hotels welcomed Maori guests.' Turbott surmounted the difficulties by asking Te Puea to go to Waikato Hospital for a test and x-ray, which she did willingly; and then persuading the Hamilton Rotary Club to join forces with her in building a hostel in Frankton for Maori visitors. She also allowed Turbott to put a hut on the Turangawaewae farm so that an infectious case could be treated away from contact with his own family, but close to a Maori environment.

'The response of the people, reluctant at first, gathered momentum. Families with TB cases had them treated and district nurses kept an eye on all contacts. After some years, it seemed that there were no more secondary cases.'[14] Dr Turbott was delighted at the way he and Te Puea had been able to work together. 'We must pay tribute to the helpfulness and willing cooperation of this enlightened and capable Waikato leader,' he concluded in one of his annual reports.[15]

In 1943 Te Puea decided to consolidate the results of the Health Department's programme by trying to persuade Maori from outside Turangawaewae to seek medical treatment. She had tried to operate a clinic from the pa but the health of her own doctor, Douglas Martin, was not up to such a project. She had heard of another Waikato doctor whose reputation was high among Maori. Dr Rachel Monk and her husband Frank had come to New Zealand in 1939 as Jewish refugees from Czechoslovakia. After she had acquired New Zealand qualifications at Otago University, the Health Department had posted Dr Monk to the mining town of Pukemiro, about twelve miles from Ngaruawahia. She quickly established a strong practice that included a large number of Maori, some of whom came from as far as Tuakau to consult her.[16]

Te Puea had Captain Werohia drive her to Pukemiro to meet the Monks. She told them about her plan for a clinic at Turangawaewae where Maori could come for treatment in a Maori environment. Consultations would be held in Mahinarangi, and Te Puea herself would be reassuringly present for these and subsequent house calls in Ngaruawahia. Dr Monk agreed to the proposal and initially came to the pa for one afternoon a week. She charged nothing for consultation, taking only the Social Security subsidies. The scheme was a modification of Te Puea's original plan to use Mahinarangi as a hospital.

Confidence in the clinic spread more rapidly than Te Puea or Dr Monk had anticipated. Within a few months the doctor was coming twice a week, Monday and Friday afternoons, and seeing up to thirty patients each time. They came from further afield than Ngaruawahia, as Te Puea had hoped they would: from Tuakau in the north to Te Kuiti in the south. Dr Monk was helped with administration, interpreting and nursing care by Mrs Maira Moke and either Sister Irene Hobbs or Heeni Wharemaru.

The location of the clinic was moved to the previously abandoned Turangawaewae House (the former Parliament House) on the west side of the river. Te Puea, encouraged by the Rev. A. J. Seamer, hoped eventually to turn this into a full-scale hospital and money was raised for this purpose during the last two wartime regattas and with concerts. But, as had happened in 1929, the proposal was defeated by public health regulations; after Dr Monk moved to Auckland in 1946 no more was heard of it.[17]

The long-term goal had been achieved by this time, however. The standard of Maori health in Waikato was now comparable to that of the European. And Maori patients showed less reluctance about consulting doctors. Later arrivals, like Dr Margaret McDowall, found that people would follow Te Puea's advice and example on medical matters.[18]

The one campaign that Te Puea suspended throughout the war was that of settling the raupatu, the 800,000 acres confiscated in 1864. This grievance had underlain almost every disagreement Te Puea had had with Pakeha authority. The fact that the Sim Commission had found in Waikato's favour in 1928 only made the lack of a final settlement more frustrating.† 'It is

---

† The commission had been set up by Gordon Coates to inquire 'into the root cause of the reactionary influences, resentment and suspicion' among Maori whose land had been confiscated. It found that in Waikato's case, 'the Natives were treated as rebels and war declared against them before they had engaged in war of any kind and in the circumstances they had no alternative but to fight in their own self-defence. In their eyes the fight was not against the Queen's sovereignty, but a struggle for house and home' (Commission Report, p. 11).

beyond the understanding of myself and my people . . . that in spite of the finding of the honourable men of this Commission, no reparation acceptable to Waikato and practicable for New Zealand has yet been arranged,' Te Puea told Acheson in 1939, '[and] that a wrong nearly 80 years old should be permitted to continue to grind Waikato Maoris down . . . and compel many of them to feel life to be very harsh.'[19]

There was another side to this, of course. Some observers believed that it was the shared grievance of the confiscation that had held the Kingitanga together for so long. And part of the reason for the delay in settlement was Waikato's inability to decide what was acceptable. The commission had suggested an annual payment of £3000 (and Taranaki had accepted their recommended settlement of £5000 a year). Te Rata had told Ngata that hapu would have to decide the matter;[20] and hapu had been utterly unable to agree in subsequent marae discussion. A large section of Waikato opinion, led by Marae Edwards, still demanded that 'as the land was taken, so should land be returned'.[21]

The basis for the conservative opinion was not simply idealism or rapaciousness, although it has been represented in both these lights. It was primarily an expression of the belief that money taken in compensation for land that had been fought over was contaminated. 'We won't take black pennies', was one cry; and, 'you don't eat your ancestors'.[22] The fact that the bones of ancestors lay in this land for which money was being offered, and that this money would be used to buy the necessities of life, meant the recipients would indeed be 'eating' their ancestors.

There were further attempts at settlement in the 1930s. With Koroki's and Te Puea's encouragement, Pei Jones set up a rangatahi (young people's) group headed by Tumate Mahuta to carry on negotiations with the Coalition Government during the Depression and later with the Labour Government.[23] Tumate indicated that Waikato would no longer press for the return of the land confiscated, and offers of money and alternative lands were considered over two years.

When Michael Joseph Savage visited Turangawaewae in July 1936 he promised a settlement that would be no less than the offer of the Forbes' Government (£5000 per year). From this point negotiations bogged down. Tumate was pressing for £10,000 per annum.

While Savage was in London at a Prime Ministers' Conference, Frank Langstone offered Waikato a large block of Crown land near Taupo. Tumate and Jones were on the verge of accepting when a telegram arrived for Langstone saying they had not been authorised by Koroki to negotiate on behalf of Waikato. It was sent from Morrinsville and signed by Tarapipipi, the Kingmaker. Jones and Tumate returned to Waikato in confusion.[24]†

Negotiations were postponed by mutual agreement during the war but resumed in 1945 with Te Puea indicating she was fully prepared to accept a monetary settlement.[25] Waikato now had a powerful and perceptive ally in government offices in the person of Mick Jones, then Private Secretary to H. G.R. Mason, Minister of Native Affairs.‡ In March 1946 the Government reached what turned out to be an interim settlement of Ngai Tahu claims, and in April Prime Minister Fraser and Mason came to Turangawaewae, well briefed by Mick Jones on local feeling. After a day of fruitless discussion on the marae on 20 April (in which some spokesmen called for statutory recognition of the Maori kingship as a prerequisite for settlement), Fraser asked Pei Jones to bring a group of elders to the Waipa Hotel that night.

We were conducted to Mr Fraser in his big bedroom. The elders were invited to make themselves comfortable on the Prime Minister's bed and the rest of us sat on chairs. 'Now,' said the Prime Minister, 'we can talk man to man without the worry of saying things for the benefit of the hundreds out there on the marae today. My Government is prepared to make a fair settlement on the same basis as was made with Sir Maui Pomare for his Taranaki people.' [Jones] pointed out to the Prime Minister that Mr Savage had made a similar promise ten years earlier. 'All right then,' the Prime Minister replied. 'You ask the elders whether an extra £50,000 spread over ten years will be acceptable.' One of the elders said, 'Make it £10,000 for the first year and spread £40,000 over 40 years,' 'That is fair enough,' said the Prime Minister.[26]

The eventual offer made on the marae the following day was for £6000 per year for fifty years and £5000 thereafter in perpetuity. The boldness of the move took the conservative spokesmen by surprise. Before disagreement could erupt yet again, Te Puea told Roore Edwards to get to his feet and accept. He stood up and said, 'Kua oti te take nei,' which Mick

---

† Shortly afterwards, on 29 April 1938, Tumate died. According to Alex McKay (letter to Eric Ramsden, 15/12/38), it was a case of mate Maori — 'his mana was insulted by Tarapipipi, he died.' At the tangi Tarapipipi was ritually insulted by Ngati Pikiao, both by exposure of the body in posture dances and the brandishing of a weapon within inches of his head. It was the last occasion in Waikato that such actions were performed publicly.
‡ Eric Ramsden was to write in his diary the following year: 'In effect, Rotohiko [Mick Jones] is Native Minister today.' (Eric Ramsden, Diary, 2/10/47. R.P.)

Jones translated to Fraser as 'the matter is finalised satisfactorily'.[27] In this manner a sore that had festered for eighty-two years was at last on the way to being healed.

Formal Waikato acceptance was signed on 22 April by Te Puea, her brother Wanakore Herangi, Roore Edwards and Ngapaka Kukutai. Then the Tainui Trust Board was established to administer the annual payments. The first board was made up of members nominated by Te Puea. They included Pei Jones as chairman, Ted Tukere (son of Tukere Te Anga) as secretary, Roore Edwards, Hori Paki, Ngapaka Kukutai and Te Uira Manihera. Subsequent members were elected.

When the first cheque was received on 1 February 1947, the board went to Waahi and laid £1000 before Koroki: £500 for his personal use and £500 to commemorate the Waikato who had shed blood for the Kingitanga. Te Puea said to him: 'It was because of the setting up of a king that men took up arms and were killed in battle. Therefore, Son, on you this day rests all these things which have been spoken of.'[28]

The subsequent deliberations and decisions of the board did not produce universal satisfaction. It rejected a suggestion by Tonga Mahuta that the entire annual sum be used to purchase one farm each year for a hapu affected by the confiscation. Instead, in the opinion of some spokesmen, it frittered money away.[29] Most funds were spent on administration costs, grants to marae towards the costs of functions, contributions to Koroki for entertainment, and educational assistance to Waikato students. (A letter to the *New Zealand Herald* in July 1948 claimed that the board had been dominated by Te Puea and its funds wasted on Turangawaewae; it called for a public enquiry.[30]) Te Puea herself was occasionally angered by the board when it did not automatically endorse her proposals.† And the board was sometimes embarrassed by her insistence on grants that they felt were unjustified (such as one to help Maharaia Winiata study abroad in 1952[31]).

But the quality of life in Waikato was markedly different as a result of the interim settlement. There was far less haranguing over past injustices; Koroki was never again short of money for tangi and hospitality as he had frequently and embarrassingly been in the 1930s and 1940s; and, perhaps most importantly, the lingering image of Waikato as a band of disloyal desperados was removed. As Te Puea put it:

---

† She told Leslie Kelly in 1948 that she knew 'nothing of their doings . . . the only time she had endeavoured to address the board, she had been told to leave as she was not a member.' (Leslie Kelly to Eric Ramsden, 10/10/48. R.P.)

Our ancestors have been vindicated in the sight of New Zealand . . . The people now know that justice is on our side. Money can never wipe away the blood that has been shed. No settlement can ever efface the tears that have fallen. And those who suffered most are no longer with us. No, money is not everything. But it means much to know we have been proved right.'[32]

And there this particular matter rested until the 1980s.[†]

---

† See page 320.

14

Return of Ru and conflicts

War's end in 1945 did nothing to interrupt the flow of VIP guests requiring extensive ceremonial attention. Turangawaewae had become an essential stop on Government-arranged itineraries. One of the first such visits was by Lord Louis and Lady Mountbatten on 8 April 1946. Mountbatten shot up in the estimation of his hosts when he began his speech by reciting the Tainui haka *Ka Mate Ka Mate* which he had learnt twenty-six years before. Te Puea impressed him as 'a most remarkable woman in every way'; but he was greatly disappointed by Koroki's reticence.[1]

Subsequent visits included Lord and Lady Bledisloe on 25 March 1947 (on a return visit to New Zealand), and the new Governor-General Sir Bernard Freyberg on 29 March. Both occasions were poignant — the Bledisloes' because of the number of people who had died since their last visit twelve years before; and Freyberg's because, as former Commander of the New Zealand Division, he was regarded as bearer of the deaths of members of the Maori Battalion. Koroki presented the Governor-General with an illuminated address that paid tribute to his 'inspiring and courageous leadership during a time of direst peril', and commemorated 'the spirits of our fallen sons whose blood has enriched . . . the classic battlefields of Greece, Crete, El Alamein, Tripoli, Tunisia and Italy.'[2] The war, especially the Battle of El Alamein, was again a subject for Waikato oratory when Field-Marshal Montgomery visited the marae three months later. Doubts about Waikato's loyalty had been well and truly banished.

Although Te Puea sometimes spoke of her entertainment role as if it were a burden, she would have been offended if these people had passed through Ngaruawahia without a stop at the pa. Each visit was, in her eyes, a recognition of Koroki's mana and an affirmation of Turangawaewae's role as a national marae.† (Theoretically Waitangi had been planned to serve this purpose; in fact it could not because it lacked traditional Maori associations and the support of a well-organised tangata whenua group.) In the eyes of officialdom, Turangawaewae's attraction lay in its creditable appearance, the engaging personality of Te Puea, and the ability of its inhabitants to turn on what Sir Charles Fergusson had referred to twenty years before as 'a good show'.[3]

In June and July 1947, Te Puea reversed roles of hostess and guest for five weeks and made her only trip outside New Zealand. There had been previous invitations — to Honolulu in 1934, for example, and to Sydney for the city's 150th anniversary celebrations in 1938. But on each occasion the promised financial support had not materialised and plans had been abandoned.

In 1947 Te Puea was invited to Tonga for the double wedding of Queen Salote's sons, Tupoutoa-Tungi and Tuipelehake.‡ She was strongly tempted to make the trip. She had entertained parties of Tongans and Cook Islanders in the 1930s and 1940s, including those of Makeanui Tinirau (1934) and Salote (1936), and had become interested in these territories. She knew Rarotongans through their marriage into the Orakei community. She had also taken up the cause of Rio Tario, who had been imprisoned in 1945 after the New Zealand Agent in Aitutaki had accused him of stealing £250. Tario claimed that the accusation was unjustified. Te Puea was keen to visit the island personally to determine if he had been as badly treated as he alleged.[4]

She raised the matter with Peter Fraser in Mahinarangi early in 1947. The first Mick Jones knew of it was when Fraser called him over in the meeting house and said: 'Do you know what the lady is suggesting, Mr Jones?' 'No idea, Sir.' 'She's suggesting you accompany her on a trip to the Islands.' Jones was nonplussed. 'Isn't it up to you to decide, Sir?' And Fraser said, 'Well if that's the case then of course you must go.'[5]

Fraser arranged for the RNZAF to provide a Dakota aircraft and a crew of five (Flt-Lt 'Mac' McLean, a co-pilot, a flying engineer, a wireless operator and a steward). The Maori party was made up of sixteen passengers, each

---

† Judge Acheson had written to Eric Ramsden in November 1940: 'She feels she has only a certain period of health and life left so . . . she is beginning to begrudge the time required for the entertainment of visitors.' (R.P.)
‡ Later to become King and Prime Minister respectively.

Princess Piki, Te Puea, Mick Jones and Tumokai leave for the
Pacific Islands in June 1947. Turongo House

of whom paid £90 towards fares and donations to entertainment en route.
Te Puea led the group with Mick Jones, on full pay from the Native Affairs
Department, acting as spokesman and organiser. Others included Tumokai,
Koroki's fifteen-year-old daughter Piki,[†] the Rev. Eruera Te Tuhi as chaplain,
Sister Heeni Wharemaru, and Dr S. Hass, who had taken over as Te Puea's
physician after Dr Douglas Martin became ill (he died in 1949).

They flew out of Auckland on 7 June and headed for Norfolk Island, New
Caledonia, Fiji, Tonga (where the wedding ceremonies were to begin on 9
June), Aitutaki, Rarotonga, Samoa, and back to Auckland via Fiji. At each
stop-over they were to be looked after by diplomats, administrators, and
local Island dignitaries.

For Te Puea the 6000-mile journey was far more than a holiday; it had
deeply sentimental significance for her, like that of her visit to Cape Reinga.
She was conscious that she was tracing the path of her ancestors, the route

---

† Te Puea brought Piki along to accustom her to attention at public functions and to teach her
how to 'take her place'. She had apparently decided by this time that the girl should
succeed Koroki and should be better prepared for the responsibility than her father had
been. From this time the press made reference to 'Princess Piki'.

back to some mythical and perhaps actual Hawaiki. It was a pilgrimage to be treated with reverence. She told Tumokai that as their predecessors had committed themselves to the care of Tangaroa, god of the sea, so they would entrust themselves to Tawhirimatea, god of wind and air; and she believed in the existence of both deities.[6]

The party arrived in Nukualofa on 8 June and for the next week, in Mick Jones' words, its members 'lived like lords'.[7] At the wedding functions, which continued over a week, they were given places of honour (at the feast on 10 June, for example, Te Puea and Tumokai sat on Queen Salote's left at the official table). Salote also invited Te Puea, Tumokai, Piki, Mick Jones and the Rev. Te Tuhi to a special audience at which she thanked Te Puea for her many kindnesses to the Tongan people, especially for hospitality at Turangawaewae. Te Puea gave the Queen a gift of £50 for her welfare work, tiki for her sons and paua shell necklaces for the brides.[8]

They left Tonga early on Sunday 15 June. The same morning the plane crossed the International Dateline and Te Puea made her first mistake in thirty years of diary-keeping. As she made her entry for Sunday, Flt-Lt McLean leaned over her shoulder and said, 'Oh no, Te Puea, today's Saturday.' She said, 'You're crazy, Mac, it's Sunday.' So he explained. In a subsequent letter to Alex McKay she complained: 'Te porangi te mahi o te Pakeha' — how crazy Pakeha ways are.[9]

Those who knew Te Puea well had not seen her so happy and high-spirited for many years. The trip seemed to rejuvenate her — she suffered no illness, showed no sign of anxiety when the aircraft passed through severe turbulence, and seemed to thrive on the tropical climate of heat and hedonism. Some of the more cantankerously prudish attitudes she had acquired in recent years fell away. She made Sister Heeni get up and join the uninhibited dancing in Aitutaki and Rarotonga, something she had not allowed her to do at home; and when Heeni complained that she did not know what to do, Te Puea told her to 'get up and wriggle around'.[10]

While the ceremonies in Tonga had been the major object of the trip, the party agreed subsequently that Aitutaki was the highlight. It was partly because of a similarity of language (they found Aitutaki Maori more intelligible than other Polynesian dialects), partly the warmth of the hospitality (which on occasions included six meals in the course of a day), and partly because of a sequence of events that made them feel they had indeed come to an ancestral home.

The 'happenings' began as they approached Aitutaki. Mick Jones, the worst passenger, was feeling dizzy and sick. About thirty miles from the island Te Puea nudged Tumokai and told him to look out their window, which was alongside the wing. A small rainbow arched over the wing from the tip to the fuselage. She pointed it out to Jones and said, 'Don't be scared, Roto. That's the old people travelling with us and taking care of us.' A few minutes later Jones called out to them from the other side of the plane and told them to look below. Three thousand feet beneath them, just over the surface of the sea, they saw a moving waterspout and looked down into its funnel as they moved over it.

The island itself was covered with rain cloud when they tried to land. After some difficulty the plane was guided by radio and touched down in pouring rain. As soon as it finished taxiing a group of old people came forward and began to call out greetings that were familiar to the Maori aboard. 'Oromai, Te Puea, oromai te Ariki vaine' (Come forward, Te Puea, come forward the female Ariki). As the first members of the party came down the gangway the cloud lifted and within a few minutes they were bathed in sunshine and could see the island's peak. A litter was waiting to carry Te Puea to the reception but she refused to climb on it. 'Ko tera te Ariki,' she said pointing to Piki. There is the Ariki.

The older islanders were excited by the circumstances of the arrival. One of the orators explained why:

> He told us that a discoverer of Aitutaki, and one of its heroes, had been the navigator Ru. Ru had sailed from Raiatea into a savage storm. At the height of it, he saw this rainbow ahead of the canoe. His crew began to call out to him, 'E Ru, he korero.' Explain. They thought it was a sign of danger. But he just took them right underneath it and it didn't move away from them.
>
> When they were under the arch they struck a whirlpool and this began to suck the canoe down into the sea. And Ru began an old karakia that invokes the god of the sea:

> Tangaroa i te titi, Tangaroa i te tata,
> Whakawateangia te kare o te moana,
> Whakawateangia nga kapua o te rangi,
> Kia tae au ki te whenua
> I tumanakohia e au.'

Calm the oceans, clear the clouds from the skies, that I might reach the land that I am seeking. After he'd said this the whirlpool stopped, the rainbow disappeared and the sky cleared. And there was this mountain rising up out of the sea, out of Aitutaki. And he named it Te Araura after the one he'd left behind.

Princess Piki, King Koroki's eventual successor, is carried on a litter at Mangaia in the Cook Islands. Turongo House

Well, after some years Ru decided to leave Aitutaki. He sailed off towards Aotearoa. As he disappeared south he said to his people, 'Ki te kore au e hoki mai, he wa tona.' If I don't return this time, there'll be a time when I shall. When he'd finished explaining this to us, the old fellow went up to Te Puea and said, 'Oromai, Te Puea, oromai te uri o Ru.' Welcome back as the descendant of Ru. He referred our journey back to his ancestor because of all those things that had happened to us. Te Puea had come back in place of Ru. And they made the old lady a gift of land because of it.[11]

From Aitutaki the Dakota flew to Rarotonga, and from there to Samoa, Fiji and Auckland. At Rarotonga the crew said their goodbyes before they started for home. They were unwilling to dismantle the expedition. 'I've been right through the tropics in wartime,' Flt-Lt McLean told Te Puea, 'but I've never seen anything like this. I've never seen the inside of people the way I did on this trip. Let's just keep going and do the world. I'd never get tired of it.'[12] The feeling was mutual. After their return to New Zealand Te Puea gave McLean a greenstone pendant, her highest token of respect and affection.[13]

Home again to a New Zealand winter, Te Puea caught a chill immediately and was forced to bed for over a month. She wrote grumpily to a friend in the Islands that her illness was caused by 'coming back to this cold and terrible country'.[14] She would have happily stayed in the tropics if there had been an opportunity. Apart from brief excursions to the pa for hui, well wrapped up, she remained in bed until the end of September when she headed for Wellington to try to wrest another favour from Peter Fraser.

This time she was looking for a government loan of £25,000 to build a sufficiently large hall to settle the marae's accommodation and entertainment difficulties (and to provide a balcony overlooking the river from which guests could watch canoe displays). She wanted to reduce her dependence on the army's marquees and trestle tables. The two-storeyed building was to be called Aotearoa and was to serve as a memorial to members of the Maori Battalion who had lost their lives in World War Two. It was also intended to provide an additional asset for the marae in time for the planned royal visit of King George VI and Queen Elizabeth in March 1949.[15] Te Puea hoped that such a cluster of worthy intentions would make the project universally acceptable, even at a time when public funds and building materials were scarce. She already had some money in hand originally collected for the health clinic during the war. Fraser was sympathetic; he even agreed to a timber allocation and to make carpenters available from the Housing Department.[16]

When Te Puea released information to the press the following year, however, it provoked a fiercely unfavourable reaction. The *New Zealand Herald* editorialised that the Government was only trying 'to curry political favour with the Maoris . . . At best the whole project would be extravagant; in the midst of a housing famine, which affects both Maori and Pakeha, it is little short of an outrage . . . It will be ironical if Mr Fraser confirms the Government's part in the plan while the Railway Department badly needs a building of equal size to shelter its buses every night in Auckland.'[17]

Te Puea replied most effectively to this last point: 'Possibly the Prime Minister will regard the shelter of human beings at night as more worthy of consideration than the shelter of buses.' She went on: 'Much . . . is said about encouraging Maoris to return to the pa and cultivate their ancient crafts . . . Now, when a scheme is planned to foster life at the pa and save our people from sleeping in tents or in the open, such a scheme is hotly assailed.'[18]

The Prime Minister, however, had begun to back down. In reply to a question in Parliament from R. M. Algie, he said it was not a government project. 'Princess Te Puea had approached him and said the tribe could furnish the labour and the material. The scheme would have to be considered in the light of other requirements.'[19]

Soon afterwards Fraser withdrew all government support. He told Te

Puea by letter that there was no prospect of completing the building in time for the planned royal visit. 'Support would be given, however, to any building project at the pa when some leeway on the housing shortage had been made up.'[20] Te Puea would have none of the alternative proposal. She felt deceived. She told the press that she was 'hurt and disappointed . . . I have finished with the whole business and do not intend to carry on with the work even when materials are available.'[21]†

More than anything else the key to Te Puea's success as a leader was a combination of appealing personal qualities that could be summed up in Maori terms as ihi, wehi and mana, and in European eyes as charisma. She not only led confidently and astutely, she inspired others to follow. Henry Kelliher spoke approvingly of her 'dynamic personality and tremendous drive'.[22] Judge Acheson voiced the quality that drove people to make sacrifices for her: 'I was filled with admiration at the marvellous ability of Te Puea to fill . . . myself and others with a desire to help her . . . [she] has an intellect of the highest order.'[23]

Eric Ramsden went even further in his assessment: 'I consider Te Puea to be the most outstanding woman that either race has produced in New Zealand within a century,' he wrote.[24] And, on another occasion: 'If I were asked the secret of [her] success I would say that, apart from her organising gifts and business acumen, she has a positive genius for extracting the very best from people.'[25]

And it was another of her strengths that this 'very best' came from people she had selected to be effective agents for her policies at appropriate times — people who enhanced and extended the assets she had and compensated for sensitivities or skills that birth and experience had not given her.

In the Waikato Maori world she had been able to secure her position on the basis of her inheritance and personal qualities, strengthened by the absolute loyalty and industry of workers like Tumokai, Piri Poutapu and Rangitaua Tapara. From 1927, however, she had to call on the expertise of Ngata and Balneavis to ease her into the wider Maori world and into fruitful relationships with European-based institutions. And then she had needed a

---

† The project was dropped; Te Puea made less ambitious additions to accommodation and feeding facilities at the pa in 1952. After her death, the hall proposal was revived — at first as a suggested memorial to her memory — and this resulted in the building on the same site of Kimiora, opened by Queen Elizabeth II in February 1974.

band of lieutenants who could help her front up to the European world. It was partly to raise her confidence: 'I feel shy of Pakeha when ever they come to talk to me,' she told Ramsden in 1934 (and this was not a coy girl speaking, it was a woman of fifty-one years).[26] It was also to secure the new and necessary objective of making herself intelligible to the Pakeha world. Having decided that she would use Pakeha resources, especially money and technology, she then had to cope with the fact that Europeans 'don't understand the Maori race'.[27] And she felt it had become necessary to create a Pakeha awareness and understanding of what she was trying to do. It was in this context that the commitments and contributions of Alex McKay, Eric Ramsden and Judge Acheson were so useful to her in the 1930s.

By 1948, however, Te Puea was relying on a very different set of advisers from that she had been using a decade earlier. The press releases on the Maori Battalion Hall had been prepared with the help of Maharaia Winiata, a Bay of Plenty clergyman and teacher; Biddy Pickering of Ngaruawahia was helping with correspondence; Judge Acheson was dead; Alex McKay was working for the Department of Maori Affairs in Whangarei; Eric Ramsden was complaining that Te Puea no longer saw him when she was in Wellington; and her stalwart of thirty-odd years, Piri Poutapu, had left the pa under a cloud.

Only the Methodists, especially Father Seamer and Sister Heeni, had remained close and constant advisers; and the Jones brothers — although in the case of the latter, the influence of Mick was waxing and that of Pei waning as the younger brother drew closer to Koroki than to Te Puea.

Everybody who worked for Te Puea under the spell of her personality or her ideals had at some time to experience the sharpness of her tongue and the frostiness of her resentment. While some were sycophantic and others easily bruised, most of her lieutenants were simply prepared to weather the storms. In cases where their actions or advice had obviously been well-intentioned, Te Puea would eventually abandon rancour and resume cordial relations. Pei Jones recalled one such incident in June 1937, immediately after the big hui at Waitara.

> John Thomson (Hone Tamihana) . . . had passed away in the Hamilton Public Hospital. The body was taken through to Ngaruawahia by Hera, Te Puea's sister, and the tangi was held there. The day before the funeral the announcement was made that Te Puea, after consulting King Koroki, was making arrangements to have Hone buried on Taupiri Mountain — a signal honour.
>
> Unfortunately, the Ngati Matakores were against this proposal,

particularly Hone's brothers who had completed similar arrangements for a Masonic funeral at Kihikihi in the family plot. In the absence of my older brother, Rotohiko, the Matakores looked to me as representing the senior branch of the hapu to debate the matter with Te Puea. The talk continued for hours and into the night. Te Puea was adamant and I found myself equally determined to justify . . . my fellow tribesmen. My difficulty was further accentuated by one of Hone's younger brothers who at one time threatened to get police assistance.

Next morning it was intended to continue the debate when an unexpected turn took place with the arrival of Haunui from Waahi. Presumably, he had come to the conclusion that the funeral would be held at Kihikihi and as his party of mourners approached the body he raised his voice in a farewell chant. 'Haere, haere, haere! Haere e hoki ki to ukaipo!' (Depart and proceed homeward to the place where your midnight cries were soothed at your mother's breast).

Te Puea bowed her head. I went along to shake hands with her but she pushed me away with the remark, 'So you have got Haunui on your side too!' Haunui had not been prompted but Te Puea would not believe me. It settled the issue and that afternoon the funeral took place at Kihikihi.

Te Puea was very sore with me. For several months she did not write and if she had anything to communicate or desired some advice or information from me it was done through a third party. I was most unhappy about it all. Then one day there was to be an important discussion at Ngaruawahia. As my car drew up at the main gate it came on to rain and at the same time I saw Te Puea walking from Kimikimi toward Mahinarangi. I got out of the car and hurried towards her. She saw me coming and shrugging her shoulders hurried on. I overtook her and caught hold of her hand. 'If you and I were to hongi now, this rain will stop,' I said hurriedly but very earnestly. She hesitated and was lost for I drew her to me and we made it up with a hongi. As she pulled away, the rain ceased. Te Puea smiled, the sun came out.[28]

There were similar instances in which Te Puea was not prepared to forgive and forget, however; and the 1940s was littered with the wreckage of former relationships. One of the first causalities was Piri Poutapu.

The break came one night in 1943 during the community discussion that frequently followed the evening Pai Marire service at the pa. Te Puea announced that she was planning to draw up a will and had taken advice about it from Judge Acheson. In it she would leave one-third of the 372-acre

Turangawaewae Estate to Koroki or his successor and two-thirds to the trustees of the marae; but not until after Tumokai's death. So long as he lived Te Puea wanted him to hold the farm as her heir. It was to be her way of repaying his loyalty and providing him with security. From all but one of the audience present there was no objection.

The exception was Poutapu. He got to his feet and told Te Puea that she would be violating her own principle that everything they did was for 'the people', not for any one of them individually. 'I reminded her that this was what she had instilled into me all my life. And now she was saying that one person was to inherit the benefit of something we'd all worked for. I told her it was wrong.'[29] Te Puea was furious. She could only view the argument as disloyalty. 'I'll never forgive him,' she told Pei Jones.[30] And to Ramsden she wrote that she and Poutapu had 'parted bad friends'.[31] She never did forgive him.

The feud was a particularly tragic one. Apart from Te Puea and Tumokai, nobody had worked harder for Turangawaewae and the Kingitanga than Poutapu; nobody was more committed to Te Puea's objectives. But it was the very qualities that gave them their respective strengths that made the break irreparable: Te Puea simply could not be told that she was wrong about something, particularly something that involved a matter of principle (and in other circumstances this stubbornness had enabled her to convert the impossible into the possible, the faculty that Judge Acheson called 'her sublime courage'[32]). Poutapu too had never compromised on a principle — his refusal to do so in this case was the same impulse that had led him to decline to carve for large sums of money. The exacerbating factor was Poutapu's telling Te Puea she was being untrue to her own code, an accusation that was tantamount to a cardinal accusing the Pope of heresy.

Te Puea went ahead and had the will drawn up. It was signed on 1 December 1944 and appointed Tumokai, Judge Acheson and Ted Tukere (son of Tukere Te Anga) trustees. Subsequently she added Pei Jones and revoked Tukere's appointment. Piri Poutapu left Turangawaewae and was unable to return in Te Puea's lifetime.[†]

Another person to whom Te Puea had looked for the assumption of responsibilities in the 1940s was Poutapu's leading protégé, Inia Te Wiata; and she also found him wanting. When Te Wiata had come to Waikato from Otaki in 1933 he had been, in his own words, 'more Pakeha than anything else'. Thirteen years later his association with Te Puea and her community

---

† He returned and resumed a leadership role in the community after her death.

had left him 'a complete Maori'.[33] He was, in Poutapu's estimation, the most gifted of the apprentice carvers;[34] he had mastered action songs and haka and his voice had become known throughout the country; he had spent time learning Tainui history, genealogy and chant; he was also quietly reliable by nature. In Te Puea's mind he showed every sign of becoming a leading elder and a versatile teacher. She had agreed reluctantly to his marriage with Ivy Friar of Tangirau (for some reason Te Wiata never understood, the old lady appeared to be keeping Ivy away from men, possibly because she had considered an arranged marriage to somebody else).[35]

In 1946, as a result of energetic lobbying by his admirers, the singer was awarded a three-year scholarship to Trinity College, London. He was ready to move: the consistent praise his voice had attracted over ten years had made him ambitious to match his alleged talent with musical training (and the compliments had come from people as accomplished as the Australian bass Peter Dawson;[36] and, according to his second wife, he had become too independent to fit easily into the intrusive intimacy of Maori communal life; in particular, he was beginning to resent Te Puea's instructions on how to raise his children, and this had led him to move out of Turangawaewae and into a farm cottage.[37]

A public subscription was opened to supplement the scholarship and Sir Apirana Ngata asked all tribes to contribute. Te Wiata also performed in a series of fund-raising concerts throughout the North Island. The only person not enthusiastic about the project was Te Puea. She was adamant that his responsibilities — tribal and family — lay at home; and she feared the corrupting influences in a cosmopolitan city, away from the sanctions that she believed were necessary for the moral and physical well-being of the Maori (she was particularly fearful of his vulnerability because he was going without Ivy).[38] To her, the venture seemed personal and selfish. When Eric Ramsden, at Ngata's request, asked her to contribute £100 to the fund, Te Puea replied: 'No, not one shilling. If Ngata wanted the money for a meeting house or something for the people then I would give it. But for this, nothing.'[39] From this attitude, Ramsden noted, she could not be moved.

Ramsden had developed a close relationship with Te Wiata and asked him to be godfather to his daughter, Tiahuia. He was attracted too by the singer's sensitivity and his way with words. (He noted that Inia had said of a daughter who died that 'she did not just hold a flower . . . she caressed it.'[40]) Te Wiata wrote to him from the *Rimutaka* en route for London that he had achieved a reconciliation with Te Puea only as the ship was leaving Auckland in April 1947: 'She was at the wharf to see Lord and Lady Bledisloe off. We kissed goodbye when I was boarding the ship. Tumokai cried and so did I. Ivy feels alright now and I feel much better. We did not deserve the way she received us . . . I feel very happy to know she looks upon us again as her children.'[41]

The reconciliation was only temporary, however. When Te Wiata refused to return to New Zealand after his initial three years of study were completed, Te Puea's convictions about the corrupting effects of city and overseas life appeared to be confirmed. She simply wrote him off as somebody else who had let her down.[42] He, meanwhile, remained in London to become an internationally-known operatic and concert performer. He was eventually divorced from Ivy and married the New Zealand actress Beryl McMillan in 1959; he felt unable for many years to return to New Zealand because of the consequences of his break with Te Puea and the family he had left behind.[43]

While the circumstances surrounding the ructions with Poutapu and Te Wiata could be regarded as unfortunate, Te Puea seemed fully justified in dismissing another protégé, Leslie Kelly. Kelly was a part-Maori of Waikato ancestry who met Te Puea in the early 1930s. He became, in Mick Jones' words, 'her golden-haired boy'.[44] She wrote to Ramsden in 1939: 'I like him very much. I wish he would come and live either here or in Hamilton . . . Do you know your wish to grant him a Maori name has been granted? I have given him the name Te Putu which is the right name for him for he is a descendant of that chief.'[45] She anticipated at this time that Kelly would attend hui at Turangawaewae, graduate to being one of the organisers and — because of his charm and articulateness — eventually assume a role as a spokesman for the Kingitanga. 'He will make a real rangatira kaumatua,' she said on another occasion.[46] While Kelly's mana was growing in Te Puea's eyes, he was preparing one of the most daring plagiarisms in New Zealand literature.

In the 1930s he was living at Te Kuiti and working for the Railways Department as a fireman. He was also contributing to the *Journal of the Polynesian Society* as a highly-regarded amateur ethnologist and historian. Pei Jones was living at Te Kuiti too, working for the local office of the Native Land Court. On several occasions he asked Kelly to accompany him on weekend trips to investigate remote fortified pa sites. During these trips, Kelly learnt that Jones had accumulated a large quantity of material for a history of the Tainui tribes and he offered to type this in manuscript form. Jones accepted, gratefully. Kelly performed the task and kept carbon copies.[47]

By 1937, unbeknown to Jones or anybody else in Waikato, Kelly had offered this material to A.H. and A.W. Reed for publication. Reeds in turn approached Apirana Ngata for assistance from the Maori Purposes Fund Board, and Ngata referred the manuscript back to Kelly with suggested improvements.[48] It was composed entirely of material that Jones had compiled and drafted.†

The book, *Tainui: the story of Hoturoa and his descendants*, was finally published by the Polynesian Society over Kelly's name in 1949. Only at that point did the plagiarism become known.‡ Three years earlier, on 11 September 1946, Kelly had asked Te Puea to sign a preface that bestowed fulsome praise on him as author ('You have performed a valuable work . . . Because of the blood that is in your veins, the old people have spoken with you freely').[49] But she had not read it; Kelly had told her it was 'something from Pei for you to sign, for the Tainui book I have been typing for him'.[50]

Jones was stunned. Te Puea and the Waikato elders with whom he consulted were horrified at the magnitude of Kelly's deception. The only things that restrained Jones from taking legal action to prevent distribution of the book were Te Puea's reservation that it would expose the fact that she had signed the preface without reading it; and the general feeling that it would be unseemly to conduct litigation over material that Waikato elders regarded as highly tapu.[51]

Waikato had its own ways of punishing transgressions against the tribal code, however. Kelly became persona non grata at Turangawaewae from that time on; Te Puea spoke scathingly of him and to him, and he stopped visiting the pa. And she told Jones that 'Kelly, by acting in a deceitful manner in respect of our Tainui history, would be whakawhiua . . . she expressed . . . tapu foreboding regarding Kelly's fate.'[52]*

---

† Jones has written: 'Ye Gods! Whenever I read the dissembling manner in which Kelly gave these particulars I feel upset, and this is one reason I cannot trust myself at this stage to publicise Kelly's unscrupulous actions' (personal communication, 11/9/75).

‡ It is probable that one of the reasons Kelly went ahead with publication through the Polynesian Society is that Jones was suffering from cancer of the bowel in the 1940s and for some years was not expected to survive. After surgery in 1943, however, he made a slow but finally complete recovery. The editor of the *Journal of the Polynesian Society*, Johannes Andersen, told Jones subsequently that *Tainui* was not Kelly's only attempt at plagiarism; another was detected shortly before publication. (Pei Jones, personal communication, 11/9/75.)

* The expression 'whakawhiua' refers here to a divinely ordained punishment for transgressions of magnitude against tapu. In this case Te Puea's foreboding seemed to her followers to be fulfilled. Kelly died in unusual and painful circumstances on 6 August 1959. The Coroner's finding attributed death to 'multiple injuries received from being crushed under a railway wagon when the engine of the train he was driving fouled the main line and was

Others who worked Te Puea up to near-venomous expressions of hostility in the late 1940s included Eric Ramsden and his second wife Merenia. The course of her association with them was, like that with Poutapu, unfortunate in the light of the warmth and trust she had shared with Ramsden in earlier years.

The deterioration in this case began in 1944 when Ramsden notified Te Puea from Christchurch that he was in a relationship with Merenia ('Billy') Meteherangi Collins, a Ngai Tahu woman, and that she had become pregnant. Te Puea's first reaction was one of pure and characteristic compassion. She invited Merenia to come to Waikato to have the baby, and she offered to adopt it, a gesture that Ramsden and Merenia accepted. 'Dear Merenia,' Te Puea wrote in May 1944, 'the fact that you gave your aroha to Eriki is a very great thing to me. He is a good and honest man . . . I am looking forward to the day when you come to me . . . [and] I will await the coming of my child.'[53]

That child, a daughter, was born in August 1944. Te Puea took her at once and named her Tiahuia after her own mother.[†] She placed the girl in the care of one of the women at the pa, Te Ata Martin, but frequently had her stay at the farm. Tiahuia rapidly became a favourite: 'She is going to be the belle of Waikato,' Te Puea wrote in April 1945. 'She has the face and eyes of a grown-up and when she smiles she is just beautiful.'[54]

Things were going seriously wrong by 1946. Ramsden began to have reservations about Tiahuia's being brought up in an entirely Maori environment. He tried to recover the child and when Te Puea refused to let her go, Ramsden threatened legal action; this infuriated Te Puea who believed that when relationships became the subject of litigation they had reached an all-time low.[55†] Their correspondence, so voluminous and warm from 1928 to the mid-1940s, became more restrained. The biography of Te Puea which Ramsden had begun to work on intensively late in 1942 and hoped to complete in 1944[56] came to a standstill; he received no assistance

---

involved in a collision with another train at the Matumaoho Railway Station.' (Certificate of death, Office of the Registrar of Births, Deaths and Marriages, Wellington.)

† It was not the first time that she had given a Waikato name to a Ramsden child. In 1928 she had caused considerable controversy by naming Ramsden's son Michael 'Hoturoa', after the captain of the Tainui canoe. This name had traditionally been regarded as so tapu that Waikato Maori had not used it.

‡ Tiahuia remained at the pa until after Te Puea's death. Subsequently Ramsden brought her to Wellington (where he was working for the *Evening Post*) to be raised with his two younger children, Irihapeti and Peter.

from Te Puea after 1946 and other people, like Pei Jones, became increasingly unwilling to help or even be associated with him.[†]

The sections of the biography that Ramsden did manage to draft are disjointed and repetitive. Relatively trivial incidents are examined in detail (such as the death of Te Heuheu Tukino in 1920); and more significant ones — like the establishment of Turangawaewae — are passed over. And although Ramsden shared Te Puea's confidence for twenty years, a surprising amount of his material was drawn from other published sources, especially Judge Acheson's articles for *The Mirror*. The idiom is the mock-heroic one that Ramsden liked to adopt for Maori subjects (his title was to be *Te Puea Herangi: Princess of Maoriland*; and he has her saying things like, 'Tell them to grieve not, I shall yet be destined to complete my task'). The project seems to have been more than he could cope with. In May 1947 he wrote in his diary: 'Trying to get my papers in order to return to writing the Te Puea book. But everything is in a hopeless mess.'[57] He never returned to it.

In 1947 Ramsden and Merenia were caught up in a series of incidents that represented the nadir of their relationship with Te Puea; and which also gave weight to Te Puea's reputation as a seer. Merenia, in Te Puea's judgement, behaved badly at the Turangawaewae poukai. The old lady abused her savagely for this, and according to Ramsden, told Merenia that her punishment would be to die on the same day as herself: 'When I go, I'll make sure you go with me.'[58] And Merenia had a series of dreams in which Tawhiao appeared to her and made predictions. Ramsden recorded in his diary for 22 March 1947: 'She has told me . . . that I would die at the age of 63; that Te Puea would die in "56", that Pei would live for many years.'[59][‡]

In the final years of Te Puea's life the estrangement with Ramsden was perpetuated by his adoption of National Party politics at a time when she was inclining towards Labour (he was writing for the party paper *Freedom* as 'Te Hokioi' or 'Eriki', noms-de-plume he favoured when writing about Maori things; he also became an adviser on Maori affairs to National Party ministers after 1949). Others with whom Te Puea's relations became more

---

[†] Jones wrote to him on 26 May 1946: 'You will have to exempt me from further contributions' (R.P.).

[‡] Some of these prophecies came remarkably close to fulfilment: Merenia Ramsden did not die on the same day as Te Puea but on the same date one year later, 12 October 1953; Ramsden died in 1962 at the age of 64; Te Puea died in 1952; and Pei Jones lived until 1976.

distant, partly for political reasons, included Ngeungeu Zister (née Beamish) and George Graham of the Akarana Maori Association in Auckland.

Some of those who felt they had been discarded by Te Puea became bitterly antagonistic and shared their paranoia in letters to one another. Usually they blamed 'other advisers' for their fall from grace. George Graham told Ramsden that Te Puea was 'surrounded by a complete pack of traitors — and alongside of her she requires a strong personality to generally checkmate adverse machination. She has too long relied on personalities who are out — like so many hyenas — to attack and eat up all that she can so achieve.'[60] Leslie Kelly also wrote to Ramsden: 'In the back of my mind [is] the example of previous faithful workers being just dropped when Te Puea thought fit . . . I have no intention of being used as a sucker.'[61]

The only person who refused to discuss his disagreement with anybody or abuse Te Puea publicly, although he had reason to do so, was Piri Poutapu. He wrote a characteristic letter to Ramsden: 'I find it very difficult to write to you for fear that such correspondence may become known and it may involve you in the same fate . . . [Trouble does] exist between us, and I do not wish to go into any details with regard to that matter.'[62]

Most of the disaffected had given Te Puea some cause to reject them, some offence against her personal or tribal code of behaviour. But part of the blame for some of the disagreements did rest with Te Puea — she had become more adamant about her opinions with the passage of years and, when her health was declining, more liable to lose her temper. Where jealousy was apparent — in the case of former confidants blaming their downfall on new ones — it was inevitable that the major targets in the late 1940s should be the Jones brothers and Maharaia Winiata.

Michael Rotohiko and Pei Te Hurinui Jones accumulated an impressive record of service in the Kingitanga and Maori affairs generally.[†] Apart from Tukere Te Anga, they were the only ones among Te Puea's early Maori advisers who had received education beyond primary level, and their work as Native Agent and Native Land Court Officer respectively had given them a considerable degree of knowledge and skill in dealing with Maori land

---

† Mick Jones retired from the public service in 1963 after working with seven ministers of Native and Maori Affairs and sitting on numerous official committees and ad hoc bodies; Pei Te Hurinui was awarded an honorary doctorate by the University of Waikato in 1968 for his services to Maori language and literature, and he became president of the New Zealand Maori Council in 1970 and in this capacity welcomed Queen Elizabeth II to New Zealand on behalf of the Maori people that year; his major business concern from 1945 was the Puketapu Incorporation based in Taumaruanui.

matters. They were also highly literate in Maori and English and Pei, in addition to his books in English, his work on tribal songs with Apirana Ngata and his revision of Williams' *Dictionary of the Maori Language*, also enjoyed translating classics of English literature into Maori (*The Merchant of Venice* and FitzGerald's *The Rubaiyat of Omar Khayyam* among them).

Their roles were distinctive but complementary. From 1940, Mick had worked quietly but astutely for the Kingitanga from the office of the Minister of Native Affairs, while Pei had taken a more partisanly public role on Te Puea's behalf (as she had on his when he stood for Parliament): he organised Kingitanga functions, prepared publications and press releases and acted as a spokesman for the movement. As noted previously,[†] they had different political views which in turn reflected different ideological inclinations — Mick favoured government and public service initiatives in Maori affairs, Pei leaned more towards private enterprise approaches. And Mick was far less willing to seek attention than Pei. But they worked well together and Pei always deferred to his older brother on ceremonial occasions when they were both present.

Some critics accused Mick of subverting Te Puea to socialist principles,[63] others suggested Pei's accumulation of designations and responsibilities represented no more than a compulsion to hog the limelight.[64] But in fact both remained influential with Koroki and Te Puea because of their intelligence, their sophistication in dealing with European matters, and their willingness to drop whatever they were doing to come to the Kingitanga's assistance and work very hard on its behalf.[‡] As McKay, Ramsden and Acheson had built bridges from the Pakeha world to that of the Maori, the Jones brothers were building them just as effectively in the other direction.

From 1949 their influence with Te Puea was supplanted to some extent by that of Maharaia Winiata, who had begun to work intensively for her the previous year and was possibly the most able Maori adviser she ever had. Winiata was a member of the Ngati Ranginui and Ngaiterangi tribes of the

---

† See page 241.
‡ There were differences of interpretation here. Pei Jones objected strongly to the use of the word protégé to describe his relationship with Te Puea. 'In the case of my elder brother and me, kinship ties ruled our relationship with Te Puea and the Maori King family . . . To describe us as a protégé (i.e. person to whom another is protector or patron) . . . has quite the wrong connotation.' (Personal communication, 11/9/75.) There were others, nevertheless, who felt that without Te Puea's and Koroki's patronage, Pei Te Hurinui's position would not have remained as strong as it did (interviews Piri Poutapu and Te Uira Manihera). Robert Mahuta has commented: 'Without Te Puea's or Koroki's support Pei would have been ineffective' (personal communication).

Bay of Plenty which, although not part of Waikato proper, had always retained a close association with the Kingitanga. His father had been a life-long friend of Te Puea's and Winiata himself saw much of her after his posting to Kawhia as a Methodist minister and his marriage in 1940 to Frances Clegg, one of Te Puea's favourites among the lay workers at the pa.

His background in education was strong. He had been the first Maori to take a full training course at Trinity Methodist Theological College where he had obtained a diploma in theology; he later graduated M.A. in education from Auckland University College. He taught at primary schools and at Wesley College in Paerata becoming, at one point, acting-Principal. Apart from Ngata, he was the nearest thing to an academic that Te Puea had known.

Winiata's political and practical instincts were also strong. He had stood unsuccessfully for the Western Maori parliamentary seat in the 1945 by-election (under another family name, Piahana). He was an arresting public speaker and his press statements were succinct and pungent; he also had a considerable facility for organisation and committee work. After 1945 he put these talents to work for a large number of Maori causes including the fight to save the Orakei Marae and the Methodists' efforts to keep liquor out of the King Country.

Te Puea took to him with all the force and optimism with which she had previously embraced Leslie Kelly.[65] She decided that he would be a future repository of Waikato learning, and sent him to elders like Roore Edwards for instruction in Tainui tradition and kawa. [66] Unlike Kelly, Winiata lived up fully to expectation. Winiata for his part referred to Te Puea as 'a genius'. He told Ramsden: 'My heart is to help Waikato.'[67]

The most continuous Pakeha influence in Te Puea's life was Alex McKay. They were close from 1919 until her death and they never had a serious falling-out. Although he spoke Maori and came to understand Maori matters as well as anybody, he remained a Pakeha, confident in his own identity and background of European culture and Roman Catholicism. He was not an emotional cripple looking for a romantic cultural refuge, as were some Pakeha-Maori; nor would he accept any form of material dependence on Te Puea (which was his major motive for joining the Department of Native Affairs after a family allowance ceased). He was a strong and independent person who approved of Te Puea and the Kingitanga and was prepared to help both.

He was also one of the few people of whom it could be said that there was no personal gain for him in his relationship with Te Puea. He was never self-seeking in advice — he was frank, loyal and self-effacing. Even when he had engineered agreements or accomplishment, he refused to accept credit or limelight. This transparent honesty in his dealings with her appealed to Te Puea. They also enjoyed each other's skills as raconteurs. Some friendships with other Europeans blazed more spectacularly at times, but they proved to be more transitory.

There were two themes in McKay's dealings with Te Puea that help explain his involvement in the Kingitanga and his usefulness to its leaders. He was a self-confessed lover of ritual — he believed that human relationships and affairs were most pleasingly regulated by protocol and ceremony, and preferably through forms of both that had the durability of a tradition. His advice from a Maori point of view tended to emphasise ways in which ritual and tradition could continue to work — in particular, he was conscious of behaviour inasmuch as it increased or diminished mana and mystique; and he encouraged that which increased it.[†]

He also recognised that Te Puea would be able to carry out her selected goals most effectively if she was able to tap European resources and reserves of goodwill; hence the need to make herself intelligible to the wider Pakeha community and its institutions and his advice on how this could best be done. Such advice was always tactfully astute and showed a rare understanding of both Maori and Pakeha considerations (and this capacity was to stand McKay in good stead in his late career — from 1938 — with the Department of Native and subsequently Maori Affairs, from which he retired as assistant-secretary in 1962). If his influence diminished towards the end of Te Puea's life, it was only because his work kept him away from Ngaruawahia. And after her death, it was he more than any other person who was the active guardian of her reputation and her mana.

There were other friendships with Europeans that, while not exhibiting the same degree of intimacy as that with McKay, remained constant until Te Puea's death: those with the Rev. A. J. Seamer, Henry Kelliher (who continued to advise on business matters), Biddy Pickering, Bunny Woodhams, Roy Knight, Bill Eaddy, Colin Caddie (headmaster at Rakaumanga), and Frank and Rachel Monk.

Among the Maori supports, Rangitaua Tapara stayed close to her in spite of the break with Poutapu, her brother; elders like Roore Edwards, Peha Wharakura and Ngapaka Kukutai were always at her service; Te Uira Manihera and Sister Heeni were favourite companions; and Mono Ewe

---

† And he continued to do so in his relationships with the kahui ariki after Te Puea's death, particularly with Piki after she became Queen Te Atairangikaahu.

looked after her still at home. But it was Tumokai who remained the most solid pillar in Te Puea's life. In thirty years of marriage their commitment to each other never wavered. He continued to look to her for direction and carried out her instructions to the letter. She in turn leaned on him as the one person who could be relied upon without having to be stood over. He was tireless in his manual work, the person who automatically took the tedious jobs that nobody else wanted; and he was the troubleshooter she would dispatch to any part of Waikato when things went wrong because people were not pulling their weight.

She also confided in him completely — not for the purpose of seeking advice that he might not be competent to give, for he was not her intellectual equal; but to use him as a sounding board, an audience to whom she could clarify her thoughts and, when occasion demanded it, relieve her feelings. He was the one person with whom she could be completely honest, and the one who knew everything about her life — past and present, creditable and discreditable.

Their relationship was not one of solemn intensity, however. They frequently exhibited a playfulness together that people around them found contagious. When he became attached to something, she would hide it and give him clues until he found it. And they shared an enormous joy in the company of children and in devising treats for them.

Te Puea's earlier regret that she was unable to conceive became, in time, a regret on Tumokai's behalf. She told Ramsden in February 1940: 'Dave should have a child of his own flesh. You know how deeply he has grieved for Pirihia. It has been dreadful to hear him sobbing in the night.' Te Puea had planned that he should have a child with Papi Pokaia, her first adopted daughter. 'I would have gone away for a time for I am woman enough not to like to see what would have happened. But I would have returned in good time and taken the baby, and that would have pleased his heart.' But Papi ran away and subsequently married Rua Cooper, without Te Puea's approval.[68]

In spite of the mutual dependence that characterised their relationship and the love that brought them close, there were times when their lives seemed separated by an enormous gulf: Tumokai regarded her as an ariki with ariki powers that he could witness but not share, especially those of a spiritual or psychic character; and, like Alex McKay, he refused to speak or accept the limelight on public occasions. At hui and receptions he was rarely on the marae with the speakers and VIPs; he was far more likely to be out the back with the workers; that was how he regarded his role as mokai — the 'worker' — that his name suggested.

Nowhere was Te Puea's reliance on him made clearer than in the wording of her will. Here, amid the legal form and prosaic language, was a request: 'Knowing his devotion to the objectives for which we have both worked together for so long, I express the wish that he shall continue after my death as long as he can in the task we undertook together, and shall exercise and hold the same control and authority.'[69] Tumokai's commitment persisted. So literally did he take the request that twenty-five years after Te Puea's death he was working as hard on the Turangawaewae Estate as he ever had, at an age when most men would have been long retired.

15

Churches, schools and alcohol

By 1948 there was no sign of the suspicious attitude to the Christian churches that Te Puea had held twenty years before. 'I want to open my arms to all religions,' she told Sister Heeni Wharemaru that year. 'They are all paths to the same God.'[1] She had mellowed. Pai Marire continued to be the major religion preached and practised at Turangawaewae and morning and evening services were still held daily. But all other denominations bar Ratana were represented at hui, even the Anglicans under the leadership of Canon Karira Karaka. (Other Anglican visitors and friends had included Mutu Kapa and H. W. Williams.)

This openness was subject only to the proviso that church representatives who worked at the pa were expected to participate fully in its communal life.[2] In practice — and as a declared policy — only the Methodists were prepared to do this. The foothold they had secured through Te Puea's relationships with church leaders had been retained and consolidated by the involvement of church workers in Turangawaewae's social and religious activities. Deaconesses, among them Sisters Heeni Wharemaru, Margaret Nicholls, Irene Hobbs, Frances Clegg (later Winiata), did not hesitate to throw themselves into the less romantic chores: preparing food and doing dishes in the kitchens, serving in the dining room, cleaning the grounds, supervising dances, chaperoning the girls on trips away and driving Te Puea's cars for her or offering her the use of church vehicles. They even took part in the Pai Marire services.

In addition to their advantage of being long established in Waikato, the strength of the Methodists lay in the fact that the Maori section of the church in the twentieth century did not set out to 'reform' Maori values and tastes to fit preconceived ecclesiastical notions. Rather, the Wesleyans were prepared to adapt church ritual and practices to harmonise with Maori life. They did not feel threatened by Maori forms of worship like Pai Marire, viewing them rather as things that could either be incorporated into Christian worship or allowed to coexist comfortably alongside it (the Presbyterians in the Urewera took a similar view of Ringatu). To a large extent this policy was the fruit of A.J. Seamer's leadership of the Maori Mission and the manner in which it was carried on after 1939 by his successor, G.I. Laurenson. They in turn had been influenced by Te Puea's advice about what features of church liturgy were most appropriate for Maori congregations.[3]

Occasionally there were disagreements. While Te Puea was there to push people, the working week at the pa was a seven-day one: there were always jobs to be done on the farm and cleaning and maintenance around the marae. This unrelenting pace upset Father Seamer who told her that working on Sunday was contrary to Biblical instruction. 'I know, Father,' Te Puea told him. 'I know that. And I know people talk about it. But *you* know that I have a programme of things to be done and only a limited time in which to do it. And we believe that God's present in everything that we do. So if we're guilty, he is too.' Seamer always withdrew from such a formidable combination of theology and practicality.[4]

In spite of work programmes, however, Sister Heeni, Margaret Nicholls or Irene Hobbs always held morning Sunday School sessions at the pa; and it was Te Puea who would stop what she was doing and prowl about to round up all children not otherwise engaged, regardless of their denomination. She sent early arrivals out to hurry latecomers, and she had the sick — adults and children — carried there in their beds.

Often she came close to unnerving the deaconesses by staying to listen critically to their instruction and offering advice of her own. But her contributions, even when they implied criticism, were gentle. 'That's all very well what you told the children,' she said to Heeni after one session, 'but I remember my Dad putting it better. He used to say that when you're on your own you only think you're on your own. You might want to steal something, get away with something. That's when you have to remember that you're never really on your own at all. There are always other presences, spiritual ones, watching you, noting what you do. And if you do something wrong they'll make sure it catches up with you. That's what you should tell the children.'[5]

Te Puea's maxims reflected her belief in the value of guilt as a means of controlling social behaviour; and in the value of confession as a way of alleviating that guilt when misdemeanours had been committed. 'No matter what state your body is in,' she kept telling her children, 'you'll always feel well if your conscience is in order and your mind at rest. If they are not, you'll feel unwell and unhappy.'[6]

She also stressed that for her, most satisfaction in life had come from 'working with my hands and my body for the benefit of other people'.[7] The dignity of manual labour, the reward of eating food raised by one's own hand, the euphoric spirit of the ohu or community work force — concentration on these things may have sounded trite and sententious to the European listener. But for Te Puea they were values that had to be inculcated to ensure the survival of Turangawaewae as a nursery for Maori values; they had to be stressed in the face of European suggestions that such values were at best primitive and outmoded and at worst something to be sneered at.

Another way in which Te Puea sought to control European influences on Maori life was by advocating formal education for Kingitanga leaders. She had changed her mind completely on this issue. In the 1920s she had told Ramsden that European education diluted Maori values and weakened the power of Maori institutions; she had also seen it used too often by Maori, particularly two Maniapoto families, as a means of fleecing their own people. This latter suspicion lingered to some extent. It was aroused afresh in 1947 when she discovered that Ted Tukere, secretary of the Tainui Trust Board and promising son of Tukere Te Anga, had been forging her signature on cheques. He had to be dismissed from the board and his appointment as trustee under Te Puea's will was revoked.[†]

In spite of such setbacks, however, she had come increasingly to view education as a means of regulating the introduction of European elements into Maori life without swamping the Maori qualities. Those who had been most able to exert this control seemed to her to be those with education (and Ngata had been the prime example until his fall from power; the others who had impressed her with their 'Maori worldliness' were the Jones brothers). She stressed frequently in the 1940s that she felt at a disadvantage because she had not acquired a better command of English when she had had the opportunity.[8] This handicap had forced her to rely more heavily on European lieutenants than she might otherwise have

---

† Tukere Te Anga himself, Te Puea's cousin, had also disappointed her. She had given him and his family her former house at the pa so that he could live there and put his education and experience to work for the community. But he had not done so; in Te Puea's mind, it was a cardinal sin to lead a private life in a Maori community. He died in 1946.

chosen to do. Further, while Mahuta had ensured that his sons (including Te Rata) acquired a primary education, Koroki had had none. And this had been one of the factors contributing to his reticence and vulnerability to manipulation.[†] Her association with Peter Fraser, which had included attendance at a teachers' conference while he was Minister of Education,[9] had confirmed these views.

So Te Puea took steps to ensure that the Kingitanga leaders of the future would be better equipped than she and Koroki had been. After discussions with A.J. Seamer and Henry Kelliher, she tried to enrol Piki at boarding school in Auckland in 1944. To her annoyance, St Cuthberts did not keep a place which she believed she had reserved. Finally, she sent Piki to the Anglican Diocesan School in Hamilton as a day pupil; she boarded at the Te Rahui Methodist Hostel and Heeni Wharemaru, who ran the hostel, and Father Seamer, now living in retirement in Hamilton, kept a parental eye on her. Seven years later Te Puea had Koroki's adopted son Robert Mahuta (a member of the kahui ariki through his grandmother Piupiu) sent to Mt Albert Grammar School in Auckland, in the face of opposition from Koroki, who had wanted him to become a mechanic. She opened an account at George Court's department store so that he could buy clothes and other necessities charged to her.[‡]

To their mother, Te Atairangikaahu, Te Puea stressed that both children were to work as hard as possible and learn as much as they could; but they were not to forget that they were Maori. This education was for the benefit of the people, not themselves; the one thing she did not want in the kahui ariki as a result of education was a replacement of Maori communal sensitivity by a strongly individualist, competitive, money-grubbing instinct.[10]

One way she believed that traditional Maori values could be conserved in schools (and in the process made more intelligible to Pakeha) was by the introduction of some form of Maori studies into the curriculum. At the time there were no such courses other than in a few Maori-oriented private

---

† He did not learn to read or write until Alex McKay gave him lessons in 1937 (McKay to Eric Ramsden, 27/10/37. R.P.).

‡ Mahuta became the first member of the kahui ariki to graduate from university. In 1973 he was appointed Director of the Centre for Maori Studies and Research at the University of Waikato, Hamilton, and in 1976 he was enrolled for a doctorate in anthropology at Wolfson College, Oxford. He had been preceded as a Waikato Maori graduate by Robert Kerr of Taharoa and Pare Hopa of Gordonton. But in the mid-1970s Waikato still had a lower percentage of graduates than other major tribes.

schools. In a press release directed at the new National Minister of Education (R. M. Algie) after the 1949 General Election, Te Puea advanced a programme that was not to be accepted wholly by the Department of Education for another twenty years:

'The language, history, crafts and traditions of the Maoris should be an essential part of the curriculum throughout the country,' she said. 'Unity of Maori and Pakeha can only grow from each sharing the worthwhile elements in the other's culture. Today the Maori language can no longer be taught in the home to Maori children. It should be given a place in the schools.'[11]

Te Puea also backed Maharaia Winiata strongly when he began work in Waikato in 1949 as the country's first Maori Adult Education Officer. She listened to his proposals that hui and tangi be used as media for formal education, endorsed it, and then instructed tribal committees to help him. Winiata organised classes throughout Waikato and the King Country with the cooperation of elders like Tom Reweti of Te Kuiti. By 1950 he even had a class of elderly men at Turangawaewae learning to write their names and to read from *Janet and John* books.[12] It was the mana of Te Puea that made such classes acceptable in circumstances where they would not have been possible twenty years before.

In her emphases and choice of tactics, the Te Puea of the late 1940s spoke with a different voice from the leader of the 1920s. She still had the same objectives: upholding the Kingitanga and making Waikato a self-reliant people. But she had become less and less inclined to engage the Pakeha world in head-on confrontation. She had acquired prestige and influence in European circles; she had learned a great deal about politics; she was now inclined to state what she believed to be the Waikato or Maori case as strongly as she could, hold out for it, then make some adjustments according to what concessions her opponents seemed likely to offer. In this fashion she had achieved acceptance for Koroki as a national leader and Turangawaewae as a national marae, and an interim settlement of the raupatu issue.

'It's no good looking backwards now,' she said frequently to Heeni Wharemaru and others of her last group of protégés. 'We've got to look to the future. And that future has to include the Pakeha and Pakeha laws and even marriage to the Pakeha. We've simply got to strengthen our Maori roots so we can cope with it all and not stop being Maori.'[13]

Te Puea frequently used the churches in the 1940s to shelter Maori lifestyle with the protection of European institutions. She had clergymen speak out in favour of tangi when they were under attack by Waikato Hospital

Board officials;[14] and she began to insist that inhabitants of Turangawaewae who had married by customary declaration undergo legal church weddings. In scenes reminiscent of *Pygmalion*, she had couples in their forties and fifties married in front of Mahinarangi in the presence of their children and even grandchildren. Later there would be a wedding breakfast to emphasise that something of significance had taken place.[15]

Te Puea also used the Methodists to mount an attack on an aspect of European life that she felt was more destructive to the Maori than anything else: the sale and consumption of alcohol.† And in what was to be one of her final crusades, she sought further legislative protection for the Maori in this area.

It was not that Te Puea was now teetotal. She drank in private in her own home and in the homes of friends. In the 1930s she had enjoyed a glass of Schnapps before breakfast; later, she had drunk at night for the relief of what she believed was asthma, and for this she favoured brandy;[16] at other times she provided alcohol to entertain intimates.[17]‡ Hone Heke Rankin of Ngapuhi, who often took Te Puea a small bottle of spirits as a gift when he visited Turangawaewae, believed a certain amount of liquor was essential to her in later life to help her survive the ordeals of long public functions.[18]

She was sharply aware of two things that she cited frequently to justify her stand. One was the toll that excessive drinking took on personal health and family relationships; the other was the fact that the Maori was more vulnerable to such drinking in circumstances where he was stripped of social supports and traditional sanctions on behaviour, particularly where he felt discouraged by an inability to compete with Europeans.

The experience of her own life had reinforced these convictions. Alcohol had been a factor in her health decline in the mid-1930s and Dr Douglas Martin had said to her then that if she did not stop drinking she would kill herself. She had also seen bitter and near-murderous arguments among the kahui ariki that had been brought about and intensified by alcohol (she had been a participant in such arguments before her marriage to Tumokai).[19] And she had seen the organisation and social life of whole communities collapse when alcohol became at first an accepted part of hui and then the

---

† It could be said with equal validity that the Methodists 'used' Te Puea for the same purpose. It does not matter; both statements are true. There was a total identity of interest and objective.

‡ Because off-premise sales of alcohol to Maori were forbidden until 1948, Te Puea used a doctor's prescription to buy brandy. One of these, signed by Dr. S. Hass in November 1947, asserts that she needed it 'to strengthen her heart'.

dominant ritual (and this had distressed her particularly when she visited Parihaka in 1922; at times it had also seemed on the verge of happening at Waahi). While she rarely undercut the mana of the kingship by letting criticism slip in public, she was also terribly unhappy about Koroki's drinking bouts.[20]

The ban on drink on marae over which she exercised direct control persisted. She never served it at functions; when there were complaints, she disposed of them by saying that people who were happy in themselves needed no alcohol to make fun; and if they were not happy within themselves, then there were other ways to remedy that.[21] Marae committees, particularly the one at Turangawaewae, were authorised to fine people caught breaking this rule (and to show there were to be no exceptions she forced payment of a fine by Koroki for a Turangawaewae infringement in 1948). When Te Puea 'shouted' for her own workers, as she frequently did after the work of a large hui was completed, it was done outside the marae. When she suspected that her children or visitors were circumventing the rule by sneaking out of functions to drink in the dark, Te Puea would prowl around with a torch or switch on car headlights suddenly to catch the culprits; they would be sent home.[22]

In the eyes of some of her more worldly followers like the Jones brothers, Te Puea seemed to have become rather obsessive and excessive in her statements about alcohol in the 1940s. Pei Jones saw it as something Maori would have to learn to live with if they were to take an equal place alongside Europeans.[23] Te Puea disagreed. She accepted the benevolently paternalistic view of most Methodist church workers that because Maori seemed to have difficulty handling alcohol, they should be protected from it. Her opinions became more strident after changes in the law that gave Maori greater access to liquor in hotels and the right to take it home. 'I can't close my eyes to all the people drinking in their homes,' she told Ramsden. 'What I want is [a return to] the law of 1945 so I can go into a hotel and drive them out, women and all.'[24]

In a statement to the *New Zealand Herald* in 1949 she said that 'when drink is in a Maori home our virtue of hospitality becomes a vice . . . In Waikato we do not pray "lead us into temptation", but we do pray "lead us not into temptation". Let us be honest and admit that while we can excel in some things, the great majority of our people, and indeed many Europeans, are at the mercy of this evil foreign leviathan when it is let loose among them. It creates debauchery and sordidness and cancels moral restraints.'[25]

Te Puea's fears about alcohol came to a head between 1946 and 1949. First, a 1946 Royal Commission on Licensing recommended changes to the law to put Maori drinkers on an equal footing with Pakeha. It also cast doubts on the existence of a 'sacred pact', a moral agreement between Maniapoto chiefs and the then Minister of Native Affairs, John Bryce, under which the King Country had been opened to Europeans in the early 1880s on the condition that alcohol could not be sold within its boundaries (and in 1946 the district was still 'dry'). Then, early in December 1948, the Government passed legislation that allowed Maori women to be served liquor on licensed premises and Maori men to take alcohol off the premises.

The legislation came largely as a result of lobbying by Maori returned servicemen, who had resented the fact that they had fought alongside Pakeha soldiers for the duration of World War Two, only to return home to a situation where they did not enjoy the same rights (and one ex-soldier has described how he had to persuade Hindus to buy liquor for him in his home district[26]). Anticipating disagreement from tribal leaders and church groups, the Government allowed very little time for the hearing of evidence by the relevant select committee. Over strong last-minute protests from Koroki's council, Te Puea and church and prohibitionist groups, the legislation was rushed through Parliament.

Even more ominous in Te Puea's eyes, notice was given in the same amendment that a referendum would be held in March 1949 to determine whether the King Country would remain a no-licence area. This issue was even more charged than the general one of Maori and alcohol. It was the firm conviction of Te Puea and most Maniapoto chiefs that the King Country had been opened in 1883 for settlement by Europeans and the construction of the Main Trunk railway line only on the condition that it remained dry. Subsequent Maori reference to this agreement spoke of a 'sacred pact' between Wahanui Huatare and John Bryce. Statements by Bryce's successor as Native Minister, John Ballance, and by the Premier of the day, Robert Stout, seemed to confirm the existence of the pact. Maniapoto people had no doubts. In their popular mythology the pact had lifted the tapu off the King Country and placed it instead on liquor: the one was a consequence of the other; if the presence of the Pakeha was allowed, then there had to be some protection from his vices.

Unfortunately, there was no contemporary documentary evidence for such an agreement in parliamentary records. And the 1884 legislation which designated the district no-licence was no different from that employed for the same purpose in other districts. This led the 1946 Commission to infer that there was no pact; or, if there had been, that subsequent changes in conditions had rendered it obsolete. (It was, as Maharaia Winiata noted, a contradictory and catch-all conclusion, suggesting that the issue was predetermined.[27]) The effect of this view was that the King Country could be declared 'wet' by a 60 percent majority of voters in a referendum; and there is no doubt that the liquor trade and a large majority of Europeans in the district hoped for this outcome.

Te Puea was incensed. First, she believed in the pact and was determined that it should not be overridden without the culprits being reminded loudly that they were breaking faith with a section of the Maori people. Secondly, a change in designation threatened to introduce the problems associated with alcohol into one of the few Maori districts that did not appear to have a disproportionately high Maori crime rate. (Maori convictions between 1935 and 1944 for offences related to alcohol amounted to 0.745 per 1000 people in the King Country, compared with 1.345 in Waikato and 3.743 in Gisborne.[28]) She believed strongly that it was the responsibility of Parliament to continue to exercise legislative protection against alcohol and, if possible, to extend it. She told the *New Zealand Herald*: 'As [alcohol] is a manufactured pakeha commercial and legalised evil, it is right that Parliament in the highest interests of both Maori and pakeha should restrain it or, better still, prohibit it absolutely.'[29]

After the hurried passage of the 1948 legislation and notice of the King Country referendum, Te Puea sent Peter Fraser a telegram protesting against a breach of trust. 'Governments change but we thought the good faith of the British Crown was permanent,' she suggested, twisting the knife.[30] Fraser, a teetotaller, smarted under this and under additional accusations that, as Minister of Maori Affairs,[†] he had gone back on an undertaking to consult with Maori leaders before proposing major legislation affecting the race (he had made this promise in 1945). His response was to invite a deputation to Parliament on 30 March 1949 to make submissions to him on the King Country question. Annoyingly for the Maori protesters, the referendum was to take place three weeks before the Wellington visit, which casts doubt on the value of making submissions and on the Prime Minister's sincerity.[‡]

None the less Te Puea and the King Country Maori Executive Committee accepted the invitation and threw themselves into what was — in Maori terms — a high-powered operation. The Methodist Church and the New Zealand Alliance provided money and documentary resources for the

---

† The term 'Native' had been dropped from all official references in 1947.
‡ As it turned out, this referendum made no difference. Although a preponderance of European residents was in favour of restoration, the Maori vote failed to reach the requisite 60 percent.

submissions. Maharaia Winiata, Tita Wetere and others worked day and night for several weeks collating historical and statistical evidence. A petition was circulated by Methodist church workers within the King Country asking for the retention of no-licence status. Te Puea sent out a letter under Koroki's letterhead to all members of the King Country tribes saying: 'I implore you to retain our mana and our rangatiratanga which are unique to us and do not have equivalents among other coloured peoples; uphold this sacred inheritance.'[31]

Finally, Te Puea and A.J. Seamer persuaded Koroki that he must lead the deputation. As she told the King, the original pact had been blessed by the mana of Tawhiao and the Maniapoto chiefs united under him; it was necessary that its existence be upheld by the hereditary successors to that mana.[32] While this arrangement was logical according to the Kingitanga view, at another level it was something of a propaganda coup: it was the first time a Maori king had adopted such a stance within New Zealand (Tawhiao's and Te Rata's missions to the British Crown having taken place abroad). Te Puea also prepared signed 'Members' tickets' for the delegation that included Koroki's coat of arms, instructions on when and where to assemble, and permission to bring friends; it had the appearance of an invitation to a State function.

Te Puea's handling of the campaign was more sophisticated and better supported than anything she had mounted previously. But on this occasion her word was not law: the issue exposed cracks in the ranks of the King Movement supporters.

Pei Jones, believing an extension of licensing was inevitable, had formed a committee of young Maniapoto leaders to try to wrest some money from the liquor trade for tribal welfare projects. In return, the committee would undertake to diminish Maori opposition to changes in the law. One of the members, Tony Ormsby, held discussions with representatives of the trade who agreed that potential licencees would have no difficulty paying £500 a year each into a welfare fund. According to Jones, they referred to the sum as 'peanuts' in comparison with the expected income. The committee then sent a petition to Parliament through the Member for Waikato, Sir Walter Broadfoot, formally requesting that provision be made for such an arrangement in any new legislation.[33]

Te Puea and Seamer were upset about this move. Having decided to hold out for a continuation of total prohibition, they wanted no splits in the movement. Jones and Seamer exchanged angry words at a Te Kuiti hui, the latter asking for the withdrawal of the petition in the interests of the morals and health of the Maori people. Jones retaliated by telling him the churches had no right to become involved in the issue; it only injected elements of emotional stress that made matters more difficult to discuss and resolve. Jones also said that church sponsorship of the prohibition petition resulted in a misleading number of signatures — people who liked their drink and wanted greater access to it were signing because they felt they could not refuse a request by a minister or a deaconess. Worst of all, Jones concluded, the prohibition group would ensure that neither Maori side would achieve its objective: the King Country would be licensed and the Maori people would receive no benefits from the move; they would only suffer as a consequence of greater opportunities for drinking.

This disagreement exacerbated an element of strain in Te Puea's relationship with Jones; it never entirely disappeared. It was made even worse by Pei's insistence that it was singularly inappropriate for Koroki to act as figurehead for the prohibition group. The King's fondness for alcohol was well known among Maori leaders. Some months after the Wellington mission, as Koroki was driving Jones to Huntly up the west bank road to avoid police patrols, the King told him he was well aware that he had been wearing 'the wrong colours'; but he said he had been manipulated into the position and felt he had had little choice.[34]

The day of the deputation was a festive one. Early in the morning of 30 March 1949, Koroki, Te Puea and hundreds of supporters arrived in Wellington by special train. They were taken to the Ngati Poneke hall close to the station, welcomed by local elders and given breakfast. At 10.30 they assembled at Parliament steps and at 11 o'clock 600 people entered Parliament Buildings to meet Peter Fraser in his twin roles of Prime Minister and Minister of Maori Affairs. They represented 150 King Country hapu among them.

The deputation spokesmen, Winiata and Wetere, presented Fraser with a petition for a continuation of prohibition in the district signed by 4050 people — 2300 King Country residents over the age of twenty-one, 1400 under twenty-one, and 350 Maniapoto living outside their home territory. They read from a twenty-three-page statement signed by Koroki and '32 leading chiefs of the King Country'. This outlined the Maniapoto view of the pact, referred to liquor as 'a devitalising and demoralising agent', and cited figures that suggested offences relating to drunkenness were lower in the King Country than elsewhere. The statement concluded by asking Fraser, as 'protector under the Crown of the Maori race', to refer the question to the Trusteeship Committee of the United Nations.

Fraser thanked the delegation and its spokesmen and promised to consider the submission. Then he gave the entire party a cup of tea which,

Prime Minister Peter Fraser prepares to meet King Koroki in Parliament in the course of the presentation of the King Country Pact petition, March 1949.

Irene Hobbs

as one member noted, meant 'a long session of standing round, but one which the older folk bore in a spirit of forbearance.'[35] Indeed, that was the spirit of the day: self-sacrifice in a worthy but hopeless cause.

The euphoria that the exercise had generated — the spectacle of 600 Maori marching into Parliament behind their King — disguised for a time the fact that it achieved nothing. In Government eyes it had probably not been expected to; it was simply a way of containing and then allaying the misgivings of a morally-roused pressure group. Licences were granted to King Country charter clubs over the next two years and, after a further referendum in 1954, to hotels. The King Country was made wet after all.

Te Puea was embittered by the result, part of which she lived to see. It strengthened her conviction that politicians, no matter how charming they could be as individuals, were devious and untrustworthy in their public roles. She was especially upset because she had lobbied Parliament and public opinion more energetically in this cause than in any other.[36] She failed to see that it was a lost cause, and had been so from its inception.

Certainly, there had been merit in the Maori case: liquor, if not the cause of Maori social problems, was an exacerbating factor; it continued to be so;

it was true that the liquor trade with its vested commercial interest in the sale of liquor was disproportionately influential in deciding matters of public interest (but the fact that breweries donated funds to both major political parties meant that neither was prepared to curb that influence); it was also true that the preparation of the case against the maintenance of the King Country Pact showed all the shortcomings of the European insistence on working from documentary records and ignoring oral and traditional ones — it was indeed 'incomplete and Pakeha-coloured' as the statement Winiata had written for Koroki alleged.

But the mood of Parliament, political parties and the country as a whole was moving towards self-reliance for the Maori through equal opportunity rather than through protectionism; and equal opportunity meant equal risk. New Zealanders generally drank to excess and if the Maori displayed a higher casualty rate than the European it was because he had been stripped of more social supports. What public policy should have considered then was how to restore those supports. It did not begin to do so seriously for another generation. Meanwhile, Te Puea's worst fears about the effects of alcohol on the Maori appeared to be confirmed.

16

Last years

A film taken at Turangawaewae in February 1950 shows Te Puea to be a fragile woman, prematurely aged. The occasion was a visit by 700 Empire Games competitors. She appears surprisingly short (a little over five feet tall), slight, and wearing a bright blue and white floral dress; over this hangs the familiar sackcloth apron with its wide, sensible pockets. She has her scarf round her head and is carrying a wide-brimmed straw hat that she brought back from the Islands. Her eyes, squinting slightly against the sun, are protected by a pair of dark glasses.

She seems at least ten years older than her sixty-six years; except that she is charged with nervous energy. She darts among clusters of guests who tower over her. As she talks she gestures with her hands and shrugs her shoulders a great deal; when she listens she is intent. She leans coquettishly against the male visitors as she becomes aware of being filmed; she does this easily, unselfconsciously, and the men like it. Her whole aura is that of a woman who is confident among people, accustomed to being the centre of attention, and who knows how to cajole and manipulate and keep large numbers of people occupied.[1]

She enjoyed these garden parties. Like the hui, poukai and tangihanga throughout Waikato, they were functioning more efficiently now than at any time previously: the organisation and the calendar of annual events that she had built up like a church liturgy to give the Kingitanga substance and cohesion — both were now a way of life for thousands of Maori on dozens of marae. (According to an estimate in 1951, the participating membership of the King Movement was then about 20,000 people.[2]) Pakeha no longer regarded the cycle of functions as threatening or even peculiar; many participated as workers or guests.

At the centre of the organisation, the Tekaumarua or Council of Twelve Elders that she had established for Koroki in the late 1930s — based on that

Te Puea entertains members of the British Empire games team, February 1950.
Turongo house

which had assisted Tawhiao and Mahuta — advised the King on matters of broad policy, made decisions about ritual and kawa, and published movement news in *Te Paki o Matariki*. Individual marae supporting the kingship were administered by home committees who planned local functions and coordinated with those in other parts of Waikato, Maniapoto, Hauraki and the Bay of Plenty. No sooner was one poukai or anniversary hui completed than somebody was planning the next on another marae and everybody else anticipating it. Life for Kingitanga supporters had become a forward-looking one of participation in distinctively Maori activities that reinforced positive feelings of group and individual identity. Te Puea's objective of the 1920s and 1930s — to make Waikato 'a people once again' — was achieved.

Robert Mahuta, Koroki's adopted son, grew up in the King's household in the late 1940s and early 1950s. He said that the calendar of movement activities planned and consolidated by Te Puea gave him and his contemporaries 'an alternative set of symbols and values, and indeed an alternative lifestyle, from that of the forty-hour week, quarter-acre section and mortgage . . . The poukai gatherings, life crises rituals and many other hui staged by the movement provide a network of occasions within which people can come together to laugh, sing, play, work and talk about those things they deem are important. It is at these hui that dreams are recounted,

Tawhiao's promise of the millennium is retold, and people's hopes for the future are revitalised.'[3] And Maharaia Winiata said the Kingitanga was, for its members, a 'more intimate covering for their spirit [that] keeps them warm in the wider atmosphere about them.'[4]

The poukai and coronation hui cemented the movement more than anything else. Not only did they bring people together regularly to intensify their shared aspirations, they also acted as what Acheson called 'verbal newspapers . . . the only effective means of spreading tribal or political views.'[5] They were for Waikato what the Ringatu 'Twelfths' were for Tuhoe, and they had the same effect: they reinforced a feeling of tribe while expressing sentiments that transcended those of tribe.

The land development schemes and subsequent marae and meeting house building programme of the 1930s and 1940s had extended the base for these activities and brought in larger numbers of people as participants as well as spectators. Voluntary contributions made at the twenty-five-odd poukai helped keep local marae solvent, while a portion of this money, periodic tribal levies, the whitebait tribute and contributions from the Tainui Trust Board gave Koroki and the central organisation based on Turongo House the funds to initiate hui and development programmes.[†]

Turangawaewae itself had a permanent population at this time of just under 200 residents. Here too day-to-day organisation was in the hands of a committee, chaired by Roy Moke. This planned and controlled hui and fund-raising, and was responsible for maintenance of facilities and the behaviour of inhabitants and visitors; from the early 1950s it also controlled

---

[†] The only feature of Kingitanga organisation that diminished in function and importance during Te Puea's lifetime was the institution of the Kingmaker. After Tarapipipi's death in 1941, Ngati Haua remained handicapped by poverty and internal squabbling. The role of Kingmaker shrank to a purely ceremonial one and remained so, although his representatives continued to sit on Koroki's and then Te Atairangikaahu's councils. A major source of contention was that Ngati Haua maintained that not only was the title of Kingmaker hereditary, but also that of Tumuaki or chairman of the King's council of advisors; the rest of Waikato disagreed and when Koroki's council was set up it was under non-Ngati Haua chairmanship. Tension between Turangawaewae and Rukumoana intensified almost to the point of violence on two occasions: when Te Puea wanted Tarapipipi buried on Taupiri and Ngati Haua wanted to inter his body under Mahuta's statue at Rukumoana (and both sides believed they won — according to a Ngati Haua spokesman, the body finally buried on Taupiri was not that of Tarapipipi); and in 1966 when Ranginui Tamehana, a grandson of Tupu Taingakawa, removed the Kingitanga's coronation throne from Kauhanganui at Rukumoana to Mahinarangi. This last action was regarded by the remainder of Ngati Haua as a further diminution of Ngati Haua's mana. (Interviews, Winara Samuels and Alex McKay.)

the activities of marae wardens who wore uniforms and carried out supervisory duties.

Te Puea's role was no longer indispensable. She still liked to patrol the area to ensure that necessary work was being undertaken, and to look for evidence of drinking, misbehaviour and untidiness; but it was no longer necessary that she do so; her organisation was capable now of functioning without her. In the jargon of anthropology, she had successfully 'routinised her charisma'.[6] It was enough now for her lieutenants to say, 'Te Puea wouldn't like that,' or, 'That isn't worthy of the old lady'; and people would conform to the standards demanded of them. Her continual physical presence was no longer necessary to move people: she had become a mythic figure in her own lifetime.[†] The mixture of affection and awe that residents of the pa displayed towards her in these years was also apparent in their nicknames for Te Puea: 'the Giant', 'the Witch' and, most commonly, simply 'Ma'.

The independent functioning of Kingitanga organisation released Te Puea for a more private life than she had been able to enjoy for the previous thirty years. Although she was increasingly in demand for the honorary designations of public life,[‡] she travelled about less frequently. She was able to be an energetic hostess when occasion demanded because she was using the farm more often as a refuge and a means of recuperation. Under Tumokai's supervision it was supporting itself and helping to feed the pa. It carried a dairy herd, pigs, and large crops of vegetables, especially potatoes and kumara. She was also determined to reopen the Raungawari farm and, for the last three years of her life, she went up there for days at a time to begin to clear it.[*] On both farms, among children and animals, Te Puea worked and renewed herself.

---

† And was an even more dominant one after her death. In the 1950s Waikato magistrates became fond of telling Maori offenders that 'this would never have happened if Princess Te Puea had still been alive'. This brought protests from Piri Poutapu — by then back at the pa — and Maharaia Winiata that many of the offenders had nothing to do with Turangawaewae and in some cases had no connection with Waikato tribes.

‡ She was much sought-after to be patroness of organisations like the Maori Women's Welfare League, established in 1951 to help Maori women adjust to changing economic and social circumstances. She was also reputed to have been a Justice of the Peace; but Justice Department records hold no evidence that she was so appointed (see personal communication from the Secretary of Justice, 12/1/77; and from National Archives, 26/1/77).

* Tumokai carried on this work after her death and brought the farm into production; but he was unable to manage two properties simultaneously and returned full-time to the Turangawaewae farm in the late 1960s.

Although only she, Tumokai and Momo slept permanently in the farm-house on the Turangawaewae Estate, she had huts built around it to house her floating extended family. She almost always had young people staying. Sometimes it was Herangi nieces and nephews, sometimes children from the pa like Tiahuia Ramsden, sometimes girls from Te Rahui Hostel in Hamilton, where Sister Heeni was matron; always during the school holidays she had Piki there. She had a firm but easy relationship with the younger ones and there was competition to be allowed to stay. As she had always done, she knew what pleased children. She would show them where to pick raspberries, for example, then say: 'Go over to the milking shed. See Uncle Dave and he'll give you some cream.'[7]

On a typical day, Sister Heeni remembered, Te Puea would get up early, help Momo round the house, feed whoever was staying — at the farmhouse kitchen table — feed the dogs and cats, prepare morning tea for the workers in the fields and take it out to drink with them. Then, if it was sunny, she would potter about in her own vegetable and flower gardens, for which she always stole clippings if she saw something bright and beautiful that she did not already have. As she worked she liked to chat, and to use whatever she was doing as a source of homilies for any captives within earshot ('always keep things clean, always keep things tidy: these are the things that bring you satisfaction').[8] In the afternoons she might visit the pa and weed and sweep there, which always brought others rushing out to help; or she might sit in the fields on an orange box, supervising planting or harvesting.

If Te Puea had one quality that was a source of irritation in all this, it was her unwillingness to relinquish supervisory roles. She did not want to let go of anything; although she had always delegated jobs and involved her supporters in organisation, she was convinced that if she absented herself entirely the farm and the pa would slide into slothfulness and debauchery. She continued, like a parent, to treat her workers as her children. The only ones she trusted completely to carry on without her were Tumokai, Momo and Rangitaua.

In the evenings she tackled correspondence with Biddy Pickering, who was able to give her the most professional secretarial service she had ever had. And she continued to keep her diary, obsessively entering her move-ments of the day and any monies received or spent. At night she always found sleeping difficult because her breathing became difficult. She would sit up late and read or write, straining her failing eyesight, and then walk around in an effort to relieve the congestion in her lungs and the tightness in her chest. She and Tumokai believed the condition was asthma; in fact, as Dr Margaret McDowall established later, the discomfort was brought on by progressive bronchiectasis that worsened as she lay prone.[9] On such nights she sometimes allowed herself a measure of brandy or schnapps.

She continued to be frugal to the point of austerity in her daily habits. But this very austerity heightened her enjoyment of the odd extravagance with which she indulged her vanity and her liking for occasional luxuries. Sometimes it would be a new dress from bright material bought at Courts in Hamilton and made up by Doris Eaddy. The ultimate extravagance she allowed herself was a huge black limousine, a 1948 Chrysler Windsor, in which she was driven about like a Cabinet Minister.

(Contrary to published rumours,[10] the car was neither a gift nor a bribe from the Labour Government. She told Peter Fraser in 1949 that she wanted help to buy a new car; he sent her with Mick Jones to see Walter Nash, Minister of Finance, who took her to Todd Motors; there she was prevailed upon to take a large black Austin but she refused, saying it looked too much like a hearse; instead, she insisted that she wanted one 'just like Mr Nash's'; which she got.[11] It was paid for by the sale of two other vehicles from the Turangawaewae Estate.[12])

The new car elevated Te Puea's style but did not change her habits. Bill Eaddy remembered her and Tumokai driving into his service station to fill up for a long journey; there was a strong smell of dried shark from the boot. Her earlier drivers, Sister Heeni, Irene Hobbs, Frances Winiata and Maera Moke, were reticent to chance their hand with the vehicle and risk its splendid and extensive body. But Te Puea did not plan to become a remote authority figure; she encouraged them quietly, sitting in the front with them until they gained confidence.[13] Only Tumokai was able to handle it at once.†

The most memorable hui at Turangawaewae that year was one in honour of Peter Buck, who had been knighted in 1947. In February 1949 he began a farewell tour of New Zealand that included visits to twenty-six maraes; it was occasioned by an earlier operation for abdominal cancer which had produced the prognosis that he would not live more than three months.‡

Buck and Te Puea do not appear to have met before this visit (or, if they had, neither could recall it). When he was working as a medical officer in Waikato she had not emerged as a leader; while he was in Parliament

---

† The imposing vehicle reduced some other people to consternation. Muriwai Tawhiao, asked to clean it, was caught by Tumokai soaping the engine.
‡ In fact he survived a further three years.

representing Northern Maori there had been little contact between that electorate and Waikato; later there had been the war and Buck's Health Department duties in Wellington; he had left New Zealand permanently in 1927 and returned only once, briefly, in 1935. They knew of each other, however, through their respective public reputations (Ngata had begun talking about Te Puea in his letters to Buck as early as 1927). Each respected the other: to Te Puea, Buck was an eminent tohunga, the only one to distinguish the Maori race abroad;[†] and to Buck, Te Puea was one of the few progressive community leaders who had promoted his views on the need for sanitation and hard work.[14]

But they do not seem to have entirely liked what they knew about each other. Asked by Ramsden for assistance with his Te Puea biography, Buck replied: 'I cannot think of any personal reminiscences of her . . . when I was Health Officer they were not very cooperative.'[15] It is difficult to believe that Buck had no relevant recollections. His own field notebooks are scattered with references to Mahuta, members of the kahui ariki, even visits to Te Puea's Searancke cousins at Te Kopua.[16] The relevant factor seems to have been that they were not favourable references. In May 1907, for example, Buck travelled to Waahi and slept the night in the meeting house. He spoke to Te Marae and Mahuta who 'made a great fuss' of him; the following day he went to Te Kopua to examine William Searancke and his family and noted that people there were 'a better class than Waikato'.[17]

It is possible that Buck also did not want to be party to a book eulogising Te Puea and Waikato. In addition to his reservations based on their earlier lack of cooperation on health policies, he had also disapproved strongly of Te Puea's pacifist stance in World War One, when he served at the front as an enthusiastic combatant; and he had never approved of movements that upheld the 'mana motuhake' — the right of the Maori to govern themselves separately — as the Kingitanga had done (this phrase was, in fact, the motto on Tawhiao's Te Paki o Matariki coat of arms).[18]

For her part, Te Puea had heard of and disliked Buck's frequent references to what he called his 'mongrel' status, and his suggestion that the Maori part of his background was the inferior element, a handicap he had been forced to overcome.[19] She also could not help but be conscious that Buck had chosen to work abroad as an expatriate rather than among his own people. Nevertheless Buck had been the first Maori to fly a banner

---

† Unable to pursue anthropology in New Zealand, he had become Director of the Bishop Museum in Honolulu and held a chair of anthropology at Yale University.

abroad successfully other than in wartime (and three years later Te Puea was to encourage Maharaia Winiata to do the same). He had become a legend, she had supported Ramsden's moves to secure him a knighthood,[20] and she was proud that the first marae he stood on in fourteen years was Turangawaewae. She was further flattered when Lady Buck told her in Turongo that the food served in the Waldorf-Astoria in New York was no better than that at Turangawaewae. From Ngaruawahia, Buck left with Ngata to inspect the land development scheme at Horohoro (the one Te Puea had been offered and had refused in 1929).[†]

The visit had a sequel that was to involve Te Puea and revive her intimacy with Ngata. He and Buck conceived the idea of a series of celebrations to mark the sexcentenary of the so-called 'Great Fleet' canoe migration of Polynesians to New Zealand.[‡] The hui would not be simply a commemoration of a significant anniversary: they would serve to raise Maori consciousness and pride, particularly by emphasising the scale of Polynesian seafaring and exploration at a time when Europeans had yet to enter the Pacific or cross the Atlantic; and they would be an appropriate peg on which to hang a range of educational programmes and competitions. Buck promised to return to New Zealand for the celebrations if he was able, although he must have known the prospect was unlikely. And the mana of his name helped to sell the project to dozens of tribal committees in urban and rural areas.

Te Puea first heard of the proposal at the Turangawaewae reception for Buck. She approved wholeheartedly and saw it as another step towards

---

[†] More than anything else, of course, Buck was Ngata's friend. In spite of differences of temperament and emphases they had shared a great deal, particularly intelligence and erudition (and, from their concurrent parliamentary terms, a dislike for what they regarded as Pomare's pro-European antics). Their correspondence is a mine of perceptive comment on the changes that European contact was forcing on the Maori. Buck believed that Ngata, had he so chosen, could have become an ethnologist of worldwide distinction; Ngata in turn had worked hard and unsuccessfully to establish a position for Buck back in New Zealand. Jock McEwen's description of the friends' reunion in 1949 is a moving indication of the depth of distinctively Maori feeling that they shared: 'We went into the lounge of the hotel where Te Rangi Hiroa was staying. The room was crowded with people from many parts of the world. Sir Apirana stood at the door and eventually saw his old friend at the furthest corner of the room. He began the traditional tangi which brought a sudden hush. The two Maoris walked towards each other chanting as they went, oblivious of the throng around them. They met in the centre of the room and pressed noses in the old Polynesian greeting and wept. [It] was a meeting which I shall never forget.' (Condliffe 1971, p. 8.)

[‡] At this time there was a general acceptance that a fleet of canoes containing the ancestors of the major tribes had made landfall in New Zealand around 1350 AD. Strong doubts have since been cast on the fleet concept (see Simmons 1976).

winning acceptance of Turangawaewae as a national marae and a focal point for kotahitanga under the mana of Koroki.[21] She wrote to Ngata and suggested that the celebrations culminate in a grand finale at Turangawaewae in October 1950, coinciding with the King's coronation hui.[22] Ngata agreed, and six major marae began to prepare for the chain of functions.

The project revived in Te Puea's mind one she had launched unsuccessfully for the 1940 national centenary: the creation of a fleet of canoes representing each major tribal district. This time there was no question of building a fleet – resources were as scarce as they had been in the late 1930s; and Piri Poutapu — the only man capable of heading such a venture — was exiled from the pa. She settled on a less ambitious and more symbolic representation of the original idea; she instructed her nephew Tamati Herangi, now in charge of the Turangawaewae Carving School, to prepare nine model canoes for presentation at the Turangawaewae hui to the descendants of each: Tainui, Takitimu, Kurahaupo, Tokomaru, Te Arawa, Mataatua, Aotea, Horouta and Ngatokimatawhaorua.

At Te Puea's suggestion too, Maharaia Winiata became involved full-time in the preparations. He saw this series of hui as an excellent opportunity to dramatise and extend the programmes of Maori adult education that he had been conducting from Auckland and Waikato marae.[23] He consulted Ngata and the two men drew up a plan for the objectives and course of each hui.

> A close investigation by Maori authorities into the orally kept traditions of the canoes, an exchange of information on the canoes, a study of the lore, the history and literature of the people. A dash of colour and pageantry in the dances and rituals performed on the marae, a display of the characteristic oratory of the elders . . . and the discussion of matters affecting Maori welfare, land development, economic advancement, preservation of Maori culture, and education.[24]

In addition, capitalising on the interest generated by the Empire Games in Auckland in February 1950, the Ngaruawahia hui was to include a national Maori sports competition with teams formed on a tribal basis.

The programme was identical to that conceived by Ngata in the 1920s for the cultural and economic advancement of his people. It had lapsed on a national scale since his resignation from office in 1934. The only difference was that this time the primary organiser and spokesman was to be Winiata rather than the ageing and failing elder statesman.

Winiata threw himself into the work of organisation. He travelled to all major tribal districts, supervised the setting up of local committees for the discussion of canoe traditions and recruiting for sports competitions, released press statements that were planned so as to build up to a climax for the October hui, and prepared a series of broadcasts in English and Maori on Maori settlement theories and traditions. His hope, he told the New Zealand *Listener*, was that 'the talks will succeed in expressing something of the intense pride which is undoubtedly stirring in my people in this anniversary year.'[25] He also planned to involve wider New Zealand society: 'The sense of community, the generous hospitality displayed at the celebrations . . . these are gifts of the Maori to the emerging race of New Zealanders.'[26]

All this Winiata undertook with the blessing of Ngata and Te Puea. Both were too ill and too tired to lay the groundwork as they would have done in previous years; but both were confident that Winiata was the person to carry on in their stead. Both had marked him as an heir apparent.

The round of hui began at Te Kaha on 21 January 1950. It continued at Gisborne on 24 February, Otaki on 18 March, Hastings on 22 August and Whakatane on 22 September. Ngata's death on 14 July[†] generated intense expressions of emotion at the later meetings and a strong feeling that the Maori people were indeed entering a new phase of political and cultural development.

The final hui was held as planned at Turangawaewae from 5 October to 10 October. Winiata edited a special booklet for the participants that summarised in Maori the major canoe traditions and highlighted that of Tainui. Expectations for a large crowd were high; early press reports spoke of a probable attendance of 12,000 people and an army of women that was working day and night 'peeling thirty tons of potatoes and six tons of kumaras'.[27]

The event itself was a disappointment. Torrential rain over the whole week kept thousands of spectators and potential participants away (the final attendance was about 3000). The plane that was to bring Prime Minister Sidney Holland and the new Maori Affairs Minister E. B. Corbett was unable to take off from Paraparaumu Airport.[‡] In their absence the senior guests of honour were Walter Nash representing the Leader of the Opposition (Peter Fraser had had a stroke and then a heart attack at the beginning of the month), and the Members of Parliament Eruera Tirikatene, Iriaka Ratana

---

† See page 305.
‡ Labour had lost office in November 1949; Sidney Holland had led the National Party to a 12-seat majority in Parliament.

and Hilda Ross.[†] Although the press described the event as 'a fitting climax to Princess Te Puea's work',[28] she was intensely disappointed at the low attendance and the curtailment of activities. In addition, her health suffered one of its periodic setbacks and she spent most of the week in a wheelchair.[29]

Cheated of the fulsome attention that she had hoped the celebrations would attract for Koroki and Turangawaewae, Te Puea revived another crusade that had been close to her heart for the same reasons: securing a visit to Turangawaewae by British royalty. In her eyes, such a visit was to be — literally — the crowning touch of her work. It would be a final and public demonstration that the feuds of the past were healed and that the Waikato people were fully committed to being citizens of New Zealand and the British Commonwealth. In addition, it would confirm Koroki as the senior Maori ariki and Turangawaewae as the paramount Maori venue for the reception of national guests. Te Puea had gone some way towards achieving this status with the steady stream of VIP visitors since the war; some, like the Mount-battens, had been 'almost Royalty',[30] and it was now taken for granted that successive Governors-General and Prime Ministers would call there.

But the ultimate gesture of recognition had to be the reception of a British monarch by a Maori King, and she had nourished this dream since the Prince of Wales was hustled through Ngaruawahia in 1919.[31] She had sustained it in spite of the by-passing of Ngaruawahia in favour of Rotorua for the Duke and Duchess of York's visit in 1927 and that of the Duke of Gloucester in 1935. As a result of Peter Fraser's sympathy, it had seemed that she would achieve the objective in March 1949. The Government had prepared an itinerary for the visit of King George VI and Queen Elizabeth that included Maori receptions at Waitangi, Ngaruawahia, Rotorua and the East Coast. At the eleventh hour, Te Puea was robbed: the visit was post-poned because of the King's illness. And when the tour was re-organised under the National Government in 1950 Ngaruawahia was excluded. As in the past, there was to be a single Maori reception at Rotorua.

Te Puea was outraged at this reversal. Although the Maori Affairs Minister Ernest Corbett claimed that the reasons were the King's health and stated preference,[32] Waikato did not believe him. They were certain there was a strong element of revenge by the new Government for the Kingitanga's past

---

† Nash was to involve himself closely in Maori affairs after Fraser's death in December 1950. He formed a belated but intimate relationship with Te Puea (and with her kaumatua Hori Paki). After the Coronation hui in 1951 he wrote to her that 'if at any time there is any Maori subject you desire me to give consideration to, I will be more than pleased to do so.' (Walter Nash to Te Puea, 11/10/51. W.P.)

separatism, for Maori support of the Labour Party, and in particular for Te Puea's close relationship with Peter Fraser. Certainly Sidney Holland displayed considerable impatience with Waikato's request for a place on the itinerary. No Prime Minister since William Massey had come to office with so little contact with Maori and so little interest in Maori affairs. He viewed them as a homogeneous group whose elements of diversity were solely the consequence of internal squabbling.[33] To him, Maori were simply Maori and they were fortunate to get even one special reception at Rotorua (and even this he had initially opposed[34]). The main justification for the single reception, he believed, was that as native inhabitants they were a distinctive touch to be flourished at visitors until such time as they were safely assimilated into the majority culture; and it was Holland's hope that assimilation would be accomplished as quickly and as painlessly as possible.[35]

Dissatisfaction with the new itinerary was first discussed publicly at the sexcentennial hui at Turangawaewae in October 1950. Representatives of the visiting tribes supported the suggestion that a stop at Ngaruawahia should be restored to the programme (as visitors, of course, it would have been less than polite not to have done so; but this did reduce any appearance of mere partisanship in Waikato's case). Te Puea subsequently summarised the case in a press statement released through Winiata. She said the exclusion of Ngaruawahia insulted Maori aristocracy and belittled the royal visitors:

> It would not be right for King Koroki's followers to attend the national Maori welcome at Rotorua, having failed to receive the Royal couple when they passed within a stone's throw of the Maori King's house . . . The King and his people wanted a chance to dispel murmurings which alleged they were disloyal to the British throne . . . At all previous Royal visits the Maori King has asked, she said, for Ngaruawahia to be included, but always without avail. The tribes wanted to demonstrate their loyalty on their own marae . . . the pah would be of more interest to Royalty than the Pukekohe market gardens or the Huntly collieries [which were included in the tour] . . . It is strange to Maori eyes to see the party stop at Pukekohe and Huntly and pass through the ancient territory of the Maori King, neglect his pah and palace, and go straight on to Hamilton to stop for several days. Maori etiquette is being violated.[36]

Corbett paid his first visit to Ngaruawahia as Minister of Maori Affairs in March 1951. Roore Edwards, speaking on the marae on behalf of Koroki and Te Puea, asked him to reinstate Ngaruawahia on the itinerary. The minister replied this was impossible because the choice had been King

George's.[37] Te Puea felt insulted by the reply and, according to Winiata, 'would not swallow her spit' to reopen the matter with the Prime Minister. But at a meeting on 18 March held in conjunction with the Ngaruawahia Poukai, a group made up of Waikato, Maniapoto, Taranaki, North Auckland and Bay of Plenty representatives formed what they called 'the Te Puea Herangi Advisory Committee' to pursue the matter, with Winiata as secretary. This resolved to carry on the fight on as many fronts as possible. The same day Winiata sent a letter in Te Puea's name to Lord Bledisloe in Gloucestershire, asking for advice and support from the English end, and one over his own name to Prime Minister Holland.

The letter to Holland repeated the arguments in favour of Turangawaewae as a venue for a Maori welcome. It stressed that Waikato wanted the royal couple to 'receive from these subjects of theirs, long overcast with the shadows of the troubles of the sixties, the deep sincere expressions of loyalty and love for the descendant of the Great Queen Mother, Victoria. Here at Turangawaewae, in a manner impossible elsewhere, a genuine Maori atmosphere can be produced in a brief programme . . . that will truly convey to their Majesties the core of the traditional culture of their Maori subjects.' Winiata also quoted the Undersecretary for Internal Affairs as saying that people were still free to re-open the question; since King George was said to have made the decision, Winiata invited Holland to support an approach, 'through the usual channels, to the King himself'.[38]

He then tried to enlist Eric Ramsden's help on the strength of the latter's former commitment to the Kingitanga and current membership of the National Party. He suggested in his letter that Ngaruawahia had indeed been excluded for political reasons.[39] Ramsden was not to be easily wooed, however. His letters in reply show him to be torn between a desire to flaunt his newly-acquired political influence on the one hand, and on the other to punish Te Puea and Waikato for what he viewed as their rejection of him.

'Other influences have cut across the path and I have been ignored,' Ramsden wrote, referring to Mick Jones' relationship with Te Puea. 'Twice she has been to Wellington and not seen me. I could have seen her either time . . . after the years of service I have given to her cause, I have naturally felt disappointed.'[40] But if anybody could secure modifications in the tour itinerary, Ramsden suggested, it would be him or Hoeroa Marumaru.†

---

† Marumaru was a Maori vice-president of the National Party and had stood as the National candidate for Western Maori in 1946 and 1949; in 1950 he was appointed to the Legislative Council in place of Apirana Ngata. His wife had accompanied Te Puea on the trip to the Islands in 1947.

'Hoeroa, I can assure you, is the most influential Maori in this country today, and that must remain so while the present Government remains in office. Mr Holland is always ready to listen to Hoeroa and he accords me the same privilege.'[41] But Ramsden warned Winiata that 'the Prime Minister is most touchy', and that 'behind the scenes Hoeroa and I had the greatest difficulty in securing a Maori hui at all . . . The Government is not afraid of political repercussions . . . [It] is in office without a single Maori member. The Maori people had the remedy in its own hands.'[42]

The most that Ramsden could offer was the possibility of a compromise: that Koroki and Te Puea be introduced to King George and Queen Elizabeth at Huntly Station when the train stopped there. This should 'satisfy the dignity of both sides,' he wrote, and he forwarded the suggestion to Corbett.

By April 1951 the ripples that Winiata had started had spread and reaction began to flow back to Turangawaewae, much of it contradictory. In a letter marked 'Secret — only to you', Holland wrote that it was 'the King [who] had decided there will be one Maori function only.' But he was appalled at the suggestion that Te Puea and the supporting tribes make an independent approach to Buckingham Palace. 'It would not be in order for your people to do so,' he told Winiata. 'His Majesty could not allow himself to deal directly with any individual groups of people, no matter how strong a claim they may have, and to expect him to vary decisions which have been arrived only after the closest consultation between himself and the representatives of the Government would produce quite an untenable situation.' In framing the itinerary, 'proper regard was made to the claims and desires of both the Pakeha and the Maori people.' The Prime Minister showed no understanding of the Waikato case in his conclusion that a single function at Rotorua would 'provide an opportunity for the Maori people to adjust their own internal problems and join together to show in a fitting manner their loyalty and devotion to the Crown.'[43]

Meanwhile Lord Bledisloe had taken a different view. He told Te Puea that he and his wife 'entirely shared' her opinions about the visit, and that he had written to the King's secretary Sir Alan Lascelles to put her suggestion to the King. 'I now understand,' he concluded, 'that the itinerary is not finally settled and there should not be any difficulty (if your Prime Minister and present Governor-General approve) in making some modifications.'[44]

This held out some hope; and the information that it was the New Zealand Government and not the King who wanted a single Maori function was reinforced by letters from the Governor-General Sir Bernard Freyberg, who said arrangements were a matter for 'the Government alone';[45] and from a Buckingham Palace secretary who said the programme had been entrusted 'to the Prime Minister of New Zealand'[46] (this last letter was in reply to one Te Puea had sent to Lord Mountbatten).

Subsequent correspondence bogged down in repetition and stalemate. Waikato refused to send Te Puea and Koroki to Huntly Railway Station and suggested instead that Queen Elizabeth and Princess Margaret visit Turangawaewae if the King's health was indeed not up to such a visit.[47] This in turn was unacceptable to the Government. Early in 1952, when it was decided that Princess Elizabeth and the Duke of Edinburgh should visit New Zealand instead of the ailing King, Te Puea sent them an invitation through Lord Mountbatten to visit Turangawaewae.[48] The whole cycle began again: Buckingham Palace referred her back to the New Zealand Government, and Holland refused to alter the new itinerary — the third — so as to include Ngaruawahia.

By now the Prime Minister was unable to plead the King's state of health and personal preference as justification; it had become simply a matter of not backing down. To do so, he said, would lead to a flood of requests for visits from other parts of the country not included in the programme. And there the matter rested until after Te Puea's death in October 1952.[†]

As hopes for a royal visit seemed to be fading, Te Puea's attention was taken up by the Kingitanga succession. There was no doubt in her mind that Piki was heir apparent – that was one of the reasons she had taken her to the Islands in 1947. Koroki had no sons; his eldest daughter Julia was not regarded as legitimate; his adopted son Robert was not of a sufficiently direct line of descent to be considered eligible. The only possibility of the succession by-passing Koroki's descendant was that of a potential claim on behalf of Tonga Mahuta's son Tumate, known as Charlie (he became chief organiser at Waahi after his father's death in 1947).

Such a claim would have reflected the continuing ambition on the part of Waahi members of the kahui ariki to restore the headquarters and focus of the Kingitanga to their pa; in particular, they sought to transfer the annual coronation hui back to Waahi and completed a new hall with this end in

---

† Te Puea did not live to see what she would have regarded as the culmination of her efforts to win official acceptance for the Kingitanga. On 30 December 1953, fourteen months after her death, Queen Elizabeth II and the Duke of Edinburgh visited Turangawaewae for twenty minutes. In that time, according to the *Auckland Star* of 31 December, 'there ended a feud that has lasted a hundred years'. The visit was repeated on 8 February 1974 and on subsequent occasions.

view in the late 1940s. Feelings about Te Puea from this branch of the family remained ambivalent. They all knew they needed her — like a strong parent — to push them along and rally the people behind public projects. But they resented her bullying and the fact that she had drawn the limelight away from Waahi.

While her uncle Haunui and cousin Tonga were alive, these feelings had a measure of overt leadership (they tried to get government support for their development plans independent of Te Puea in 1945, for example[49]). After their deaths, Mahuta family resistance to Te Puea tended to be passive. On some occasions, knowing that Te Puea was coming to seek him out for criticism or advice he did not want, Koroki would simply absent himself.[50] And right up to Te Puea's death he refused to make Turongo his permanent home, something she had set her heart on.

But Te Puea did get her way with Piki, so much so that Koroki was heard to say she was more her child than his.[51] It was Te Puea who had decided on education at the Diocesan School in Hamilton, and she had kept the girl with her at the farm during the holidays. Her allowance was limited strictly; much was expected of her by way of responsible leadership and conformity to tribal expectations; and the watchdog for these expectations was Te Puea. Piki's own evaluation of their relationship was that 'she was hard on me'.[52] Unmindful of her mother's and her own reaction to arranged marriages, Te Puea was also determined to select Piki's husband; she had two names in mind.[53]

The problem that then arose was that Piki was as independent in her choice of relationships as most other members of the kahui ariki had been at the same age. She took up determinedly with Whatumoana, son of Wetere and Frances Paki and grandson of Hori. Te Puea was furious: this was no part of her scheme of things. She believed that Frances Paki's Aupouri line was not sufficiently senior to justify a kahui ariki connection; and she suspected the Paki clan of designs to infiltrate the family (one of Hori's daughters had already married Charlie Mahuta). She went to Rakaumanga and abused the old patriach, warning him to keep his mokopuna in line. (Her words to him were: 'E Hori, isn't your longing for me satisfied?') She was also merciless to Piki in her condemnation of the relationship.

These outbursts, marked by over-reaction and vituperative language, were more than anything a sign of Te Puea's steadily declining health. Her compulsion to work and to dominate people drove her on; but her judgement was affected by pain and fatigue. The instinct that had showed her in earlier days where to draw the lines of conflict, when to hold out and when to be flexible, was now impaired. Her mind and body had not seized up in full stride as she had often expected they would; they were running down slowly.

And yet her achievements were monumental, and her awareness of this fact made her more expectant that her demands would be met. She had come back to her people when they were fragmented and demoralised. In forty years of relentless work she had restored to them their system of rural-based extended families, their communal patterns of living, their traditional leadership and their cultural activities. In addition to these more general goals, she had won a large measure of European acceptance of the Kingitanga and helped secure compensation for the confiscations; and she had established a model pa and a system of Kingitanga organisation that would both survive her. Her large objectives were achieved; and being achieved, they ensured that the movement no longer had to play a political role to survive. From the 1950s, it was to persist and to meet the aspirations of its members as a focal point for Maori values and a rallying point for Maori activities.

17

Towards
Te Rerenga Wairua

The years 1950 and 1951 brought a spate of deaths and reminders of deaths. There was Ngata in July 1950, Bishop Bennett in September, Peter Fraser in December; in 1951 there was her cousin Te Rauangaanga, her brother Wanakore in April and Peter Buck in December. In addition, the Government had opened a memorial chapel to Gordon Coates at Matakohe in May 1950 and Te Puea and Tumokai made a pilgrimage there to place a sprig of red manuka on the former Prime Minister's grave.[1]

These were all people whose lives and careers had been bound up with her own, people who had been well and strong in the years when her life had seemed to be in danger. The accumulation of bereavements weighed her down with a sense of her own mortality and made her vulnerable state of health still more precarious.

She was affected most by Ngata's death on 14 July 1950. In spite of the fact that their relationship had been ambivalent, sometimes bitter, she felt her spirit twined round his. He more than anybody else had led her into contact with other tribes; he had showed her the advantages of cooperation with governments and the Department of Native Affairs; he had launched the land development schemes that had re-established Waikato farming. He had an intellect and erudition the equal of any man, yet he had remained Maori to the core. She had also understood and loved him for his amorous peccadillos.[2] 'Part of my light has gone out with him,' she told Tumokai.[3]

Tumokai drove her to Waiomatatini, the marae where twenty-three years before they had spent Christmas with their children in surroundings that had seemed like home. She remained the length of the tangi but never left the Chrysler; she sat hunched in the back seat surrounded by pillows and communed with the spirit that had gone. But the mourners were aware she was there; she was a more dominant presence for not being visible. 'We knew there was something powerful in that black car,' said Tom Te Maro. 'We all felt it and gave it a wide berth. And sometimes people saw a face looking out, white with silver hair and heavy eyes. She seemed more like a ghost than Api's tupapaku.'[4]

After the tangi Te Puea recorded what appears to have been her only radio broadcast: a poroporoaki to Ngata on the Maori Programme. It was done in Maori at Waahi, in the stylised idiom of traditional funeral farewells. Her voice sounded faint and constricted, and the congestion in her lungs was audible when she breathed. But there was also a sound of determination, the tone of somebody accustomed to pushing a weak body to its limits:

> The spirit of our elder Ngata lies fallen on the East Coast. I am deeply grieved and I lament for him. He was the man who upheld the treasures of the old Maori world. Depart, my elder. The whole world knew of your work. Depart. The old Maori world ceases with you. The mana and the tapu of that world have gone with you. Depart, my friend, return to Hawaiki, to your ancestors who will open their arms to you. And my greetings to you, the people, who are left his orphans.[5]

Te Puea collapsed after the recording session and went to bed for several months. In a letter to Mick Jones on 10 August she described herself as 'very weak. We will look to you to carry out our wishes.'[6] And two months later, at Koroki's coronation hui, Leslie Kelly met her being pushed in a wheelchair. 'She looked terrible,' he told Ramsden, 'shrunken and very dark in the skin and very feeble . . . as if she might die at any moment.'[7]

Te Puea's health had been declining steadily through the 1940s, with a sharp dip in 1944 when she appeared to suffer a heart attack.[8] In addition, she developed progressive bronchiectasis that congested her lungs and lengthened the windpipe. This made breathing more difficult and exacerbated the heart condition. Her eyes — the source of so much admiration in earlier years — deteriorated: they watered frequently and her sight began to fail. (She wore glasses from the late 1930s, but most reluctantly; she always tried to take them off for photographs.) Her hands frequently trembled and the legibility of her handwriting declined.

And yet she was always unwilling to convalesce. After collapses, she had beds made up, at first in the porch of Kimikimi and then, after 1938, on a verandah in Turongo. She always feared that work would not get done if she was not there to supervise. Frequently between 1950 and 1952 Dr Margaret McDowall (who had taken over Dr Hass's practice) found her too ill to work, but sitting up on an orange box directing kumara planting on the farm or building work inside the pa. From 1950 too she was in and out of a wheelchair as congestive heart failure came and went, swelling her ankles and legs to the point where she could not walk.

Dr McDowall sent her to Waikato Hospital in January 1951 for an X-ray to confirm that the bronchiectasis was not a recurrence of tuberculosis.[9] She was sent home with the futile instruction to 'take things quietly'.[10] (Which she never would. In her entry in the 1951 edition of Who's Who, the final section reads: 'Have no recreations. When I am not working I sleep.'[11])

In May Te Puea and Tumokai decided to go to Te Kao. Northland held warm associations for them. They had gone to Ahipara on previous occasions when she was run down and each time enjoyed the heat, the beach, the sea air and the fresh seafood.[12] She had met Judge Acheson there and been reunited with her northern relative Mutu Kapa; through these two she had been introduced to the Te Kao community, among whom she had found further Tainui connections and felt completely at home. These earlier trips had seemed more like holidays than anything else she could remember. And now her need to be recharged was stronger than it had ever been.

The occasion for the visit was the unveiling of tombstones for Te Aupouri elders. Among them was one for Te Paea Eru Ihaka, mother of the Rev. Kingi Ihaka, who had died in 1949. Kingi Ihaka was Te Puea's godchild. He had been christened Kingi Matutaera after one of Te Puea's nephews, a son of Te Ngaehe's, who had been taken to Te Kao by Mutu Kapa; and the nephew had been named after his great-grandfather Tawhiao. In 1951 Ihaka was stationed in Masterton as a young curate. Te Puea told him that Waikato would escort him home for the unveilings.

When the party left Turangawaewae on the morning of 11 May it had grown to include Ngati Maniapoto and Ngati Pikiao representatives.[13] Te Puea and Tumokai travelled in front in the Chrysler with the Ihakas, and Koroki followed; behind them were ten more cars and three buses. They stopped for the night at Te Iringa Marae near Kaikohe. Before the party could sleep, however, the Ngapuhi hosts launched a strong attack on the Kingitanga. They accused Koroki of aggrandisement and said that Ngapuhi recognised one sovereign only, the British one. It was a familiar litany and Te Puea's old warhorse Roore Edwards rose for the defence.† He confronted

---

† He was to die exactly one year later in May 1952.

them with the fact that their representatives had been among those who established the kingship and selected Potatau. The arguing did not stop until the early hours of the following morning when Ihaka scolded his kinsmen for breaking the conventions of hospitality.

Saturday 12 May was a clear sunny day. The convoy stopped for lunch at Kaitaia and most of the men slipped away to hotels for a drink. Te Puea, annoyed at being abandoned, asked the Rev. Heemi Rihimona where everybody was. He bent and whispered that the men were in the pub. 'Pack of bastards,' Te Puea shouted, burning the old man's ears. Like the Methodists, she came down hard on drinking; but frequently at the expense of language.

By mid-afternoon when the party was about twenty miles south of Te Kao it ran into sudden and torrential rain. The roads beyond Kaitaia had metal, clay or sand surfaces, and in wet conditions forced traffic to crawl. It was four o'clock by the time they reached Waihopo, about ten miles from Te Kao. Here further progress was impossible because a stream that ran over the road, normally just four metres wide, had swollen to 100 metres and deepened. There was nothing to do but wait and hope that the water would drop.

As the passengers sat in the unusually dim afternoon light, a lightning display began to illuminate the sky to the north. It started with great flashing sheets; then, at the centre of each flash, the lightning forked – first one filament and then several at a time. They ran down the sky from right and left but all finished at the same part of the horizon, like jagged arrows pointing to the same place: Te Rerenga Wairua, the Leaping-off Place of Spirits.

In the first car Tumokai and the Ihakas watched through the windscreen in silence. But Te Puea, hunched forward in the front with a shawl round her shoulders, kept her head bowed and began to pray aloud. At one point the Ihakas' three-year-old son Tom leaned towards her and said, 'Ghosts, Nannie, ghosts.' But she took no notice. Finally, when Tumokai took her arm, she lifted her head and looked at him. She had been crying. She said simply: 'Te tikanga Maori, e Tu.' The Maori sign.[†]

The convoy was halted for six hours. Many of the cars were affected by water and before they could move off again required attention from Koroki and Tumokai, the only mechanics in the group. They reached Te Kao around

---

† In traditional mythology forked lightning over burial places was an omen of death, as in the waiata: 'See where the lightning flashes two-forked over Tauwhare, what is it but a sign of coming death' (Nga Moteatea, Vol. I, p. 15).

midnight and the weather was transformed for the second time that day. The sky, which is like a vast upturned bowl over that part of the country because of the flatness of the landscape, shimmered with stars. The Te Kao people were waiting outside to welcome them.

During the reception inside the hall, Te Puea made one of her rare public speeches. After greeting and thanking the Te Kao people, she asked the Ngati Tipa members of the Waikato party to stand; and then the Ihaka family. 'These are your relatives,' she said to both groups, who were meeting for the first time (Paea Ihaka's paternal grandmother had come from Waikato).[†]

The following morning a dozen tombstones were unveiled, Te Paea Ihaka's by Koroki. After the ceremony Te Puea told Tumokai that she wanted to visit Te Rerenga Wairua once more. So, early in the afternoon, they slipped away from the hui and drove to Cape Reinga in the company of the Aupouri elders Heemi Manera and Hohepa Kanara. The landscape had changed since their earlier visit in 1929. A lighthouse complex that had previously stood on the island off Cape Maria van Diemen to the west had been installed at the cape in 1941.

This time Te Puea was unable to manage the difficult walk down to the pohutukawa tree, the actual leaping-off place. Instead she stood in sight of it on the hill above, below the lighthouse, and prayed for several minutes. Then she asked to be taken into the building. The keeper, Mr S. Schofield, was delighted when he found out who she was. He invited her to sign the visitors' book. 'What's the date?' she asked him. 'The thirteenth,' he said, 'Sunday May the thirteenth.' Te Puea nodded. 'What an unlucky day to sign anything,' she said as she wrote her name. Then she and Tumokai started for home.

From the cape she fell into a deep sleep. She did not wake when the car went through Te Kao, and Tumokai had difficulty rousing her at Kaikohe that night. The following day she slept all the way through to Ngaruawahia. It was her last major trip. She was not well enough again to leave Waikato.[14]

T e Puea's major business preoccupation in 1951 was raising money to buy a sawmill at Ngaruawahia and finding timber for it from Maori blocks. The mill had run into difficulties under its previous owners when the supply of

---

† To Kingi Ihaka, it was obvious that 'one of the main purposes of the visit was to knit the relationship between Waikato and Aupouri' (interview 9.5.75). A particular motive for this may have been Te Puea's acceptance that Piki would eventually marry Whatumoana Paki, whose mother Frances had come from Te Kao.

local timber was exhausted. Te Puea, advised by Ngahihi Hughes of Otoro-hanga, saw the venture as one that should bring additional income for the farm and pa; and at the same time provide materials for Maori residential and community buildings throughout Waikato. In particular, she wanted to build a new dining room and yet another meeting house at Turangawaewae. While this was under discussion she went to Kawhia with Tumokai on 31 August to inspect a stand of trees and make arrangements for felling it. She was feeling feverish and unwell. The timber was on a section of a farm that was difficult to reach, so they travelled in Tumokai's truck, which could cope with the terrain more easily than the car; the cabin was draughty and uncomfortable. By the time they got home on Sunday night Te Puea was so ill that Dr McDowall was called at 11 p.m. She found the old lady had bilateral pneumonia, and that her condition was critical.

Te Puea refused to go to hospital and so Dr McDowall sat with her on Monday night to see her through the crisis. By 2 a.m. on Tuesday her pulse was stronger and McDowall concluded that her patient had 'turned the corner'. She left her to sleep. In the morning Te Puea told McDowall that she had to go down to the pa because she had a letter from the King 'commanding' that she do so. (Koroki was convinced she was about to die and wanted her at Turongo.) McDowall said it was out of the question. But when she returned at six that evening Te Puea had gone. Three days later, from her bed at Turongo, she was supervising the wedding of four couples on the marae.[15]

A worsening of her bronchiectasis prevented Te Puea fully recovering from pneumonia. In October she coughed up half a pint of blood. By January 1952 she was so ill again that when Dr McDowall insisted on hospitalisation Te Puea agreed. She was still bringing up blood and in addition was suffering from chest pains and shortness of breath.

She wanted to be in charge of arrangements for her own comfort, however; and while she managed to make herself understood in English, her choice of words was not always correct. She rang Bunny Woodhams from the farm and told him that she needed 'a man's morning coat'. Woodhams, accustomed to odd requests at short notice (she once asked for a red carpet), assumed that Koroki or Tumokai was going to a function that required formal dress. As he tried to think where he might find such a garment, he began to mutter aloud about the irksome nature of formalities. She cut him short, 'No, you silly,' she said. 'You don't know what I'm talking about. I need a morning coat. The kind you put on in the morning when you get out of bed.' What she wanted was a warm man's dressing gown.[16]

Te Puea spent seven weeks in Waikato Hospital. She improved rapidly but was easily exhausted by visitors, of whom she had far too many. They came in dozens and brought fruit, vegetables and flowers, which she in turn distributed among the staff and other patients. The nursing notes on her hospital record alternate between 'patient bright and happy' and 'has been tired by visitors'.[17] By the end of January she had improved sufficiently to call Sister Heeni in on four occasions to take her out for drives. On one of these she appeared at Bunny Woodhams' office at Court's in Hamilton, wearing her dressing gown and slippers. He was alarmed and asked what was wrong. She said nothing, she just wanted to talk; she was fed up with the hospital. So he fetched a cup of tea and they talked for half an hour. Then Woodhams had a phone call from Bill Herewini, the District Maori Welfare Officer, who asked if he had seen Te Puea. 'Why?' said Woodhams. 'Because she's walked out of hospital and nobody can find her anywhere.'[18]

Te Puea was also answering correspondence, with Biddy Pickering's help, from dozens of wellwishers. One message had come from the secretary of the New Zealand Communist Party, Vic Wilcox. Te Puea wrote back: 'My thoughts went back to the time when you and your party came over to Orakei Pa to build that manuka fence; often I think about it and when I read your kind message it filled my eyes with tears . . . I have been fighting all this time. I am not finished yet.'[19]

She was discharged on 5 February. Her hospital report noted that the symptoms associated with heart failure had improved slowly, and that she was anxious to return home: 'We actually kept her in much longer than she would have liked.'[20]

The following day King George VI died at Sandringham. This had particular consequences in the Maori world: it meant that royal tour arrangements would be further postponed; and it raised the prospect of a Maori delegation to London for the coronation of Queen Elizabeth in June the following year. Te Puea's Ngati Rangitane friend Hoeroa Marumaru (whose wife had accompanied her on the Islands trip in 1947) was determined to organise such a group, and that it should include all the big names of Maoridom. When he spoke to Alex McKay at Wellington Railway Station late in February, he told him he was taking Te Puea out of New Zealand for the second time. McKay was doubtful that her health would be up to such a trip and said so. 'Well,' said Marumaru, 'you tell her that I'm going. And that I'm taking her with me. And that I'm not taking no for an answer.'[21]

A large mortgage on the Turangawaewae Estate enabled Te Puea to buy the sawmill by March. She had taken this step against the strong advice of Pei Jones, who was now working full time for the Puketapu Timber Incorporation, a venture that also involved milling. He was convinced that the mill could not operate economically, particularly if she went ahead and used a large stand of timber on Maungatautari Mountain, as she planned to do. Told of Jones' opposition, Te Puea's other advisers assured her that he was simply jealous of competition.[22] She was also disposed to disregard his advice because of disagreements on other matters including King Country licensing and the affairs of the Tainui Trust Board, of which Jones was then chairman.

On 26 June Te Puea was back in hospital suffering severely from congestive heart failure. Her ankles and legs were swollen again and she could not walk; the chest pains and breathlessness had returned more acutely than before. Her admission report attributed the relapse to her inability to stop working.[23] Everybody was worried about her, including Te Puea herself. She brought Momo Ewe with her and an additional bed was made up in Te Puea's room. Visitors were restricted to Tumokai, Biddy Pickering and Sister Heeni. Her lawyer was allowed in once for the signing of documents relating to the sawmill.

She left hospital for a few hours on 13 July to attend a small hui at the pa which, according to newspaper reports, was in honour of the 82-year-old Australian composer Alfred Hill. In fact she was more conscious that it was the last function that Maharaia and Frances Winiata would attend before they left for Edinburgh, where he was to undertake a doctoral thesis on a Nuffield Fellowship. Mindful of what had happened to Inia Te Wiata's marriage, Te Puea insisted that they should both go.[24]

Five days later she was discharged again. The swelling had receded; she was able, temporarily, to walk. The following day she wrote to Aroha Jones, Mick's youngest daughter: 'Waikato Hospital . . . pushed me out, not sick enough to have a room. So I am in Turongo for a few days . . . Uncle Dave is working in the sawmill. He is very well and we have plenty of firewood.'[25] In fact, Te Puea had left hospital at her own insistence. Dr McDowall was angry and Tumokai anxious; but the patient was adamant. She was worried that the new buildings at the pa — the meeting house Pare Hauraki and a new dining room — would not be completed in time for opening at the coronation hui in October unless she was there. As in the past, she intended to supervise the construction down to the finest detail.

She also wanted to say goodbye privately to the Winiatas. Maharaia and Frances were taken into the side bedroom at Turongo where she lay propped up on pillows. Maharaia was shocked and embarrassed by her appearance. Death seemed inevitable, he wrote later that year.[26] They talked for a while and then Te Puea told them she wanted to bless them. So they knelt by her bed in turn while she laid her hands on their heads and prayed over them. Then she gave them each a greenstone pendant, and to Maha a copy of one of Tawhiao's prayerbooks, marked and annotated in the King's own hand. She told him that although he was Ngati Ranginui, he was to work hard overseas and then come back and put his additional qualifications to work for Waikato and the Kingitanga. 'That finally bound me to Te Puea and Koroki and all they stood for,' he wrote. 'I feel as if I belong to Waikato more than I do my own people. Whatever manly or . . . Maori qualities I have came from them, especially from Te Puea.'[27]†

Early in August a reluctant Tumokai told Te Puea that the mill was in serious trouble. They had planned to set it on its feet by completing the Maungatautari contract. But after several weeks in the bush, he had come to the conclusion that the operation was impossible; the terrain was too steep, the mature trees too scattered. The time and expenditure needed to get the logs out could only result in huge losses. In the short term, there was no way of meeting repayment commitments on the mill let alone showing a profit.‡ This news and the depression it brought did nothing to improve her health. There was consolation only in the fact that the mill had been able to produce enough timber for the new marae buildings.

On 11 August Momo, Mihi Haggie and other women at the pa decided something had to be done to cheer Te Puea up. They threw a party to celebrate the thirty-first anniversary of the marae and made an elaborate and tiered cake. Te Puea came and did appear to enjoy herself. She ate well for the first time in months. In her after-dinner speech she was full of gratitude for the gesture.[28]

Throughout September and the first week in October she went out doggedly each day in the wheelchair to the marae, sometimes from the farm, sometimes from Turongo. She dismissed the disaster of the mill from her mind and focused her whole attention on the near-impossible task of getting the house Pare Hauraki and the dining room ready for 7 October. It was the goal that drove her from her bed each morning when she should have stayed in it; when she should, in fact, have been in hospital. 'She was

---

† Winiata was awarded a doctorate by Edinburgh University in December 1954. He was the first Maori to study on an overseas fellowship and the first to be awarded a non-medical doctorate. His thesis, *The Changing Role of the Leader in Maori Society*, was dedicated to 'my kuia and ariki Te Puea Herangi and Koroki Te Rata Mahuta'. Winiata was regarded as the most promising Maori academic since Buck; he died suddenly on 6 April 1960 at the age of 47.
‡ The whole of Te Puea's diary for 1952, including the section dealing with the sawmill venture, disappeared immediately after her death (interview Alex McKay).

driving herself to death,' Dr McDowall said. 'And yet it was the same willpower that was keeping her alive.'[29]

In one final attempt at Kingitanga reorganisation, Te Puea suggested to Koroki's council that it would be preferable to hold the coronation anniversary on the weekend nearest the date rather than on the day itself. The idea was not acceptable. Their reply, she told journalist Mel Taylor early in October, was that 'the sun, the moon and the stars cannot be changed'; neither could the Coronation Day. But, said Te Puea, what about the kings of England? They changed their birthday dates. That was nothing to do with Waikato, the council told her.[30]

The crowds had begun to arrive by Monday 6 October. Te Puea, in the wheelchair still, was as much in evidence as at any previous hui. 'Though not yet completely recovered from the illness which forced her into hospital earlier in the year, [she] watches, supervises, organises and is proud,' Taylor reported. She joked with people as she met them and was as incisive as ever in her instructions to workers; but she looked terrible. She seemed hunched and shrunken; her skin was black and parchment-like, her eyes yellow. When Dr McDowall suggested she return home to bed, she said: 'No. I want to see everything.'[31]

The new buildings were opened by Koroki on Tuesday 8 October, the anniversary day. That night, staying at Turongo with Raukura Paki close by, Te Puea appeared to suffer a heart attack and Dr McDowall was called. She also asked for Father Seamer and Sister Heeni brought him up from Hamilton. The following morning she insisted on getting up again to watch the service and speeches.

On Thursday morning, Alex McKay — up from Wellington for the hui and also sleeping in Turongo — got up early to make Te Puea a cup of tea. The phone rang and he answered it from the kitchen. The call was from Parewanui to say that Hoeroa Marumaru had suffered a heart attack and died the night before; they would delay the burial for as long as it was necessary to get Te Puea there. McKay said there was no question of her travelling. He replaced the receiver and took Te Puea her tea in silence. 'Well?' she said. 'Aren't you going to tell me?' 'Tell you what?' asked McKay. 'That Hoeroa has gone,' Te Puea said, looking straight at him.

On Saturday she asked to be wheeled round the grounds of the pa. She had one final look to ensure that the rubbish was cleared away and everything was in order. Then she told Sister Hobbs to take her back to the farm. At home, Momo and Raukura helped the old lady into bed. She asked them to take all her clothes outside and hang them in the long shed, and to cover each hanger with a coat or jacket of Tumokai's. Then she fell into a deep sleep.

That night at the pa Tumokai's sister Nukupera Te Waru dreamed she could hear three voices singing from the river, one man and two women. She said next morning the man had been Hoeroa Marumaru and one of the women Te Puea. They had sung a Waikato version of the lament *Enari Te Titi* which said, in part: 'I look over the water and imagine I see canoes coming to rescue me. But they are only phantom vessels.'[32]

Te Puea talking to John Allenby, October 1952, hours before her death.
Auckland Star

All through Sunday 12 October Te Puea lay semi-conscious, her eyes closed, breathing with difficulty. Her feet, legs and back were cold. Momo rubbed them for a while in the morning and was relieved by Sister Heeni; nobody else dared touch the old lady. But she was not without company. Throughout the day a small crowd assembled in the house. They came in silently and filled the sitting room-bedroom in a half-circle around the open side of Te Puea's box bed; others sat in the kitchen. The women were wearing black and Momo too slipped away to borrow a cardigan; she did not want to have anything coloured on, she told Dr McDowall. To spare Te Puea's eyes there was no light. In the dimness, Tumokai, Momo, Rangitaua and the women in black — the children of other years — talked softly and waited. In the evening they were joined by Koroki and Te Atairangikaahu.

At the end, Te Puea spoke only Maori. She opened her eyes at one point and looked at the people round the bed. 'Ki te mate ana au ko ta koutou mahi i muri nei he porangi,' she said. When I've gone, you folk will all go mad. And, late in the evening, she reached out and pulled Momo's head down to her lips. 'Koatu tenei ki a Tumokai,' she whispered. Give this to Tumokai. With the other hand she tugged a small purse out of her nightdress. There was £25 in it. Tumokai put it in the safe by the back door and never touched it again.

A few minutes after 9 p.m. Te Puea's heart failed. She died quietly, her eyes still closed. She was sixty-eight years old.[33]

Te Puea's body lies in state in front of Mahinarangi. Irene hobbs

Te Puea's open casket lay on the porch of Mahinarangi for seven days. The funeral ceremonies were the largest seen in New Zealand outside those for Prime Ministers who had died in office. Newspapers estimated that over 10,000 mourners paid respects over a week, among them the Prime Minister Sidney Holland and the Leader of the Opposition, Walter Nash. More than 300 telegrams of condolence arrived from overseas. One thousand floral tributes lay on the marae.

On the fifth day of the tangi an Arawa and Tuwharetoa party broke with the Waikato custom of alternating host and visiting speakers. One, a Tuwharetoa orator named Heemi Pitiroi, finished a speech which Te Kani Te Ua of Ngati Porou described as 'uncalled for . . . pure skite'.[34] He signalled his wife to join him in a patere in front of Te Puea's body. Te Mamae Pitiroi did so, trembling violently. The husband led off with the first line, but jumbled the words; the rest of the party followed uncertainly. Then his wife twisted around and pitched forward on the ground. Tuwharetoa finished the song and then bent to attend to her; she was dead. Her body was laid for a time alongside Te Puea's.†

Mourners approach the coffin. Irene hobbs

† The family of Heemi and Mamae Pitiroi view the incident in a different light from Te Kani Te Ua. They point out that Mamae had been strongly advised by her doctor not to attend the tangi because of her serious heart condition; and that they regard the circumstances of her departure from life as a privilege — doing what she most loved doing and was celebrated for, and lying in state alongside Te Puea.

When the hearse pulled up at Taupiri Mountain for the burial on 19 October, the cortège stretched nearly two miles and was two and three cars deep in places. A plan to ferry the body downriver was thwarted: in Piri Poutapu's absence, the canoes were in disrepair. A light rain was falling and the river covered in mist as the mourners climbed up the mountain to lay Te Puea among the remains of the kahui ariki. The rain became torrential as the coffin was lowered into the grave.

Final farewells on Taupiri, in pouring rain: Mick Jones, Tumokai and Alex McKay. Turongo House

The burial prayers were led, in turn, by Karira Karaka, Ngapaka Kukutai, Mutu Kapa, G.I. Laurenson and Eruera Te Tuhi, her Anglican and Methodist friends. At the end one of Te Puea's girls, a teenager, became hysterical and tried to throw herself into the open grave. Tumokai stepped forward, held her, and two women began to chant the familiar ritual: 'Rire rire hau pai marire.' The girl became still and put her arm around Tumokai, joining in. And the Hauhau service was the last. There was to be no tombstone in keeping with Tawhiao's injunction that in death the kahui ariki were to be indistinguishable from the humble.

Piki married Whatumoana Paki. She was raised to the kingship on 23 May 1966 after Koroki's death on 18 May, the first woman to head the movement. At succession she took her mother's name, Te Atairangikaahu. Many of Te Puea's lieutenants remained involved in the Kingitanga until the late 1970s. Piri Poutapu died in 1975, Pei Jones in 1976, Mick Jones in 1977, and Alex McKay and Te Uira Manihera in 1980. Maharaia Winiata had died earlier in 1960 and Eric Ramsden in 1962. Tumokai, who was to die in 1985, had survived long enough to contribute to both a book and a television documentary on Te Puea's life.

Of all those left behind, nobody had to make more painful adjustments after Te Puea's death than Tumokai. He was just a worker again, no longer a consort; and there were strong resentments about the life interest in the farm that Te Puea had bequeathed him. When he returned there after the tangi he found the house stripped of everything with which Te Puea had had contact: bedclothes, crockery, cutlery; an instance of muru. He had to go and buy two mugs so that he and Momo could have a cup of tea. But the clothing in the long shed, covered by his own, remained. Later that year, when he was away at Raungawari, the shed caught fire. Momo, Papi and her husband Rua Cooper managed to throw the garments clear. Cooper built another shed at once and Momo hung the dresses, evening gowns, skirts, blouses and cardigans at the far end. Within a week a swarm of bees had settled around the entrance; they stung anybody who came near the door. Only Tumokai was able to enter the shed unmolested and he did so every few months to sweep it clean. Twenty-four years later the bees and clothes — now encrusted in honeycomb — were there still.

Epilogue:
Resolution of Raupatu

Te Puea's and Tainui's acceptance of the raupatu settlement proposed by
Peter Fraser at Easter 1946 had been based on the assumption that it was a
'take-it-or-leave-it' offer. After more than a decade of intermittent discussion
between Tainui and the Crown, there was no new ground to be covered.
There were no legal remedies available to contest the proposal or seek to
have it enlarged. And there was a possibility that the Labour Government
would lose office at the end of that year and be replaced by a National one
actively opposed to any kind of settlement of Maori grievances.

With these considerations uppermost, and mindful of the tribe's depressed
social and economic circumstances, especially the difficulties Koroki faced
trying to uphold the mana of the Kingitanga by offering and reciprocating
hospitality, Te Puea decided that the time had come to accept the offer on
the negotiating table: a payment of £10,000 for the first year, £6000 a year
for fifty years, and thereafter £5000 a year (later $15,000) in perpetuity. She
saw this settlement above all else as an admission of culpability on the part
of the Crown and a vindication of the Kingitanga's historical stance. Waikato
as a whole shared that view.

There was always a vocal minority that disagreed, however, both at the
time and subsequently. A Maniapoto Welfare Committee warned Peter
Fraser in 1946 that they rejected the settlement and would not let the issue
rest. In 1947 a petition from Te Hau Tanawhea and 2646 others was
presented to Parliament asking that land confiscated from Waikato in the
1860s be returned. The principles underlying objections to the accepted
offer from the Crown were those which had been voiced by Waikato
kaumatua from the time negotiations began in the wake of the Sim
Commission's 1928 report, which had found that the confiscation of
Waikato lands in the 1860s was 'excessive':

> I riro whenua atu, me hoki whenua mai.
> Ko te moni hei utu mo te hara.

As land was taken, so land should be returned.
Money is simply the payment for the wrongs committed.

According to this view, the annual payments from Government which permitted the operation of the Tainui Trust Board were some compensation for the 'sin' of confiscation itself. But they did not address the primary grievance, the loss of 485,625 hectares of tribal land and the accompanying loss of livelihood and mana.

In the years following Te Puea's death in 1952, dissatisfaction with the size and nature of the settlement grew. It was fuelled partly by the realisation that the sums involved made no provision for inflation and the rising value of the land lost. Consequently payments were progressively devalued with every year that passed (Crown research in 1989 estimated conservatively that the Tainui Trust Board had been deprived of more than $6.5 million on the basis of inflation alone).

Secondly, Maori expectations about the possibility of resolving historical grievances satisfactorily were being raised by a slowly developing recognition on the part of the country as a whole of the damage that colonisation and conquest had inflicted on Maori. There was also a growing national consensus that the Crown had persistently and consistently breached articles of the Treaty of Waitangi, especially article two, throughout the second half of the nineteenth century and into the twentieth. The Maori Land March of 1975, led by Whina Cooper, had dramatised these issues and focused Maori anger and grief at the loss of land and of economic and cultural resources; it had also won a large measure of support from Pakeha New Zealanders.

That same year, reflecting the change in expectations and giving further momentum to it, the third Labour Government established the Waitangi Tribunal. This forum, chaired by the Chief Judge of the Maori Land Court, was given powers to investigate contemporary breaches of the Treaty by the Crown or by local authorities and to recommend remedies to the Government. The Government would then negotiate an appropriate settlement with claimants. A decade later the fourth Labour Government made the tribunal's jurisdiction retrospective so that breaches of the spirit or the letter of the Treaty could be investigated back to 1840.

The extension of the tribunal's powers had at least three predominant effects. The steam and substance drained out of Maori protests on such national occasions as Waitangi Day commemorations (it became increasingly difficult to accuse the Crown of not caring about breaches of the Treaty when a mechanism had been devised specifically to identify and propose remedies for such breaches). It resulted in an avalanche of claims which looked likely to engage the tribunal for at least two decades. And it further raised Maori hopes that wrongs committed over the previous 150 years might at last have a real chance of being addressed and resolved, and that economic resources lost to iwi as a result of Crown action might in some measure be restored. Tainui was one of the first iwi to recognise and take advantage of the tribunal's extended powers and to set in motion renewed negotiations with the Crown.

The person most directly responsible for the adoption of the strategy was Robert Te Kotahi Mahuta, member of the kahui ariki and adopted son of King Koroki and his wife Te Atairangikaahu. After his secondary education, Mahuta had for a time worked in Huntly coal mines and then joined the New Zealand Army. In the late 1960s he enrolled at Auckland University and graduated with a B.A. in Maori and anthropology, and subsequently with an M.A. When the newly established University of Waikato advertised for a director of its Centre for Maori Studies and Research, Mahuta applied and was duly appointed in 1972. With the strong support of his mentor and colleague, Professor James Ritchie, Mahuta focused the work of the centre on 'action oriented' research that would produce improved economic, social and cultural conditions for Maori communities and tribes.

Two of the centre's major projects involved compensation for the Waahi community for the detrimental environmental effects caused by the building and operation of the coal-fired Huntly Power Station, and an attempt to establish tribal property rights to coal being extracted from State-owned mines and land within the confiscation boundaries. The second of these campaigns was ignited by the fourth Labour Government's creation of a State Owned Enterprise, Coalcorp, to operate the mines; and the related decision to sell this and other SOEs to the private sector, as part of a strategy to reduce government debt and shrink the involvement of the Crown in commercial activities. This new direction in government policy, part of economic restructuring and reform of the State sector initiated by Finance Minister Roger Douglas, raised the prospect that Crown resources which could have been available to settle compensation claims might in fact be lost to the State and consequently to Maori claimants. The projected sale of Coalcorp was of particular concern to the Tainui Trust Board, which had identified coal as one of the strategic assets which could be used in part-settlement of any future Tainui claim against the Crown.

In March 1987, therefore, on behalf of the Tainui Trust Board, Robert Mahuta filed two claims with the Waitangi Tribunal. One sought to restrain the powers of the new State Owned Enterprises Act, which was to be used by the Government as a mechanism for selling off State assets. The other was a new claim for compensation for the land confiscation of the 1860s. These initiatives set off a chain of events that led eventually to a renewed round of bargaining between Tainui and the Crown.

Tainui was unable to obtain an early tribunal hearing on the Coalcorp issue and the Government was unwilling to give the tribe the assurances it sought over recognition of potential ownership of coal and the mining rights to it. So the Tainui Trust Board decided to seek judicial clarification of how the State Owned Enterprises Act affected these issues and how they related to the tribe's overall claim for compensation for the confiscations. A hearing began in the Court of Appeal in Wellington in August 1989. Around 1000 people, mainly Tainui, marched to the court in support of the tribe's leaders and lawyers. It was a scene reminiscent of Te Puea's presentation of the King Country Pact petition to Peter Fraser at Parliament four decades earlier.

The judgment, delivered in October, could not have been more favourable to Tainui. It noted that a considerable part of the lands confiscated in the 1860s had been taken in clear breach of the Treaty of Waitangi. It also affirmed that coal mining rights were a legitimate part of Tainui's claim against the Crown and were therefore eligible for inclusion in any settlement. The Court President, Sir Robin Cooke, went on to say that the 1946 settlement had been 'trivial ... Some form of more real and constructive compensation is obviously called for if the Treaty is to be honoured.'[1] Sir Robin viewed Tainui's willingness to negotiate with the Crown as an alternative to Waitangi Tribunal hearings or further court action. But he made it clear that the tribe could return to court if the Government declined to negotiate.

This decision laid the foundation for what followed: five years of hard-nosed and highly specific discussions between the Tainui Trust Board and the Crown. For the first year negotiations involved the fourth Labour Government and progressed as far as a statement of each side's position (Tainui sought a settlement involving land and money, part ownership of Coalcorp and disclosure of all reports and information available to the Crown; the Government sought to restrict settlement to an adjustment of the 1946 level of payments to allow for inflation — from $15,000 a year to around $220,000, with a lump sum of $6.7 million to compensate for previous income lost as a consequence of inflation; plus 'enhancement' of this sum to the tune of a further $20 million).

Once a National Government returned to office towards the end of 1990, the new Prime Minister, Jim Bolger, and the minister responsible for Treaty claims, Doug Graham, exhibited a stronger determination to bring the negotiations to settlement. They achieved this goal, remarkably, in the face of considerable opposition within their own caucus. When a 'heads of agreement' document was eventually signed by Tainui and Crown representatives in December 1994, it included the following provisions:

- The Crown would apologise for the confiscation of Waikato-Tainui lands.
- An acknowledgement that the confiscated territory had a minimum modern value of $12 billion.
- An agreement to transfer to Tainui over a period of five years 14,483 hectares of current Crown lands in Waikato (this would include the Hopuhopu Army Camp, which would subsequently house the tribe's new administrative headquarters, and the land on which the University of Waikato stood).
- Payment of $170 million to Tainui to acquire further assets, including land, in compensation for the gap between the value of the land taken and that returned.
- An agreement that Tainui would relinquish all further claims within the confiscation area, excluding those to the Waikato River and west coast harbours, which had never been officially confiscated and would eventually become the subject of future negotiations.

After consultation on both sides, Te Arikinui Te Atairangikaahu and Robert Mahuta signed a deed of settlement on behalf of Tainui that incorporated these measures. Principal signatories for the Crown were Bolger and Graham. The necessary legislation, the Waikato-Tainui Raupatu Claims Settlement Act, was passed by the New Zealand Parliament in November 1995 and signed into law that same month, with an apology to Tainui by Queen Elizabeth II, who was visiting the country at the time. Thus did the great-great-granddaughter of Queen Victoria, monarch at the time of the Waikato War and confiscations, make the final gesture to heal what had been a suppurating sore on the New Zealand body politic for 130 years; and she did it in the presence of Te Arikinui Te Atairangikaahu, great-great-granddaughter of Tawhiao.

Tainui chief negotiator Robert Mahuta, himself a great-great-grandson of Tawhiao, and a great-nephew and protégé of Te Puea Herangi, noted that the agreement with the Crown led to a dissolution of the old Tainui Trust Board in 1999. It was replaced by Te Kauhanganui, a Tainui tribal council based on Tawhiao's parliament and made up of representatives of the sixty-one marae which had been signatories to the settlement.

'[In] the end,' he wrote, 'the mana of Waikato stands revealed again: we have restored wealth to the tribe; we have our own governance; we can attend to the needs of our people ourselves. This is what was guaranteed to us in the Treaty of Waitangi. It is what our ancestors sought when they agreed to hold the Kingitanga for the motu ... The past has its purposes, but no one lives there. Part of our credo is to take risks and accept the consequences; we always move from the known into the unknown.'[2]

In January 2001, within months of making this statement, Sir Robert Mahuta died, worn out by the combined effects of diabetes and the stress of bringing the raupatu issue to closure. He was buried at the front of the Tainui Endowed College at Hopuhopu, one of the fruits of compensation, in view of Taupiri Mountain and the Waikato River.

What Mahuta acknowledged to the end of his life, however, was that in seeking settlement of the raupatu he had been seeking fulfilment of Te Puea Herangi's vision: to make Waikato a recognisable people once again; and to restore the Kingitanga to the position it had held in Tawhiao's time, as a safe place where the mana of all its people might be protected.

Glossary of Maori words[†]

Aotearoa	a Maori name for New Zealand
ariki	paramount chief or senior chief
aroha	love, caring
atua	guardian deity
atuatanga	spirituality, godliness
haka	vigorous posture dance, usually of defiance
hapu	basic tribal grouping, section of an iwi
hara	fault, sin
hongi	nose-pressing greeting
hue	gourd
hui	gathering, meeting
ihi	power, inspiring awe
kahui ariki	Waikato 'royal family', usually defined as descendants of Tawhiao
kai	food
kainga	home, settlement
karakia	prayer, service
karanga	calling visitors forward, usually on to a marae
kauhanganui	assembly, parliament
kaumarua	twelve, Maori King's council of twelve advisers; in a Ringatu context, the twelfth day of the month, on which a service is held
kaumatua	male elder
kawa	marae procedure, protocol
kiekie	straw-like plant used for plaiting
Kingi	King
Kingitanga	Maori King Movement
kotahitanga	movement for inter-tribal unity
kuia	female elder

---

† The brief explanations given are appropriate for text references; in other contexts meanings may vary.

kumara	sweet potato
kupapa	loyalist (to Crown in New Zealand Wars)
kumete	wooden bowl
makutu	black magic
mana	prestige, authority
mana motuhake	separate mana or nationhood of the Maori people
mangai	mouth; in the case of T. W. Ratana, Mouthpiece of God
marae	courtyard for conduct of ceremony, usually in front of a meeting house, also can refer to settlement around such a courtyard
matakite	intuition, second sight
mauri	life-force, aura
mimi	urinate
mokopuna	grandchild, descendant
muru	legitimate plundering in compensation for alleged offences
ngeri	chant with actions
noa	common, profane
ohaoha	injunction
pa	Maori settlement, sometimes fortified in pre-European times
Pakeha	non-Maori, European
panui	announcement, pamphlet disseminating announcement
papakainga	settlement site, especially on marae reserve
pataka	storehouse
patere	form of song-chant, usually assertive
patu	short-handled fighting club
poi	plaited ball on cord used in action songs
poroporoaki	farewell
poukai	hui at which marae supporting the King Movement demonstrate loyalty, contribute to funds, meet the incumbent leader and discuss movement affairs
pounamu	New Zealand nephrite, greenstone
powhiri	song-welcome to a marae
ponga	tree fern
pukana	eye-widening gesture in haka, patere or action song
rangatira	chief, chiefly
rangatiratanga	leadership, aristocracy, authority

raupatu	confiscation of Waikato territory in 1864
raupo	bulrush
runanga	tribal council
taiaha	long club used formerly for fighting and latterly for performing ceremonial challenges
Tainui	canoe which brought ancestors of Waikato, Maniapoto and Hauraki tribes to New Zealand, also name of people who belong to those tribes
tangata whenua	hosts, people of the land
tangi	weep, mourning ceremony
tangihanga	mourning ceremony for dead
tapu	sacred, forbidden
taonga	treasured possession
taurekareka	slave, scoundrel
tekoteko	carved figure, usually on top of meeting-house gable
tena koe	traditional formal greeting
tiki	carved figure, usually worn as neck ornament
tino pai	very good
tohunga	chosen one, expert, priest
tukutuku	woven wall panels inside meeting house
tumuaki	president or chairman
tupapaku	corpse
tupuna	ancestor
waahi tapu	sacred place
wahine	woman
Waikato	longest river in New Zealand, group name for tribes who come from that river's catchment
waka	canoe
waka huia	carved box, formerly for holding huia feathers
wehi	capacity to inspire awe
wero	ceremonial challenge to visitors conducted on marae
whakapapa	genealogy
whakatauki	saying, proverb
whanau	extended family
whare	house
whare karakia	house of prayer

Family tree

Principal members of the kahui ariki mentioned in text

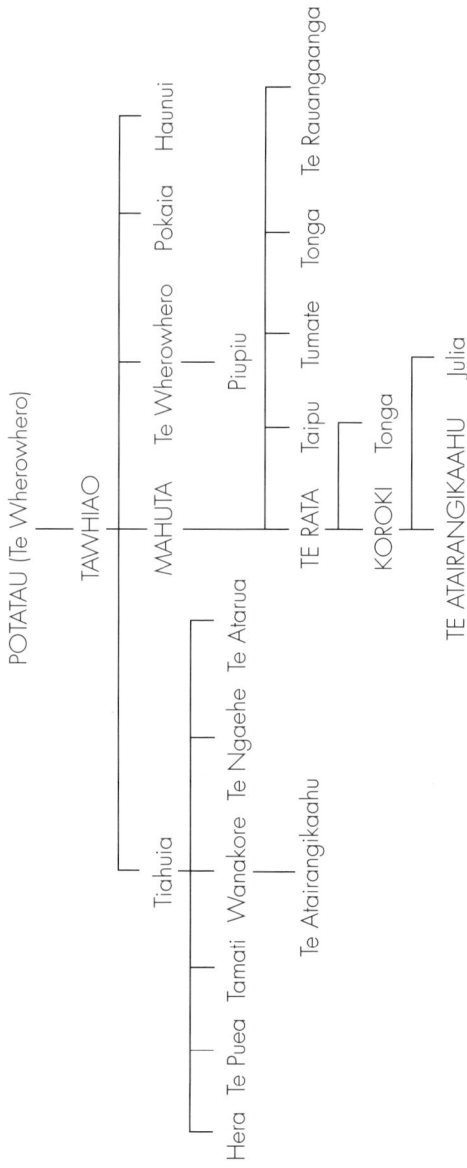

POTATAU (Te Wherowhero)

TAWHIAO

MAHUTA — Te Wherowhero — Pokaia — Haunui

Piupiu

TE RATA — Taipu — Tumate — Tonga — Te Rauangaanga

KOROKI — Tonga

TE ATAIRANGIKAAHU — Julia

Tiahuia

Hera — Te Puea — Tamati — Wanakore — Te Ngaehe — Te Atarua

Te Atairangikaahu

Note on sources

While I have acknowledged the major sources for this book in the preface, some additional comments should be made.

The Ramsden Papers in the Alexander Turnbull Library include a draft biography dating from the 1940s, *Te Puea Herangi, Princess of Maoriland*, by Eric Ramsden. It is sketchy in some sections, repetitive in others, and written in the idiom of a bygone era. But the source material for it — the notes Ramsden kept from his conversations with Te Puea, her father, Te Uira Te Heuheu and others — is a mine of useful information, as are the letters from Maori correspondents who included Te Puea. Ramsden was an amateur scholar and a collector who sought to become involved in the public affairs of his day and to keep every piece of paper that came his way. The Ngata-Buck correspondence, which he also secured, contains the most perceptive and articulate analysis of contemporary Maori matters yet placed on record. I have drawn too from this.

Material in the National Archives, although patchy and frequently difficult to locate, was rewarding. I drew extensively from Native Health records for information on disease and epidemics in Waikato; and on Native Affairs archives for government and departmental views of the Kingitanga and Te Puea's work. These latter were most satisfyingly detailed for some years (those of Gordon Coates' term of office and the 1934 Royal Commission investigation, for example), and non-existent for others, apparently as a consequence of ministers removing files when they left office. In one intriguing instance, that of a security investigation of Waikato leaders during World War Two, the relevant file had been catalogued and deposited with the archives and then inexplicably removed.

The *Appendices to the Journal of the House of Representatives* hold a mass of detailed information, particularly for the late nineteenth and early twentieth century years, and for Apirana Ngata's term of office.

Te Puea's personal papers, in the instances where I have cited them (see preface), are attributed to the Turongo House Collection at Turangawaewae Marae, which is not open for public inspection.

Additional papers in private hands came to light in the course of research. The most voluminous and rewarding were those of Michael Rotohiko (Mick)

Jones, and the late Dr Maharaia Winiata. The former filled many gaps in the Native Affairs archives, and included treasures such as Te Puea's handwritten notes of evidence for the 1934 Royal Commission. This evidence was missing from the commission's files in the National Archives. It is one of those examples of interminable Maori garrulousness for which posterity can be grateful, even if members of the commission were not: by presenting lengthy details about her childhood and early years at Turangawaewae, Te Puea compiled what amounts to a potted autobiography, part of which is a summary of her diary to 1934. At the time of writing this book, the Winiata papers were still held by Mrs Frances Winiata and Mr Jones's had been passed to the National Archives. The papers of the late Dr Pei Te Hurinui Jones were also inspected.

The majority of the taped interviews I conducted with major informants have been placed in the Alexander Turnbull Library for eventual public use with certain restrictions on confidential matters. I have not given dates in the footnotes for the lengthier interviews which went on over several weeks. The shorter and less substantial ones I have identified by time and place.

Two further sources require acknowledgement. For information on issues and events leading to the imposition of conscription on Waikato during World War One I am indebted entirely and gratefully to the research of Professor Peter O'Connor. In Chapter 4 I have quoted extensively from his paper 'The Recruitment of Maori Soldiers, 1914–1918'. An Auckland University masters thesis by William Worger, 'Te Puea, the Kingitanga and Waikato', did not contribute factually to this book, but it provided helpful interpretive insights on Te Puea's behaviour in the wider context of New Zealand life up to the 1930s.

To simplify the numbered footnotes I have used abbreviations for the names of people and sources consulted most frequently. They are:

AJHR   *Appendices to the Journal of the House of Representatives.*
AM   Alex McKay (Edward Alexander McKay).
ATL   Alexander Turnbull Library, Wellington.
ER   Eric Ramsden.
HW   Heeni Wharemaru.
Int   Interview.
MA   Archives of the Department of Maori Affairs (until 1947 the Department of Native Affairs), held in the National Archives, Wellington.
MJ   Michael Rotohiko Jones (Mick Jones).
MJP   Michael Jones Papers.

MWP	Maharaia Winiata Papers.
NZ	Ngeungeu Zister (née Beamish).
NZPD	New Zealand Parliamentary Debates.
PJ	Pei Te Hurinui Jones.
PP	Piri Poutapu.
RM	Robert Mahuta.
RP	Ramsden Papers.
THC	Turongo House Collection.
TK	Tumokai Katipa.
TP	Te Puea.
TPB	Eric Ramsden's draft biography of Te Puea entitled *Te Puea Herangi, Princess of Maoriland*, in Ramsden Papers, Alexander Turnbull Library.
TPL	Letter from Te Puea, to Eric Ramsden unless otherwise stated.
WS	Winara Samuels.

Sources by chapter

Prologue

1. Hochstetter, *Neuseeland*, Stuttgart 1867, p. 456.
2. Cowan, quoted by ER in TPB, Ch. 3, p. 9.
3. Hochstetter, quoted by Featon, pp. 8–9.
4. For example, see Ngata, quoted by Worger, p. 9.
5. Int RM.
6. Andersen and Petersen, p. 233.
7. PJ, 1968, p. 137.
8. PJ, *ibid.*, p. 138.
9. PJ, *ibid.*
10. PJ, *ibid.*
11. Williams, p. 67.
12. PJ, *op. cit.*, p. 141.
13. This account of the origin of poukai from an interview with Whitiora Cooper, November 1973.
14. Int RM.
15. PJ, *op. cit.*, p. 142.
16. Ngata to ER, Wellington, 27 July 1947. RP.
17. PJ, *op. cit.*, p. 143
18. Ngata to Sutherland, 18 April 1938; Ngata correspondence. WTU.
19. Fisher to ER, 24.7.43. RP.
20. See *NZ Encyclopaedia*, Vol. 3, p. 647.
21. Condliffe, 1959.
22. AJHR, 1907, H31, p. 56.
23. AJHR, 1906, G5, p. 51.
24. Te Uira Te Heuheu to ER, Ngaruawahia, 4/11/44.
25. Judge Edgar to Miss Stewart, MA, series 21, 20.
26. District Health Officer R. Makgill, 21/1/11. MA.
27. AJHR, 1905, G5, pp. 53–4.
28. Buck to ER, 26/1/45. RP.

1. Early years

1. At the outset there is disagreement about facts. Most previous accounts say she was born in 1884 (cf Ramsden, Butterworth, Worger). But Te Puea herself was uncertain and referred inquiries (such as Welfare Officer Bill Herewini seeking to formalise her social security arrangements) to the records of Mercer School. These, she said, contained the birth date given by her father. The date there is 9 November 1883. November 1883 was also used on the bereavement card sent out by King Koroki after her death.

2. Te Tahuna Herangi to ER, Ngaruawahia, 1943. RP.
3. Acheson, 1940.
4. Te Tahuna, op. cit.
5. W. Searancke to D. McLean, 15 August 1867; quoted by ER in TPB. RP.
6. Int NZ.
7. Ibid.
8. ER, 1952, p. 194.
9. Int PP.
10. Int NZ.
11. Ibid.
12. TP, handwritten notes for evidence to Royal Commission on Native Affairs prepared at Waiuku on 15 April 1934; evidence delivered in Auckland on 28 April 1934. MJP. The notes were prepared from Te Puea's diary and are virtually a summary of it to 1934. Translation by Sam Karetu.
13. Acheson, op. cit.
14. Te Paea has frequently been referred to as Tawhiao's 'sister', especially in accounts of her allegedly being offered the kingship ahead of him. PJ (personal communication 20/10/75) said this was incorrect. Te Paea was certainly Kati's [Potatau's brother's] daughter. The mistake made in various accounts is no doubt due to the use of the Maori relationship term tuahine, sister or female cousin to a male.
15. ER, Freedom, 20 October 1952.
16. TP, Royal Commission notes, op. cit.
17. Int NZ.
18. Ibid.
19. Te Uira Te Heuheu to ER, Ngaruawahia, 4 November 1944. RP.
20. ER notes, 1946. RP.
21. Int TK.
22. ER, TPB, Ch. 6, pp. 4, 5.
23. Acheson, op. cit.
24. Te Uira Te Heuheu, op. cit.
25. TPL to Lady Newall, 6 July 1944. RP.
26. Acheson, op. cit.
27. Ibid.
28. ER, Sun, 10 September 1927.
29. Int NZ.
30. AJHR, 1905, G5, pp. 53 and 54.
31. Acheson, op. cit.
32. Int Oliver Finlay, Waiuku, 12/12/74.
33. Acheson, op. cit.
34. Int NZ.
35. Acheson, op. cit.
36. TP. Royal Commission notes, op. cit.
37. Int MJ.
38. Taiporutu Mitchell to ER, quoted in TPB, Ch. 6, p. 16.
39. Acheson, op. cit.

40. TPL to Merenia Ramsden, 22 May 1944. RP. (Slightly reworded.)
41. Information on the Seccombe family comes from Alfred Seccombe of Auckland (interviewed 10/3/75), and that on Roy Seccombe from his cousin Thomas Thorn Seccombe (interviewed 17/3/75), also of Auckland; information was also supplied by Ngcungcu Zister, who knew Te Puea at the time of the relationship.
42. Int NZ.
43. *Ibid.*
44. *Ibid.*
45. Te Uira Te Heuheu, *op. cit.*
46. Ints NZ and PP.
47. Int NZ.
48. TP to ER, notes from a visit to Waikato in 1932. RP.
49. *Ibid.*
50. Int NZ.
51. Maori Women's Welfare League paper to Pan-Pacific Women's Association Conference, Auckland, 1953.
52. Int TK.
53. *Ibid.*

2. Return to the river

1. See PJ, 1968, p. 144.
2. Int NZ.
3. Int NZ and PP.
4. Int TK.
5. Acheson, 1940.
6. *Ibid.*
7. Int TK. Katipa's version of the incident is virtually the same as Acheson's but more detailed.
8. Acheson, *op. cit.*
9. *Ibid.*
10. TP, Royal Commission notes, Waiuku, 15 April 1934. MJP.
11. Int PP.
12. Int TK.
13. Int PP.
14. See Cody, 1953, pp. 88–92. I am indebted to his research for the details that follow about events in Taranaki leading to Pomare's candidacy.
15. Cody, *op. cit.*, pp. 96, 97.
16. AJHR, 1906, H34, p. 74.
17. *Ibid.*, p. 68.
18. Scott, 1975, p. 196.
19. Lady Miria Pomare to ER, 19 January 1944. RP.
20. See *Auckland Star*, 13 August 1909.
21. This account from Lady Pomare's letter, *op. cit.* Cody's account says 200 votes, which seems improbable.
22. ER notes, RP.
23. Letter to ER, 24 July 1943. RP.

24. Int Sonny Kaihau, Waiuku, 10/8/75.
25. ER, 1952, p. 196.
26. *Dominion*, 31 August 1910.
27. See, for example, *New Zealand Herald*, 17 June 1910.
28. PJ, *op. cit.*, p. 144.
29. *Ibid.*
30. TP, Royal Commission notes, *op. cit.*
31. ER, TPB, Ch. 7, p. 6; and Int PP.
32. Condliffe, 1971, p. 120.
33. See clipping dated 14 December 1909, Maori Purposes Fund Board papers, WTU, Ms 189, folder 172.
34. Ngata to ER, 27 July 1947. RP.
35. Te Uira Te Heuheu to ER, Ngaruawahia, 4 November 1944. RP.
36. Acheson, *op. cit.*
37. TPL to J.F. Cody, 7/9/45.
38. TP to PJ, quoted PJ, 1968, p. 144.
39. ER, TPB, Ch. 7, p. 7.
40. Acheson, *op. cit.*
41. TPL to J.F. Cody, *op. cit.*
42. Int TK.
43. *Ibid.*
44. Int PJ.
45. Voting figures from AJHR, 1912, H12A, pp. 39–41.
46. Int TK.
47. *Ibid.*
48. ER, TPB, Ch. 7, p. 8.
49. Int TK.
50. Int PJ, slightly different wording in personal communication from PJ, 11/9/75.
51. Int TK.
52. Acheson, *op. cit.*, and Int TK.
53. Int PJ.
54. This account from Te Whati Tamati (who had been present at Tauranganui in 1912) speaking at the Tauranganui poukai in November 1974. One response of the people there to Mahuta's statement was to complete their meeting house.
55. This description from Piri Poutapu who sighted the disturbance at the age of eleven, gave the alarm, and saw the recognisable fish.

3. Consolidation
1. Int TK.
2. PJ, 1968, p. 150.
3. ER, notes after a visit to Waikato, January 1932. RP.
4. See Te Uira Te Heuheu to ER, Ngaruawahia, 4 November 1944, RP; and Int NZ.
5. *Ibid.*
6. Int PP.

7. Int WS.
8. Gorst, 1908, p. 308.
9. Int WS.
10. See, for example, Ngata's letter to Sutherland, 18/4/38, Ngata correspondence. WTU.
11. Worger p. 24.
12. *Ibid.*, p. 25.
13. *Ibid.*, p. 24.
14. PJ, *op. cit.*, p. 145.
15. *Ibid.*, p. 146.
16. *Ibid.*, p. 146.
17. Int PP.
18. *Ibid.*
19. AJHR, 1914, H31, pp. 50, 51.
20. Maclean, 1964, pp. 235, 236.
21. Int TK.
22. *Ibid.*
23. ER, *Sun*, 10 September 1927.
24. Int PP.
25. See Acheson, Butterworth, Ramsden.
26. Acheson, 1940.
27. *Otago Daily Times*, 14 October 1952.
28. Int TK.
29. *Ibid.*
30. See *New Zealand Herald*, 11 June 1910.
31. PJ, *op. cit.*, p. 147.
32. Unidentified clipping, THC, datelined London 22 May.
33. *Ibid.* and ER, TPB, Ch. 7, p. 18.
34. Int WS.
35. ER, *op. cit.*, p. 17.
36. *Ibid.*, p. 17.
37. PJ, *op. cit.*, p. 147.
38. ER, notes from TP, Ngaruawahia, July 1944, RP.
39. *Ibid.*
40. Int MJ.
41. ER, notes from TP, Ngaruawahia, July 1944, RP.
42. Int PP, and O'Connor, 1967, p. 62.
43. Account given to a hui in January 1917, quoted in O'Connor, p. 62.
44. Ints PP and PJ.
45. Mahuta, 1974, p. 7.

4. Conscription and Pai Marire

1. Preface to Cowan, 1926, pp. IX and X.
2. O'Conner, p. 53. For information of events leading up to the imposition of conscription on Waikato I am indebted almost entirely to this study.
3. *Ibid.*, p. 61.
4. *Ibid.*, p. 65.

5. *Ibid.*, p. 54.
6. *Ibid.*, p. 54.
7. *Ibid.*, p. 62.
8. *Ibid.*, p. 62.
9. *Ibid.*, p. 63.
10. *Ibid.*, p. 64.
11. *Ibid.*, p. 66.
12. *Ibid.*, p. 66.
13. *Ibid.*, p. 66.
14. *Ibid.*, p. 66.
15. Cody, pp. 119, 120.
16. O'Connor, *op. cit.*, p. 62.
17. Worger, p. 45.
18. O'Connor, *op. cit.* p. 70.
19. PJ, 1971, p. 10.
20. ER, TPB, Ch. 8, p. 12.
21. *Ibid.*
22. O'Connor, *op. cit.*, pp. 67, 68.
23. *Ibid.*, pp. 68, 69.
24. *Ibid.*, p. 71.
25. *Ibid.*, p. 71.
26. *Ibid.*, pp. 72, 73.
27. See Defence Act 1909, 27 (3).
28. O'Connor, *op. cit.*, p. 74.
29. ER notes from TP, Ngaruawahia, July 1944. RP.
30. ER, TPB, Ch. 8, p. 18.
31. ER, notes from TP, *op. cit.*
32. *Ibid.*
33. *Ibid.*
34. *Ibid.*
35. O'Connor, *op. cit.*, p. 75.
36. *Ibid.*, p. 75.
37. *New Zealand Herald*, 12 June 1918, quoted O'Connor, p. 75.
38. Kingitanga ms, extracts in RP.
39. Te Uira Te Heuheu to ER, Ngaruawahia, 4 November 1944. RP.
40. Kingitanga ms, *op. cit.*
41. *Ibid.*
42. These telegrams were kept by Te Puea, copied by Ramsden and translations of the copies (by Pei Jones) left in the Ramsden Papers.
43. *Ibid.*
44. ER, notes from TP, *op. cit.*
45. O'Connor, *op. cit.*, pp. 81, 82.
46. Tae Tapara, statement to ER, Waiuku, July 1944. RP.
47. Lady Pomare to ER, 19 January 1944. RP.
48. *Ibid.* Cody (p. 122) says the meeting was at Waihi. Te Puea's account suggests it was at Mangatawhiri. Cody also believed that the hosts stood

in water as an additional mark of contempt. It is far more likely that this action was, as Te Puea says, unavoidable because of flooding.

49. ER, notes from TP, *op. cit.*
50. Lady Pomare, *op. cit.*
51. Ints TK, PP and RM.
52. Int TK.
53. ER, notes from TP, *op. cit.*
54. Te Uira Te Heuheu, *op. cit.*
55. Int TK.
56. Int PP.
57. Here Mokena to ER. RP.
58. O'Connor, *op. cit.* , p. 81.
59. Lady Pomare, *op. cit.*
60. Int AM, also various TPL to ER.
61. O'Connor, *op. cit.*, p. 80.
62. *Ibid.*, p. 81.
63. *Ibid.*, p. 82.
64. *Ibid.*, p. 82.
65. ER, notes from TP, *op. cit.*

5. Turangawaewae: Preparations

1. AJHR, 1920, H31, p. 27.
2. Maclean, 1964, p. 202.
3. AJHR, 1920, H31, p. 13.
4. Scott, p. 198.
5. Int TK.
6. AJHR, 1920, H31, pp. 23 and 26.
7. Int TK.
8. *Ibid.*
9. *Ibid.*
10. *Ibid.*
11. *Ibid.*
12. TP, Royal Commission notes, Waiuku, 15 April 1934. MJP.
13. Worger, p. 50.
14. TP, Waiuku notes, *op. cit.*
15. ER, notes from TP, Ngaruawahia, 6 September 1946. RP.
16. ER, TPB.
17. *Weekly News*, 27 March 1919, clipping in THC.
18. Int PP; and PJ 1971, p. 6.
19. For example the NZBC's series of Maori films on television, *Tangata Whenua*, November and December 1974.
20. Int PP; also *Auckland Star*, 28 April 1936. RP.
21. TP, Waiuku notes, *op. cit.*
22. *Taranaki Daily News*, 21 October 1952, quoting Tiaki Hira at Te Puea's tangi.
23. PJ, *op. cit.*, p. 7.

24. Int PP.
25. *Ibid.*
26. Int PJ.
27. Int PP.
28. TP to ER, Ngaruawahia, July 1944, RP.
29. Int PJ.
30. Int PP.
31. *Ibid.*
32. PJ, 1971, p. 8.

6. Turangawaewae: The long march

1. Int PP.
2. *Ibid.*
3. *Ibid.*
4. *Ibid.*
5. *Ibid.*
6. *Ibid.*
7. TP, Royal Commission notes, Waiuku, 15 April 1934. MJP.
8. *Ibid.*
9. *Ibid.*
10. Ints PP and G. I. Laurenson, 10/8/75.
11. Ints PP and TK.
12. Int AM.
13. TP, Waiuku notes, *op. cit.*
14. Int TK.
15. *Ibid.*
16. Int PP.
17. PJ, notes for TPB, RP.
18. Int TK.
19. *Ibid.*
20. TP, Waiuku notes, *op. cit.*
21. Clipping dated only 1923. THC.
22. Ints PP and TK.
23. PJ, *op. cit.*
24. Ngahuia Te Awekotuku, personal communication, 28/7/76.
25. Int TK.
26. TP, Waiuku notes, *op. cit.*
27. Maori Women's Welfare League papers to Pan-Pacific Women's Association Conference, Auckland 1953.
28. TP, Waiuku notes, *op. cit.*
29. Int TK; and ER, 1952, p. 193.
30. Acheson, 1940.
31. Phillipps, 1955, p. 201.
32. Int TK.
33. ER, TPB, Ch. 1.
34. TP, Waiuku notes, *op. cit.*
35. *The Sun*, 10 September 1927.

36. Int NZ.
37. ER, *Evening Post*, 18 January 1958.
38. *New Zealand Herald*, 6 November 1963.
39. ER, TPB, Ch. 1, p. 17.
40. *Auckland Star*, 1/5/28.
41. ER, TPB, Ch. 1, p. 17.
42. ER, *The Sun*, 10 September 1927.
43. Acheson, *op. cit.*

7. An end to isolation
1. TP, Royal Commission notes, Waiuku, 15 April 1934, MJP.
2. *Ibid.*
3. ER, *The Sun*, 10/9/27.
4. Int TK.
5. Roberts pp. 321–2.
6. Waiuku notes, *op. cit.*
7. *Ibid.*
8. Ngata to Buck, 7/6/29. RP.
9. Ngata to Sutherland, 19.4.38, Ngata Correspondence. WTU.
10. *Ibid.*
11. Ngata to Buck, 7/6/29. RP.
12. Ngata to Buck, 5/1/29. RP.
13. Ngata to Buck, 2/9/33. RP.
14. Buck to Ngata, 20/9/25. RP.
15. Ngata to Sutherland, 18.4.38, Ngata Correspondence. WTU.
16. Waiuku notes, *op. cit.*
17. *Ibid.*
18. Int TK.
19. TPL, 10/5/34. RP.
20. TPL to *New Zealand Herald*, 10/3/32.
21. Int TK.
22. For example, ER, notes after a visit to Waikato, January 1932. RP.
23. Waiuku notes, *op. cit.*
24. Ngata to ER, 27/7/47. RP.
25. TPL to Coates, 11/12/28. MA.
26. NZPD, 1934, Vol. 240, p. 1200.
27. Worger, p. 64.
28. Int TK.
29. Waiuku notes, *op. cit.*
30. PJ, 1971, p. 16.
31. *Ibid.*
32. Ngata to ER, 27/7/47. RP.
33. Waiuku notes, *op. cit.*
34. Ngata to ER, 27/7/47. RP.
35. Keesing, *Maori Progress on the East Coast*, quoted by Worger, p. 102.
36. *NZ Picturegoer*, Vol. 1, no. 29. 22 June 1928. MA.
37. Waiuku notes, *op. cit.*

38. Int TK.
39. ER, TPB, Ch. 8, p. 12. RP.
40. MA.
41. *Ibid.*
42. TPL to Ngata, 9/2/31. MJP.
43. Balneavis to TP, 6/10/28. MA.
44. Waiuku notes, *op. cit.*
45. TPL, 19/9/28, RP; and Balneavis notes, MA.
46. *Dominion*, 1/9/28.
47. TPL, 19/9/28. RP.
48. Int TK.

8. Mahinarangi: A coming together

1. TPL, 8/12/28. RP.
2. TPL to Coates, 11/12/28. MA.
3. *Ibid.*
4. TPL, 12/1/29. RP.
5. TPL, 8/12/28. RP.
6. *Ibid.*
7. Worger, p. 108.
8. TPL, 12/1/29. RP.
9. Int TK.
10. Int AM.
11. Int TK.
12. Peter Hallinan, personal communication, undated 1975.
13. Ngata to Buck, 26/3/29. RP.
14. PJ, 1971, p. 8.
15. ER, TPB, Ch. 1, p. 21. RP.
16. *Ibid.*, p. 10.
17. Ngata to ER, 27/7/47. RP.
18. PJ to ER, notes for TPB. RP.
19. PJ, 1971, pp. 26–7.
20. *The Sun*, 19/3/29.
21. PJ to ER, notes for TPB. RP.
22. Int PJ.
23. Roberts, pp. 321–2.

9. Back to the land

1. Int TK.
2. Acheson, 1940.
3. *Ibid.*
4. NZPD, 1928, Vol. 219, p. 643
5. Tukere Te Anga to Undersecretary, 12/7/29. MA.
6. TPL, 17/1/33. RP.
7. Int MJ.
8. ER notes. RP.

9. Native Land Amendment and Native Land Claims Adjustment Act, 1929, section 23.
10. Worger, p. 116.
11. *Ibid.*
12. TP, Royal Commission notes, Waiuku, 15 April 1934. MJP.
13. *Ibid.* and Int AM.
14. *Ibid.*
15. *Ibid.*
16. Worger, p. 128.
17. AJHR, 1931, G10.
18. Waiuku notes, *op. cit.*
19. *Ibid.*
20. *Ibid.*
21. *Ibid.*
22. Int TK.
23. Tukere Te Anga to Ngata, 25/10/29. MA.
24. Ngata to Buck, 30/3/32. RP.
25. TPL, 30/3/32. RP.
26. Ngata to Buck, 9/9/33. RP.
27. ER, notes after a visit to Waikato, January 1932. RP.
28. Waiuku notes, *op. cit.*
29. ER, notes after a visit to Waikato, *op. cit.*
30. TPL, 27/5/31. RP.
31. TPL, 14/6/33. RP.
32. ER, notes after a visit to Waikato, *op. cit.*
33. TPL, 2/9/31. RP.
34. TPL to Ngata, 28/5/31. MJP.
35. See various letters, MJP.
36. TPL, 4/9/32. RP.
37. TPL, 4/9/32. RP.
38. TPL, 2/2/34. RP.
39. Worger, p. 116.
40. *Ibid.*, p. 155.
41. *NZ Truth*, 31/3/32.
42. Ngata to Buck, 17/9/32. RP.
43. See Report of the Commission on Native Affairs, AJHR, 1934, G11.
44. Worger, P. 163.
45. NZPD, 1934, Vol. 240, p. 1151.
46. Ted Williams, personal communication, 10/2/77.
47. Waiuku notes, *op. cit.*
48. Ngata to Public Accounts Committee (1933). MA.
49. Waiuku notes, *op. cit.*
50. NZPD, 1934, Vol. 240, p. 1245.
51. TPL, 10/5/34.
52. Worger, p. 168.
53. Frank Langstone, notes for speech at opening of Turongo House. MJP.

54. *Ibid.*
55. Int TK.
56. TPL, January 1932. RP.
57. *Auckland Star*, 28/4/36.
58. Int MJ.
59. TPL, 4/12/40. RP.

10. Tohunga and parsons

1. TPL, 16/10/33. RP.
2. *Ibid.*
3. Int PJ.
4. TPL; and TPB, Ch. 13, p. 16. RP.
5. TPL, 16/10/33. RP.
6. Int PJ.
7. TPL, 16/10/33. RP
8. Ints PP, RM.
9. Acheson, 1940.
10. *Ibid.*
11. Int TK.
12. TPL, 22/9/35. RP.
13. This information from Alex McKay. The Mater Misericordiae Hospital was unable to locate records to confirm the account; the main hospital block was opened in March 1936, and the X-ray department began to operate in June of that year (personal communication from Sister M. de Montfort, 1/12/76).
14. AM to ER, 14/7/36. RP.
15. AM to ER, 5/8/36. RP.
16. *Ibid.*
17. Int TK. Acheson (1940) gives a slightly different account of this story that shows signs of having been filtered through his imagination.
18. AM to ER, 26/10/37. RP.
19. Int AM.
20. Int Bunny Woodhams.
21. TPL, 2/2/41. RP.
22. Int TK.
23. TPL, 2/2/41. RP.
24. Int Te Uira Manihera.
25. *Ibid.*
26. TPL, 2/2/41. RP.
27. *Ibid.*
28. Acheson, *op. cit.*
29. Henry Kelliher, personal communication, 8/5/75.
30. Int AM.
31. *Ibid.*
32. For a general account of Te Puea's religious beliefs I am indebted to lengthy discussions with Piri Poutapu and Tumokai Katipa. Both noted that the beliefs were also their own, and that they had acquired them

from Te Puea. I used part of their articulation of Pai Marire principles in an earlier article, 'Ngakahikatea', published in the *New Zealand Listener* on 16 August 1975. I have not drawn from Paul Clark's book *Hauhau, the Pai Marire Search For Maori Identity* because it threw little light on Pai Marire in Waikato and inferred that practice of the religion had died out in the nineteenth century.

33. Int TK.
34. Acheson, *op. cit.*
35. Ints TK, PP.
36. ER, notes after New Zealand visit 1934; and notes after visit in 1940. RP.
37. Int TK.
38. TPL, 8/8/33. RP.
39. TPL, 17/8/39. RP.
40. Int TK.
41. ER, notes, 5 February 1940. RP.
42. Tukere Te Anga to Ngata, 25/10/29. MA.
43. Tae Tapara, interview with ER, undated. RP.
44. TP to ER. RP.
45. Int. TK.
46. *Ibid.*
47. *Ibid.*
48. *Ibid.*
49. Ints TK, PP.
50. TPL, 9/2/42. RP.
51. ER, TPB, Ch. 6, p. 11. RP.
52. Int TK.
53. *Ibid.*
54. TP to ER, notes. RP.
55. Int PP.
56. ER, notes 'Te Puea makes a home'. RP.
57. Int TK.
58. Int NZ.
59. *Ibid.*
60. Int HW.
61. Int G.I. Laurenson, 10/8/75.
62. TPL, 8/8/33. RP.
63. Ints PP, G.I. Laurenson.
64. NZPD, 1903, Vol 142, p. 1141.
65. TP to ER, notes. RP.
66. *Ibid.*
67. ER, notes of an interview with Bishop Cherrington, Hamilton, 12/9/46. RP.
68. ER, notes. RP.
69. ER, note in TPB, Ch. 6. RP.
70. Worger, p. 105.
71. Int AM.
72. TPL, 8/8/33. RP.

73. Int G.I. Laurenson, 10/8/75.
74. Int TK.
75. Int C.G. Scrimgeour.
76. C.G. Scrimgeour, personal communication, undated, 1976.
77. *Ibid.*
78. Int AM.
79. Clark, p. 74; int RM.
80. Int PP.
81. Int G.I. Laurenson, 10/8/75.

11. A river culture

1. PJ, 1968, p. 151.
2. Letter from the Central Executive and Members of Parliament of the New Zealand Labour Party to 'King Koroki, the elders and people of the Maori race', 11/10/33. MJP.
3. PJ, *op. cit.*, p. 152.
4. *Ibid*, p. 153.
5. Clipping dated 5/2/34. MA.
6. PJ, *op. cit.*, p. 153.
7. *Ibid.*, p. 154.
8. Int TK.
9. Buick, p. 78.
10. TPL, 8/4/34. RP.
11. PJ, *op. cit.*, p. 153.
12. *Ibid.*, p. 154.
13. TPL, 21/7/34. RP.
14. Int TK.
15. Int PJ.
16. Acheson, 1940.
17. Int PP.
18. ER, Diary, 27/2/47. RP.
19. Acheson, *op. cit.*
20. PP to ER, quoted in TPB, Ch. 12, p. 6. RP.
21. Int PP.
22. Int PJ.
23. TPL, 18/4/35. RP.
24. PJ, notes to ER for TPB. RP.
25. Ngata to ER, 3/8/36. RP.
26. TPL, 18/4/35. RP.
27. AM to ER, 18/8/36. RP.
28. *Te Paki o Matariki*, 4/5/35. RP.
29. TP in TPB, Ch. 11, p. 9. RP.
30. Worger, p. 143.
31. Int PP.
32. TPL, 11/11/35. RP.
33. Ints PP and G.I. Laurenson.
34. Int PP.

35. *Ibid.*
36. AM to ER, 17/4/36. RP.
37. Int PP and story NZ *Herald*, 30/1/71. The *Herald* account is correct in substance, but incorrect in some details.
38. Int PP.
39. AM to ER, 10/6/36. RP.
40. AM to ER, undated. RP.
41. AM to ER, dated 14 October only. RP.
42. Undated clipping. RP.
43. Unidentified clipping, May 1937. MWP.
44. Int Te Uira Manihera.
45. TPL to Te Uira Manihera, 21/3/37.
46. Int PP.
47. Downes and Harcourt, p. 112.
48. Int AM.
49. *Ibid.*
50. Int PP.
51. Inia Te Wiata to ER, Diary, 27/2/47. RP.
52. Int AM.
53. Text of Governor-General's speech. MJP.
54. ER, Diary, 27/2/47; corrected slightly in interview with AM.
55. ER, TPB, Ch. 12, p. 10. RP.
56. Ngata to Sutherland, 18/4/38, Ngata Correspondence. WTU.
57. AM to ER, 15/12/38. RP.
58. Ngata to Sutherland, undated, *op. cit.*
59. Langstone to TP, 11/4/38. MJP.
60. *Ibid.*
61. ER, notes. RP.
62. Langstone to TP, 1/8/38. MJP.
63. Int PJ.
64. Acheson to ER, 18/11/40. RP.
65. TPL, 4/12/40. RP.
66. Acheson, 1940.

12. War and politics

1. Int PJ.
2. *Ibid.*
3. Letter from the Central Executive and Members of Parliament of the New Zealand Labour Party, 11/10/33. MJP.
4. Int PJ.
5. *Ibid.*
6. TPL, 2/2/41. RP.
7. TP to ER, TPB, Ch. 12, p. 16. RP.
8. Int MJ.
9. *Ibid.*
10. John A. Lee, personal communication, 29/10/76.
11. Int MJ.

12. TPL, 25/2/39. RP.
13. Int MJ.
14. TPL to ER. RP.
15. TPL to Peter Fraser, undated. RP.
16. *Ibid.*
17. *Ibid.*
18. TPL, 17/8/39. RP.
19. NZPD, 1939, Vol. 254, p. 724 and following.
20. Langstone to TP, 31/1/40. RP.
21. Galway to TP, 31/1/40. RP.
22. Int PP.
23. *NZ Truth*, 14/2/40.
24. Int PJ.
25. Int AM.
26. TPL to Savage, 20/9/39. RP.
27. TPL, 12/11/39. RP.
28. TPL, 11/7/41. RP.
29. Henderson, p. 70.
30. K. Allott, personal communication, 13/3/75.
31. TPL, 2/2/41. RP.
32. TPL, 22/4/42. RP.
33. ER, carbon copy of letter for publication, RP. I was unable to verify if the letter had been published.
34. Wood, p. 156.
35. *Ibid.*, p. 158.
36. *Ibid.*, pp. 161–2.
37. Int MJ.
38. Int PP.
39. TPL, 22/4/42. RP.
40. Int PJ.
41. TPL, 4/11/42. RP.
42. Wood, p. 160.
43. TPL, 6/7/40, RP; and Ngapaka Kukutai to Peter Fraser at Wellington Conference, July 1942.
44. Int AM.
45. *Ibid.*
46. TPL, 26/10/41. RP.
47. TPL, 4/11/42. RP.
48. Powles, personal communication, 11/11/74.
49. Int AM.
50. Int PJ. An official report of this conference is titled 'Conference held at Wellington on July 1 and July 2, 1942. Between the Prime Minister and Te Puea Herangi CBE and other leaders of the Waikato people, with reference to the Maori war effort.' Copies are held in the Maori Affairs section of National Archives and by Robert Mahuta. Members of the Waikato party were not given an opportunity to read these minutes and verify the record, and they disagreed with it in some important respects

(interview Pei Jones). I have quoted from Pei Jones and from the Waikato report of the meeting, set out in a special edition of *Te Paki o Matariki* and translated by Mick Jones.

51. Undated *Te Paki O Matariki.* MJP.
52. PJ, 1968.
53. Int PJ.
54. TPL, 3/1/43. RP.
55. ER, notes, RP; also Cowan, 1908.
56. TPL, 25/2/39. RP.
57. Int AM.
58. *Ibid.*
59. Samuel White to TP, 20/11/42. RP.
60. TPL, 3/1/43. RP.
61. Int Bunny Woodhams, 27/4/75.
62. Int HW.
63. *Ibid.*
64. *Ibid.*
65. *Ibid.*
66. *Te Paki o Matariki*, 19/12/43, for example.
67. TPL, 22/4/43. RP.
68. *Ibid.*
69. ER, Diary entries for October 1947. RP.
70. Int MJ.
71. TPL, 14/12/42. RP.
72. TPL, 20/6/43. (Slightly reworded.)

13. Raupatu and other causes
1. TPL, 9/12/42. RP.
2. TPL, 14/12/42. RP.
3. Most of this information from Kawharu, 1975, pp. 6–17; also personal communication I. H. Kawharu; and undated clippings, MWP.
4. Bill Eaddy, personal communication.
5. *Ibid.*
6. TPL, 20/6/47. RP. (Slightly reworded.)
7. *In Print*, June 1943. MWP.
8. *Auckland Star*, 26/8/49. MWP.
9. TPL, 20/6/43, RP; and Bill Eaddy, personal communication.
10. TPL, 20/6/43. RP. (Slightly reworded.)
11. Bill Eaddy, personal communication.
12. *Ibid.*
13. H.B. Turbott, personal communication, 21/3/77.
14. *Ibid.*
15. H.B. Turbott, Medical Officer of Health, Hamilton; Annual Report, 1939, records of Hamilton Health Department Office.
16. Int Frank Monk.
17. *Ibid.*
18. Int Margaret McDowall, 27/9/75.

19. Acheson, 1940.
20. PJ, 1968, p. 150.
21. *Ibid.*
22. Int Herepo Rongo, August 1973.
23. PJ, *op. cit.*, p. 150.
24. PJ, 1971.
25. TPL, 4/8/45. RP.
26. PJ, 1968, p. 158.
27. Leslie Kelly to ER, October 1947. RP.
28. ER, notes. RP.
29. Int AM.
30. *NZ Herald*, 7/7/48. MWP.
31. Int PJ.
32. ER, TPB, Ch. 15, p. 12. RP.

14. Return of Ru and conflicts

1. Louis Mountbatten, Diary for 8 April 1946; personal communication, 2/9/76.
2. Koroki to Freyberg, 29/3/47. MJP.
3. Sir Charles Fergusson, Diary for 30 April 1928; personal communication Lord Ballantrae.
4. Int TK.
5. Int MJ.
6. Int TK.
7. MJ to his family, 15/6/47. MJP.
8. *Ibid.*
9. Ints TK and AM.
10. Int HW.
11. Int TK.
12. *Ibid.*
13. Int HW.
14. Undated letter begun by TP but never sent. THC.
15. *NZ Herald*, 30/6/48. MWP.
16. *Ibid.*
17. *NZ Herald* 1/7/48. MWP.
18. *NZ Herald* 7/7/48. MWP.
19. *NZ Herald* 2/7/48. MWP.
20. Undated clipping. MWP.
21. *Ibid.*
22. Kelliher, personal communication, 8/4/75.
23. Acheson to ER, 18/11/40. RP.
24. ER, TPB, Ch. 1, p. 12.
25. ER, clippings. RP.
26. TPL, 1934. RP.
27. TPL, 27/10/31. RP.
28. PJ, notes for TPB; version here edited as result of interview.
29. Int PP.

30. Int PJ.
31. TPL, 26/2/43. RP.
32. Acheson to ER, 18/11/40. RP.
33. ER, Diary, 27/2/47. RP.
34. Int PP.
35. Beryl Te Wiata, personal communication, 12/3/77.
36. Te Wiata, 1976, p. 27.
37. Beryl Te Wiata, personal communication, *op. cit.*
38. Int PP.
39. ER, Diary, 27/2/47. RP.
40. *Ibid.*
41. Inia Te Wiata to ER, 5/5/47. RP.
42. Int PP.
43. Beryl Te Wiata, personal communication, *op. cit.*
44. Int MJ.
45. TPL, 17/8/39. RP.
46. TPL, 10/12/39. RP.
47. PJ, personal communication, 11/9/75.
48. Letters A.W. Reed to A.T. Ngata, 16/4/37; A.T. Ngata to L.G. Kelly, 13/5/37; and others following. Held by PJ in 1975.
49. Preface, Kelly, 1949.
50. TP to PJ, recounted in personal communication, 11/9/75.
51. Int PJ.
52. PJ, personal communication, 11/9/75.
53. TPL to Merenia Ramsden, 22/5/44. RP. (Slightly reworded.)
54. TPL, 4/4/45. RP. (Slightly reworded.)
55. Int PJ.
56. ER, letters to Pat Lawlor, personal communication, April 1975.
57. ER, Diary, 6/5/47. RP.
58. Int Tiahuia Grey (née Ramsden); also TPL, 23/5/47. RP.
59. ER, Diary, 22//3/47. RP.
60. Graham to ER, 1/3/44. RP.
61. Kelly to ER, 15/10/50. RP.
62. PP to ER, 12/2/44. RP.
63. ER, Diary, entries for October 1947. RP.
64. Int Te Uira Manihera.
65. Int PJ.
66. Int Frances Winiata.
67. Winiata to ER, 2/4/51. RP.
68. ER, TPB, Ch. 13, p. 11. RP.
69. Te Puea's will, 7 December 1944. RP.

15. Churches, schools and alcohol
1. Int HW.
2. Int F. I. Hobbs, 10/8/75.
3. Int G. I. Laurenson, 10/8/75.
4. Int HW.

5. *Ibid.*
6. *Ibid.*
7. Int MJ.
8. TPL to Merenia Ramsden, 4/5/44. RP.
9. TPL, 25/2/39. RP.
10. Int RM.
11. TP, undated clipping. MWP.
12. Int Frances Winiata.
13. Int HW.
14. Int PJ.
15. Int F. I. Hobbs.
16. Int TK.
17. Int MJ.
18. ER, notes from Hone Heke Rankin. RP.
19. Int TK.
20. Personal communication.
21. Int HW.
22. Int F. I. Hobbs.
23. Int PJ.
24. TPL, 25/7/49. RP. (Slightly reworded.)
25. TP, undated clipping. MWP.
26. See John Rangihau in King, 1975, p. 228.
27. Int Frances Winiata.
28. Statement signed by King Koroki, to Fraser, 30/3/49. MWP.
29. TP, *NZ Herald*, 3/11/49. MWP.
30. TP, telegram to Fraser, 12/11/48. MWP.
31. TPL to King Country tribes, 28/2/49. MWP.
32. Int RM.
33. Int PJ.
34. *Ibid.*
35. F. I. Hobbs, personal communication, undated.
36. Int TK.

16. Last years

1. 16 mm film taken by Dudley Wright, February 1950.
2. *Who's Who*, Wellington, 1951, p. 134.
3. RM, 'The Maori King Movement', unpublished paper, University of Waikato, 1974.
4. Winiata, 1958.
5. Acheson, 1940.
6. Kawharu, 1975, p. 9.
7. Int HW.
8. *Ibid.*
9. Int Margaret McDowall, 27/9/75.
10. ER, *People*, 1951.
11. Int MJ.
12. Int AM.

13. Int HW.
14. Int PJ.
15. Buck to ER, 26/1/45. RP.
16. Buck, Field Notes, Bishop Museum, Honolulu, Gr. 1. box 1.1, bk. 1.
17. *Ibid.*
18. See Condliffe, 1971, p. 126.
19. Int PJ.
20. M. J. Savage to TP, 2/11/39. RP.
21. Int RM.
22. Winiata, 1950.
23. Int Frances Winiata.
24. Winiata, 1950.
25. Winiata, *New Zealand Listener*, undated clipping. MWP.
26. Winiata, 1950.
27. Undated clipping. MWP.
28. Undated clipping. MWP.
29. Kelly to ER, 15/10/50. RP.
30. Int PJ.
31. Int PP.
32. *NZ Herald*, 12/3/51.
33. See letter from Holland to Maharaia Winiata, 17/4/51. MWP.
34. ER to Winiata, 24/3/51. MWP.
35. Int PJ.
36. Undated clipping, MWP. This statement was made in 1952 when Te Puea was in hospital and it refers to the subsequent plan for a visit by the then-Princess Elizabeth and Prince Phillip. But it summarises the considerations she had voiced over the two preceding years.
37. *NZ Herald*, 12/3/51. MWP.
38. Winiata to Holland, 18/3/51. MWP.
39. Winiata to ER, 22/3/51. MWP.
40. ER to Winiata, 24/3/51. MWP.
41. ER to Winiata, 30/3/51. MWP.
42. ER to Winiata, 30/3/51, and 24/3/51. MWP.
43. Holland to Winiata, 17/4/51. MWP.
44. Lord Bledisloe to TP, 7/4/51. MWP.
45. Freyberg to TP, 23/4/51. MWP.
46. Buckingham Palace to TP, 31/1/52. MWP.
47. ER to Winiata, undated. MWP.
48. Buckingham Palace to TP, 31/1/52. MWP.
49. TPL, 4/4/45. RP.
50. Int RM.
51. *Ibid.*
52. Int Te Arikinui Te Atairangikaahu.
53. Int TK.

17. Towards Rerenga Wairua
1. Int TK.

2. Int NZ.
3. Int TK.
4. Int Tom Te Maro, July 1975.
5. NZBC Archives.
6. TPL to MJ, 10/8/50. MJP.
7. Leslie Kelly to ER, 15/10/50. RP.
8. TPL, 29/3/44. RP.
9. Int Margaret McDowall, 27/9/75.
10. Hospital notes, Waikato Hospital Records.
11. Who's Who, Wellington, 1951, p. 191.
12. TPL, 18/4/35.
13. The story of this trip comes from interviews with the Rev. Kingi Ihaka and Tumokai Katipa.
14. Int TK.
15. Int Margaret McDowall.
16. Int Bunny Woodhams, 27/4/75.
17. Hospital notes, Waikato Hospital Records.
18. Int Bunny Woodhams.
19. People's Voice, 13/2/52. MA.
20. Hospital notes, Waikato Hospital Records.
21. Int AM.
22. Int PJ.
23. Hospital notes, Waikato Hospital Records.
24. Int PP.
25. TPL to Aroha Jones, 18/7/52. MJP.
26. Maharaia Winiata to ER, 22/10/52. RP.
27. Ibid.
28. Int PJ; and PJ, 1971, p. 40.
29. Int Margaret McDowall.
30. Auckland Star, 6/10/52.
31. Int Margaret McDowall.
32. Int TK.
33. The information on Te Puea's last days is taken from interviews with Tumokai Katipa, Alex McKay, Heeni Wharemaru, F.I. Hobbs and Margaret McDowall.
34. Te Kani Te Ua to ER, 2/11/52. RP.

Epilogue

1. McCan, p. 281.
2. McCan, pp. 332, 333. I am indebted to this book for much of the factual material in the Epilogue; and to Sir Robert Mahuta for discussion of the relevant issues.

Bibliography

Unpublished

A. MAJOR INTERVIEWS

With Tumokai Katipa, Piri Poutapu, Alex McKay, Ngeungeu Zister, Michael Rotohiko Jones, Pei Te Hurinui Jones, Robert Mahuta, Winara Samuels, Heeni Wharemaru, Te Uira Manihera, Whitiora Cooper, Wetere Paki, Ngakahikatea Whirihana, Herepo Rongo, Frances Winiata, F.I. Hobbs, G.I. Laurenson, B.E. Woodhams, Kingi Ihaka, Margaret McDowall, Frank Monk, Bill Eaddy, Hoeroa Marumaru, Sir Henry Kelliher, Stanley Newton, Oliver Finlay. Tapes, transcripts and notes of these have been deposited with the Alexander Turnbull Library, Wellington.

B. PRIVATE PAPERS

McDonnell Papers, Alexander Turnbull Library.
Maharaia Winiata Papers, held by Frances Winiata, Auckland.
Michael Rotohiko Jones Papers, National Archives, Wellington.
Pei Te Hurinui Jones Papers, held by Brian Jones, Taumarunui.
Ramsden Papers, Alexander Turnbull Library.
Turongo House Collection of letters, photographs, clippings and Te Puea Herangi's diary, held at Turangawaewae Marae, Ngaruawahia.

C. OFFICIAL PAPERS

'Conference held at Wellington on July 1 and July 2, 1942. Between the Prime Minister and Te Puea Herangi CBE and other leaders of the Waikato people, with reference to the Maori war effort.' Copies held by Robert Mahuta and National Archives (Maori Affairs).
Health Department Archives, National Archives.
Maori Affairs Archives, National Archives.

D. THESES AND RESEARCH PAPERS

Butterworth, G.V., 'The Politics of Adaptation. The Career of Sir Apirana Ngata 1874–1928', MA thesis, Victoria University, 1969.
Farland, B.H., 'The Political Career of J.G. Coates', MA thesis, Victoria University, 1965.
McClean, Sheila, 'Maori Representation: 1905 to 1948', MA thesis, Auckland University College, 1949.

Mahuta, Robert, 'The Maori King Movement', unpublished paper, University of Waikato, 1974.

Raureti, Moana, 'The Ratana Movement', Dip. Soc. Sci. thesis, Victoria University College, 1954.

Winiata, Maharaia, 'The Changing Role of the Leader in Maori Society', PhD thesis, Edinburgh University, 1954.

Worger, William Hewlett, 'Te Puea, the Kingitanga and Waikato', MA thesis, University of Auckland, 1975.

Published

A. BOOKS

Andersen, J.C. and Petersen, G.C., *The Mair Family*, Reed, Wellington, 1956.

Bassett, Michael, *Coates of Kaipara*, Auckland University Press, Auckland, 1995.

Belich, James, *The New Zealand Wars and the Victorian Interpretation of Racial Conflict*, Auckland University Press, Auckland, 1986.

Buck, Peter, *Vikings of the Sunrise*, Frederick A. Stokes, New York, 1938.

Buick, T.L., *Waitangi Ninety-four Years After*, Thomas Avery and Sons Ltd, New Plymouth, 1934.

Clark, Paul, *Hauhau, the Pai Marire Search For Maori Identity*, Auckland University Press, Auckland, 1975.

Cody, J.F., *Man of Two Worlds, Sir Maui Pomare*, Reed, Wellington, 1953.

Condliffe, J.B., *New Zealand in the Making*, Allen and Unwin, London, 1959.

Condliffe, J.B., *Te Rangi Hiroa*, Whitcombe and Tombs, Christchurch, 1971.

Cowan, James, *New Zealand or Aotearoa*, Dept. of Tourist and Health Resorts, Wellington, 1908.

Cowan, James, *The Maoris in the Great War*, Whitcombe and Tombs, Wellington, 1926.

Downes, Peter and Harcourt, Peter, *Voices in the Air*, Methuen, Radio New Zealand, Wellington, 1976.

Featon, John, *The Waikato War, 1863–1864*, J.H. Field, Auckland, 1879.

Gorst, J.E., *New Zealand Revisited*, Pitman and Sons, London, 1908.

Gorst, J.E., *The Maori King*, Macmillan, London, 1864.

Grayland, E.C., *Famous New Zealanders*, Whitcombe and Tombs, Christchurch, 1968.

Henderson, James McLeod, *Ratana, the Man, the Church, the Political Movement*, Reed, Wellington, 1972.

Jones, Pei Te Hurinui, *King Potatau*, Polynesian Society, Wellington, 1959.

Jones, Pei Te Hurinui, *Mahinarangi*, J.C. Ekdahl, Hawera, 1946.

Kawharu, I.H. (ed.), *Conflict and Compromise*, Reed, Wellington, 1975.

Kawharu, I.H., *Orakei a Ngati Whatua Community*, NZ Council for Educational Research, Wellington, 1975.

Kelly, Leslie George (Te Putu), *Tainui; the Story of Hoturoa and His Descendants*, Polynesian Society, Wellington, 1949.

King, Michael, *Moko — Tattooing in the Twentieth Century*, Alister Taylor, Wellington, 1972.

King, Michael (ed.), *Te Ao Hurihuri*, Hicks Smith and Sons, Wellington, 1975.

King, Michael, *Te Puea Herangi, From Darkness to Light*, Kete Raukura series, Department of Education, Wellington, 1984.

King, Michael, *Whina, A Biography of Whina Cooper*, Penguin, Auckland, 1991.

King, Michael, 'Between Two Worlds' in *The Oxford History of New Zealand*, Oxford University Press, Auckland, 2000.

Koroki, My King, Turongo House, Ngaruawahia, 1999.

Laurenson, G.I., *Te Hahi Weteriana*, Wesley Historical Society, Auckland, 1972.

Maclean, F.S., *Challenge for Health*, Government Printer, Wellington, 1964.

McCan, David, *Whatiwhatihoe, The Waikato Raupatu Claim*, Huia, Wellington, 2001.

Ngata, A.T., *Nga Moteatea*, Vols I and II, Polynesian Society, Wellington, 1959.

Norris, H.C.M., *Armed Settlers*, Paul's Book Arcade, Hamilton, 1963.

Oppenheim, R.S., *Maori Death Customs*, Reed, Wellington, 1973.

Parsonson, Ann, and others, 'Te Kirihaehae Te Puea Herangi' in *Dictionary of New Zealand Biography*, vol. 3, pp. 208–211.

Phillipps, W.J., *Carved Maori Houses of the Western and Northern Areas of New Zealand*, Government Printer, Wellington, 1955.

Pocock, J.G.A. (ed.), *The Maori and New Zealand Politics*, Blackwood and Janet Paul, Hamilton, 1965.

Pomare, M., *The Maori*, Melbourne, 1905.

Ramsden, Eric, *Sir Apirana Ngata*, Reed, Wellington, 1948.

Roberts, G.T., *Kohikohinga*, Whitcombe and Tombs, Christchurch, 1929.

Salmond, Anne, *Hui*, Reed, Wellington, 1975.

Schwimmer, E.G. (ed.), *The Maori People in the Nineteen-Sixties*, Blackwood and Janet Paul, Auckland, 1968.

Scott, Dick, *Ask That Mountain, the Story of Parihaka*, Heinemann-Southern Cross, Auckland, 1975.

Simmons, David Roy, *The Great New Zealand Myth: a study of the discovery and origin traditions of the Maori*, Reed, Wellington, 1976.

Sinclair, Keith, *The Origins of the Maori Wars*, N.Z. University Press, Wellington, 1961.

Sorrenson, M.P.K. (ed.), *Na To Aroha, The Correspondence Between Sir Apirana Ngata and Sir Peter Buck 1925–50*, 3 vols, 1986-88.

Stokes, Evelyn, *Wiremu Tamihana Rangatira*, Huia, Wellington, 2002.

Sutch, W.B., *Poverty and Progress in New Zealand*, Reed, Wellington, 1969.

Sutherland, I.L.G. (ed.), *The Maori People Today*, N.Z. Institute of International Affairs, Wellington, 1940.

Tawhiao, King or Prophet, Turongo House, Ngaruawahia, 2000.

Te Wiata, Beryl, *The Most Happy Fella*, Reed, Wellington, 1976.

Walker, Ranginui, *He Tipua, The Life and Times of Sir Apirana Ngata*, Viking, Auckland, 2001.

Williams, J.A., *Politics of the New Zealand Maori. Protest and Cooperation, 1891–1909*, Oxford University Press, Auckland, 1969.

Winiata, Maharaia, *The Changing Role of the Leader in Maori Society*, Blackwood and Janet Paul, Auckland, 1967.

Wood, F.L.W., *The New Zealand People at War*, Dept. of Internal Affairs, Wellington, 1958.

B. PAMPHLETS, ARTICLES AND ADDRESSES

Acheson, F.O.V., 'Princess Te Puea Speaks', in *New Zealand Mirror*, Vol. 18, nos 7 to 11, 1940.

Burton, E., 'Princess Te Puea', in *Overseas*, London, June 1939.

Butterworth, G.V., 'Te Puea Herangi', in *New Zealand's Heritage*, Part 95, pp. 2652–2656.

Cowan, James, 'Te Puea Herangi: Princess of Waikato and Leader of Her People', in *New Zealand Railways Magazine*, Vol. 11, no. 6, 1 September, 1936.

Dansey, Harry, 'Just Call Me Te Puea Said the Princess', in *NZ Woman's Weekly* 9 October 1972.

Gordon, P. and Rolleston, W., 'Maori Electoral Issues', in *Te Maori*, Vol. 3, no. 1, 1972.

Jones, Pei Te Hurinui, 'Maori Kings', in *The Maori People in the Nineteen-Sixties* (E.G. Schwimmer, ed.), Wellington, 1968.

Jones, Pei Te Hurinui, 'Turangawaewae' (pamphlet), Ngaruawahia, 1971.

Mahuika, Api, 'Leadership: Inherited and Achieved', in *Te Ao Hurihuri*, (M. King. ed.), Wellington, 1975.

M.H., 'Te Puea Herangi OBE [sic], Her Work For the Maori People', in *Women Today*, 1 July 1937.

New Zealand Pan-Pacific Women's Association, 'Te Puea Herangi CBE', paper prepared by the Maori Women's Welfare League, 1953.

Ngata, A.T., 'Waikato of a Hundred Taniwhas', in *Te Ao Hou*, no. 17, December 1956.

O'Connor, P.S., 'The Recruitment of Maori Soldiers 1914–1918', in *Political Science 19*, 1967, pp. 48–83.

Ramsden, Eric, 'Princess of Maoriland', in *Reed's New Zealand Christmas Annual*, 1947/48.

Ramsden, Eric, 'Princess Te Puea, the Maker of Maori Kings', in *People*, 3 January 1951.

Ramsden, Eric, 'Te Puea Herangi CBE 1884–1952', in *Journal of the Polynesian Society*, Vol. 61, 1952, pp. 192–208.

Sorrenson, M.P.K., 'The Maori King Movement 1858–1885', in *Studies of a Small Democracy* (R. Chapman and K. Sinclair eds.), Auckland, 1963.

Winiata, Maharaia, 'Founding of the Maori King Movement' (pamphlet), Ngaruawahia, 1958.

Winiata, Maharaia, 'Tainui Sexcentennial Canoe Celebrations', (pamphlet), Hamilton, 1950.

Winiata, Maharaia, 'The Changing Face of Maori Leadership', 1966 (typescript, Alexander Turnbull Library).

C. OFFICIAL PAPERS

Appendices to the Journals of the House of Representatives.
Commission to inquire into the report upon the Departments of Government
concerned with the administration of Native Affairs, Wellington, 1934.
Confiscated native lands and other grievances, Royal Commission, Wellington,
1928.
New Zealand Parliamentary Debates.
New Zealand Parliamentary Record, 1840–1949.

D. NEWSPAPERS

Auckland Star
Dominion
Evening Post
Huntly Press
New Zealand Herald
New Zealand Truth
Sun
Te Paki O Matariki
Waikato Times

E. RECORDINGS AND FILMS

Film of Te Puea Herangi and canoe building shot in the 1930s and 1940s by
R.G.H. Manley, print initially held by South Pacific Television, Auckland;
edited by Merata Mita and released in 1990 as documentary film *Mana
Waka*.
Recording of the opening of Turongo House, 1938, held by Robert Mahuta.
Te Puea Herangi's poroporoaki to Sir Apirana Ngata, NZBC archives.
Te Puea Herangi on film shot in February 1950 by D.E. Wright, Leigh.

Index